LIVING LITURGY™

Sunday Missal

2027

Celebrating the Eucharist

LITURGICAL PRESS
Collegeville, Minnesota

litpress.org

Published with the approval of the
Committee on Divine Worship
United States Conference of Catholic Bishops

Nihil Obstat: Reverend Robert C. Harren, J.C.L., *Censor Librorum*

Imprimatur: ✠ Most Reverend Patrick M. Neary, C.S.C., Bishop of Saint Cloud,
April 17, 2026

Cover design by Monica Bokinskie. Art by Br. Martin Erspamer, OSB, a monk of St. Meinrad Archabbey, Indiana.

ISSN 1949-1166
ISBN 979-8-4008-0215-7

Contents

The Order of Mass

The Introductory Rites

Entrance Chant

STAND

Sign of the Cross

Priest: In the name of the Father, and of the Son, and of the Holy Spirit.

People: **Amen.**

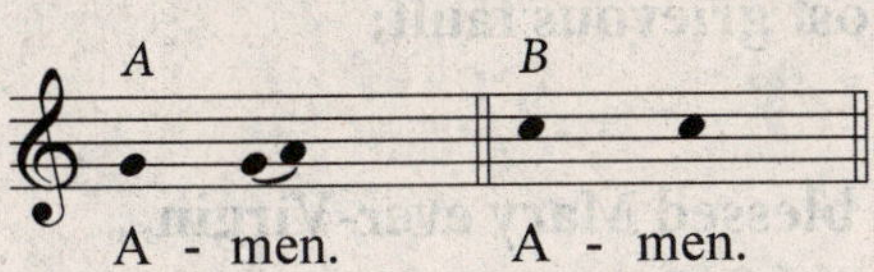

Greeting

A Priest: The grace of our Lord Jesus Christ,
and the love of God,
and the communion of the Holy Spirit
be with you all.

People: **And with your spirit.**

B Priest: Grace to you and peace from God our Father
and the Lord Jesus Christ.

People: **And with your spirit.**

C Priest: The Lord be with you.

People: **And with your spirit.**

[From time to time on Sundays, especially in Easter Time, instead of the customary Penitential Act, the blessing and sprinkling of water may take place as a reminder of Baptism.]

Penitential Act

A Priest: Brethren (brothers and sisters), let us
acknowledge our sins,
and so prepare ourselves to celebrate the sacred
mysteries. (Pause)

All: **I confess to almighty God**
and to you, my brothers and sisters,
that I have greatly sinned,
in my thoughts and in my words,
in what I have done and in what I have failed to do,

And, striking their breast, they say:

through my fault, through my fault,
through my most grievous fault;

Then they continue:

therefore I ask blessed Mary ever-Virgin,
all the Angels and Saints,
and you, my brothers and sisters,
to pray for me to the Lord our God.

Priest: May almighty God have mercy on us,
forgive us our sins,
and bring us to everlasting life.

People: **Amen.**

B Priest: Brethren (brothers and sisters), let us acknowledge our sins,
and so prepare ourselves to celebrate the sacred mysteries. (Pause)

Priest: Have mercy on us, O Lord.

People: **For we have sinned against you.**

Priest: Show us, O Lord, your mercy.

People: **And grant us your salvation.**

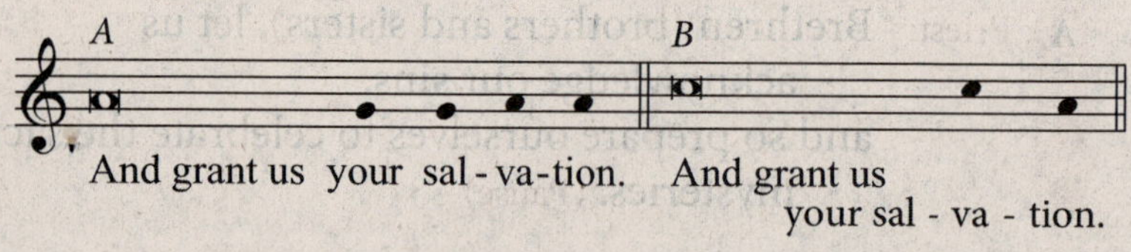

Priest: May almighty God have mercy on us,
forgive us our sins,
and bring us to everlasting life.

People: **Amen.**

C Priest: Brethren (brothers and sisters), let us acknowledge our sins,
and so prepare ourselves to celebrate the sacred mysteries. (Pause)

Priest (Deacon or another minister):
You were sent to heal the contrite of heart:
Lord, have mercy. Or: Kyrie, eleison.

People: **Lord, have mercy.** Or: **Kyrie, eleison.**

Priest: You came to call sinners:
Christ, have mercy. Or: Christe, eleison.

People: **Christ, have mercy.** Or: **Christe, eleison.**

Priest: You are seated at the right hand of the Father to intercede for us:
Lord, have mercy. Or: Kyrie, eleison.

People: **Lord, have mercy.** Or: **Kyrie, eleison.**

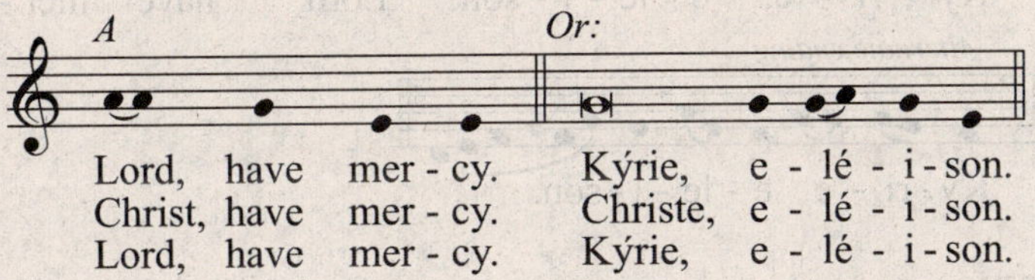

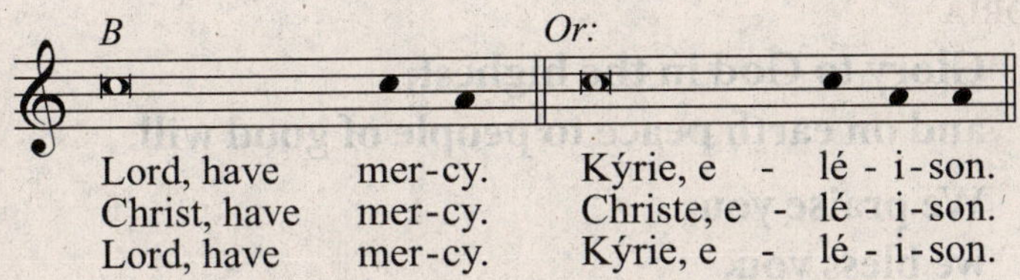

Priest: May almighty God have mercy on us,
forgive us our sins,
and bring us to everlasting life.

People: **Amen.**

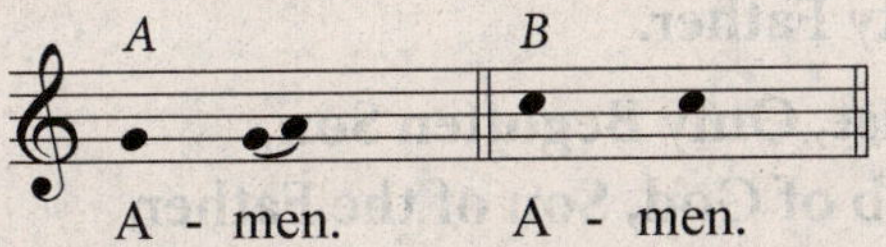

Kyrie

The Kyrie, eleison (Lord, have mercy) invocations follow, unless they have just occurred in a formula of the Penitential Act.

℣. Lord, have mercy. ℟. **Lord, have mercy.**
℣. Christ, have mercy. ℟. **Christ, have mercy.**
℣. Lord, have mercy. ℟. **Lord, have mercy.**

Or:

℣. Kyrie, eleison. ℟. **Kyrie, eleison.**
℣. Christe, eleison. ℟. **Christe, eleison.**
℣. Kyrie, eleison. ℟. **Kyrie, eleison.**

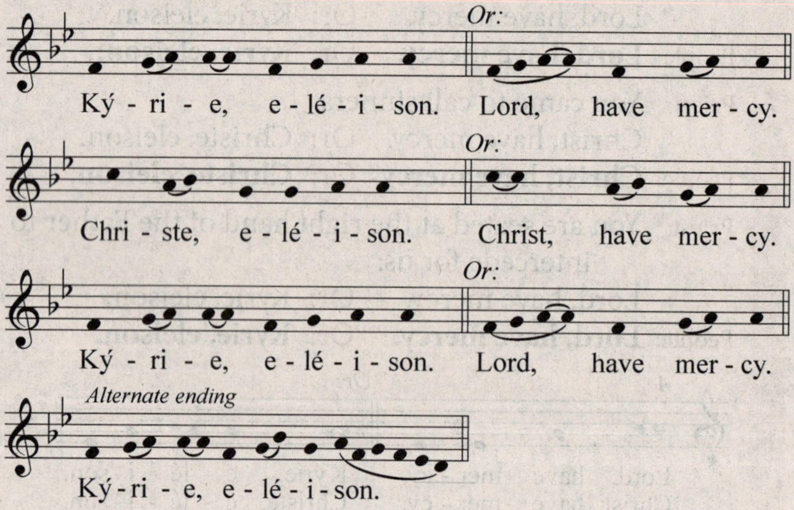

Gloria

All: **Glory to God in the highest,**
and on earth peace to people of good will.

We praise you,
we bless you,
we adore you,
we glorify you,
we give you thanks for your great glory,
Lord God, heavenly King,
O God, almighty Father.

Lord Jesus Christ, Only Begotten Son,
Lord God, Lamb of God, Son of the Father,

you take away the sins of the world,
have mercy on us;
you take away the sins of the world,
receive our prayer;
you are seated at the right hand of the Father,
have mercy on us.

For you alone are the Holy One,
you alone are the Lord,
you alone are the Most High,
Jesus Christ,
with the Holy Spirit,
in the glory of God the Father.
Amen.

Collect (Opening Prayer)

Priest: Let us pray.

All pray in silence with the Priest for a while.

Then the Priest, with hands extended, says the Collect prayer, at the end of which the people acclaim:

Amen.

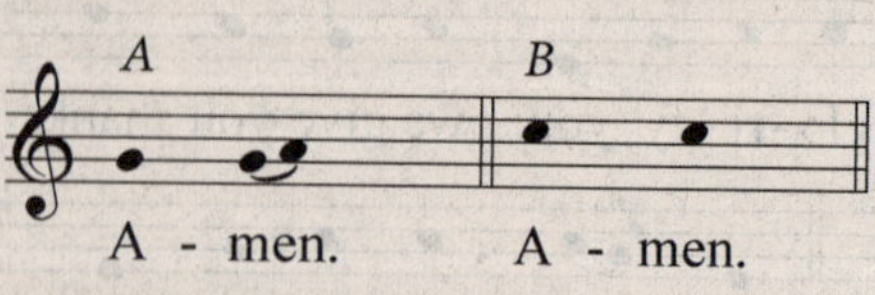

The Liturgy of the Word

First Reading

SIT

Then the reader goes to the ambo and reads the First Reading, while all sit and listen.

To indicate the end of the reading, the reader acclaims:

The word of the Lord.

All: **Thanks be to God.**

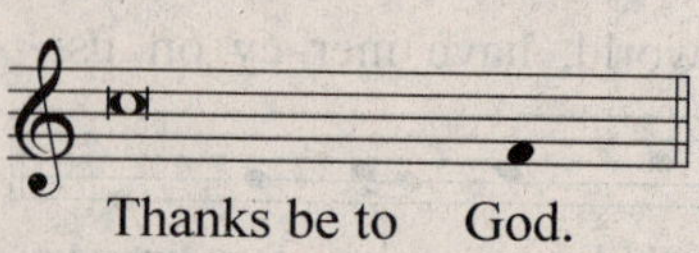

Responsorial Psalm

The psalmist or cantor sings or says the Psalm, with the people making the response.

Second Reading

After this, if there is to be a Second Reading, a reader reads it from the ambo, as above.

To indicate the end of the reading, the reader acclaims:

The word of the Lord.

All: **Thanks be to God.**

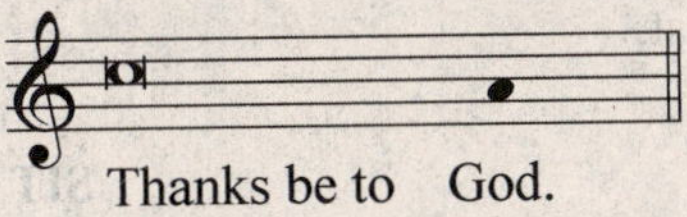

Gospel Acclamation

STAND

There follows the Alleluia or another chant laid down by the rubrics, as the liturgical time requires.

Gospel Dialogue

Deacon or Priest: The Lord be with you.

People: **And with your spirit.**

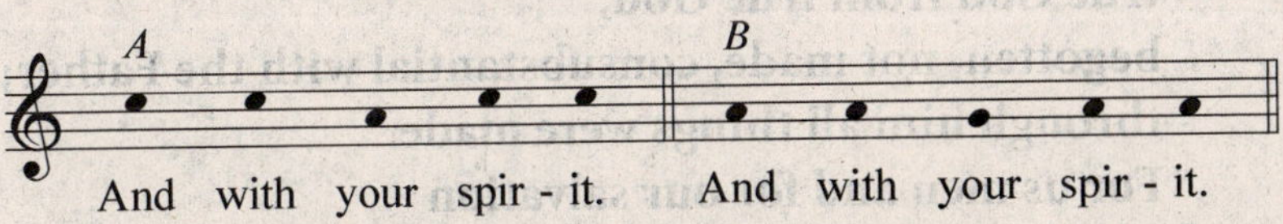

Deacon or Priest: A reading from the holy Gospel according to N.

People: **Glory to you, O Lord.**

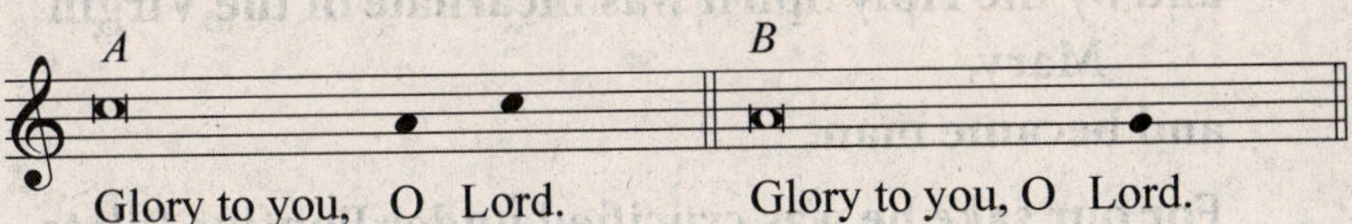

Gospel Reading

At the end of the Gospel, the Deacon, or the Priest, acclaims:

The Gospel of the Lord.

All: **Praise to you, Lord Jesus Christ.**

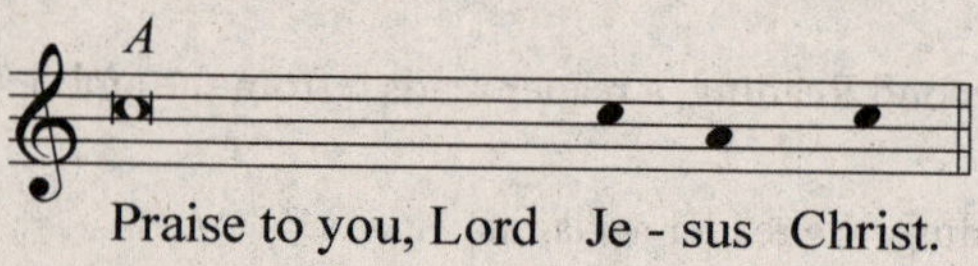

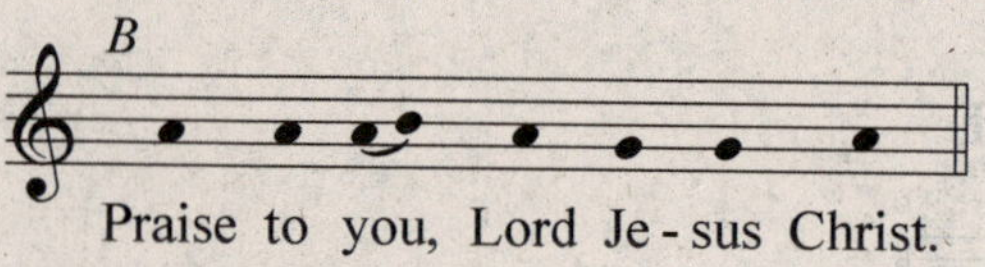

Homily **SIT**

Profession of Faith **STAND**

All: **I believe in one God,**
the Father almighty,
maker of heaven and earth,
of all things visible and invisible.

I believe in one Lord Jesus Christ,
the Only Begotten Son of God,
born of the Father before all ages.
God from God, Light from Light,
true God from true God,
begotten, not made, consubstantial with the Father;
through him all things were made.
For us men and for our salvation
he came down from heaven,

At the words that follow, up to and including and became man, all bow.

and by the Holy Spirit was incarnate of the Virgin Mary,
and became man.

For our sake he was crucified under Pontius Pilate,
he suffered death and was buried,
and rose again on the third day
in accordance with the Scriptures.

He ascended into heaven
and is seated at the right hand of the Father.
He will come again in glory
to judge the living and the dead
and his kingdom will have no end.

I believe in the Holy Spirit, the Lord, the giver of life,
who proceeds from the Father and the Son,
who with the Father and the Son is adored and glorified,
who has spoken through the prophets.

I believe in one, holy, catholic and apostolic Church.
I confess one Baptism for the forgiveness of sins
and I look forward to the resurrection of the dead
and the life of the world to come. Amen.

At the words that follow, up to and including and became man, *all bow.*

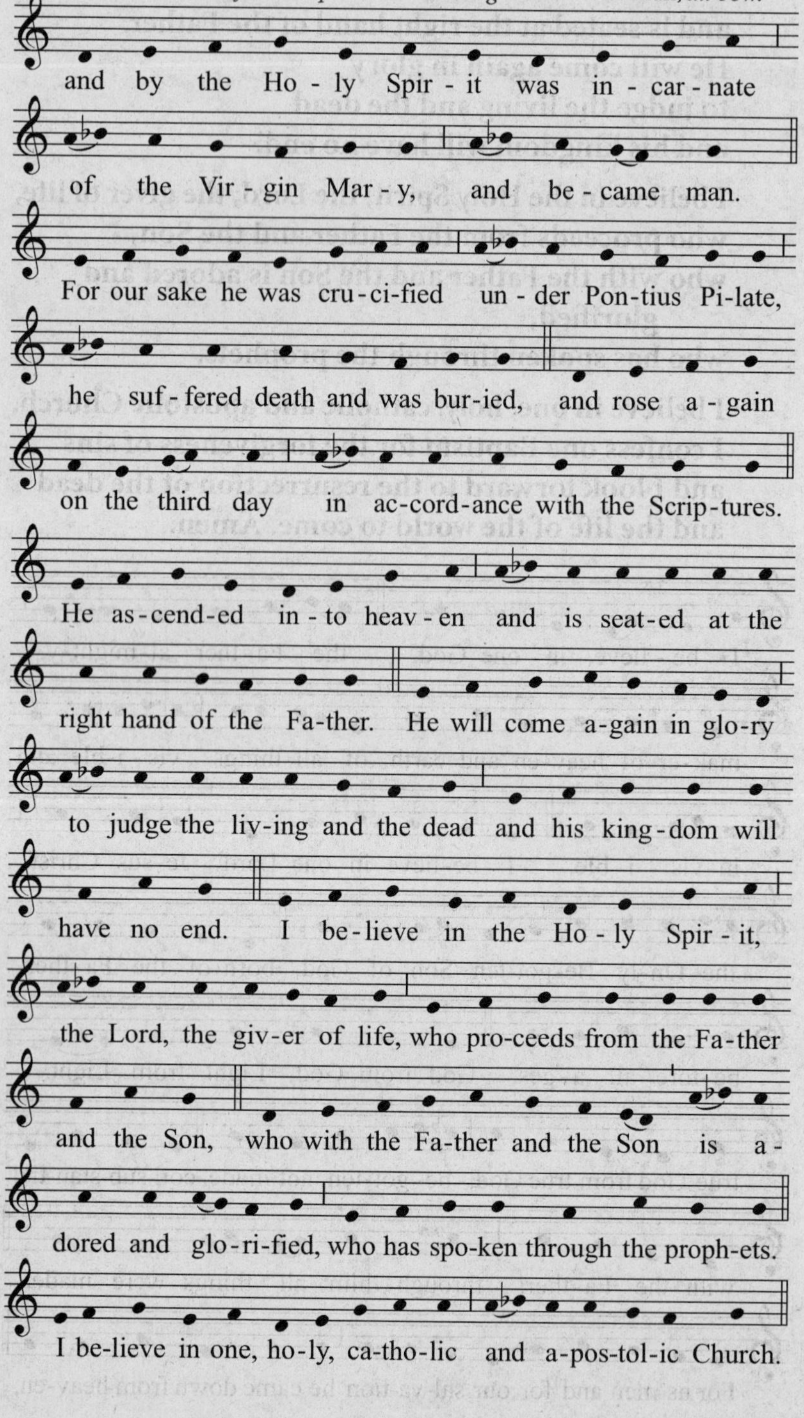

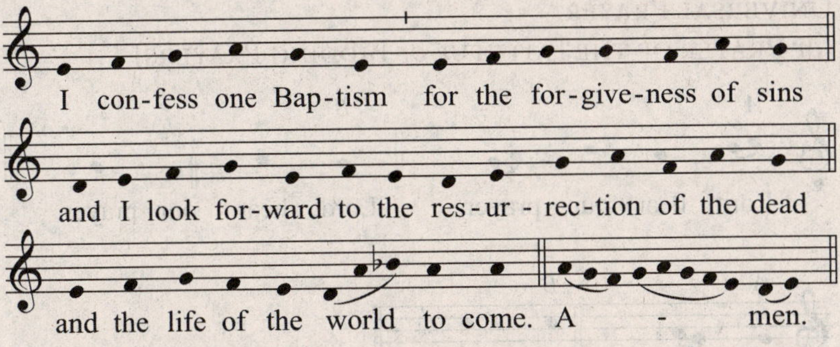

Instead of the Niceno-Constantinopolitan Creed, especially during Lent and Easter Time, the baptismal Symbol of the Roman Church, known as the Apostles' Creed, may be used.

All: **I believe in God,**
the Father almighty,
Creator of heaven and earth,
and in Jesus Christ, his only Son, our Lord,

At the words that follow, up to and including the Virgin Mary, all bow.

who was conceived by the Holy Spirit,
born of the Virgin Mary,
suffered under Pontius Pilate,
was crucified, died and was buried;
he descended into hell;
on the third day he rose again from the dead;
he ascended into heaven,
and is seated at the right hand of God the Father almighty;
from there he will come to judge the living and the dead.

I believe in the Holy Spirit,
the holy catholic Church,
the communion of saints,
the forgiveness of sins,
the resurrection of the body,
and life everlasting. Amen.

Universal Prayer
(*or* Prayer of the Faithful *or* Bidding Prayers)

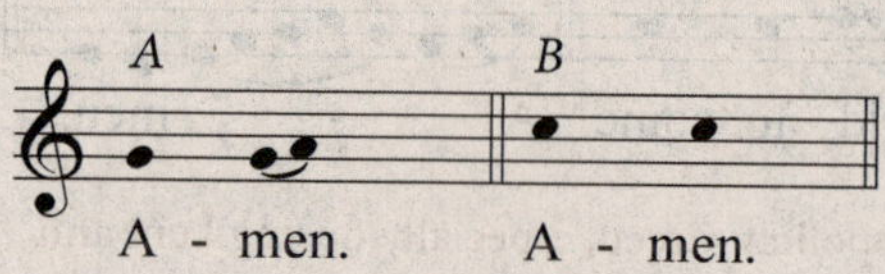

The Liturgy of the Eucharist

Presentation and Preparation of the Gifts **SIT**

The Priest, standing at the altar, takes the paten with the bread and holds it slightly raised above the altar with both hands, saying in a low voice:

Blessed are you, Lord God of all creation,
for through your goodness we have received
the bread we offer you:
fruit of the earth and work of human hands,
it will become for us the bread of life.

If, however, the Offertory Chant is not sung, the Priest may speak these words aloud; at the end, the people may acclaim:

Blessed be God for ever.

The Priest then takes the chalice and holds it slightly raised above the altar with both hands, saying in a low voice:

Blessed are you, Lord God of all creation,
for through your goodness we have received
the wine we offer you:
fruit of the vine and work of human hands,
it will become our spiritual drink.

If, however, the Offertory Chant is not sung, the Priest may speak these words aloud; at the end, the people may acclaim:

Blessed be God for ever.

Standing at the middle of the altar, facing the people, extending and then joining his hands, he says:

Pray, brethren (brothers and sisters),
that my sacrifice and yours
may be acceptable to God,
the almighty Father.

The people rise and reply: **STAND**

May the Lord accept the sacrifice at your hands
for the praise and glory of his name,
for our good
and the good of all his holy Church.

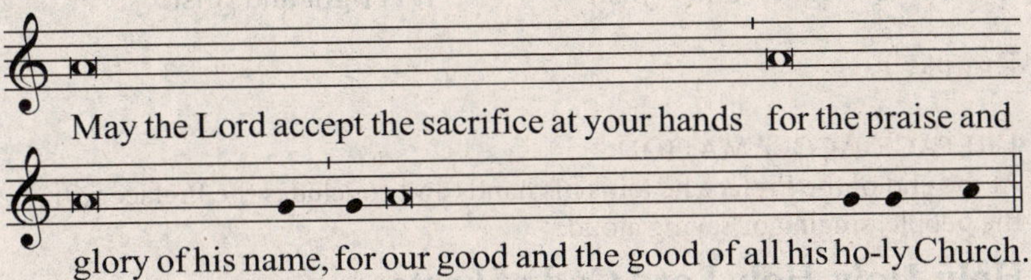

Prayer over the Offerings

Then the Priest, with hands extended, says the Prayer over the Offerings, at the end of which the people acclaim:

Amen.

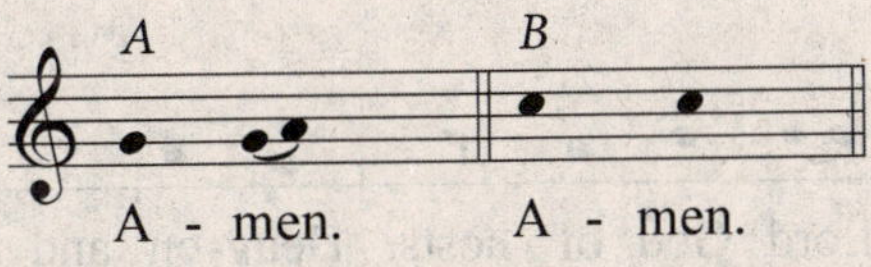

The Eucharistic Prayer

Priest: The Lord be with you.

People: **And with your spirit.**

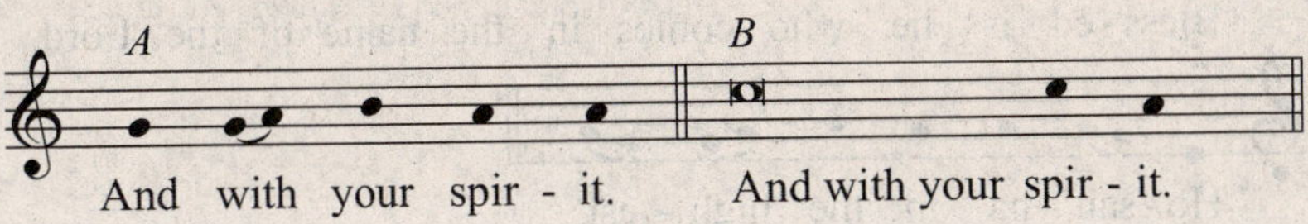

Priest: Lift up your hearts.

People: **We lift them up to the Lord.**

Priest: Let us give thanks to the Lord our God.

People: **It is right and just.**

Preface

Preface Acclamation

At the end of the Preface he joins his hands and concludes the Preface with the people, singing or saying aloud:

Holy, Holy, Holy Lord God of hosts.
Heaven and earth are full of your glory.
Hosanna in the highest.
Blessed is he who comes in the name of the Lord.
Hosanna in the highest.

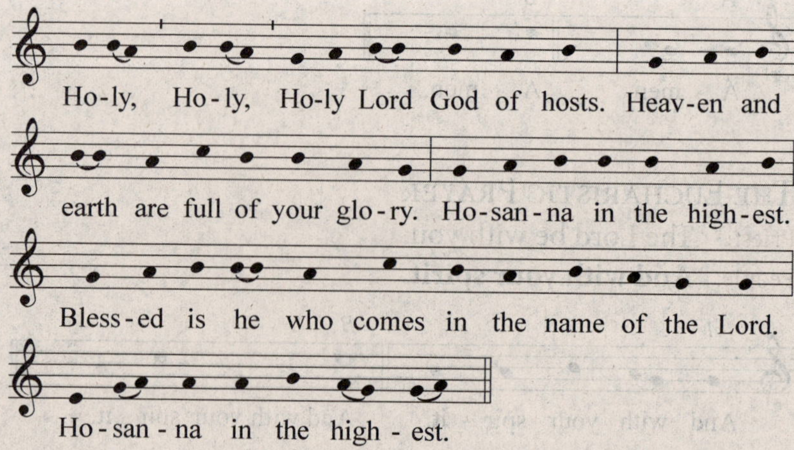

Or:

Sanctus, Sanctus, Sanctus Dóminus Deus Sábaoth.
Pleni sunt cæli et terra glória tua.
Hosánna in excélsis.
Benedíctus qui venit in nómine Dómini.
Hosánna in excélsis.

[In addition to the Eucharistic Prayers provided below, on some occasions the priest may use the authorized Eucharistic Prayers for Reconciliation, pages 471–476, or Eucharistic Prayers for Use in Masses for Various Needs.]

Eucharistic Prayer I (The Roman Canon) **KNEEL**

Priest:
To you, therefore, most merciful Father,
we make humble prayer and petition
through Jesus Christ, your Son, our Lord:
that you accept
and bless ✠ these gifts, these offerings,
these holy and unblemished sacrifices,
which we offer you firstly
for your holy catholic Church.
Be pleased to grant her peace,
to guard, unite and govern her
throughout the whole world,
together with your servant N. our Pope
and N. our Bishop,*
and all those who, holding to the truth,
hand on the catholic and apostolic faith.

Commemoration of the Living
Remember, Lord, your servants N. and N.
and all gathered here,
whose faith and devotion are known to you.
For them, we offer you this sacrifice of praise
or they offer it for themselves
and all who are dear to them:
for the redemption of their souls,
in hope of health and well-being,
and paying their homage to you,
the eternal God, living and true.

* Mention may be made here of the Coadjutor Bishop, or Auxiliary Bishops, as noted in the *General Instruction of the Roman Missal*, no. 149.

Within the Action

In communion with those whose memory we venerate,
especially the glorious ever-Virgin Mary,
Mother of our God and Lord, Jesus Christ,
† and blessed Joseph, her Spouse,
your blessed Apostles and Martyrs,
Peter and Paul, Andrew,
(James, John,
Thomas, James, Philip,
Bartholomew, Matthew,
Simon and Jude;
Linus, Cletus, Clement, Sixtus,
Cornelius, Cyprian,
Lawrence, Chrysogonus,
John and Paul,
Cosmas and Damian)
and all your Saints;
we ask that through their merits and prayers,
in all things we may be defended
by your protecting help.
(Through Christ our Lord. Amen.)

On the Nativity of the Lord and throughout the Octave

Celebrating the most sacred night (day)
on which blessed Mary the immaculate Virgin
brought forth the Savior for this world,
and in communion with those whose memory we venerate,
especially the glorious ever-Virgin Mary,
Mother of our God and Lord, Jesus Christ, †

On the Epiphany of the Lord

Celebrating the most sacred day
on which your Only Begotten Son,
eternal with you in your glory,
appeared in a human body, truly sharing our flesh,
and in communion with those whose memory we venerate,
especially the glorious ever-Virgin Mary,
Mother of our God and Lord, Jesus Christ, †

From the Mass of the Easter Vigil until the Second Sunday of Easter

Celebrating the most sacred night (day)
of the Resurrection of our Lord Jesus Christ in the flesh,
and in communion with those whose memory we venerate,
especially the glorious ever-Virgin Mary,
Mother of our God and Lord, Jesus Christ, †

On the Ascension of the Lord
Celebrating the most sacred day
on which your Only Begotten Son, our Lord,
placed at the right hand of your glory
our weak human nature,
which he had united to himself,
and in communion with those whose memory we venerate,
especially the glorious ever-Virgin Mary,
Mother of our God and Lord, Jesus Christ, †

On Pentecost Sunday
Celebrating the most sacred day of Pentecost,
on which the Holy Spirit
appeared to the Apostles in tongues of fire,
and in communion with those whose memory we venerate,
especially the glorious ever-Virgin Mary,
Mother of our God and Lord, Jesus Christ, †

Therefore, Lord, we pray:
graciously accept this oblation of our service,
that of your whole family;
order our days in your peace,
and command that we be delivered from eternal damnation
and counted among the flock of those you have chosen.
(Through Christ our Lord. Amen.)

From the Mass of the Easter Vigil until the Second Sunday of Easter
Therefore, Lord, we pray:
graciously accept this oblation of our service,
that of your whole family,
which we make to you
also for those to whom you have been pleased to give
the new birth of water and the Holy Spirit,
granting them forgiveness of all their sins;
order our days in your peace,
and command that we be delivered from eternal damnation
and counted among the flock of those you have chosen.
(Through Christ our Lord. Amen.)

Be pleased, O God, we pray,
to bless, acknowledge,
and approve this offering in every respect;
make it spiritual and acceptable,
so that it may become for us
the Body and Blood of your most beloved Son,
our Lord Jesus Christ.

On the day before he was to suffer,
he took bread in his holy and venerable hands,
and with eyes raised to heaven
to you, O God, his almighty Father,
giving you thanks, he said the blessing,
broke the bread
and gave it to his disciples, saying:

TAKE THIS, ALL OF YOU, AND EAT OF IT,
FOR THIS IS MY BODY,
WHICH WILL BE GIVEN UP FOR YOU.

In a similar way, when supper was ended,
he took this precious chalice
in his holy and venerable hands,
and once more giving you thanks, he said the blessing
and gave the chalice to his disciples, saying:

TAKE THIS, ALL OF YOU, AND DRINK FROM IT,
FOR THIS IS THE CHALICE OF MY BLOOD,
THE BLOOD OF THE NEW AND ETERNAL COVENANT,
WHICH WILL BE POURED OUT FOR YOU AND FOR MANY
FOR THE FORGIVENESS OF SINS.

DO THIS IN MEMORY OF ME.

The mystery of faith.

And the people continue, acclaiming:

A **We proclaim your Death, O Lord,**
and profess your Resurrection
until you come again.

B **When we eat this Bread and drink this Cup,**
we proclaim your Death, O Lord,
until you come again.

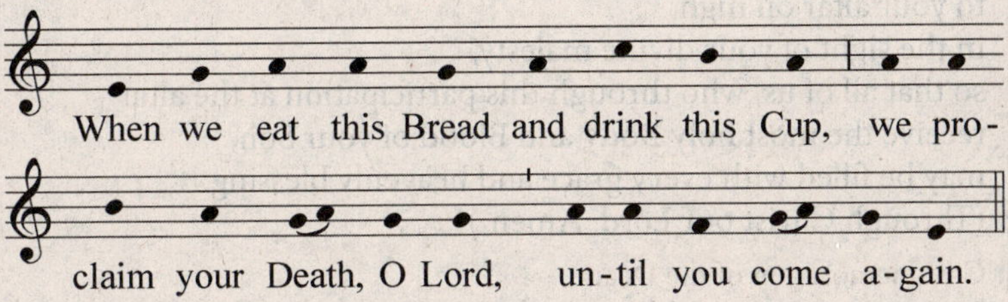

C **Save us, Savior of the world,**
for by your Cross and Resurrection
you have set us free.

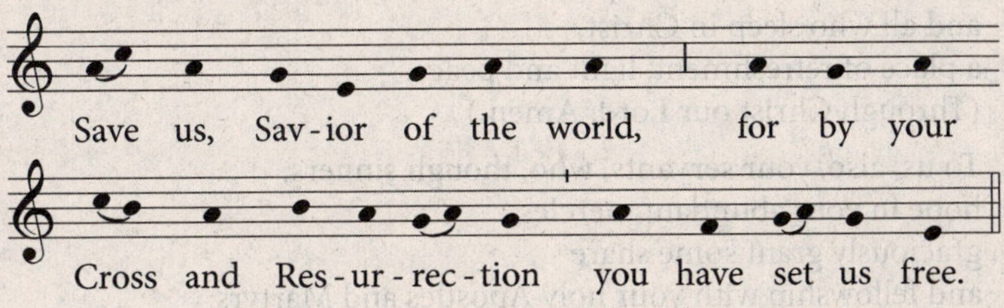

Priest:
Therefore, O Lord,
as we celebrate the memorial of the blessed Passion,
the Resurrection from the dead,
and the glorious Ascension into heaven
of Christ, your Son, our Lord,
we, your servants and your holy people,
offer to your glorious majesty
from the gifts that you have given us,
this pure victim,
this holy victim,
this spotless victim,
the holy Bread of eternal life
and the Chalice of everlasting salvation.

Be pleased to look upon these offerings
with a serene and kindly countenance,
and to accept them,
as once you were pleased to accept
the gifts of your servant Abel the just,
the sacrifice of Abraham, our father in faith,
and the offering of your high priest Melchizedek,
a holy sacrifice, a spotless victim.

In humble prayer we ask you, almighty God:
command that these gifts be borne
by the hands of your holy Angel
to your altar on high
in the sight of your divine majesty,
so that all of us, who through this participation at the altar
receive the most holy Body and Blood of your Son,
may be filled with every grace and heavenly blessing.
(Through Christ our Lord. Amen.)

Commemoration of the Dead

Remember also, Lord, your servants N. and N.,
who have gone before us with the sign of faith
and rest in the sleep of peace.

Grant them, O Lord, we pray,
and all who sleep in Christ,
a place of refreshment, light and peace.
(Through Christ our Lord. Amen.)

To us, also, your servants, who, though sinners,
hope in your abundant mercies,
graciously grant some share
and fellowship with your holy Apostles and Martyrs:
with John the Baptist, Stephen,
Matthias, Barnabas,
(Ignatius, Alexander,
Marcellinus, Peter,
Felicity, Perpetua,
Agatha, Lucy,
Agnes, Cecilia, Anastasia)
and all your Saints;
admit us, we beseech you,
into their company,
not weighing our merits,
but granting us your pardon,
through Christ our Lord.

Through whom
you continue to make all these good things, O Lord;
you sanctify them, fill them with life,
bless them, and bestow them upon us.

Through him, and with him, and in him,
O God, almighty Father,
in the unity of the Holy Spirit,
all glory and honor is yours,
for ever and ever.

People: **Amen.**

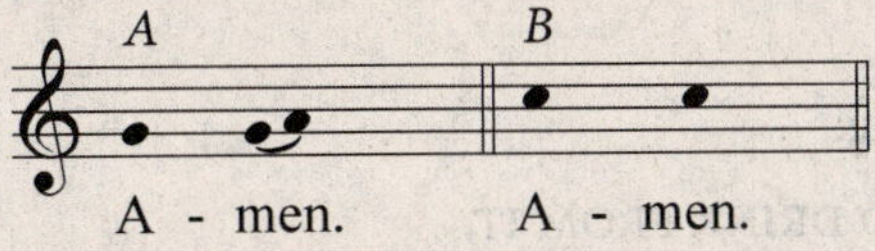

Then follows the Communion Rite, page 30.

Eucharistic Prayer II

Preface

It is truly right and just, our duty and our salvation,
always and everywhere to give you thanks, Father most holy,
through your beloved Son, Jesus Christ,
your Word through whom you made all things,
whom you sent as our Savior and Redeemer,
incarnate by the Holy Spirit and born of the Virgin.

Fulfilling your will and gaining for you a holy people,
he stretched out his hands as he endured his Passion,
so as to break the bonds of death and manifest the resurrection.

And so, with the Angels and all the Saints
we declare your glory,
as with one voice we acclaim:

Holy, Holy, Holy Lord God of hosts.
Heaven and earth are full of your glory.
Hosanna in the highest.
Blessed is he who comes in the name of the Lord.
Hosanna in the highest.

Priest:

You are indeed Holy, O Lord,
the fount of all holiness.
Make holy, therefore, these gifts, we pray,
by sending down your Spirit upon them like the dewfall,
so that they may become for us
the Body and ✠ Blood of our Lord Jesus Christ.

At the time he was betrayed
and entered willingly into his Passion,
he took bread and, giving thanks, broke it,
and gave it to his disciples, saying:

TAKE THIS, ALL OF YOU, AND EAT OF IT,
FOR THIS IS MY BODY,
WHICH WILL BE GIVEN UP FOR YOU.

In a similar way, when supper was ended,
he took the chalice
and, once more giving thanks,
he gave it to his disciples, saying:

TAKE THIS, ALL OF YOU, AND DRINK FROM IT,
FOR THIS IS THE CHALICE OF MY BLOOD,
THE BLOOD OF THE NEW AND ETERNAL COVENANT,
WHICH WILL BE POURED OUT FOR YOU AND FOR MANY
FOR THE FORGIVENESS OF SINS.

DO THIS IN MEMORY OF ME.

The mystery of faith.

People:

A **We proclaim your Death, O Lord,
and profess your Resurrection
until you come again.**

B **When we eat this Bread and drink this Cup,
we proclaim your Death, O Lord,
until you come again.**

C **Save us, Savior of the world,
for by your Cross and Resurrection
you have set us free.**

Priest:
Therefore, as we celebrate
the memorial of his Death and Resurrection,
we offer you, Lord,
the Bread of life and the Chalice of salvation,
giving thanks that you have held us worthy
to be in your presence and minister to you.

Humbly we pray
that, partaking of the Body and Blood of Christ,
we may be gathered into one by the Holy Spirit.

Remember, Lord, your Church,
spread throughout the world,
and bring her to the fullness of charity,
together with N. our Pope and N. our Bishop*
and all the clergy.

* Mention may be made here of the Coadjutor Bishop, or Auxiliary Bishops, as noted in the *General Instruction of the Roman Missal*, no. 149.

In Masses for the Dead, the following may be added:
Remember your servant N.,
whom you have called (today)
from this world to yourself.
Grant that he (she) who was united with your Son in a death like his,
may also be one with him in his Resurrection.

Remember also our brothers and sisters
who have fallen asleep in the hope of the resurrection,
and all who have died in your mercy:
welcome them into the light of your face.
Have mercy on us all, we pray,
that with the Blessed Virgin Mary, Mother of God,
with blessed Joseph, her Spouse,
with the blessed Apostles,
and all the Saints who have pleased you throughout the ages,
we may merit to be coheirs to eternal life,
and may praise and glorify you
through your Son, Jesus Christ.

Through him, and with him, and in him,
O God, almighty Father,
in the unity of the Holy Spirit,
all glory and honor is yours,
for ever and ever.

People: **Amen.**

Then follows the Communion Rite, page 30.

Eucharistic Prayer III

Priest:
You are indeed Holy, O Lord,
and all you have created
rightly gives you praise,
for through your Son our Lord Jesus Christ,
by the power and working of the Holy Spirit,
you give life to all things and make them holy,
and you never cease to gather a people to yourself,
so that from the rising of the sun to its setting
a pure sacrifice may be offered to your name.

Therefore, O Lord, we humbly implore you:
by the same Spirit graciously make holy
these gifts we have brought to you for consecration,
that they may become the Body and ✠ Blood
of your Son our Lord Jesus Christ,
at whose command we celebrate these mysteries.

For on the night he was betrayed
he himself took bread,
and, giving you thanks, he said the blessing,
broke the bread and gave it to his disciples, saying:

TAKE THIS, ALL OF YOU, AND EAT OF IT,
FOR THIS IS MY BODY,
WHICH WILL BE GIVEN UP FOR YOU.

In a similar way, when supper was ended,
he took the chalice,
and, giving you thanks, he said the blessing,
and gave the chalice to his disciples, saying:

TAKE THIS, ALL OF YOU, AND DRINK FROM IT,
FOR THIS IS THE CHALICE OF MY BLOOD,
THE BLOOD OF THE NEW AND ETERNAL COVENANT,
WHICH WILL BE POURED OUT FOR YOU AND FOR MANY
FOR THE FORGIVENESS OF SINS.

DO THIS IN MEMORY OF ME.

The mystery of faith.

People:

A **We proclaim your Death, O Lord,
and profess your Resurrection
until you come again.**

B **When we eat this Bread and drink this Cup,
we proclaim your Death, O Lord,
until you come again.**

C **Save us, Savior of the world,
for by your Cross and Resurrection
you have set us free.**

Priest:
Therefore, O Lord, as we celebrate the memorial
of the saving Passion of your Son,
his wondrous Resurrection
and Ascension into heaven,
and as we look forward to his second coming,
we offer you in thanksgiving
this holy and living sacrifice.

Look, we pray, upon the oblation of your Church
and, recognizing the sacrificial Victim by whose death
you willed to reconcile us to yourself,
grant that we, who are nourished

by the Body and Blood of your Son
and filled with his Holy Spirit,
may become one body, one spirit in Christ.

May he make of us
an eternal offering to you,
so that we may obtain an inheritance with your elect,
especially with the most Blessed Virgin Mary, Mother of God,
with blessed Joseph, her Spouse,
with your blessed Apostles and glorious Martyrs
(with Saint N.: the Saint of the day or Patron Saint)
and with all the Saints,
on whose constant intercession in your presence
we rely for unfailing help.

May this Sacrifice of our reconciliation,
we pray, O Lord,
advance the peace and salvation of all the world.
Be pleased to confirm in faith and charity
your pilgrim Church on earth,
with your servant N. our Pope and N. our Bishop,*
the Order of Bishops, all the clergy,
and the entire people you have gained for your own.

Listen graciously to the prayers of this family,
whom you have summoned before you:
in your compassion, O merciful Father,
gather to yourself all your children
scattered throughout the world.

† To our departed brothers and sisters
and to all who were pleasing to you
at their passing from this life,
give kind admittance to your kingdom.
There we hope to enjoy for ever the fullness of your glory
through Christ our Lord,
through whom you bestow on the world all that is good. †

When this Eucharistic Prayer is used in Masses for the Dead, the following may be said:

† Remember your servant N.
whom you have called (today)
from this world to yourself.
Grant that he (she) who was united with your Son in a death like his,
may also be one with him in his Resurrection,

* Mention may be made here of the Coadjutor Bishop, or Auxiliary Bishops, as noted in the *General Instruction of the Roman Missal*, no. 149.

when from the earth
he will raise up in the flesh those who have died,
and transform our lowly body
after the pattern of his own glorious body.
To our departed brothers and sisters, too,
and to all who were pleasing to you
at their passing from this life,
give kind admittance to your kingdom.
There we hope to enjoy for ever the fullness of your glory,
when you will wipe away every tear from our eyes.
For seeing you, our God, as you are,
we shall be like you for all the ages
and praise you without end,
through Christ our Lord,
through whom you bestow on the world all that is good. †

Through him, and with him, and in him,
O God, almighty Father,
in the unity of the Holy Spirit,
all glory and honor is yours,
for ever and ever.

People: **Amen.**

Then follows the Communion Rite, page 30.

Eucharistic Prayer IV

Preface

It is truly right to give you thanks,
truly just to give you glory, Father most holy,
for you are the one God living and true,
existing before all ages and abiding for all eternity,
dwelling in unapproachable light;
yet you, who alone are good, the source of life,
have made all that is,
so that you might fill your creatures with blessings
and bring joy to many of them by the glory of your light.

And so, in your presence are countless hosts of Angels,
who serve you day and night
and, gazing upon the glory of your face,
glorify you without ceasing.

With them we, too, confess your name in exultation,
giving voice to every creature under heaven,
as we acclaim:

Holy, Holy, Holy Lord God of hosts.
Heaven and earth are full of your glory.
Hosanna in the highest.
Blessed is he who comes in the name of the Lord.
Hosanna in the highest.

Priest:
We give you praise, Father most holy,
for you are great
and you have fashioned all your works
in wisdom and in love.
You formed man in your own image
and entrusted the whole world to his care,
so that in serving you alone, the Creator,
he might have dominion over all creatures.
And when through disobedience he had lost your friendship,
you did not abandon him to the domain of death.
For you came in mercy to the aid of all,
so that those who seek might find you.
Time and again you offered them covenants
and through the prophets
taught them to look forward to salvation.

And you so loved the world, Father most holy,
that in the fullness of time
you sent your Only Begotten Son to be our Savior.
Made incarnate by the Holy Spirit
and born of the Virgin Mary,
he shared our human nature
in all things but sin.
To the poor he proclaimed the good news of salvation,
to prisoners, freedom,
and to the sorrowful of heart, joy.
To accomplish your plan,
he gave himself up to death,
and, rising from the dead,
he destroyed death and restored life.

And that we might live no longer for ourselves
but for him who died and rose again for us,
he sent the Holy Spirit from you, Father,
as the first fruits for those who believe,
so that, bringing to perfection his work in the world,
he might sanctify creation to the full.

Therefore, O Lord, we pray:
may this same Holy Spirit
graciously sanctify these offerings,
that they may become
the Body and ✠ Blood of our Lord Jesus Christ
for the celebration of this great mystery,
which he himself left us
as an eternal covenant.

For when the hour had come
for him to be glorified by you, Father most holy,
having loved his own who were in the world,
he loved them to the end:
and while they were at supper,
he took bread, blessed and broke it,
and gave it to his disciples, saying:

TAKE THIS, ALL OF YOU, AND EAT OF IT,
FOR THIS IS MY BODY,
WHICH WILL BE GIVEN UP FOR YOU.

In a similar way,
taking the chalice filled with the fruit of the vine,
he gave thanks,
and gave the chalice to his disciples, saying:

TAKE THIS, ALL OF YOU, AND DRINK FROM IT,
FOR THIS IS THE CHALICE OF MY BLOOD,
THE BLOOD OF THE NEW AND ETERNAL COVENANT,
WHICH WILL BE POURED OUT FOR YOU AND FOR MANY
FOR THE FORGIVENESS OF SINS.

DO THIS IN MEMORY OF ME.

The mystery of faith.

People:

A **We proclaim your Death, O Lord,**
and profess your Resurrection
until you come again.

B **When we eat this Bread and drink this Cup,**
we proclaim your Death, O Lord,
until you come again.

C **Save us, Savior of the world,**
for by your Cross and Resurrection
you have set us free.

Priest:
Therefore, O Lord,
as we now celebrate the memorial of our redemption,
we remember Christ's Death
and his descent to the realm of the dead,
we proclaim his Resurrection
and his Ascension to your right hand,
and, as we await his coming in glory,
we offer you his Body and Blood,
the sacrifice acceptable to you
which brings salvation to the whole world.

Look, O Lord, upon the Sacrifice
which you yourself have provided for your Church,
and grant in your loving kindness
to all who partake of this one Bread and one Chalice
that, gathered into one body by the Holy Spirit,
they may truly become a living sacrifice in Christ
to the praise of your glory.

Therefore, Lord, remember now
all for whom we offer this sacrifice:
especially your servant N. our Pope,
N. our Bishop,* and the whole Order of Bishops,
all the clergy,
those who take part in this offering,
those gathered here before you,
your entire people,
and all who seek you with a sincere heart.

Remember also
those who have died in the peace of your Christ
and all the dead,
whose faith you alone have known.

To all of us, your children,
grant, O merciful Father,
that we may enter into a heavenly inheritance
with the Blessed Virgin Mary, Mother of God,
with blessed Joseph, her Spouse,
and with your Apostles and Saints in your kingdom.
There, with the whole of creation,
freed from the corruption of sin and death,
may we glorify you through Christ our Lord,
through whom you bestow on the world all that is good.

* Mention may be made here of the Coadjutor Bishop, or Auxiliary Bishops, as noted in the *General Instruction of the Roman Missal*, no. 149.

EUCH IV

Through him, and with him, and in him,
O God, almighty Father,
in the unity of the Holy Spirit,
all glory and honor is yours,
for ever and ever.

People: **Amen.**

The Communion Rite **STAND**

The Lord's Prayer

Priest: At the Savior's command
and formed by divine teaching,
we dare to say:

All: **Our Father, who art in heaven,**
hallowed be thy name;
thy kingdom come,
thy will be done
on earth as it is in heaven.
Give us this day our daily bread,
and forgive us our trespasses,
as we forgive those who trespass against us;
and lead us not into temptation,
but deliver us from evil.

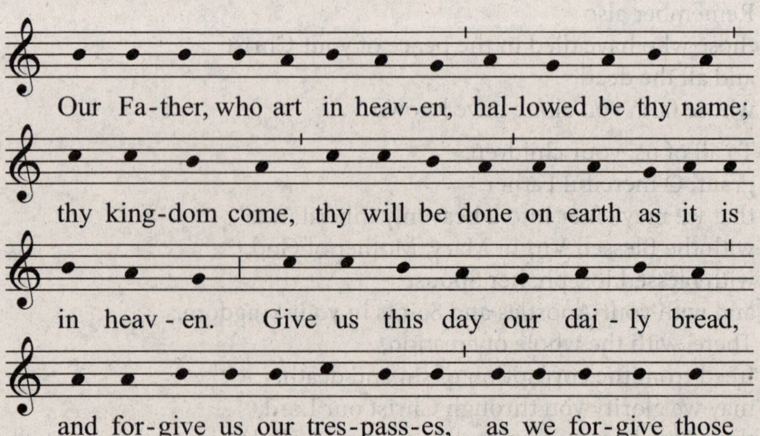

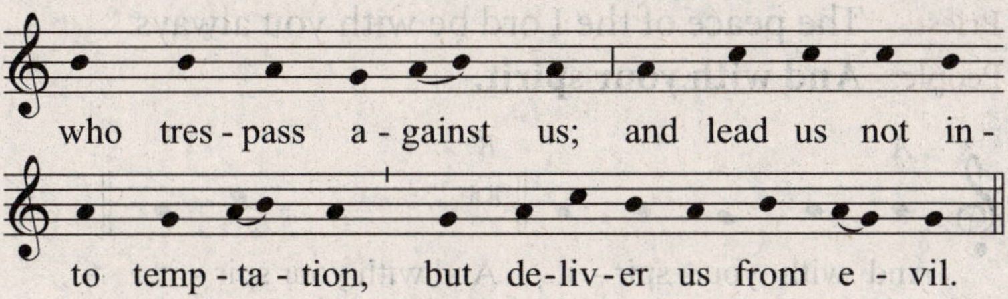

Priest: Deliver us, Lord, we pray, from every evil,
graciously grant peace in our days,
that, by the help of your mercy,
we may be always free from sin
and safe from all distress,
as we await the blessed hope
and the coming of our Savior, Jesus Christ.

All: **For the kingdom,**
the power and the glory are yours
now and for ever.

Sign of Peace

Priest: Lord Jesus Christ,
who said to your Apostles:
Peace I leave you, my peace I give you,
look not on our sins,
but on the faith of your Church,
and graciously grant her peace and unity
in accordance with your will.
Who live and reign for ever and ever.

People: **Amen.**

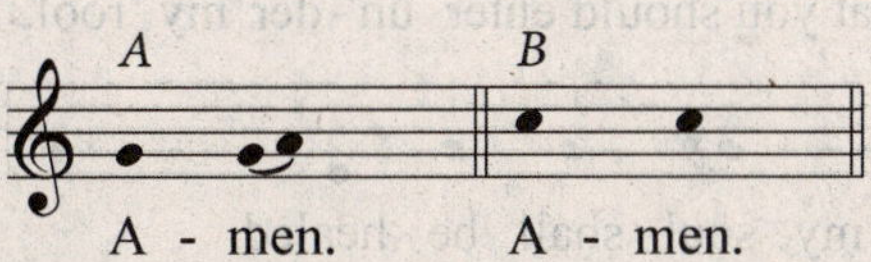

Priest: The peace of the Lord be with you always.

People: **And with your spirit.**

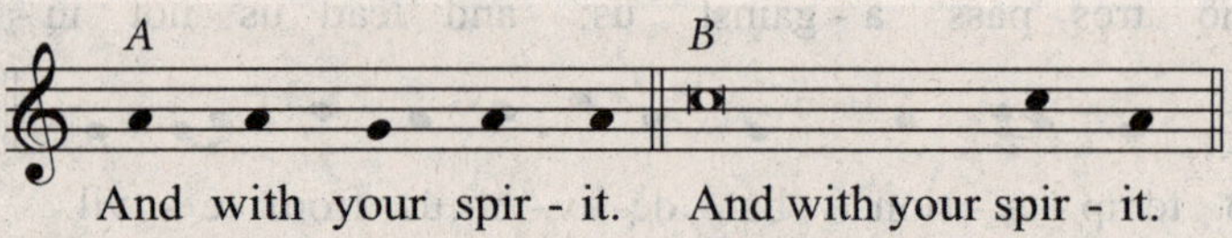

Then, if appropriate, the Deacon, or the Priest, adds:

Let us offer each other the sign of peace.

Fraction of the Bread

All: **Lamb of God, you take away the sins of the world,**
have mercy on us.
Lamb of God, you take away the sins of the world,
have mercy on us.
Lamb of God, you take away the sins of the world,
grant us peace.

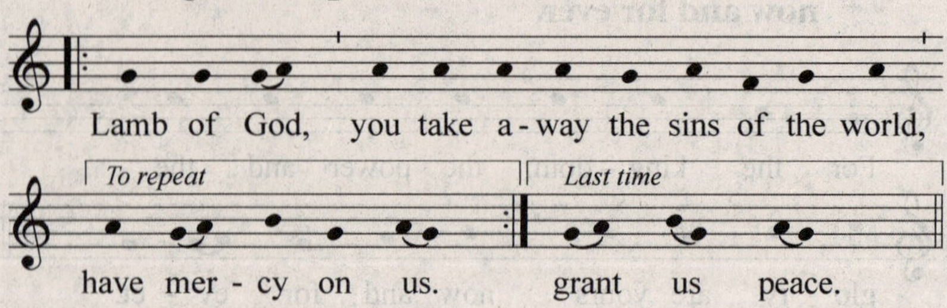

Invitation to Communion

KNEEL

Priest: Behold the Lamb of God,
behold him who takes away the sins of the world.
Blessed are those called to the supper of the Lamb.

All: **Lord, I am not worthy**
that you should enter under my roof,
but only say the word
and my soul shall be healed.

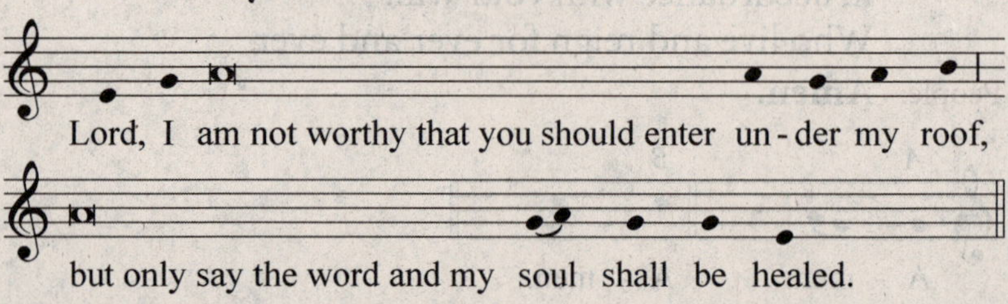

Communion **STAND**

The Priest says to each of the communicants: The Body of Christ.

The communicant replies: **Amen.**

Prayer after Communion **STAND**

The Priest says: Let us pray.

At the end the people acclaim: **Amen.**

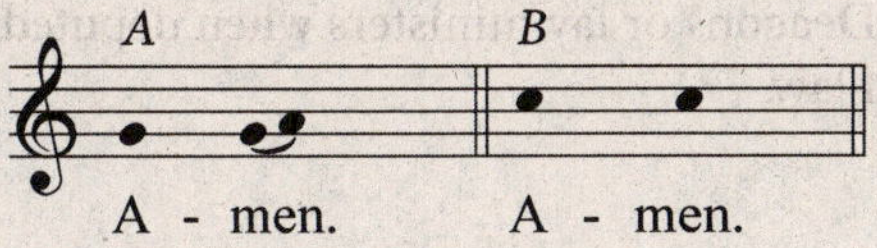

The Concluding Rites

Final Blessing

Priest: The Lord be with you.

People: **And with your spirit.**

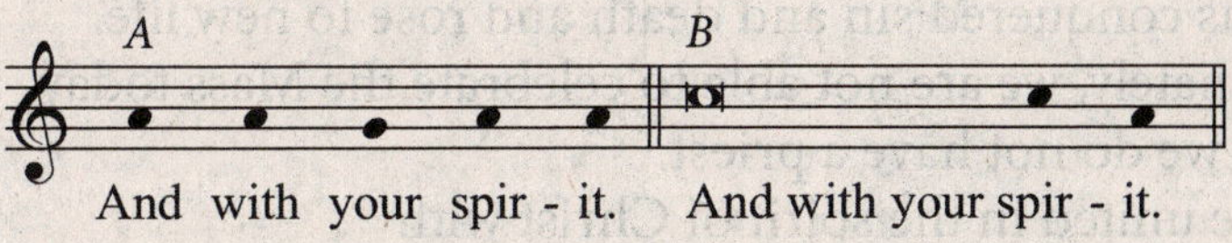

Priest: May almighty God bless you,
the Father, and the Son, ✠ and the Holy Spirit.

People: **Amen.**

Dismissal

The Deacon, or the Priest himself:

Go forth, the Mass is ended.

Or:

Go and announce the Gospel of the Lord.

Or:

Go in peace, glorifying the Lord by your life.

Or:

Go in peace.

People: **Thanks be to God.**

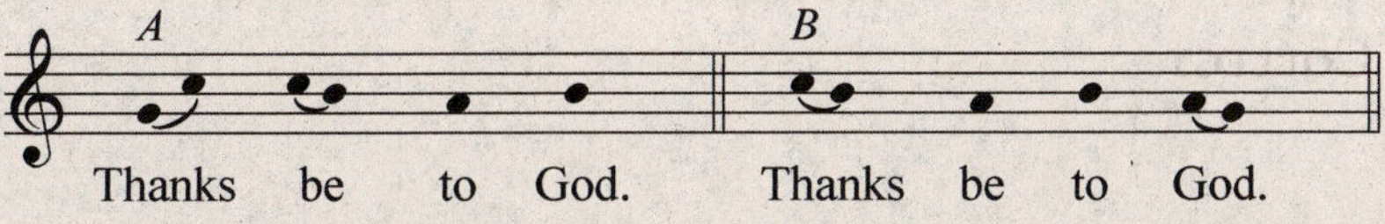

Sunday Celebration of the Liturgy of the Word

[With Holy Communion]

This prayer service is adapted from *Sunday Celebrations in the Absence of a Priest* and may be used by Deacons or lay ministers when deputed in accordance with the norm of law.

Introductory Rites

Introduction

Deacon or lay leader:

We gather here to celebrate the Lord's Day.
Sunday has been called the Lord's Day because
 it was on this day
that Jesus conquered sin and death and rose to new life.
Unfortunately, we are not able to celebrate the Mass today
because we do not have a priest.
Let us be united in the spirit of Christ with
 the Church around the world
and celebrate our redemption in Christ's suffering,
 Death and Resurrection.

Sign of the Cross **STAND**

Deacon or lay leader:

In the name of the Father, and of the Son, and of the Holy Spirit.

All respond: **Amen.**

Greeting

Deacon or lay leader:

Grace and peace to you from God our Father
and from the Lord Jesus Christ.
Blessed be God for ever.

All: **Blessed be God for ever.**

Collect

Liturgy of the Word of God — SIT

First Reading

Responsorial Psalm

Second Reading

Gospel Acclamation — STAND

Gospel

Homily or Reflection on the Readings — SIT

Period of Silence

Profession of Faith — STAND

[The Nicene Creed can be found on page 8.]

Apostles' Creed

I believe in God,
the Father almighty,
Creator of heaven and earth,
and in Jesus Christ, his only Son, our Lord,

At the words that follow, up to and including the Virgin Mary, all bow.

who was conceived by the Holy Spirit,
born of the Virgin Mary,
suffered under Pontius Pilate,
was crucified, died and was buried;
he descended into hell;
on the third day he rose again from the dead;
he ascended into heaven,
and is seated at the right hand of God the Father almighty;
from there he will come to judge the living and the dead.

I believe in the Holy Spirit,
the holy catholic Church,
the communion of saints,
the forgiveness of sins,

the resurrection of the body,
and life everlasting. Amen.

Prayer of the Faithful

Communion Rite

Lord's Prayer

Deacon or lay leader:

The Father provides us with food for eternal life.
Let us pray for nourishment and strength.

All say:

Our Father, who art in heaven,
hallowed be thy name;
thy kingdom come,
thy will be done
on earth as it is in heaven.
Give us this day our daily bread,
and forgive us our trespasses,
as we forgive those who trespass against us;
and lead us not into temptation,
but deliver us from evil.
Amen.

Invitation to Communion — KNEEL

Deacon or lay leader:

Behold the Lamb of God,
behold him who takes away the sins of the world.
Blessed are those called to the supper of the Lamb.

All say:

Lord, I am not worthy
that you should enter under my roof,
but only say the word
and my soul shall be healed.

Communion

Act of Thanksgiving — STAND

Concluding Rite

Invitation to Pray for Vocations to the Priesthood

Deacon or lay leader:

Mindful of the Lord's word, "Ask the Master of the harvest to send out laborers for the harvest," let us pray for an increase of vocations to the Priesthood. May our prayer hasten the day when we will be able to take part in the celebration of the Holy Eucharist every Sunday.

Blessing

Deacon: The Lord be with you.

All: **And with your spirit.**

And he blesses the people, saying:

May almighty God bless you,
the Father, and the Son, ✠ and the Holy Spirit.

All reply: **Amen.**

If, however, the minister is neither a Priest nor a Deacon, while invoking God's blessing and signing himself (herself), he (she) says:

May the Lord bless us,
protect us from all evil
and lead us to everlasting life.

Or:

May the almighty and merciful Lord bless us and keep us,
the Father, and the Son, and the Holy Spirit.

All reply: **Amen.**

Finally, the minister says:

Go in peace.

All reply: **Thanks be to God.**

Then, after making an appropriate sign of reverence, the minister leaves.

Sign of Peace

First Sunday of Advent

November 29, 2026

Reflection on the Gospel

The gospel that begins our new liturgical year admonishes us, the faithful, to watch and be alert. Why? Because, simply, we do not know. In this pericope what is unknown is "when the lord of the house is coming." But for each of us today, this gospel calls us to embrace the unknown, as another expression goes, and to participate, actively, in our lives of faith instead of anticipating. So in fact, the gospel is calling us, really, to not know—and to be okay with not knowing.

—Living Liturgy™, *First Sunday of Advent 2026*

ENTRANCE ANTIPHON (Cf. Psalm 25[24]:1-3)

To you, I lift up my soul, O my God.
In you, I have trusted; let me not be put to shame.
Nor let my enemies exult over me;
and let none who hope in you be put to shame.

COLLECT

Grant your faithful, we pray, almighty God,
the resolve to run forth to meet your Christ
with righteous deeds at his coming,
so that, gathered at his right hand,
they may be worthy to possess the heavenly Kingdom.
Through our Lord Jesus Christ, your Son,
who lives and reigns with you in the unity of the Holy Spirit,
God, for ever and ever. All: **Amen.**

READING I (L 2) (Isaiah 63:16b-17, 19b; 64:2-7)

A reading from the Book of the Prophet Isaiah

Oh, that you would rend the heavens and come down!

You, LORD, are our father,
our redeemer you are named forever.
Why do you let us wander, O LORD, from your ways,
and harden our hearts so that we fear you not?
Return for the sake of your servants,
the tribes of your heritage.
Oh, that you would rend the heavens and come down,
with the mountains quaking before you,
while you wrought awesome deeds we could not hope for,
such as they had not heard of from of old.
No ear has ever heard, no eye ever seen, any God but you
doing such deeds for those who wait for him.
Would that you might meet us doing right,
that we were mindful of you in our ways!
Behold, you are angry, and we are sinful;
all of us have become like unclean people,
all our good deeds are like polluted rags;
we have all withered like leaves,
and our guilt carries us away like the wind.
There is none who calls upon your name,
who rouses himself to cling to you;
for you have hidden your face from us
and have delivered us up to our guilt.
Yet, O LORD, you are our father;
we are the clay and you the potter:
we are all the work of your hands.

The word of the Lord. All: **Thanks be to God.**

Responsorial Psalm 80

Psalm 80:2-3, 15-16, 18-19

℟. (4) **Lord, make us turn to you; let us see your face and we shall be saved.**

O shepherd of Israel, hearken,
from your throne upon the cherubim, shine forth.
Rouse your power,
and come to save us. ℟.

Once again, O Lord of hosts,
look down from heaven, and see;
take care of this vine,
and protect what your right hand has planted,
the son of man whom you yourself made strong. ℟.

May your help be with the man of your right hand,
with the son of man whom you yourself made strong.
Then we will no more withdraw from you;
give us new life, and we will call upon your name. ℟.

Reading II (1 Corinthians 1:3-9)

A reading from the first Letter of Saint Paul to the Corinthians

We wait for the revelation of our Lord Jesus Christ.

Brothers and sisters:
Grace to you and peace from God our Father
and the Lord Jesus Christ.

I give thanks to my God always on your account
for the grace of God bestowed on you in Christ Jesus,

that in him you were enriched in every way,
with all discourse and all knowledge,
as the testimony to Christ was confirmed among you,
so that you are not lacking in any spiritual gift
as you wait for the revelation of our Lord Jesus Christ.
He will keep you firm to the end,
irreproachable on the day of our Lord Jesus Christ.
God is faithful,
and by him you were called to fellowship with his Son,
Jesus Christ our Lord.

The word of the Lord. All: **Thanks be to God.**

GOSPEL (Mark 13:33-37)

ALLELUIA (Psalm 85:8)

℣. Alleluia, alleluia. ℟. **Alleluia, alleluia.**
℣. Show us Lord, your love;
and grant us your salvation. ℟.

✠ **A reading from the holy Gospel according to Mark**

All: **Glory to you, O Lord.**

Be watchful! You do not know when the Lord of the house is coming.

Jesus said to his disciples:
"Be watchful! Be alert!
You do not know when the time will come.
It is like a man traveling abroad.
He leaves home and places his servants in charge,
each with his own work,
and orders the gatekeeper to be on the watch.
Watch, therefore;
you do not know when the Lord of the house is coming,
whether in the evening, or at midnight,
or at cockcrow, or in the morning.
May he not come suddenly and find you sleeping.
What I say to you, I say to all: 'Watch!'"

The Gospel of the Lord. All: **Praise to you, Lord Jesus Christ.**

Prayer over the Offerings

Accept, we pray, O Lord, these offerings we make,
gathered from among your gifts to us,
and may what you grant us to celebrate devoutly here below
gain for us the prize of eternal redemption.
Through Christ our Lord. All: **Amen.**

Communion Antiphon (Psalm 85[84]:13)

The Lord will bestow his bounty, and our earth shall yield its increase.

Prayer after Communion

May these mysteries, O Lord,
in which we have participated,
profit us, we pray,
for even now, as we walk amid passing things,
you teach us by them to love the things of heaven
and hold fast to what endures.
Through Christ our Lord. All: **Amen.**

Second Sunday of Advent

December 6, 2026

Reflection on the Gospel

In this gospel, John the Baptist teaches us by his words and example: how do we today prepare for the coming of the Lord? Christmas, we will recall, exists as a celebration of not only the eternal Word taking on human flesh, but of that second coming at the end of human time. Taking John's example, we might today choose to live more simply and to more freely share with those we encounter the way our lives have been impacted by our faith and our relationship with Jesus.

—Living Liturgy™, *Second Sunday of Advent 2026*

Entrance Antiphon (Cf. Isaiah 30:19, 30)

O people of Sion, behold,
the Lord will come to save the nations,
and the Lord will make the glory of his voice heard
in the joy of your heart.

Collect

Almighty and merciful God,
may no earthly undertaking hinder those
who set out in haste to meet your Son,
but may our learning of heavenly wisdom
gain us admittance to his company.
Who lives and reigns with you in the unity of the Holy Spirit,
God, for ever and ever. All: **Amen.**

Reading I (L 5) (Isaiah 40:1-5, 9-11)

A reading from the Book of the Prophet Isaiah

Prepare the way of the Lord.

Comfort, give comfort to my people,
says your God.
Speak tenderly to Jerusalem, and proclaim to her
that her service is at an end,
her guilt is expiated;
indeed, she has received from the hand of the Lord
double for all her sins.

A voice cries out:
In the desert prepare the way of the Lord!
Make straight in the wasteland a highway for our God!
Every valley shall be filled in,
every mountain and hill shall be made low;
the rugged land shall be made a plain,
the rough country, a broad valley.
Then the glory of the Lord shall be revealed,
and all people shall see it together;
for the mouth of the Lord has spoken.

Go up onto a high mountain,
Zion, herald of glad tidings;

cry out at the top of your voice,
Jerusalem, herald of good news!
Fear not to cry out
and say to the cities of Judah:
Here is your God!
Here comes with power
the Lord God,
who rules by his strong arm;
here is his reward with him,
his recompense before him.
Like a shepherd he feeds his flock;
in his arms he gathers the lambs,
carrying them in his bosom,
and leading the ewes with care.

The word of the Lord. All: **Thanks be to God.**

Responsorial Psalm 85

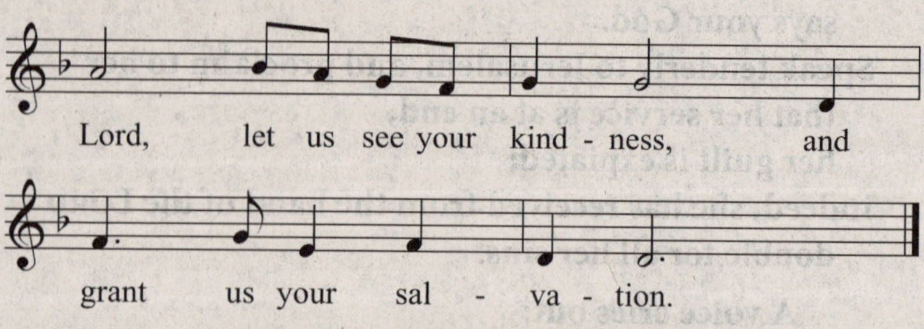

Psalm 85:9-10, 11-12, 13-14

℟. (8) **Lord, let us see your kindness, and grant us your salvation.**

I will hear what God proclaims;
the Lord—for he proclaims peace to his people.
Near indeed is his salvation to those who fear him,
glory dwelling in our land. ℟.

Kindness and truth shall meet;
justice and peace shall kiss.

Truth shall spring out of the earth,
and justice shall look down from heaven. ℟.

The Lord himself will give his benefits;
our land shall yield its increase.
Justice shall walk before him,
and prepare the way of his steps. ℟.

Reading II (2 Peter 3:8-14)

A reading from the second Letter of Saint Peter

We await new heavens and a new earth.

Do not ignore this one fact, beloved,
that with the Lord one day is like a thousand years
and a thousand years like one day.
The Lord does not delay his promise, as some regard "delay,"
but he is patient with you,
not wishing that any should perish
but that all should come to repentance.
But the day of the Lord will come like a thief,
and then the heavens will pass away with a mighty roar
and the elements will be dissolved by fire,
and the earth and everything done on it will be found out.

Since everything is to be dissolved in this way,
what sort of persons ought you to be,
conducting yourselves in holiness and devotion,
waiting for and hastening the coming of the day of God,
because of which the heavens will be dissolved in flames
and the elements melted by fire.
But according to his promise
we await new heavens and a new earth
in which righteousness dwells.

Therefore, beloved, since you await these things,
be eager to be found without spot or blemish before him, at peace.

The word of the Lord. All: **Thanks be to God.**

GOSPEL (Mark 1:1-8)
ALLELUIA (Luke 3:4, 6)

℣. Alleluia, alleluia. ℟. **Alleluia, alleluia.**
℣. Prepare the way of the Lord, make straight his paths:
all flesh shall see the salvation of God. ℟.

✠ **A reading from the holy Gospel according to Mark**

All: **Glory to you, O Lord.**

Make straight the paths of the Lord.

The beginning of the gospel of Jesus Christ the Son of God.

As it is written in Isaiah the prophet:
Behold, I am sending my messenger ahead of you;
he will prepare your way.
A voice of one crying out in the desert:
"Prepare the way of the Lord,
make straight his paths."
John the Baptist appeared in the desert
proclaiming a baptism of repentance for the forgiveness of sins.
People of the whole Judean countryside
and all the inhabitants of Jerusalem
were going out to him
and were being baptized by him in the Jordan River
as they acknowledged their sins.
John was clothed in camel's hair,
with a leather belt around his waist.
He fed on locusts and wild honey.
And this is what he proclaimed:
"One mightier than I is coming after me.

I am not worthy to stoop and loosen the thongs of his sandals.
I have baptized you with water;
he will baptize you with the Holy Spirit."

The Gospel of the Lord. All: **Praise to you, Lord Jesus Christ.**

Prayer over the Offerings

Be pleased, O Lord, with our humble prayers and offerings,
and, since we have no merits to plead our cause,
come, we pray, to our rescue
with the protection of your mercy.
Through Christ our Lord. All: **Amen.**

Communion Antiphon (Baruch 5:5; 4:36)

Jerusalem, arise and stand upon the heights,
and behold the joy which comes to you from God.

Prayer after Communion

Replenished by the food of spiritual nourishment,
we humbly beseech you, O Lord,
that, through our partaking in this mystery,
you may teach us to judge wisely the things of earth
and hold firm to the things of heaven.
Through Christ our Lord. All: **Amen.**

The Immaculate Conception of the Blessed Virgin Mary

December 8, 2026

Reflection on the Gospel

God speaks to us as did the angel to Mary in this gospel: "Do not be afraid." Why might we be afraid? Because so often God's call to us is shrouded in the unknown. Have you ever had that itch, that mysterious prod in your side that makes you feel called to something else—but you can't quite put your finger on it? And yet each time it's been God, calling not to personal desires, knowledge, or power but to faith in the divine mystery and mission. "How can this be?" indeed.

—Living Liturgy™, *The Immaculate Conception of the Blessed Virgin Mary 2026*

Entrance Antiphon (Isaiah 61:10)

I rejoice heartily in the Lord,
in my God is the joy of my soul;
for he has clothed me with a robe of salvation,
and wrapped me in a mantle of justice,
like a bride adorned with her jewels.

Collect

O God, who by the Immaculate Conception of the Blessed Virgin
prepared a worthy dwelling for your Son,
grant, we pray,
that, as you preserved her from every stain
by virtue of the Death of your Son, which you foresaw,
so, through her intercession,
we, too, may be cleansed and admitted to your presence.
Through our Lord Jesus Christ, your Son,
who lives and reigns with you in the unity of the Holy Spirit,
God, for ever and ever. All: **Amen.**

Reading I (L 689) (Genesis 3:9-15, 20)

A reading from the Book of Genesis

I will put enmity between your offspring and hers.

After the man, Adam, had eaten of the tree,
the LORD God called to the man and asked him,
"Where are you?"
He answered, "I heard you in the garden;
but I was afraid, because I was naked,
so I hid myself."
Then he asked, "Who told you that you were naked?
You have eaten, then,
from the tree of which I had forbidden you to eat!"
The man replied, "The woman whom you put here with me—
she gave me fruit from the tree, and so I ate it."
The LORD God then asked the woman,
"Why did you do such a thing?"
The woman answered, "The serpent tricked me into it, so I ate it."

Then the LORD God said to the serpent:
"Because you have done this, you shall be banned
from all the animals
and from all the wild creatures;
on your belly shall you crawl,
and dirt shall you eat
all the days of your life.
I will put enmity between you and the woman,
and between your offspring and hers;
he will strike at your head,
while you strike at his heel."

The man called his wife Eve,
because she became the mother of all the living.

The word of the Lord. All: **Thanks be to God.**

Responsorial Psalm 98

Psalm 98:1, 2-3ab, 3cd-4

℟. (1a) **Sing to the Lord a new song, for he has done marvelous deeds.**

Sing to the Lord a new song,
for he has done wondrous deeds;
His right hand has won victory for him,
his holy arm. ℟.

The Lord has made his salvation known:
in the sight of the nations he has revealed his justice.
He has remembered his kindness and his faithfulness
toward the house of Israel. ℟.

All the ends of the earth have seen
the salvation by our God.
Sing joyfully to the Lord, all you lands;
break into song; sing praise. ℟.

Reading II (Ephesians 1:3-6, 11-12)

A reading from the Letter of Saint Paul to the Ephesians

He chose us in Christ before the foundation of the world.

Brothers and sisters:
Blessed be the God and Father of our Lord Jesus Christ,
who has blessed us in Christ
with every spiritual blessing in the heavens,
as he chose us in him, before the foundation of the world,
to be holy and without blemish before him.

In love he destined us for adoption to himself through Jesus Christ,
in accord with the favor of his will,
for the praise of the glory of his grace
that he granted us in the beloved.

In him we were also chosen,
destined in accord with the purpose of the One
who accomplishes all things according to the intention of his will,
so that we might exist for the praise of his glory,
we who first hoped in Christ.

The word of the Lord. All: **Thanks be to God.**

GOSPEL (Luke 1:26-38)

ALLELUIA (*See* Luke 1:28)

℣. Alleluia, alleluia. ℟. **Alleluia, alleluia.**
℣. Hail, Mary, full of grace, the Lord is with you;
blessed are you among women. ℟.

✠ **A reading from the holy Gospel according to Luke**

All: **Glory to you, O Lord.**

Hail, full of grace! The Lord is with you.

The angel Gabriel was sent from God
to a town of Galilee called Nazareth,
to a virgin betrothed to a man named Joseph,
of the house of David,
and the virgin's name was Mary.
And coming to her, he said,
"Hail, full of grace! The Lord is with you."
But she was greatly troubled at what was said
and pondered what sort of greeting this might be.
Then the angel said to her,
"Do not be afraid, Mary,
for you have found favor with God.
Behold, you will conceive in your womb and bear a son,
and you shall name him Jesus.

He will be great and will be called Son of the Most High,
and the Lord God will give him the throne of David his father,
and he will rule over the house of Jacob forever,
and of his Kingdom there will be no end."
But Mary said to the angel,
"How can this be,
since I have no relations with a man?"
And the angel said to her in reply,
"The Holy Spirit will come upon you,
and the power of the Most High will overshadow you.
Therefore the child to be born
will be called holy, the Son of God.
And behold, Elizabeth, your relative,
has also conceived a son in her old age,
and this is the sixth month for her who was called barren;
for nothing will be impossible for God."
Mary said, "Behold, I am the handmaid of the Lord.
May it be done to me according to your word."
Then the angel departed from her.

The Gospel of the Lord. All: **Praise to you, Lord Jesus Christ.**

Prayer over the Offerings

Graciously accept the saving sacrifice
which we offer you, O Lord,
on the Solemnity of the Immaculate Conception
of the Blessed Virgin Mary,
and grant that, as we profess her,
on account of your prevenient grace,
to be untouched by any stain of sin,
so, through her intercession,
we may be delivered from all our faults.
Through Christ our Lord. All: **Amen.**

Communion Antiphon

Glorious things are spoken of you, O Mary,
for from you arose the sun of justice,
Christ our God.

Prayer after Communion

May the Sacrament we have received,
O Lord our God,
heal in us the wounds of that fault
from which in a singular way
you preserved Blessed Mary in her Immaculate Conception.
Through Christ our Lord. All: **Amen.**

Third Sunday of Advent

December 13, 2026

Reflection on the Gospel

Christian paradox is perhaps best expressed in mystery—God's truth beyond all human understanding. In our Scriptures, these paradoxes abound: both greatness and lowliness, both strength and weakness, both light and darkness, both first and last, both humanity and divinity, both life and death, both one and many. In today's gospel, John the Baptist, while decidedly unjoyful, calls each of us to a most joyful pursuit: following the one true light in the darkness, which the darkness could not overcome.

—Living Liturgy™, *Third Sunday of Advent 2026*

Entrance Antiphon (Philippians 4:4-5)

Rejoice in the Lord always; again I say, rejoice.
Indeed, the Lord is near.

Collect

O God, who see how your people
faithfully await the feast of the Lord's Nativity,
enable us, we pray,
to attain the joys of so great a salvation
and to celebrate them always
with solemn worship and glad rejoicing.
Through our Lord Jesus Christ, your Son,
who lives and reigns with you in the unity of the Holy Spirit,
God, for ever and ever. All: **Amen.**

READING I (L 8) (Isaiah 61:1-2a, 10-11)

A reading from the Book of the Prophet Isaiah

I rejoice heartily in the Lord.

The spirit of the Lord GOD is upon me,
because the LORD has anointed me;
he has sent me to bring glad tidings to the poor,
to heal the brokenhearted,
to proclaim liberty to the captives
and release to the prisoners,
to announce a year of favor from the LORD
and a day of vindication by our God.

I rejoice heartily in the LORD,
in my God is the joy of my soul;
for he has clothed me with a robe of salvation
and wrapped me in a mantle of justice,
like a bridegroom adorned with a diadem,
like a bride bedecked with her jewels.
As the earth brings forth its plants,
and a garden makes its growth spring up,
so will the Lord GOD make justice and praise
spring up before all the nations.

The word of the Lord. All: **Thanks be to God.**

RESPONSORIAL PSALM

Luke 1:46-48, 49-50, 53-54

℟. (Isaiah 61:10b) **My soul rejoices in my God.**

My soul proclaims the greatness of the Lord;
my spirit rejoices in God my Savior,
for he has looked upon his lowly servant.
From this day all generations will call me blessed: ℟.

The Almighty has done great things for me,
and holy is his Name.
He has mercy on those who fear him
in every generation. ℟.

He has filled the hungry with good things,
and the rich he has sent away empty.
He has come to the help of his servant Israel
for he has remembered his promise of mercy. ℟.

READING II (1 Thessalonians 5:16-24)

A reading from the first Letter of Saint Paul to the Thessalonians

May you entirely, spirit, soul, and body, be preserved blameless for the coming of our Lord Jesus Christ.

Brothers and sisters:
Rejoice always. Pray without ceasing.
In all circumstances give thanks,
for this is the will of God for you in Christ Jesus.
Do not quench the Spirit.
Do not despise prophetic utterances.
Test everything; retain what is good.
Refrain from every kind of evil.
May the God of peace make you perfectly holy
and may you entirely, spirit, soul, and body,
be preserved blameless for the coming of our Lord Jesus Christ.
The one who calls you is faithful,
and he will also accomplish it.

The word of the Lord. All: **Thanks be to God.**

GOSPEL (John 1:6-8, 19-28)

ALLELUIA (Isaiah 61:1 (cited in Luke 4:18))

℣. Alleluia, alleluia. ℟. **Alleluia, alleluia.**
℣. The Spirit of the Lord is upon me,
because he has anointed me
to bring glad tidings to the poor. ℟.

✠ **A reading from the holy Gospel according to John**

All: **Glory to you, O Lord.**

There is one among you whom you do not recognize.

A man named John was sent from God.
He came for testimony, to testify to the light,
so that all might believe through him.
He was not the light,
but came to testify to the light.

And this is the testimony of John.
When the Jews from Jerusalem sent priests
and Levites to him
to ask him, "Who are you?"
he admitted and did not deny it,
but admitted, "I am not the Christ."
So they asked him,
"What are you then? Are you Elijah?"
And he said, "I am not."
"Are you the Prophet?"
He answered, "No."
So they said to him,
"Who are you, so we can give an answer to those who sent us?
What do you have to say for yourself?"
He said:
"I am *the voice of one crying out in the desert,*
'*make straight the way of the Lord,*'
as Isaiah the prophet said."
Some Pharisees were also sent.
They asked him,
"Why then do you baptize
if you are not the Christ or Elijah or the Prophet?"
John answered them,
"I baptize with water;
but there is one among you whom you do not recognize,

the one who is coming after me,
whose sandal strap I am not worthy to untie."
This happened in Bethany across the Jordan,
where John was baptizing.

The Gospel of the Lord. All: **Praise to you, Lord Jesus Christ.**

Prayer over the Offerings

May the sacrifice of our worship, Lord, we pray,
be offered to you unceasingly,
to complete what was begun in sacred mystery
and powerfully accomplish for us your saving work.
Through Christ our Lord. All: **Amen.**

Communion Antiphon (Cf. Isaiah 35:4)

Say to the faint of heart: Be strong and do not fear.
Behold, our God will come, and he will save us.

Prayer after Communion

We implore your mercy, Lord,
that this divine sustenance may cleanse us of our faults
and prepare us for the coming feasts.
Through Christ our Lord. All: **Amen.**

Fourth Sunday of Advent

December 20, 2026

Reflection on the Gospel

It seems that even before Mary knew of her calling to become the mother of God incarnate that she must have already learned her faith well: from her parents, from rabbis and other holy men and women, and perhaps even from the ritual practices of her faith. Just as this gospel passage has been repetitive this Advent, the consistent presence of loved ones and faith-filled teachers, and the regular and unfailing practice of the rituals of her faith, surely embedded in Mary all that we know her to be.

—Living Liturgy™, *Fourth Sunday of Advent 2026*

ENTRANCE ANTIPHON (Cf. Isaiah 45:8)

Drop down dew from above, you heavens,
and let the clouds rain down the Just One;
let the earth be opened and bring forth a Savior.

COLLECT

Pour forth, we beseech you, O Lord,
your grace into our hearts,
that we, to whom the Incarnation of Christ your Son
was made known by the message of an Angel,
may by his Passion and Cross
be brought to the glory of his Resurrection.
Who lives and reigns with you in the unity of the Holy Spirit,
God, for ever and ever. All: **Amen.**

READING I (L 11) (2 Samuel 7:1-5, 8b-12, 14a, 16)

A reading from the second Book of Samuel

The kingdom of David shall endure forever before the Lord.

When King David was settled in his palace,
and the LORD had given him rest from his enemies on every side,
he said to Nathan the prophet,

"Here I am living in a house of cedar,
while the ark of God dwells in a tent!"
Nathan answered the king,
"Go, do whatever you have in mind,
for the LORD is with you."
But that night the LORD spoke to Nathan and said:
"Go, tell my servant David, 'Thus says the LORD:
Should you build me a house to dwell in?

" 'It was I who took you from the pasture
and from the care of the flock
to be commander of my people Israel.
I have been with you wherever you went,
and I have destroyed all your enemies before you.
And I will make you famous like the great ones of the earth.
I will fix a place for my people Israel;
I will plant them so that they may dwell in their place
without further disturbance.
Neither shall the wicked continue to afflict them as they did of old,
since the time I first appointed judges over my people Israel.
I will give you rest from all your enemies.
The LORD also reveals to you
that he will establish a house for you.
And when your time comes and you rest with your ancestors,
I will raise up your heir after you, sprung from your loins,
and I will make his kingdom firm.
I will be a father to him,
and he shall be a son to me.
Your house and your kingdom shall endure forever before me;
your throne shall stand firm forever.' "

The word of the Lord. All: **Thanks be to God.**

Responsorial Psalm 89

Psalm 89:2-3, 4-5, 27, 29

℟. (2a) **Forever I will sing the goodness of the Lord.**

The promises of the Lord I will sing forever;
  through all generations my mouth shall proclaim
    your faithfulness.
For you have said, "My kindness is established forever";
  in heaven you have confirmed your faithfulness. ℟.

"I have made a covenant with my chosen one,
  I have sworn to David my servant:
forever will I confirm your posterity
  and establish your throne for all generations." ℟.

"He shall say of me, 'You are my father,
  my God, the Rock, my savior.'
Forever I will maintain my kindness toward him,
  and my covenant with him stands firm." ℟.

Reading II (Romans 16:25-27)

A reading from the Letter of Saint Paul to the Romans

The mystery kept secret for long ages has now been manifested.

Brothers and sisters:
To him who can strengthen you,
according to my gospel and the proclamation of Jesus Christ,
according to the revelation of the mystery kept secret for long ages
but now manifested through the prophetic writings and,
according to the command of the eternal God,
made known to all nations to bring about the obedience of faith,

to the only wise God, through Jesus Christ
be glory forever and ever. Amen.

The word of the Lord. All: **Thanks be to God.**

GOSPEL (Luke 1:26-38)
ALLELUIA (Luke 1:38)
℣. Alleluia, alleluia. ℟. **Alleluia, alleluia.**
℣. Behold, I am the handmaid of the Lord.
May it be done to me according to your word. ℟.

✠ **A reading from the holy Gospel according to Luke**

All: **Glory to you, O Lord.**

Behold, you will conceive in your womb and bear a son.

The angel Gabriel was sent from God
to a town of Galilee called Nazareth,
to a virgin betrothed to a man named Joseph,
of the house of David,
and the virgin's name was Mary.
And coming to her, he said,
"Hail, full of grace! The Lord is with you."
But she was greatly troubled at what was said
and pondered what sort of greeting this might be.
Then the angel said to her,
"Do not be afraid, Mary,
for you have found favor with God.

"Behold, you will conceive in your womb and bear a son,
and you shall name him Jesus.
He will be great and will be called Son of the Most High,
and the Lord God will give him the throne of David
his father,
and he will rule over the house of Jacob forever,
and of his kingdom there will be no end."
But Mary said to the angel,
"How can this be,
since I have no relations with a man?"

And the angel said to her in reply,
"The Holy Spirit will come upon you,
and the power of the Most High will overshadow you.
Therefore the child to be born
will be called holy, the Son of God.
And behold, Elizabeth, your relative,
has also conceived a son in her old age,
and this is the sixth month for her who was called barren;
for nothing will be impossible for God."
Mary said, "Behold, I am the handmaid of the Lord.
May it be done to me according to your word."
Then the angel departed from her.

The Gospel of the Lord. All: **Praise to you, Lord Jesus Christ.**

Prayer over the Offerings

May the Holy Spirit, O Lord,
sanctify these gifts laid upon your altar,
just as he filled with his power the womb of the Blessed Virgin Mary.
Through Christ our Lord. All: **Amen.**

Communion Antiphon (Isaiah 7:14)

Behold, a Virgin shall conceive and bear a son;
and his name will be called Emmanuel.

Prayer after Communion

Having received this pledge of eternal redemption,
we pray, almighty God,
that, as the feast day of our salvation draws ever nearer,
so we may press forward all the more eagerly
to the worthy celebration of the mystery of your Son's Nativity.
Who lives and reigns for ever and ever. All: **Amen.**

The Nativity of the Lord (Christmas)

AT THE VIGIL MASS

December 24, 2026

Reflection on the Gospel

The gospel today details Joseph's response to learning of Mary's pregnancy before their marriage and consummation. At first, with at least some compassion, he does not want to shame Mary as would have been common. Yet after his dream and the divine message of the angel, he welcomes the quite untraditional family experience. This gospel invites families to ponder the value in one another and what we can learn from one another. How do we help each other grow in holiness and faith?

—Living Liturgy™, *The Nativity of the Lord (Christmas) 2026*

Entrance Antiphon (Cf. Exodus 16:6-7)

Today you will know that the Lord will come, and he will
save us,
and in the morning you will see his glory.

Collect

O God, who gladden us year by year
as we wait in hope for our redemption,
grant that, just as we joyfully welcome
your Only Begotten Son as our Redeemer,
we may also merit to face him confidently
when he comes again as our Judge.
Who lives and reigns with you in the unity of the Holy Spirit,
God, for ever and ever. All: **Amen.**

Reading I (L 13) (Isaiah 62:1-5)

A reading from the Book of the Prophet Isaiah

The Lord delights in you.

For Zion's sake I will not be silent,
for Jerusalem's sake I will not be quiet,

until her vindication shines forth like the dawn
and her victory like a burning torch.

Nations shall behold your vindication,
and all the kings your glory;
you shall be called by a new name
pronounced by the mouth of the LORD.
You shall be a glorious crown in the hand of the LORD,
a royal diadem held by your God.
No more shall people call you "Forsaken,"
or your land "Desolate,"
but you shall be called "My Delight,"
and your land "Espoused."
For the LORD delights in you
and makes your land his spouse.
As a young man marries a virgin,
your Builder shall marry you;
and as a bridegroom rejoices in his bride
so shall your God rejoice in you.

The word of the Lord. All: **Thanks be to God.**

RESPONSORIAL PSALM 89

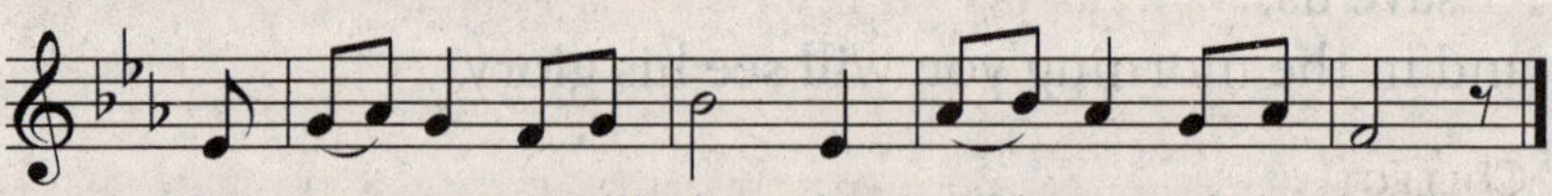

Text: Refrain, *Lectionary for Mass,* © 1969, 1981, 1997, ICEL
Music: *The Collegeville Psalter,* © 2017, Paul Inwood.

Psalm 89:4-5, 16-17, 27, 29

℟. (2a) **For ever I will sing the goodness of the Lord.**

I have made a covenant with my chosen one,
I have sworn to David my servant:
forever will I confirm your posterity
and establish your throne for all generations. ℟.

Blessed the people who know the joyful shout;
in the light of your countenance, O LORD, they walk.

At your name they rejoice all the day,
and through your justice they are exalted. ℟.

He shall say of me, "You are my father,
my God, the Rock, my savior."
Forever I will maintain my kindness toward him,
and my covenant with him stands firm. ℟.

READING II (Acts of the Apostles 13:16-17, 22-25)

A reading from the Acts of the Apostles

Paul bears witness to Christ, the Son of David.

When Paul reached Antioch in Pisidia and entered the synagogue,
he stood up, motioned with his hand, and said,
"Fellow Israelites and you others who are God-fearing, listen.
The God of this people Israel chose our ancestors
and exalted the people during their sojourn in the land of Egypt.
With uplifted arm he led them out of it.
Then he removed Saul and raised up David as king;
of him he testified,
'I have found David, son of Jesse, a man after my own heart;
he will carry out my every wish.'
From this man's descendants God, according to his promise,
has brought to Israel a savior, Jesus.
John heralded his coming by proclaiming a baptism of repentance
to all the people of Israel;
and as John was completing his course, he would say,
'What do you suppose that I am? I am not he.
Behold, one is coming after me;
I am not worthy to unfasten the sandals of his feet.'"

The word of the Lord. All: **Thanks be to God.**

GOSPEL (Matthew 1:1-25) *or* Shorter Form [ ] (Matthew 1:18-25)

ALLELUIA

℣. Alleluia, alleluia. ℟. **Alleluia, alleluia.**

℣. Tomorrow the wickedness of the earth will be destroyed:
the Savior of the world will reign over us. ℟.

✠ **A reading from the holy Gospel according to Matthew**

All: **Glory to you, O Lord.**

The genealogy of Jesus Christ, the Son of David.

The book of the genealogy of Jesus Christ,
the son of David, the son of Abraham.

Abraham became the father of Isaac,
Isaac the father of Jacob,
Jacob the father of Judah and his brothers.
Judah became the father of Perez and Zerah,
whose mother was Tamar.
Perez became the father of Hezron,
Hezron the father of Ram,
Ram the father of Amminadab.
Amminadab became the father of Nahshon,
Nahshon the father of Salmon,
Salmon the father of Boaz,
whose mother was Rahab.
Boaz became the father of Obed,
whose mother was Ruth.
Obed became the father of Jesse,
Jesse the father of David the king.

David became the father of Solomon,
whose mother had been the wife of Uriah.
Solomon became the father of Rehoboam,
Rehoboam the father of Abijah,
Abijah the father of Asaph.
Asaph became the father of Jehoshaphat,
Jehoshaphat the father of Joram,
Joram the father of Uzziah.

Uzziah became the father of Jotham,
Jotham the father of Ahaz,
Ahaz the father of Hezekiah.
Hezekiah became the father of Manasseh,
Manasseh the father of Amos,
Amos the father of Josiah.
Josiah became the father of Jechoniah and his brothers
at the time of the Babylonian exile.

After the Babylonian exile,
Jechoniah became the father of Shealtiel,
Shealtiel the father of Zerubbabel,
Zerubbabel the father of Abiud.
Abiud became the father of Eliakim,
Eliakim the father of Azor,
Azor the father of Zadok.
Zadok became the father of Achim,
Achim the father of Eliud,
Eliud the father of Eleazar.
Eleazar became the father of Matthan,
Matthan the father of Jacob,
Jacob the father of Joseph, the husband of Mary.
Of her was born Jesus who is called the Christ.

Thus the total number of generations
from Abraham to David
is fourteen generations;
from David to the Babylonian exile,
fourteen generations;
from the Babylonian exile to the Christ,
fourteen generations.

Now [this is how the birth of Jesus Christ came about.
When his mother Mary was betrothed to Joseph,
but before they lived together,
she was found with child through the Holy Spirit.
Joseph her husband, since he was a righteous man,
yet unwilling to expose her to shame,
decided to divorce her quietly.

Such was his intention when, behold,
the angel of the Lord appeared to him in a dream and said,
"Joseph, son of David,
do not be afraid to take Mary your wife into your home.
For it is through the Holy Spirit
that this child has been conceived in her.
She will bear a son and you are to name him Jesus,
because he will save his people from their sins."
All this took place to fulfill
what the Lord had said through the prophet:
Behold, the virgin shall conceive and bear a son,
and they shall name him Emmanuel,
which means "God is with us."
When Joseph awoke,
he did as the angel of the Lord had commanded him
and took his wife into his home.
He had no relations with her until she bore a son,
and he named him Jesus.]

The Gospel of the Lord. All: **Praise to you, Lord Jesus Christ.**

PRAYER OVER THE OFFERINGS
As we look forward, O Lord,
to the coming festivities,
may we serve you all the more eagerly
for knowing that in them
you make manifest the beginnings of our redemption.
Through Christ our Lord. All: **Amen.**

COMMUNION ANTIPHON (Cf. Isaiah 40:5)
The glory of the Lord will be revealed,
and all flesh will see the salvation of our God.

PRAYER AFTER COMMUNION
Grant, O Lord, we pray,
that we may draw new vigor
from celebrating the Nativity of your Only Begotten Son,
by whose heavenly mystery we receive both food and drink.
Who lives and reigns for ever and ever. All: **Amen.**

The Nativity of the Lord

AT THE MASS DURING THE NIGHT

December 25, 2026

Reflection on the Gospel

Imagine Mary and Joseph, approaching their last chance for lodging that night, tired and worn, desperation perhaps obvious on their faces. Who would have noticed all this? The innkeeper, of course. We can further imagine the innkeeper having an almost unthinkable idea: "Well . . . I could offer you . . . what about the animal pen around the back?" It's not hard to imagine Mary and Joseph exuding immense gratefulness for such a strange offering. We often have more to give than we know.

—Living Liturgy™, *The Nativity of the Lord (Mass during the Night) 2026*

Entrance Antiphon (Psalm 2:7)

The Lord said to me: You are my Son.
It is I who have begotten you this day.

Or:

Let us all rejoice in the Lord, for our Savior has been born in the world.
Today true peace has come down to us from heaven.

Collect

O God, who have made this most sacred night
radiant with the splendor of the true light,
grant, we pray, that we, who have known the mysteries of his light on earth,
may also delight in his gladness in heaven.
Who lives and reigns with you in the unity of the Holy Spirit,
God, for ever and ever. All: **Amen.**

Reading I (L 14) (Isaiah 9:1-6)

A reading from the Book of the Prophet Isaiah

A son is given us.

The people who walked in darkness
have seen a great light;
upon those who dwelt in the land of gloom
a light has shone.
You have brought them abundant joy
and great rejoicing,
as they rejoice before you as at the harvest,
as people make merry when dividing spoils.
For the yoke that burdened them,
the pole on their shoulder,
and the rod of their taskmaster
you have smashed, as on the day of Midian.
For every boot that tramped in battle,
every cloak rolled in blood,
will be burned as fuel for flames.
For a child is born to us, a son is given us;
upon his shoulder dominion rests.
They name him Wonder-Counselor, God-Hero,
Father-Forever, Prince of Peace.
His dominion is vast
and forever peaceful,
from David's throne, and over his kingdom,
which he confirms and sustains
by judgment and justice,
both now and forever.
The zeal of the Lord of hosts will do this!

The word of the Lord. All: **Thanks be to God.**

Responsorial Psalm 96

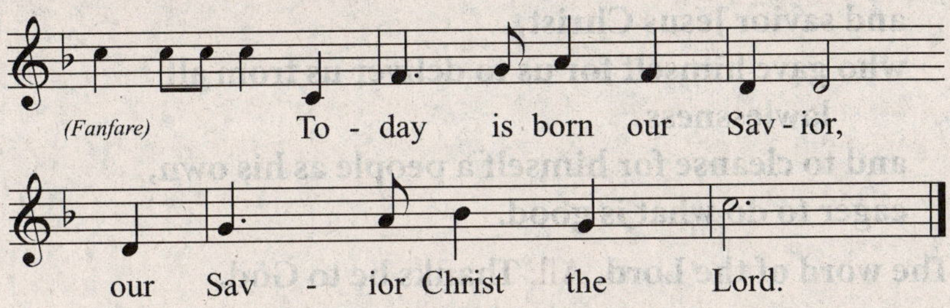

Psalm 96:1-2, 2-3, 11-12, 13

℞. (Luke 2:11) **Today is born our Savior, Christ the Lord.**

Sing to the LORD a new song;
sing to the LORD, all you lands.
Sing to the LORD; bless his name. ℞.

Announce his salvation, day after day.
Tell his glory among the nations;
among all peoples, his wondrous deeds. ℞.

Let the heavens be glad and the earth rejoice;
let the sea and what fills it resound;
let the plains be joyful and all that is in them!
Then shall all the trees of the forest exult. ℞.

They shall exult before the LORD, for he comes;
for he comes to rule the earth.
He shall rule the world with justice
and the peoples with his constancy. ℞.

Reading II (Titus 2:11-14)

A reading from the Letter of Saint Paul to Titus

The grace of God has appeared to all.

Beloved:
The grace of God has appeared, saving all
and training us to reject godless ways and worldly desires
and to live temperately, justly, and devoutly in this age,
as we await the blessed hope,

the appearance of the glory of our great God
and savior Jesus Christ,
who gave himself for us to deliver us from all lawlessness
and to cleanse for himself a people as his own,
eager to do what is good.

The word of the Lord. All: **Thanks be to God.**

GOSPEL (Luke 2:1-14)

ALLELUIA (Luke 2:10-11)

℣. Alleluia, alleluia. ℟. **Alleluia, alleluia.**
℣. I proclaim to you good news of great joy:
today a Savior is born for us,
Christ the Lord. ℟.

✠ **A reading from the holy Gospel according to Luke**

All: **Glory to you, O Lord.**

Today a Savior has been born for you.

In those days a decree went out from Caesar Augustus
that the whole world should be enrolled.
This was the first enrollment,
when Quirinius was governor of Syria.
So all went to be enrolled, each to his own town.
And Joseph too went up from Galilee from the town of Nazareth
to Judea, to the city of David that is called Bethlehem,
because he was of the house and family of David,
to be enrolled with Mary, his betrothed, who was with child.
While they were there,
the time came for her to have her child,
and she gave birth to her firstborn son.
She wrapped him in swaddling clothes and laid him in a manger,
because there was no room for them in the inn.

Now there were shepherds in that region living in the fields
and keeping the night watch over their flock.
The angel of the Lord appeared to them
and the glory of the Lord shone around them,
and they were struck with great fear.
The angel said to them,
"Do not be afraid;
for behold, I proclaim to you good news of great joy
that will be for all the people.
For today in the city of David
a savior has been born for you who is Christ and Lord.
And this will be a sign for you:
you will find an infant wrapped in swaddling clothes
and lying in a manger."
And suddenly there was a multitude of the heavenly host
with the angel,
praising God and saying:
"Glory to God in the highest
and on earth peace to those on whom his favor
rests."

The Gospel of the Lord. All: **Praise to you, Lord Jesus Christ.**

Prayer over the Offerings

May the oblation of this day's feast
be pleasing to you, O Lord, we pray,
that through this most holy exchange
we may be found in the likeness of Christ,
in whom our nature is united to you.
Who lives and reigns for ever and ever. All: **Amen.**

Communion Antiphon (John 1:14)

The Word became flesh, and we have seen his glory.

Prayer after Communion

Grant us, we pray, O Lord our God,
that we, who are gladdened by participation
in the feast of our Redeemer's Nativity,
may through an honorable way of life become worthy of union with him.
Who lives and reigns for ever and ever. All: **Amen.**

AT THE MASS AT DAWN

There is Christian paradox embedded within this morning's gospel. The stillness of nighttime has been disrupted by the singing of the angels to the shepherds: a paradox of quietude and jubilation. The shepherds visit a baby, lying still in the manger, then go forth, offering praise and glory for what they've just experienced. Indeed, it is only through faith and the power of God that such opposites become paradox; not side by side any longer, these opposites are made one in Christ. This is divine mystery.

—Living Liturgy™, *The Nativity of the Lord (Mass at Dawn) 2026*

Entrance Antiphon (Cf. Isaiah 9:1, 5; Luke 1:33)

Today a light will shine upon us, for the Lord is born for us;
and he will be called Wondrous God,
Prince of peace, Father of future ages:
and his reign will be without end.

Collect

Grant, we pray, almighty God,
that, as we are bathed in the new radiance of your incarnate Word,
the light of faith, which illumines our minds,
may also shine through in our deeds.
Through our Lord Jesus Christ, your Son,
who lives and reigns with you in the unity of the Holy Spirit,
God, for ever and ever. All: **Amen.**

Reading I (L 15) (Isaiah 62:11-12)

A reading from the Book of the Prophet Isaiah

Behold, your Savior comes!

See, the Lord proclaims
to the ends of the earth:
say to daughter Zion,
your savior comes!
Here is his reward with him,
his recompense before him.

They shall be called the holy people,
the redeemed of the LORD,
and you shall be called "Frequented,"
a city that is not forsaken.

The word of the Lord. All: **Thanks be to God.**

RESPONSORIAL PSALM 97

Text: Refrain, *Lectionary for Mass,* © 1969, 1981, 1997, ICEL
Music: *The Collegeville Psalter*, © 2017, Paul Inwood.

Psalm 97:1, 6, 11-12

℟. **A light will shine on us this day: the Lord is born for us.**

The LORD is king; let the earth rejoice;
let the many isles be glad.
The heavens proclaim his justice,
and all peoples see his glory. ℟.

Light dawns for the just;
and gladness, for the upright of heart.
Be glad in the LORD, you just,
and give thanks to his holy name. ℟.

READING II (Titus 3:4-7)

A reading from the Letter of Saint Paul to Titus

Because of his mercy, he saved us.

Beloved:
When the kindness and generous love
of God our savior appeared,
not because of any righteous deeds we had done
but because of his mercy,

he saved us through the bath of rebirth
and renewal by the Holy Spirit,
whom he richly poured out on us
through Jesus Christ our savior,
so that we might be justified by his grace
and become heirs in hope of eternal life.

The word of the Lord. All: **Thanks be to God.**

GOSPEL (Luke 2:15-20)

ALLELUIA (Luke 2:14)

℣. Alleluia, alleluia. ℟. **Alleluia, alleluia.**
℣. Glory to God in the highest,
and on earth peace to those
on whom his favor rests. ℟.

✠ **A reading from the holy Gospel according to Luke**

All: **Glory to you, O Lord.**

The shepherds found Mary and Joseph and the infant.

When the angels went away from them to heaven,
the shepherds said to one another,
"Let us go, then, to Bethlehem
to see this thing that has taken place,
which the Lord has made known to us."
So they went in haste and found Mary and Joseph,
and the infant lying in the manger.
When they saw this,
they made known the message
that had been told them about this child.
All who heard it were amazed
by what had been told them by the shepherds.
And Mary kept all these things,
reflecting on them in her heart.
Then the shepherds returned,
glorifying and praising God
for all they had heard and seen,
just as it had been told to them.

The Gospel of the Lord. All: **Praise to you, Lord Jesus Christ.**

Prayer over the Offerings

May our offerings be worthy, we pray, O Lord,
of the mysteries of the Nativity this day,
that, just as Christ was born a man and also shone forth as God,
so these earthly gifts may confer on us what is divine.
Through Christ our Lord. All: **Amen.**

Communion Antiphon (Cf. Zechariah 9:9)

Rejoice, O Daughter Sion; lift up praise, Daughter Jerusalem:
Behold, your King will come, the Holy One and Savior of the world.

Prayer after Communion

Grant us, Lord, as we honor with joyful devotion
the Nativity of your Son,
that we may come to know with fullness of faith
the hidden depths of this mystery
and to love them ever more and more.
Through Christ our Lord. All: **Amen.**

AT THE MASS DURING THE DAY

The incarnation is the core mystery of our faith. It is fitting that humanity should be saved by one such as ourselves; that we were—and are—redeemed in this way is a profound testament to human dignity. This dignity is not dependent on gender, race, ethnicity, education, accomplishments, or even belief: each human being has worth and dignity. Recognizing a divine presence in the hearts and souls of all around us cannot help but inform and transform our interactions with one another, especially on this solemnity of the incarnation.

—Living Liturgy™, *The Nativity of the Lord (Mass during the Day) 2026*

Entrance Antiphon (Cf. Isaiah 9:5)

A child is born for us, and a son is given to us;
his scepter of power rests upon his shoulder,
and his name will be called Messenger of great counsel.

COLLECT

O God, who wonderfully created the dignity of human nature
and still more wonderfully restored it,
grant, we pray,
that we may share in the divinity of Christ,
who humbled himself to share in our humanity.
Who lives and reigns with you in the unity of the Holy Spirit,
God, for ever and ever. All: **Amen.**

READING I (L 16) (Isaiah 52:7-10)

A reading from the Book of the Prophet Isaiah

All the ends of the earth will behold the salvation of our God.

How beautiful upon the mountains
are the feet of him who brings glad tidings,
announcing peace, bearing good news,
announcing salvation, and saying to Zion,
"Your God is King!"

Hark! Your sentinels raise a cry,
together they shout for joy,
for they see directly, before their eyes,
the LORD restoring Zion.
Break out together in song,
O ruins of Jerusalem!
For the LORD comforts his people,
he redeems Jerusalem.
The LORD has bared his holy arm
in the sight of all the nations;
all the ends of the earth will behold
the salvation of our God.

The word of the Lord. All: **Thanks be to God.**

Responsorial Psalm 98

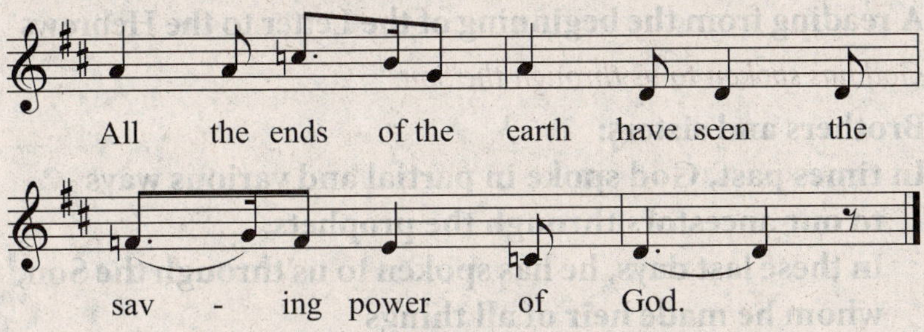

Psalm 98:1, 2-3, 3-4, 5-6

℟. (3c) **All the ends of the earth have seen the saving power of God.**

Sing to the Lord a new song,
for he has done wondrous deeds;
his right hand has won victory for him,
his holy arm. ℟.

The Lord has made his salvation known:
in the sight of the nations he has revealed his justice.
He has remembered his kindness and his faithfulness
toward the house of Israel. ℟.

All the ends of the earth have seen
the salvation by our God.
Sing joyfully to the Lord, all you lands;
break into song; sing praise. ℟.

Sing praise to the Lord with the harp,
with the harp and melodious song.
With trumpets and the sound of the horn
sing joyfully before the King, the Lord. ℟.

READING II (Hebrews 1:1-6)

A reading from the beginning of the Letter to the Hebrews

God has spoken to us through the Son.

Brothers and sisters:
In times past, God spoke in partial and various ways
to our ancestors through the prophets;
in these last days, he has spoken to us through the Son,
whom he made heir of all things
and through whom he created the universe,
who is the refulgence of his glory,
the very imprint of his being,
and who sustains all things by his mighty word.
When he had accomplished purification from sins,
he took his seat at the right hand of the Majesty
on high,
as far superior to the angels
as the name he has inherited is more excellent than
theirs.

For to which of the angels did God ever say:
You are my son; this day I have begotten you?
Or again:
I will be a father to him, and he shall be a son to me?
And again, when he leads the firstborn into the world,
he says:
Let all the angels of God worship him.

The word of the Lord. All: **Thanks be to God.**

GOSPEL (John 1:1-18) *or* Shorter Form [ ] (John 1:1-5, 9-14)

ALLELUIA

℣. Alleluia, alleluia. ℟. **Alleluia, alleluia.**
℣. A holy day has dawned upon us.
Come, you nations, and adore the Lord.
For today a great light has come upon the earth. ℟.

✠ **A reading from the beginning of the holy Gospel according to John**

All: **Glory to you, O Lord.**

The Word became flesh and made his dwelling among us.

[In the beginning was the Word,
and the Word was with God,
and the Word was God.
He was in the beginning with God.
All things came to be through him,
and without him nothing came to be.
What came to be through him was life,
and this life was the light of the human race;
the light shines in the darkness,
and the darkness has not overcome it.]

A man named John was sent from God.
He came for testimony, to testify to the light,
so that all might believe through him.
He was not the light,
but came to testify to the light.
[The true light, which enlightens everyone, was coming into the world.
He was in the world,
and the world came to be through him,
but the world did not know him.
He came to what was his own,
but his own people did not accept him.

But to those who did accept him
he gave power to become children of God,
to those who believe in his name,
who were born not by natural generation
nor by human choice nor by a man's decision
but of God.
And the Word became flesh
and made his dwelling among us,

and we saw his glory,
the glory as of the Father's only Son,
full of grace and truth.]
John testified to him and cried out, saying,
"This was he of whom I said,
'The one who is coming after me ranks ahead of me
because he existed before me.'"
From his fullness we have all received,
grace in place of grace,
because while the law was given through Moses,
grace and truth came through Jesus Christ.
No one has ever seen God.
The only Son, God, who is at the Father's side,
has revealed him.

The Gospel of the Lord. All: **Praise to you, Lord Jesus Christ.**

Prayer over the Offerings

Make acceptable, O Lord, our oblation on this solemn day,
when you manifested the reconciliation
that makes us wholly pleasing in your sight
and inaugurated for us the fullness of divine worship.
Through Christ our Lord. All: **Amen.**

Communion Antiphon (Cf. Psalm 98[97]:3)

All the ends of the earth have seen the salvation of our God.

Prayer after Communion

Grant, O merciful God,
that, just as the Savior of the world, born this day,
is the author of divine generation for us,
so he may be the giver even of immortality.
Who lives and reigns for ever and ever. All: **Amen.**

The Holy Family of Jesus, Mary, and Joseph

SUNDAY WITHIN THE OCTAVE OF THE NATIVITY OF THE LORD (Christmas)

December 27, 2026

Reflection on the Gospel

The elders of our faith communities have done and seen a lot of living. Along with holy wisdom, a long life grants to those blest with these years a certain perspective—sometimes optimistic, sometimes pessimistic, occasionally both at the same time! Simeon and Anna speak about the child as the living embodiment of the hopes and expectations of all Jews awaiting the restoration of God's rule in Israel. The birth of Jesus brings these promises to fulfillment, but perhaps not in the earthly way that was hoped for and expected.

—Living Liturgy™, *The Holy Family of Jesus, Mary, and Joseph 2026*

Entrance Antiphon (Luke 2:16)

The shepherds went in haste,
and found Mary and Joseph and the Infant lying in a manger.

Collect

O God, who were pleased to give us
the shining example of the Holy Family,
graciously grant that we may imitate them
in practicing the virtues of family life and in the bonds of charity,
and so, in the joy of your house,
delight one day in eternal rewards.
Through our Lord Jesus Christ, your Son,
who lives and reigns with you in the unity of the Holy Spirit,
God, for ever and ever. All: **Amen.**

READING I (L 17)

A (Sirach 3:2-6, 12-14)

A reading from the Book of Sirach

Those who fear the Lord honor their parents.

God sets a father in honor over his children;
a mother's authority he confirms over her sons.
Whoever honors his father atones for sins,
and preserves himself from them.
When he prays, he is heard;
he stores up riches who reveres his mother.
Whoever honors his father is gladdened by children,
and, when he prays, is heard.
Whoever reveres his father will live a long life;
he who obeys his father brings comfort to his mother.

My son, take care of your father when he is old;
grieve him not as long as he lives.
Even if his mind fail, be considerate of him;
revile him not all the days of his life;
kindness to a father will not be forgotten,
firmly planted against the debt of your sins
—a house raised in justice to you.

The word of the Lord. All: **Thanks be to God.**

Or:

B (Genesis 15:1-6; 21:1-3)

A reading from the Book of Genesis

Your own issue shall be your heir.

The word of the LORD came to Abram in a vision, saying:
"Fear not, Abram!
I am your shield;
I will make your reward very great."
But Abram said,
"O Lord GOD, what good will your gifts be,
if I keep on being childless
and have as my heir the steward of my house, Eliezer?"

Abram continued,
“See, you have given me no offspring,
and so one of my servants will be my heir.”
Then the word of the Lord came to him:
“No, that one shall not be your heir;
your own issue shall be your heir.”
The Lord took Abram outside and said,
“Look up at the sky and count the stars, if you can.
Just so,” he added, “shall your descendants be.”
Abram put his faith in the Lord,
who credited it to him as an act of righteousness.

The Lord took note of Sarah as he had said he would;
he did for her as he had promised.
Sarah became pregnant and bore Abraham a son in his old age,
at the set time that God had stated.
Abraham gave the name Isaac to this son of his
whom Sarah bore him.

The word of the Lord. All: **Thanks be to God.**

Responsorial Psalm 128 *or* 105

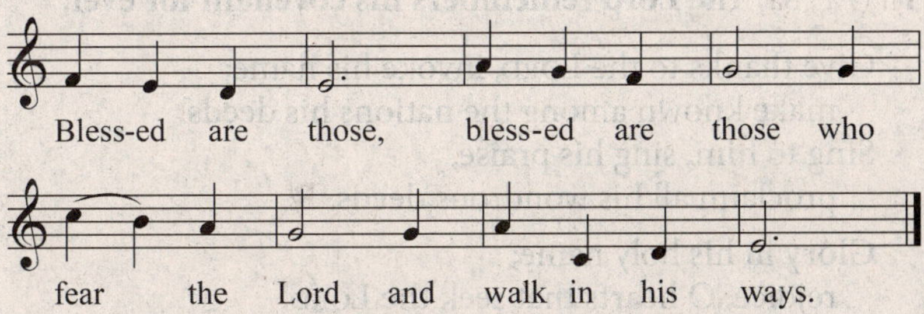

A Psalm 128:1-2, 3, 4-5

℟. (*See* 1) **Blessed are those who fear the Lord and walk in his ways.**

Blessed is everyone who fears the Lord,
who walks in his ways!

(continued)

For you shall eat the fruit of your handiwork;
blessed shall you be, and favored. ℟.

Your wife shall be like a fruitful vine
in the recesses of your home;
your children like olive plants
around your table. ℟.

Behold, thus is the man blessed
who fears the LORD.
The LORD bless you from Zion:
may you see the prosperity of Jerusalem
all the days of your life. ℟.

Or:

B Psalm 105:1-2, 3-4, 5-6, 8-9

℟. (7a , 8a) **The Lord remembers his covenant for ever.**

Give thanks to the LORD, invoke his name;
make known among the nations his deeds.
Sing to him, sing his praise,
proclaim all his wondrous deeds. ℟.

Glory in his holy name;
rejoice, O hearts that seek the LORD!
Look to the LORD in his strength;
constantly seek his face. ℟.

You descendants of Abraham, his servants,
sons of Jacob, his chosen ones!
He, the LORD, is our God;
throughout the earth his judgments prevail. ℟.

He remembers forever his covenant
which he made binding for a thousand generations

which he entered into with Abraham
and by his oath to Isaac. ℟.

READING II

A (Colossians 3:12-21) *or* Shorter Form [ ] (Colossians 3:12-17)

A reading from the Letter of Saint Paul to the Colossians

Family life in the Lord.

[**Brothers and sisters:**
Put on, as God's chosen ones, holy and beloved,
heartfelt compassion, kindness, humility, gentleness,
and patience,
bearing with one another and forgiving one another,
if one has a grievance against another;
as the Lord has forgiven you, so must you also do.
And over all these put on love,
that is, the bond of perfection.
And let the peace of Christ control your hearts,
the peace into which you were also called in one body.
And be thankful.
Let the word of Christ dwell in you richly,
as in all wisdom you teach and admonish one another,
singing psalms, hymns, and spiritual songs
with gratitude in your hearts to God.
And whatever you do, in word or in deed,
do everything in the name of the Lord Jesus,
giving thanks to God the Father through him.]

Wives, be subordinate to your husbands,
as is proper in the Lord.
Husbands, love your wives,
and avoid any bitterness toward them.
Children, obey your parents in everything,
for this is pleasing to the Lord.
Fathers, do not provoke your children,
so they may not become discouraged.

The word of the Lord. All: **Thanks be to God.**

Or:

B (Hebrews 11:8, 11-12, 17-19)

A reading from the Letter of Saint Paul to the Hebrews

The faith of Abraham, Sarah, and Isaac.

Brothers and sisters:
By faith Abraham obeyed when he was called to go out to a place
that he was to receive as an inheritance;
he went out, not knowing where he was to go.
By faith he received power to generate,
even though he was past the normal age
—and Sarah herself was sterile—
for he thought that the one who had made the promise was trustworthy.
So it was that there came forth from one man,
himself as good as dead,
descendants as numerous as the stars in the sky
and as countless as the sands on the seashore.
By faith Abraham, when put to the test, offered up Isaac,
and he who had received the promises was ready to offer his only son,
of whom it was said,
"Through Isaac descendants shall bear your name."
He reasoned that God was able to raise even from the dead,
and he received Isaac back as a symbol.

The word of the Lord. All: **Thanks be to God.**

GOSPEL (Luke 2:22-40) *or* Shorter Form [ ] (Luke 2:22, 39-40)

ALLELUIA (Colossians 3:15a, 16a)

℣. Alleluia, alleluia. ℟. **Alleluia, alleluia.**
℣. Let the peace of Christ control your hearts;
let the word of Christ dwell in you richly. ℟.

Or:

ALLELUIA (Hebrews 1:1-2)

℣. Alleluia, alleluia. ℟. **Alleluia, alleluia.**

℣. In the past God spoke to our ancestors through the prophets;
in these last days, he has spoken to us through the Son. ℟.

✠ **A reading from the holy Gospel according to Luke**

All: **Glory to you, O Lord.**

The child grew and became strong, filled with wisdom.

[When the days were completed for their purification
according to the law of Moses,
they took him up to Jerusalem
to present him to the Lord,
just as it is written in the law of the Lord,]
Every male that opens the womb shall be consecrated to the Lord,
and to offer the sacrifice of
a pair of turtledoves or two young pigeons,
in accordance with the dictate in the law of the Lord.

Now there was a man in Jerusalem whose name was Simeon.
This man was righteous and devout,
awaiting the consolation of Israel,
and the Holy Spirit was upon him.
It had been revealed to him by the Holy Spirit
that he should not see death
before he had seen the Christ of the Lord.
He came in the Spirit into the temple;
and when the parents brought in the child Jesus
to perform the custom of the law in regard to him,
he took him into his arms and blessed God, saying:
"Now, Master, you may let your servant go
in peace, according to your word,
for my eyes have seen your salvation,
which you prepared in sight of all the peoples,

a light for revelation to the Gentiles,
and glory for your people Israel."
The child's father and mother were amazed at what was said about him;
and Simeon blessed them and said to Mary his mother,
"Behold, this child is destined
for the fall and rise of many in Israel,
and to be a sign that will be contradicted
—and you yourself a sword will pierce—
so that the thoughts of many hearts may be revealed."
There was also a prophetess, Anna,
the daughter of Phanuel, of the tribe of Asher.
She was advanced in years,
having lived seven years with her husband after her marriage,
and then as a widow until she was eighty-four.
She never left the temple,
but worshiped night and day with fasting and prayer.
And coming forward at that very time,
she gave thanks to God and spoke about the child
to all who were awaiting the redemption of Jerusalem.

[**When they had fulfilled all the prescriptions**
of the law of the Lord,
they returned to Galilee,
to their own town of Nazareth.
The child grew and became strong, filled with wisdom;
and the favor of God was upon him.]

The Gospel of the Lord. All: **Praise to you, Lord Jesus Christ.**

Prayer over the Offerings

We offer you, Lord, the sacrifice of conciliation,
humbly asking that,
through the intercession of the Virgin Mother of God and Saint Joseph,
you may establish our families firmly in your grace and your peace.
Through Christ our Lord. All: **Amen.**

COMMUNION ANTIPHON (Baruch 3:38)
Our God has appeared on the earth, and lived among us.

PRAYER AFTER COMMUNION
Bring those you refresh with this heavenly Sacrament,
most merciful Father,
to imitate constantly the example of the Holy Family,
so that, after the trials of this world,
we may share their company for ever.
Through Christ our Lord. All: **Amen.**

Solemnity of Mary, the Holy Mother of God

OCTAVE DAY OF THE NATIVITY OF THE LORD (Christmas)

January 1, 2027 (First Friday)

(World Day of Peace)

Reflection on the Gospel
In addition to celebrating the Theotokos, *the "God-Bearer" today, January 1 is also the World Day of Peace. Mary herself is a shining example of peace, justice, and dignity. She is more than meek and mild, more than a lowly handmaid. Her* Magnificat *praises the God who casts down the mighty and raises the lowly. As we celebrate Mary the God-Bearer today, let us also recommit ourselves to the example given us by the Blessed Mother in prayer, in contemplation, and in action.*

—Living Liturgy™, *Mary, Mother of God 2027*

ENTRANCE ANTIPHON
Hail, Holy Mother, who gave birth to the King
who rules heaven and earth for ever.

Or:

(Cf. Isaiah 9:1, 5; Luke 1:33)
Today a light will shine upon us, for the Lord is born for us;
and he will be called Wondrous God,
Prince of peace, Father of future ages:
and his reign will be without end.

COLLECT
O God, who through the fruitful virginity of Blessed Mary
bestowed on the human race
the grace of eternal salvation,
grant, we pray,
that we may experience the intercession of her,
through whom we were found worthy
to receive the author of life,
our Lord Jesus Christ, your Son.
Who lives and reigns with you in the unity of the Holy Spirit,
God, for ever and ever. All: **Amen.**

READING I (L 18) (Numbers 6:22-27)
A reading from the Book of Numbers

They shall invoke my name upon the Israelites, and I will bless them.

The LORD said to Moses:
"Speak to Aaron and his sons and tell them:
This is how you shall bless the Israelites.
Say to them:
The LORD bless you and keep you!
The LORD let his face shine upon
you, and be gracious to you!
The LORD look upon you kindly and
give you peace!
So shall they invoke my name upon the Israelites,
and I will bless them."
The word of the Lord. All: **Thanks be to God.**

Responsorial Psalm 67

Psalm 67:2-3, 5, 6, 8

℟. (2a) **May God bless us in his mercy.**

May God have pity on us and bless us;
  may he let his face shine upon us.
So may your way be known upon earth;
  among all nations, your salvation. ℟.

May the nations be glad and exult
  because you rule the peoples in equity;
  the nations on the earth you guide. ℟.

May the peoples praise you, O God;
  may all the peoples praise you!
May God bless us,
  and may all the ends of the earth fear him! ℟.

Reading II (Galatians 4:4-7)

A reading from the Letter of Saint Paul to the Galatians

God sent his Son, born of a woman.

Brothers and sisters:
When the fullness of time had come, God sent his Son,
  born of a woman, born under the law,
  to ransom those under the law,
  so that we might receive adoption as sons.
As proof that you are sons,
  God sent the Spirit of his Son into our hearts,
  crying out, "Abba, Father!"
So you are no longer a slave but a son,
  and if a son then also an heir, through God.

The word of the Lord. All: **Thanks be to God.**

Gospel (Luke 2:16-21)

Alleluia (Hebrews 1:1-2)

℣. Alleluia, alleluia. ℟. **Alleluia, alleluia.**
℣. In the past God spoke to our ancestors through the prophets;
in these last days, he has spoken to us through the Son. ℟.

✠ **A reading from the holy Gospel according to Luke**

All: **Glory to you, O Lord.**

They found Mary and Joseph and the infant. When the eight days were completed, he was named Jesus.

The shepherds went in haste to Bethlehem and found Mary and Joseph,
and the infant lying in the manger.
When they saw this,
they made known the message
that had been told them about this child.
All who heard it were amazed
by what had been told them by the shepherds.
And Mary kept all these things,
reflecting on them in her heart.
Then the shepherds returned,
glorifying and praising God
for all they had heard and seen,
just as it had been told to them.

When eight days were completed for his circumcision,
he was named Jesus, the name given him by the angel
before he was conceived in the womb.

The Gospel of the Lord. All: **Praise to you, Lord Jesus Christ.**

Prayer over the Offerings

O God, who in your kindness begin all good things
and bring them to fulfillment,
grant to us, who find joy in the Solemnity of the holy Mother of God,
that, just as we glory in the beginnings of your grace,
so one day we may rejoice in its completion.
Through Christ our Lord. All: **Amen.**

COMMUNION ANTIPHON (Hebrews 13:8)

Jesus Christ is the same yesterday, today, and for ever.

PRAYER AFTER COMMUNION

We have received this heavenly Sacrament with joy, O Lord:
grant, we pray,
that it may lead us to eternal life,
for we rejoice to proclaim the blessed ever-Virgin Mary
Mother of your Son and Mother of the Church.
Through Christ our Lord. All: **Amen.**

The Epiphany of the Lord

AT THE VIGIL MASS

January 2, 2027

Reflection on the Gospel

Today we celebrate the visitation of the magi to the Christ Child. We hear very little in the gospel about the journey they must have taken: we know not from where they came and to where they returned, for instance. There is a practical reason that "they departed for their country by another way": to avoid Herod. Yet there is also a theological reason: everyone in Scripture who encounters the divine has their life dramatically changed. One way is by upending, literally, their life's path.

—Living Liturgy™, *Epiphany 2027*

ENTRANCE ANTIPHON (Cf. Baruch 5:5)

Arise, Jerusalem, and look to the East
and see your children gathered from the rising to the
setting of the sun.

COLLECT

May the splendor of your majesty, O Lord, we pray,
shed its light upon our hearts,

that we may pass through the shadows of this world
and reach the brightness of our eternal home.
Through our Lord Jesus Christ, your Son,
who lives and reigns with you in the unity of the Holy Spirit,
God, for ever and ever. All: **Amen.**

(Readings are those of the day.)

Prayer over the Offerings

Accept we pray, O Lord, our offerings,
in honor of the appearing of your Only Begotten Son
and the first fruits of the nations,
that to you praise may be rendered
and eternal salvation be ours.
Through Christ our Lord. All: **Amen.**

Communion Antiphon (Cf. Revelation 21:23)

The brightness of God illumined the holy city Jerusalem,
and the nations will walk by its light.

Prayer after Communion

Renewed by sacred nourishment,
we implore your mercy, O Lord,
that the star of your justice
may shine always bright in our minds
and that our true treasure may ever consist in our confession of you.
Through Christ our Lord. All: **Amen.**

Sunday, January 3

AT THE MASS DURING THE DAY

Entrance Antiphon (Cf. Malachi 3:1; 1 Chronicles 29:12)

Behold, the Lord, the Mighty One, has come;
and kingship is in his grasp, and power and dominion.

Collect

O God, who on this day
revealed your Only Begotten Son to the nations
by the guidance of a star,
grant in your mercy
that we, who know you already by faith,
may be brought to behold the beauty of your sublime glory.

Through our Lord Jesus Christ, your Son,
who lives and reigns with you in the unity of the Holy Spirit,
God, for ever and ever. All: **Amen.**

Reading I (L 20) (Isaiah 60:1-6)

A reading from the Book of the Prophet Isaiah

The glory of the Lord shines upon you.

Rise up in splendor, Jerusalem! Your light has come,
the glory of the Lord shines upon you.
See, darkness covers the earth,
and thick clouds cover the peoples;
but upon you the Lord shines,
and over you appears his glory.
Nations shall walk by your light,
and kings by your shining radiance.
Raise your eyes and look about;
they all gather and come to you:
your sons come from afar,
and your daughters in the arms of their nurses.

Then you shall be radiant at what you see,
your heart shall throb and overflow,
for the riches of the sea shall be emptied out before you,
the wealth of nations shall be brought to you.
Caravans of camels shall fill you,
dromedaries from Midian and Ephah;
all from Sheba shall come
bearing gold and frankincense,
and proclaiming the praises of the Lord.

The word of the Lord. All: **Thanks be to God.**

Responsorial Psalm 72

Psalm 72:1-2, 7-8, 10-11, 12-13

℟. (*See* 11) **Lord, every nation on earth will adore you.**

O God, with your judgment endow the king,
and with your justice, the king's son;
he shall govern your people with justice
and your afflicted ones with judgment. ℟.

Justice shall flower in his days,
and profound peace, till the moon be no more.
May he rule from sea to sea,
and from the River to the ends of the earth. ℟.

The kings of Tarshish and the Isles shall offer gifts;
the kings of Arabia and Seba shall bring tribute.
All kings shall pay him homage,
all nations shall serve him. ℟.

For he shall rescue the poor when he cries out,
and the afflicted when he has no one to help him.
He shall have pity for the lowly and the poor;
the lives of the poor he shall save. ℟.

Reading II (Ephesians 3:2-3a, 5-6)

A reading from the Letter of Saint Paul to the Ephesians

Now it has been revealed that the Gentiles are coheirs of the promise.

Brothers and sisters:
You have heard of the stewardship of God's grace
that was given to me for your benefit,
namely, that the mystery was made known to me by revelation.
It was not made known to people in other generations
as it has now been revealed
to his holy apostles and prophets by the Spirit:
that the Gentiles are coheirs, members of the same body,
and copartners in the promise in Christ Jesus through the gospel.

The word of the Lord. All: **Thanks be to God.**

GOSPEL (Matthew 2:1-12)

ALLELUIA (Matthew 2:2)

℣. Alleluia, alleluia. ℟. **Alleluia, alleluia.**
℣. We saw his star at its rising
and have come to do him homage. ℟.

✠ **A reading from the holy Gospel according to Matthew**

All: **Glory to you, O Lord.**

We saw his star at its rising and have come to do him homage.

When Jesus was born in Bethlehem of Judea,
in the days of King Herod,
behold, magi from the east arrived in Jerusalem,
saying,
"Where is the newborn king of the Jews?
We saw his star at its rising
and have come to do him homage."
When King Herod heard this,
he was greatly troubled,
and all Jerusalem with him.
Assembling all the chief priests and the scribes of the people,
he inquired of them where the Christ was to be born.
They said to him, "In Bethlehem of Judea,
for thus it has been written through the prophet:
And you, Bethlehem, land of Judah,
are by no means least among the rulers of Judah;
since from you shall come a ruler,
who is to shepherd my people Israel."
Then Herod called the magi secretly
and ascertained from them the time of the star's appearance.
He sent them to Bethlehem and said,
"Go and search diligently for the child.
When you have found him, bring me word,
that I too may go and do him homage."
After their audience with the king they set out.

And behold, the star that they had seen at its rising preceded them,
until it came and stopped over the place where the child was.
They were overjoyed at seeing the star,
and on entering the house
they saw the child with Mary his mother.
They prostrated themselves and did him homage.
Then they opened their treasures
and offered him gifts of gold, frankincense, and myrrh.
And having been warned in a dream not to return to Herod,
they departed for their country by another way.

The Gospel of the Lord. All: **Praise to you, Lord Jesus Christ.**

Prayer over the Offerings

Look with favor, Lord, we pray,
on these gifts of your Church,
in which are offered now not gold or frankincense or myrrh,
but he who by them is proclaimed,
sacrificed and received, Jesus Christ.
Who lives and reigns for ever and ever. All: **Amen.**

Communion Antiphon (Cf. Matthew 2:2)

We have seen his star in the East,
and have come with gifts to adore the Lord.

Prayer after Communion

Go before us with heavenly light, O Lord,
always and everywhere,
that we may perceive with clear sight
and revere with true affection
the mystery in which you have willed us to participate.
Through Christ our Lord. All: **Amen.**

The Baptism of the Lord

January 10, 2027

Reflection on the Gospel

John the Baptist proclaims, "One mightier than I is coming after me." When Jesus arrives and steps into the water, something extraordinary happens. The sinless Son of God joins the line of sinners waiting to be baptized. The One who has no need of cleansing identifies himself completely with our human condition. This moment is not about Jesus's repentance, but about his solidarity—with the broken, the weary, and the searching. He sanctifies the waters by entering them, making them a channel of grace for all who will follow.

—Living Liturgy™, *Baptism of the Lord 2027*

Entrance Antiphon (Cf. Matthew 3:16-17)

After the Lord was baptized, the heavens were opened,
and the Spirit descended upon him like a dove,
and the voice of the Father thundered:
This is my beloved Son, with whom I am well pleased.

Collect

Almighty ever-living God,
who, when Christ had been baptized in the River Jordan
and as the Holy Spirit descended upon him,
solemnly declared him your beloved Son,
grant that your children by adoption,
reborn of water and the Holy Spirit,
may always be well pleasing to you.
Through our Lord Jesus Christ, your Son,
who lives and reigns with you in the unity of the Holy Spirit,
God, for ever and ever. All: **Amen.**

Or:

O God, whose Only Begotten Son
has appeared in our very flesh,
grant, we pray, that we may be inwardly transformed
through him whom we recognize as outwardly like ourselves.
Who lives and reigns with you in the unity of the Holy Spirit,
God, for ever and ever. All: **Amen.**

Reading I (L 21)

A (Isaiah 42:1-4, 6-7)

A reading from the Book of the Prophet Isaiah

Behold my servant with whom I am well pleased.

Thus says the Lord:
Here is my servant whom I uphold,
my chosen one with whom I am pleased,
upon whom I have put my spirit;
he shall bring forth justice to the nations,
not crying out, not shouting,
not making his voice heard in the street.
A bruised reed he shall not break,
and a smoldering wick he shall not quench,
until he establishes justice on the earth;
the coastlands will wait for his teaching.

I, the Lord, have called you for the victory of justice,
I have grasped you by the hand;
I formed you, and set you
as a covenant of the people,
a light for the nations,
to open the eyes of the blind,
to bring out prisoners from confinement,
and from the dungeon, those who live in darkness.

The word of the Lord. All: **Thanks be to God.**

Or:

B (Isaiah 55:1-11)

A reading from the Book of Isaiah

Come to the waters: listen, that you may have life.

Thus says the Lord:
All you who are thirsty,
come to the water!
You who have no money,
come, receive grain and eat;

come, without paying and without cost,
drink wine and milk!
Why spend your money for what is not bread,
your wages for what fails to satisfy?
Heed me, and you shall eat well,
you shall delight in rich fare.
Come to me heedfully,
listen, that you may have life.
I will renew with you the everlasting covenant,
the benefits assured to David.
As I made him a witness to the peoples,
a leader and commander of nations,
so shall you summon a nation you knew not,
and nations that knew you not shall run to you,
because of the LORD, your God,
the Holy One of Israel, who has glorified you.

Seek the LORD while he may be found,
call him while he is near.
Let the scoundrel forsake his way,
and the wicked man his thoughts;
let him turn to the LORD for mercy;
to our God, who is generous in forgiving.
For my thoughts are not your thoughts,
nor are your ways my ways, says the LORD.
As high as the heavens are above the earth
so high are my ways above your ways
and my thoughts above your thoughts.

For just as from the heavens
the rain and snow come down
and do not return there
till they have watered the earth,
making it fertile and fruitful,
giving seed to the one who sows
and bread to the one who eats,

so shall my word be
that goes forth from my mouth;
my word shall not return to me void,
but shall do my will,
achieving the end for which I sent it.

The word of the Lord. All: **Thanks be to God.**

Responsorial Psalm

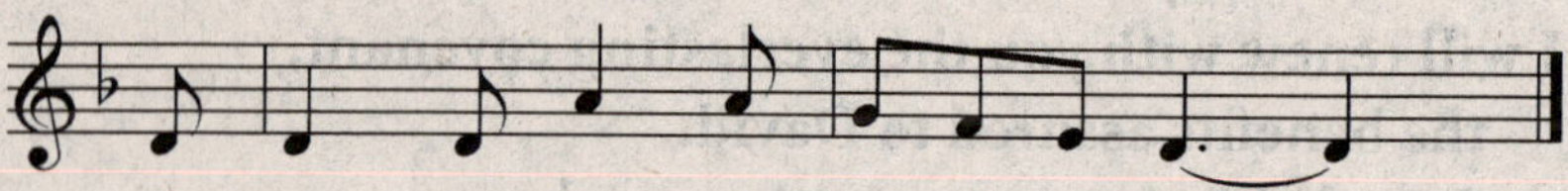

A Psalm 29:1-2, 3-4, 3, 9-10

℟. (11b) **The Lord will bless his people with peace.**

Give to the Lord, you sons of God,
give to the Lord glory and praise,
give to the Lord the glory due his name;
adore the Lord in holy attire. ℟.

The voice of the Lord is over the waters,
the Lord, over vast waters.
The voice of the Lord is mighty;
the voice of the Lord is majestic. ℟.

The God of glory thunders,
and in his temple all say, "Glory!"
The Lord is enthroned above the flood;
the Lord is enthroned as king forever. ℟.

Or:

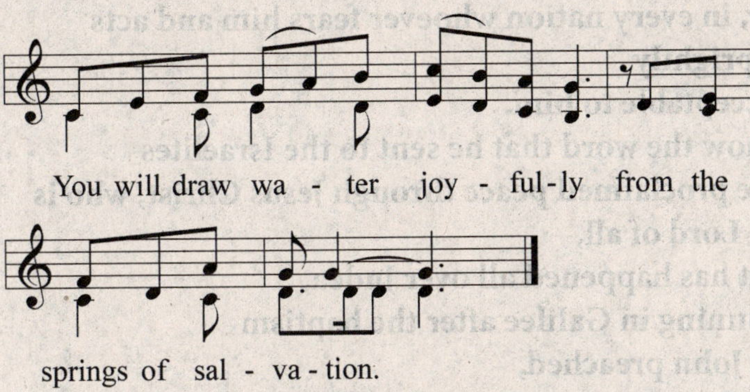

B Isaiah 12:2-3, 4bcd, 5-6

℟. (3) **You will draw water joyfully from the springs of salvation.**

God indeed is my savior;
I am confident and unafraid.
My strength and my courage is the Lord,
and he has been my savior.
With joy you will draw water
at the fountain of salvation. ℟.

Give thanks to the Lord, acclaim his name;
among the nations make known his deeds,
proclaim how exalted is his name. ℟.

Sing praise to the Lord for his glorious achievement;
let this be known throughout all the earth.
Shout with exultation, O city of Zion,
for great in your midst
is the Holy One of Israel! ℟.

Reading II

A (Acts of the Apostles 10:34-38)

A reading from the Acts of the Apostles

God anointed him with the Holy Spirit.

**Peter proceeded to speak to those gathered
in the house of Cornelius, saying:
"In truth, I see that God shows no partiality.**

Rather, in every nation whoever fears him and acts uprightly
is acceptable to him.
You know the word that he sent to the Israelites
as he proclaimed peace through Jesus Christ, who is Lord of all,
what has happened all over Judea,
beginning in Galilee after the baptism
that John preached,
how God anointed Jesus of Nazareth
with the Holy Spirit and power.
He went about doing good
and healing all those oppressed by the devil,
for God was with him."

The word of the Lord. All: **Thanks be to God.**

Or:

B (1 John 5:1-9)

A reading from the first Letter of Saint John

The Spirit and the water and the blood.

Beloved:
Everyone who believes that Jesus is the Christ is begotten by God,
and everyone who loves the Father
loves also the one begotten by him.
In this way we know that we love the children of God
when we love God and obey his commandments.
For the love of God is this,
that we keep his commandments.
And his commandments are not burdensome,
for whoever is begotten by God conquers the world.
And the victory that conquers the world is our faith.
Who indeed is the victor over the world
but the one who believes that Jesus is the Son of God?

This is the one who came through water and blood,
Jesus Christ,
not by water alone, but by water and blood.
The Spirit is the one who testifies,
and the Spirit is truth.
So there are three that testify,
the Spirit, the water, and the blood,
and the three are of one accord.
If we accept human testimony,
the testimony of God is surely greater.
Now the testimony of God is this,
that he has testified on behalf of his Son.

The word of the Lord. All: **Thanks be to God.**

GOSPEL (Mark 1:7-11)

ALLELUIA (*See* Mark 9:7)

℣. Alleluia, alleluia. ℟. **Alleluia, alleluia.**
℣. The heavens were opened and the voice of the Father thundered:
This is my beloved Son, listen to him. ℟.

Or:

ALLELUIA (*See* John 1:29)

℣. Alleluia, alleluia. ℟. **Alleluia, alleluia.**
℣. John saw Jesus approaching him, and said:
Behold the Lamb of God who takes away the sin of the world. ℟.

✠ **A reading from the holy Gospel according to Mark**

All: **Glory to you, O Lord.**

You are my beloved Son; with you I am well pleased.

This is what John the Baptist proclaimed:
"One mightier than I is coming after me.
I am not worthy to stoop and loosen the thongs of his sandals.
I have baptized you with water;
he will baptize you with the Holy Spirit."

It happened in those days that Jesus came from Nazareth of Galilee
and was baptized in the Jordan by John.
On coming up out of the water he saw the heavens being torn open
and the Spirit, like a dove, descending upon him.
And a voice came from the heavens,
"You are my beloved Son; with you I am well pleased."

The Gospel of the Lord. All: **Praise to you, Lord Jesus Christ.**

Prayer over the Offerings

Accept, O Lord, the offerings
we have brought to honor the revealing of your beloved Son,
so that the oblation of your faithful
may be transformed into the sacrifice of him
who willed in his compassion
to wash away the sins of the world.
Who lives and reigns for ever and ever. All: **Amen.**

Communion Antiphon (John 1:32, 34)

Behold the One of whom John said:
I have seen and testified that this is the Son of God.

Prayer after Communion

Nourished with these sacred gifts,
we humbly entreat your mercy, O Lord,
that, faithfully listening to your Only Begotten Son,
we may be your children in name and in truth.
Through Christ our Lord. All: **Amen.**

Second Sunday in Ordinary Time

January 17, 2027

Reflection on the Gospel

In today's gospel, God's calls reach the ears, and indeed the very souls, of people not expecting it. We, too, are charged with calling and fashioning new disciples. How do we preach the good news to those who most need to hear it? Is that message of hope and salvation brought outside the church doors somehow? Are those fallen away from the faith invited to return? Our Jewish brothers and sisters name this act of welcoming the stranger Hachnasat or'chim. *Might our church families also be blessed by our welcome?*

—Living Liturgy™, *Second Sunday in Ordinary Time 2027*

Entrance Antiphon (Psalm 66[65]:4)

All the earth shall bow down before you, O God,
and shall sing to you,
shall sing to your name, O Most High!

Collect

Almighty ever-living God,
who govern all things,
both in heaven and on earth,
mercifully hear the pleading of your people
and bestow your peace on our times.
Through our Lord Jesus Christ, your Son,
who lives and reigns with you in the unity of the Holy Spirit,
God, for ever and ever. All: **Amen.**

Reading I (L 65-B) (1 Samuel 3:3b-10, 19)

A reading from the first Book of Samuel

Speak, Lord, for your servant is listening.

Samuel was sleeping in the temple of the Lord
where the ark of God was.
The Lord called to Samuel, who answered, "Here I am."

Samuel ran to Eli and said, "Here I am. You called me."
"I did not call you," Eli said. "Go back to sleep."
So he went back to sleep.
Again the LORD called Samuel, who rose and went to Eli.
"Here I am," he said. "You called me."
But Eli answered, "I did not call you, my son. Go back to sleep."

At that time Samuel was not familiar with the LORD,
because the LORD had not revealed anything to him as yet.
The LORD called Samuel again, for the third time.
Getting up and going to Eli, he said, "Here I am. You called me."
Then Eli understood that the LORD was calling the youth.
So he said to Samuel, "Go to sleep, and if you are called, reply,
Speak, LORD, for your servant is listening."
When Samuel went to sleep in his place,
the LORD came and revealed his presence,
calling out as before, "Samuel, Samuel!"
Samuel answered, "Speak, for your servant is listening."

Samuel grew up, and the LORD was with him,
not permitting any word of his to be without effect.

The word of the Lord. All: **Thanks be to God.**

RESPONSORIAL PSALM 40

Psalm 40:2, 4, 7-8, 8-9, 10

℟. (8a and 9a) **Here am I, Lord; I come to do your will.**

I have waited, waited for the LORD,
and he stooped toward me and heard my cry.

And he put a new song into my mouth,
a hymn to our God. ℟.

Sacrifice or offering you wished not,
but ears open to obedience you gave me.
Holocausts or sin-offerings you sought not;
then said I, "Behold I come." ℟.

"In the written scroll it is prescribed for me,
to do your will, O my God, is my delight,
and your law is within my heart!" ℟.

I announced your justice in the vast assembly;
I did not restrain my lips, as you, O LORD, know. ℟.

READING II (1 Corinthians 6:13c-15a, 17-20)

A reading from the first Letter of Saint Paul to the Corinthians

Your bodies are members of Christ.

Brothers and sisters:
The body is not for immorality, but for the Lord,
and the Lord is for the body;
God raised the Lord and will also raise us by his power.

Do you not know that your bodies are members of Christ?
But whoever is joined to the Lord becomes one Spirit with him.
Avoid immorality.
Every other sin a person commits is outside the body,
but the immoral person sins against his own body.
Do you not know that your body
is a temple of the Holy Spirit within you,
whom you have from God, and that you are not your own?
For you have been purchased at a price.
Therefore glorify God in your body.
The word of the Lord. All: **Thanks be to God.**

GOSPEL (John 1:35-42)

ALLELUIA (John 1:41, 17b)

℣. Alleluia, alleluia. ℟. **Alleluia, alleluia.**
℣. We have found the Messiah:
Jesus Christ, who brings us truth and grace. ℟.

✠ **A reading from the holy Gospel according to John**

All: **Glory to you, O Lord.**

They saw where he was staying and they stayed with him.

John was standing with two of his disciples,
and as he watched Jesus walk by, he said,
"Behold, the Lamb of God."
The two disciples heard what he said and followed Jesus.
Jesus turned and saw them following him and said to them,
"What are you looking for?"
They said to him, "Rabbi"—which translated means Teacher—,
"where are you staying?"
He said to them, "Come, and you will see."
So they went and saw where Jesus was staying,
and they stayed with him that day.
It was about four in the afternoon.
Andrew, the brother of Simon Peter,
was one of the two who heard John and followed Jesus.
He first found his own brother Simon and told him,
"We have found the Messiah"—which is translated Christ.
Then he brought him to Jesus.
Jesus looked at him and said,
"You are Simon the son of John;
you will be called Cephas"—which is translated Peter.

The Gospel of the Lord. All: **Praise to you, Lord Jesus Christ.**

Prayer over the Offerings

Grant us, O Lord, we pray,
that we may participate worthily in these mysteries,
for whenever the memorial of this sacrifice is celebrated
the work of our redemption is accomplished.
Through Christ our Lord. All: **Amen.**

Communion Antiphon (Cf. Psalm 23[22]:5)

You have prepared a table before me,
and how precious is the chalice that quenches my thirst.

Or:

(1 John 4:16)
We have come to know and to believe
in the love that God has for us.

Prayer after Communion

Pour on us, O Lord, the Spirit of your love,
and in your kindness
make those you have nourished
by this one heavenly Bread
one in mind and heart.
Through Christ our Lord. All: **Amen.**

Third Sunday in Ordinary Time

January 24, 2027

Reflection on the Gospel

Jesus is always careful to meet each person where they are before inviting them into deeper holiness. Consider last week, where Jesus entered into some banter with Andrew and the other disciple and spent the whole afternoon with them. Consider that immediately upon meeting Simon, Jesus gives him a new name. Then consider today's gospel, where Jesus calls the fishermen to the ministry of evangelization and the saving of souls. Each apostle was met in a different way and brought into the work of kingdom building on different terms.

—Living Liturgy™, *Third Sunday in Ordinary Time 2027*

Entrance Antiphon (Cf. Psalm 96[95]:1, 6)

O sing a new song to the Lord;
sing to the Lord, all the earth.
In his presence are majesty and splendor,
strength and honor in his holy place.

Collect

Almighty ever-living God,
direct our actions according to your good pleasure,
that in the name of your beloved Son
we may abound in good works.
Through our Lord Jesus Christ, your Son,
who lives and reigns with you in the unity of the Holy Spirit,
God, for ever and ever. All: **Amen.**

Reading I (L 68-B) (Jonah 3:1-5, 10)

A reading from the Book of the Prophet Jonah

The Ninevites turned from their evil way.

The word of the Lord came to Jonah, saying:
"Set out for the great city of Nineveh,
and announce to it the message that I will tell you."

So Jonah made ready and went to Nineveh,
according to the LORD's bidding.
Now Nineveh was an enormously large city;
it took three days to go through it.
Jonah began his journey through the city,
and had gone but a single day's walk announcing,
"Forty days more and Nineveh shall be destroyed,"
when the people of Nineveh believed God;
they proclaimed a fast
and all of them, great and small, put on sackcloth.

When God saw by their actions how they turned from their evil way,
he repented of the evil that he had threatened to do to them;
he did not carry it out.

The word of the Lord. All: **Thanks be to God.**

RESPONSORIAL PSALM 25

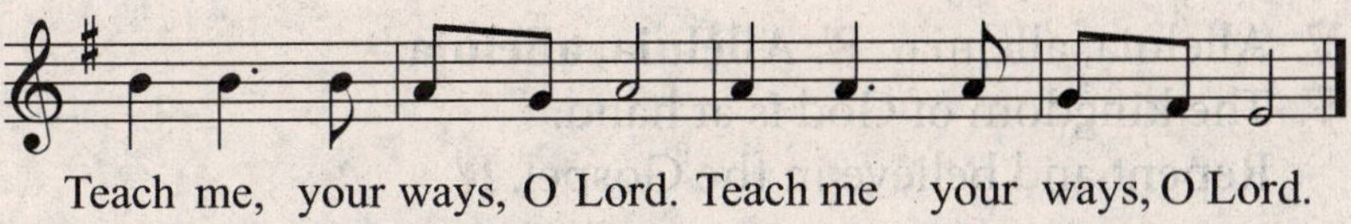

Psalm 25:4-5, 6-7, 8-9

℟. (4a) **Teach me your ways, O Lord.**

Your ways, O LORD, make known to me;
teach me your paths,
guide me in your truth and teach me,
for you are God my savior. ℟.

Remember that your compassion, O LORD,
and your love are from of old.
In your kindness remember me,
because of your goodness, O LORD. ℟.

Good and upright is the LORD;
thus he shows sinners the way.

(continued)

He guides the humble to justice
and teaches the humble his way. ℟.

READING II (1 Corinthians 7:29-31)

A reading from the first Letter of Saint Paul to the Corinthians

The world in its present form is passing away.

I tell you, brothers and sisters, the time is running out.
From now on, let those having wives act as not having them,
those weeping as not weeping,
those rejoicing as not rejoicing,
those buying as not owning,
those using the world as not using it fully.
For the world in its present form is passing away.

The word of the Lord. All: **Thanks be to God.**

GOSPEL (Mark 1:14-20)

ALLELUIA (Mark 1:15)

℣. Alleluia, alleluia. ℟. **Alleluia, alleluia.**
℣. The kingdom of God is at hand.
Repent and believe in the Gospel. ℟.

✠ **A reading from the holy Gospel according to Mark**

All: **Glory to you, O Lord.**

Repent and believe in the Gospel.

After John had been arrested,
Jesus came to Galilee proclaiming the gospel of God:
"This is the time of fulfillment.
The kingdom of God is at hand.
Repent, and believe in the gospel."

As he passed by the Sea of Galilee,
he saw Simon and his brother Andrew casting their nets into the sea;
they were fishermen.

Jesus said to them,
"Come after me, and I will make you fishers of men."
Then they abandoned their nets and followed him.
He walked along a little farther
and saw James, the son of Zebedee, and his brother John.
They too were in a boat mending their nets.
Then he called them.
So they left their father Zebedee in the boat
along with the hired men and followed him.

The Gospel of the Lord. All: **Praise to you, Lord Jesus Christ.**

PRAYER OVER THE OFFERINGS

Accept our offerings, O Lord, we pray,
and in sanctifying them
grant that they may profit us for salvation.
Through Christ our Lord. All: **Amen.**

COMMUNION ANTIPHON (Cf. Psalm 34[33]:6)

Look toward the Lord and be radiant;
let your faces not be abashed.

Or:

(John 8:12)

I am the light of the world, says the Lord;
whoever follows me will not walk in darkness,
but will have the light of life.

PRAYER AFTER COMMUNION

Grant, we pray, almighty God,
that, receiving the grace
by which you bring us to new life,
we may always glory in your gift.
Through Christ our Lord. All: **Amen.**

Fourth Sunday in Ordinary Time

January 31, 2027

Reflection on the Gospel

Last week's reflection urged readers that our welcome must be one that "meets people where they are and offers loving invitations . . ." This could be seen, potentially, as oppositional to a faith and a liturgical practice of it that speaks and lives truth (or Truth, *with a capital T). The love that was spoken of last week and the truth that is spoken of in this week's gospel are of course not oppositional at all—God* is *love and God* is *truth, after all.*

—Living Liturgy™, *Fourth Sunday in Ordinary Time 2027*

ENTRANCE ANTIPHON (Psalm 106[105]:47)

Save us, O Lord our God!
And gather us from the nations,
to give thanks to your holy name,
and make it our glory to praise you.

COLLECT

Grant us, Lord our God,
that we may honor you with all our mind,
and love everyone in truth of heart.
Through our Lord Jesus Christ, your Son,
who lives and reigns with you in the unity of the Holy Spirit,
God, for ever and ever. All: **Amen.**

READING I (L 71-B) (Deuteronomy 18:15-20)

A reading from the Book of Deuteronomy

I will raise up a prophet and I will put my words into his mouth.

Moses spoke to all the people, saying:
"A prophet like me will the LORD, your God, raise up for you
from among your own kin;
to him you shall listen.

This is exactly what you requested of the LORD, your God,
at Horeb
on the day of the assembly, when you said,
'Let us not again hear the voice of the LORD, our God,
nor see this great fire any more, lest we die.'
And the LORD said to me, 'This was well said.
I will raise up for them a prophet like you from among
their kin,
and will put my words into his mouth;
he shall tell them all that I command him.
Whoever will not listen to my words which he speaks in
my name,
I myself will make him answer for it.
But if a prophet presumes to speak in my name
an oracle that I have not commanded him to speak,
or speaks in the name of other gods, he shall die.'"

The word of the Lord. All: **Thanks be to God.**

RESPONSORIAL PSALM 95

The response is preferably sung twice after each verse

Psalm 95:1-2, 6-7, 7-9

℟. (8) **If today you hear his voice, harden not your hearts.**

Come, let us sing joyfully to the LORD;
let us acclaim the rock of our salvation.
Let us come into his presence with thanksgiving;
let us joyfully sing psalms to him. ℟.

(continued)

Come, let us bow down in worship;
 let us kneel before the LORD who made us.
For he is our God,
 and we are the people he shepherds, the flock he
  guides. ℟.

Oh, that today you would hear his voice:
 "Harden not your hearts as at Meribah,
 as in the day of Massah in the desert,
where your fathers tempted me;
 they tested me though they had seen my works." ℟.

READING II (1 Corinthians 7:32-35)

A reading from the first Letter of Saint Paul to the Corinthians

A virgin is anxious about the things of the Lord, that she may be holy.

Brothers and sisters:
I should like you to be free of anxieties.
An unmarried man is anxious about the things of the
  Lord,
 how he may please the Lord.
But a married man is anxious about the things of the
  world,
 how he may please his wife, and he is divided.
An unmarried woman or a virgin is anxious about the
  things of the Lord,
 so that she may be holy in both body and spirit.
A married woman, on the other hand,
 is anxious about the things of the world,
 how she may please her husband.
I am telling you this for your own benefit,
 not to impose a restraint upon you,
 but for the sake of propriety
 and adherence to the Lord without distraction.

The word of the Lord. All: **Thanks be to God.**

GOSPEL (Mark 1:21-28)

ALLELUIA (Matthew 4:16)

℣. Alleluia, alleluia. ℟. **Alleluia, alleluia.**

℣. The people who sit in darkness have seen a great light;
on those dwelling in a land overshadowed by death,
light has arisen. ℟.

✠ **A reading from the holy Gospel according to Mark**

All: **Glory to you, O Lord.**

He taught them as one having authority.

Then they came to Capernaum,
and on the sabbath Jesus entered the synagogue and taught.
The people were astonished at his teaching,
for he taught them as one having authority and not as the scribes.
In their synagogue was a man with an unclean spirit;
he cried out, "What have you to do with us, Jesus of Nazareth?
Have you come to destroy us?
I know who you are—the Holy One of God!"
Jesus rebuked him and said,
"Quiet! Come out of him!"
The unclean spirit convulsed him and with a loud cry came out of him.
All were amazed and asked one another,
"What is this?
A new teaching with authority.
He commands even the unclean spirits and they obey him."
His fame spread everywhere throughout the whole region of Galilee.

The Gospel of the Lord. All: **Praise to you, Lord Jesus Christ.**

Prayer over the Offerings

O Lord, we bring to your altar
these offerings of our service:
be pleased to receive them, we pray,
and transform them
into the Sacrament of our redemption.
Through Christ our Lord. All: **Amen.**

Communion Antiphon (Cf. Psalm 31[30]:17-18)

Let your face shine on your servant.
Save me in your merciful love.
O Lord, let me never be put to shame, for I call on you.

Or:

(Matthew 5:3-4)
Blessed are the poor in spirit,
for theirs is the kingdom of heaven.
Blessed are the meek, for they shall possess the land.

Prayer after Communion

Nourished by these redeeming gifts,
we pray, O Lord,
that through this help to eternal salvation
true faith may ever increase.
Through Christ our Lord. All: **Amen.**

Fifth Sunday in Ordinary Time

February 7, 2027

Reflection on the Gospel

In today's gospel, Mark tells his readers about the power of Jesus's presence. It heals physically, it cures spiritually, and because of this, even when Jesus wishes more private time, he yields to the desire of those who yearn to be near him. Knowing what to do when in the presence of the Lord can be challenging, especially if it's our first time with a profound awareness of that presence. This includes those with whom we share our welcome to be disciples of Christ.

—Living Liturgy™, *Fifth Sunday in Ordinary Time 2027*

Entrance Antiphon (Psalm 95[94]:6-7)

O come, let us worship God
and bow low before the God who made us,
for he is the Lord our God.

Collect

Keep your family safe, O Lord, with unfailing care,
that, relying solely on the hope of heavenly grace,
they may be defended always by your protection.
Through our Lord Jesus Christ, your Son,
who lives and reigns with you in the unity of the Holy Spirit,
God, for ever and ever. All: **Amen.**

Reading I (L 74-B) (Job 7:1-4, 6-7)

A reading from the Book of Job

I am filled with restlessness until the dawn.

Job spoke, saying:
Is not man's life on earth a drudgery?
Are not his days those of hirelings?
He is a slave who longs for the shade,
a hireling who waits for his wages.
So I have been assigned months of misery,
and troubled nights have been allotted to me.

If in bed I say, "When shall I arise?"
then the night drags on;
I am filled with restlessness until the dawn.
My days are swifter than a weaver's shuttle;
they come to an end without hope.
Remember that my life is like the wind;
I shall not see happiness again.

The word of the Lord. All: **Thanks be to God.**

Responsorial Psalm 147

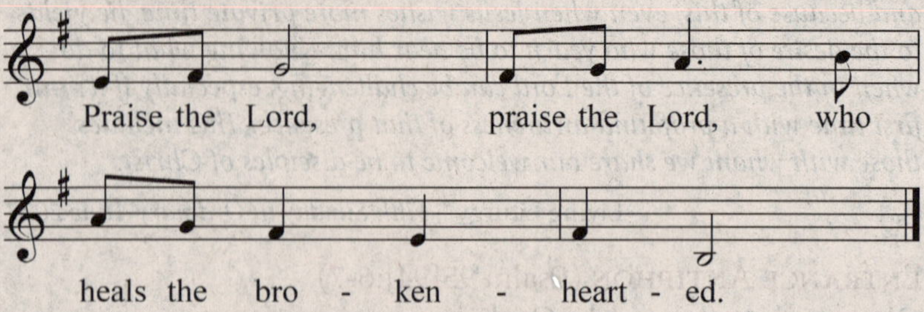

Psalm 147:1-2, 3-4, 5-6

℟. (*See* 3a) **Praise the Lord, who heals the brokenhearted.**
or: ℟. **Alleluia.**

Praise the LORD, for he is good;
sing praise to our God, for he is gracious;
it is fitting to praise him.
The LORD rebuilds Jerusalem;
the dispersed of Israel he gathers. ℟.

He heals the brokenhearted
and binds up their wounds.
He tells the number of the stars;
he calls each by name. ℟.

Great is our Lord and mighty in power;
to his wisdom there is no limit.
The LORD sustains the lowly;
the wicked he casts to the ground. ℟.

READING II (1 Corinthians 9:16-19, 22-23)

A reading from the first Letter of Saint Paul to the Corinthians

Woe to me if I do not preach the Gospel.

Brothers and sisters:
If I preach the gospel, this is no reason for me to boast,
for an obligation has been imposed on me,
and woe to me if I do not preach it!
If I do so willingly, I have a recompense,
but if unwillingly, then I have been entrusted with a stewardship.
What then is my recompense?
That, when I preach,
I offer the gospel free of charge
so as not to make full use of my right in the gospel.

Although I am free in regard to all,
I have made myself a slave to all
so as to win over as many as possible.
To the weak I became weak, to win over the weak.
I have become all things to all, to save at least some.
All this I do for the sake of the gospel,
so that I too may have a share in it.

The word of the Lord. All: **Thanks be to God.**

GOSPEL (Mark 1:29-39)

ALLELUIA (Matthew 8:17)

℣. Alleluia, alleluia. ℟. **Alleluia, alleluia.**
℣. Christ took away our infirmities
and bore our diseases. ℟.

✠ **A reading from the holy Gospel according to Mark**

All: **Glory to you, O Lord.**

Jesus cured many who were sick with various diseases.

On leaving the synagogue
Jesus entered the house of Simon and Andrew with James and John.

Simon's mother-in-law lay sick with a fever.
They immediately told him about her.
He approached, grasped her hand, and helped her up.
Then the fever left her and she waited on them.

When it was evening, after sunset,
they brought to him all who were ill or possessed by demons.
The whole town was gathered at the door.
He cured many who were sick with various diseases,
and he drove out many demons,
not permitting them to speak because they knew him.

Rising very early before dawn, he left
and went off to a deserted place, where he prayed.
Simon and those who were with him pursued him
and on finding him said, "Everyone is looking for you."
He told them, "Let us go on to the nearby villages
that I may preach there also.
For this purpose have I come."
So he went into their synagogues,
preaching and driving out demons throughout the whole of Galilee.

The Gospel of the Lord. All: **Praise to you, Lord Jesus Christ.**

PRAYER OVER THE OFFERINGS

O Lord, our God,
who once established these created things
to sustain us in our frailty,
grant, we pray,
that they may become for us now
the Sacrament of eternal life.
Through Christ our Lord. All: **Amen.**

COMMUNION ANTIPHON (Cf. Psalm 107[106]:8-9)

Let them thank the Lord for his mercy,
his wonders for the children of men,
for he satisfies the thirsty soul,
and the hungry he fills with good things.

Or:

(Matthew 5:5-6)
Blessed are those who mourn, for they shall be consoled.
Blessed are those who hunger and thirst for righteousness,
for they shall have their fill.

Prayer after Communion
O God, who have willed that we be partakers
in the one Bread and the one Chalice,
grant us, we pray, so to live
that, made one in Christ,
we may joyfully bear fruit
for the salvation of the world.
Through Christ our Lord. All: **Amen.**

Ash Wednesday

February 10, 2027

Reflection on the Gospel

We have reached the season of Lent, so now is the time for all things sad and repentant and morose and sackcloth and ashes and everything else depressing, right? No! We ought to be repentant for our sinfulness, yes. But there's more to the story. It's not like during Lent we should remember only repentance, suffering, and death. While celebrating these things, we should also remember that there is new life that arises from these very same things—there is joy and even more celebrating to come.

—Living Liturgy™, *Ash Wednesday 2027*

Entrance Antiphon (Wisdom 11:24, 25, 27)

You are merciful to all, O Lord,
and despise nothing that you have made.
You overlook people's sins, to bring them to repentance,
and you spare them, for you are the Lord our God.

Collect

Grant, O Lord, that we may begin with holy fasting
this campaign of Christian service,
so that, as we take up battle against spiritual evils,
we may be armed with weapons of self-restraint.
Through our Lord Jesus Christ, your Son,
who lives and reigns with you in the unity of the Holy Spirit,
God, for ever and ever. All: **Amen.**

Reading I (L 219) (Joel 2:12-18)

A reading from the Book of the Prophet Joel

Rend your hearts, not your garments.

Even now, says the Lord,
return to me with your whole heart,
with fasting, and weeping, and mourning;
Rend your hearts, not your garments,
and return to the Lord, your God.

For gracious and merciful is he,
slow to anger, rich in kindness,
and relenting in punishment.
Perhaps he will again relent
and leave behind him a blessing,
Offerings and libations
for the LORD, your God.

Blow the trumpet in Zion!
proclaim a fast,
call an assembly;
Gather the people,
notify the congregation;
Assemble the elders,
gather the children
and the infants at the breast;
Let the bridegroom quit his room
and the bride her chamber.
Between the porch and the altar
let the priests, the ministers of the LORD, weep,
And say, "Spare, O LORD, your people,
and make not your heritage a reproach,
with the nations ruling over them!
Why should they say among the peoples,
'Where is their God?'"

Then the LORD was stirred to concern for his land
and took pity on his people.

The word of the Lord. All: **Thanks be to God.**

RESPONSORIAL PSALM 51

Psalm 51:3-4, 5-6ab, 12-13, 14 and 17

℟. (*See* 3a) **Be merciful, O Lord, for we have sinned.**

Have mercy on me, O God, in your goodness;
in the greatness of your compassion wipe out my offense.
Thoroughly wash me from my guilt
and of my sin cleanse me. ℟.

For I acknowledge my offense,
and my sin is before me always:
"Against you only have I sinned,
and done what is evil in your sight." ℟.

A clean heart create for me, O God,
and a steadfast spirit renew within me.
Cast me not out from your presence,
and your Holy Spirit take not from me. ℟.

Give me back the joy of your salvation,
and a willing spirit sustain in me.
O Lord, open my lips,
and my mouth shall proclaim your praise. ℟.

READING II (2 Corinthians 5:20—6:2)

A reading from the second Letter of Saint Paul to the Corinthians

Be reconciled to God. Behold, now is the acceptable time.

Brothers and sisters:
We are ambassadors for Christ,
as if God were appealing through us.
We implore you on behalf of Christ,
be reconciled to God.
For our sake he made him to be sin who did not know sin,
so that we might become the righteousness of God in him.
Working together, then,
we appeal to you not to receive the grace of God in vain.
For he says:

In an acceptable time I heard you,
and on the day of salvation I helped you.

Behold, now is a very acceptable time;
behold, now is the day of salvation.

The word of the Lord. All: **Thanks be to God.**

GOSPEL (Matthew 6:1-6, 16-18)
VERSE BEFORE THE GOSPEL (*See* Psalm 95:8)

℣. Praise to you, Lord Jesus Christ, King of endless glory!
℟. **Praise to you, Lord Jesus Christ, King of endless glory!**
℣. If today you hear his voice,
harden not your hearts. ℟.

✠ **A reading from the holy Gospel according to Matthew**

All: **Glory to you, O Lord.**

Your Father who sees in secret will repay you.

Jesus said to his disciples:
"Take care not to perform righteous deeds
in order that people may see them;
otherwise, you will have no recompense from your heavenly Father.
When you give alms,
do not blow a trumpet before you,
as the hypocrites do in the synagogues and in the streets
to win the praise of others.
Amen, I say to you,
they have received their reward.
But when you give alms,
do not let your left hand know what your right is doing,
so that your almsgiving may be secret.
And your Father who sees in secret will repay you.

"When you pray,
do not be like the hypocrites,
who love to stand and pray in the synagogues and on street corners
so that others may see them.

Amen, I say to you,
they have received their reward.
But when you pray, go to your inner room,
close the door, and pray to your Father in secret.
And your Father who sees in secret will repay you.

"When you fast,
do not look gloomy like the hypocrites.
They neglect their appearance,
so that they may appear to others to be fasting.
Amen, I say to you, they have received their reward.
But when you fast,
anoint your head and wash your face,
so that you may not appear to be fasting,
except to your Father who is hidden.
And your Father who sees what is hidden will repay you."

The Gospel of the Lord. All: **Praise to you, Lord Jesus Christ.**

Blessing and Distribution of Ashes

Dear brethren (brothers and sisters), let us humbly ask God our Father
that he be pleased to bless with the abundance of his grace
these ashes, which we will put on our heads in penitence.

O God, who are moved by acts of humility
and respond with forgiveness to works of penance,
lend your merciful ear to our prayers
and in your kindness pour out the grace of your ✠ blessing
on your servants who are marked with these ashes,
that, as they follow the Lenten observances,
they may be worthy to come with minds made pure
to celebrate the Paschal Mystery of your Son.
Through Christ our Lord. All: **Amen.**

Or:

O God, who desire not the death of sinners,
but their conversion,
mercifully hear our prayers
and in your kindness be pleased to bless ✠ these ashes,
which we intend to receive upon our heads,
that we, who acknowledge we are but ashes
and shall return to dust,
may, through a steadfast observance of Lent,

gain pardon for sins and newness of life
after the likeness of your Risen Son.
Who lives and reigns for ever and ever. All: **Amen.**

To each who receives the ashes:
Repent, and believe in the Gospel.

or:

Remember that you are dust, and to dust you shall return.

The rite concludes with the Prayer of the Faithful.

Prayer over the Offerings

As we solemnly offer
the annual sacrifice for the beginning of Lent,
we entreat you, O Lord,
that, through works of penance and charity,
we may turn away from harmful pleasures
and, cleansed from our sins, may become worthy
to celebrate devoutly the Passion of your Son.
Who lives and reigns for ever and ever. All: **Amen.**

Communion Antiphon (Cf. Psalm 1:2-3)

He who ponders the law of the Lord day and night
will yield fruit in due season.

Prayer after Communion

May the Sacrament we have received sustain us, O Lord,
that our Lenten fast may be pleasing to you
and be for us a healing remedy.
Through Christ our Lord. All: **Amen.**

First Sunday of Lent

February 14, 2027

Reflection on the Gospel

It's easy to imagine Satan waiting for just the right moment, when he knew Jesus would be at his weakest. Satan presents Jesus with versions of sacred power and might that have been twisted and distorted. Persevering through the trial, Jesus begins his earthly mission by proclaiming the immediacy of the reign of God, that the old covenants of God are coming to fulfillment. Jesus's words and deeds over the next three years will make it clear that he is the living embodiment of God, the new and everlasting covenant.

—Living Liturgy™, *First Sunday of Lent 2027*

Entrance Antiphon (Cf. Psalm 91[90]:15-16)

When he calls on me, I will answer him;
I will deliver him and give him glory,
I will grant him length of days.

Collect

Grant, almighty God,
through the yearly observances of holy Lent,
that we may grow in understanding
of the riches hidden in Christ
and by worthy conduct pursue their effects.
Through our Lord Jesus Christ, your Son,
who lives and reigns with you in the unity of the Holy Spirit,
God, for ever and ever. All: **Amen.**

Reading I (L 23-B) (Genesis 9:8-15)

A reading from the Book of Genesis

God's covenant with Noah when he was delivered from the flood.

God said to Noah and to his sons with him:
"See, I am now establishing my covenant with you
and your descendants after you
and with every living creature that was with you:
all the birds, and the various tame and wild animals
that were with you and came out of the ark.
I will establish my covenant with you,
that never again shall all bodily creatures be destroyed
by the waters of a flood;
there shall not be another flood to devastate the earth."
God added:
"This is the sign that I am giving for all ages to come,
of the covenant between me and you
and every living creature with you:
I set my bow in the clouds to serve as a sign
of the covenant between me and the earth.
When I bring clouds over the earth,
and the bow appears in the clouds,
I will recall the covenant I have made
between me and you and all living beings,
so that the waters shall never again become a flood
to destroy all mortal beings."

The word of the Lord. All: **Thanks be to God.**

Responsorial Psalm 25

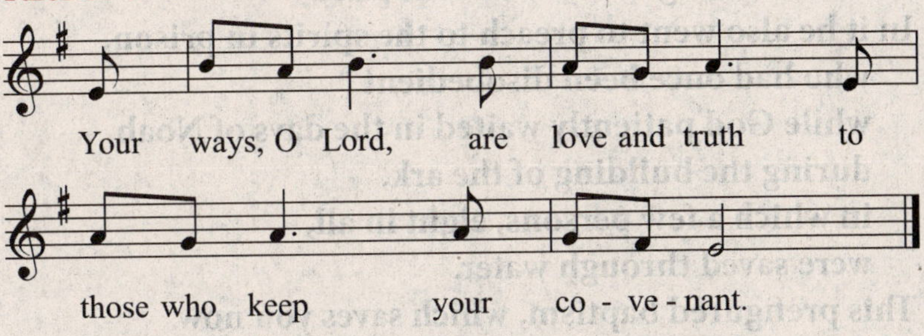

Psalm 25:4-5, 6-7, 8-9

℟. (*See* 10) **Your ways, O Lord, are love and truth to those who keep your covenant.**

Your ways, O Lord, make known to me;
teach me your paths.
Guide me in your truth and teach me,
for you are God my savior. ℟.

Remember that your compassion, O Lord,
and your love are from of old.
In your kindness remember me,
because of your goodness, O Lord. ℟.

Good and upright is the Lord,
thus he shows sinners the way.
He guides the humble to justice,
and he teaches the humble his way. ℟.

Reading II (1 Peter 3:18-22)

A reading from the first Letter of Saint Peter

The water of the flood prefigured baptism, which saves you now.

Beloved:
Christ suffered for sins once,
the righteous for the sake of the unrighteous,
that he might lead you to God.
Put to death in the flesh,
he was brought to life in the Spirit.
In it he also went to preach to the spirits in prison,
who had once been disobedient
while God patiently waited in the days of Noah
during the building of the ark,
in which a few persons, eight in all,
were saved through water.
This prefigured baptism, which saves you now.
It is not a removal of dirt from the body
but an appeal to God for a clear conscience,
through the resurrection of Jesus Christ,
who has gone into heaven

and is at the right hand of God,
with angels, authorities, and powers subject to him.

The word of the Lord. All: **Thanks be to God.**

GOSPEL (Mark 1:12-15)

VERSE BEFORE THE GOSPEL (Matthew 4:4b)

℣. Praise to you, Lord Jesus Christ, king of endless glory.
℟. **Praise to you, Lord Jesus Christ, king of endless glory.**
℣. One does not live on bread alone,
but on every word that comes forth from the mouth of God. ℟.

✠ **A reading from the holy Gospel according to Mark**

All: **Glory to you, O Lord.**

Jesus was tempted by Satan, and the angels ministered to him.

The Spirit drove Jesus out into the desert,
and he remained in the desert for forty days,
tempted by Satan.
He was among wild beasts,
and the angels ministered to him.

After John had been arrested,
Jesus came to Galilee proclaiming the gospel of God:
"This is the time of fulfillment.
The kingdom of God is at hand.
Repent, and believe in the gospel."

The Gospel of the Lord. All: **Praise to you, Lord Jesus Christ.**

PRAYER OVER THE OFFERINGS

Give us the right dispositions, O Lord, we pray,
to make these offerings,
for with them we celebrate the beginning
of this venerable and sacred time.
Through Christ our Lord. All: **Amen.**

COMMUNION ANTIPHON (Matthew 4:4)

One does not live by bread alone,
but by every word that comes forth from the mouth of God.

Or:

(Cf. Psalm 91[90]:4)
The Lord will conceal you with his pinions,
and under his wings you will trust.

Prayer after Communion

Renewed now with heavenly bread,
by which faith is nourished, hope increased,
and charity strengthened,
we pray, O Lord,
that we may learn to hunger for Christ,
the true and living Bread,
and strive to live by every word
which proceeds from your mouth.
Through Christ our Lord. All: **Amen.**

Second Sunday of Lent

February 21, 2027

Reflection on the Gospel

On this Sunday of Lent in each lectionary cycle, we always hear about the transfiguration of the Lord, one of the few passages found in each of the three Synoptic Gospels, and a moment even alluded to in Peter's second epistle. Jesus's clothes become dazzlingly white, Mark tells us, and Luke's Gospel adds that Jesus's face shone brightly like the sun. Light, considered together with darkness, is an always-present sign and symbol of our faith. There is no darkness the light cannot overcome, John's beautiful prologue reminds us.

—Living Liturgy™, *Second Sunday of Lent 2027*

Entrance Antiphon (Cf. Psalm 27[26]:8-9)

Of you my heart has spoken: Seek his face.
It is your face, O Lord, that I seek;
hide not your face from me.

Or:

(Cf. Psalm 25[24]:6, 2, 22)
Remember your compassion, O Lord,
and your merciful love, for they are from of old.
Let not our enemies exult over us.
Redeem us, O God of Israel, from all our distress.

COLLECT
O God, who have commanded us
to listen to your beloved Son,
be pleased, we pray,
to nourish us inwardly by your word,
that, with spiritual sight made pure,
we may rejoice to behold your glory.
Through our Lord Jesus Christ, your Son,
who lives and reigns with you in the unity of the Holy Spirit,
God, for ever and ever. All: **Amen.**

READING I (L 26-B) (Genesis 22:1-2, 9a, 10-13, 15-18)
A reading from the Book of Genesis

The sacrifice of Abraham, our father in faith.

**God put Abraham to the test.
He called to him, "Abraham!"
"Here I am!" he replied.
Then God said:
"Take your son Isaac, your only one, whom you love,
and go to the land of Moriah.
There you shall offer him up as a holocaust
on a height that I will point out to you."**

**When they came to the place of which God had told him,
Abraham built an altar there and arranged the wood on it.
Then he reached out and took the knife to slaughter his son.
But the LORD's messenger called to him from heaven,
"Abraham, Abraham!"
"Here I am!" he answered.
"Do not lay your hand on the boy," said the messenger.
"Do not do the least thing to him.**

I know now how devoted you are to God,
since you did not withhold from me your own beloved son."
As Abraham looked about,
he spied a ram caught by its horns in the thicket.
So he went and took the ram
and offered it up as a holocaust in place of his son.

Again the LORD's messenger called to Abraham from heaven and said:
"I swear by myself, declares the LORD,
that because you acted as you did
in not withholding from me your beloved son,
I will bless you abundantly
and make your descendants as countless
as the stars of the sky and the sands of the seashore;
your descendants shall take possession
of the gates of their enemies,
and in your descendants all the nations of the earth
shall find blessing—
all this because you obeyed my command."

The word of the Lord. All: **Thanks be to God.**

RESPONSORIAL PSALM 116

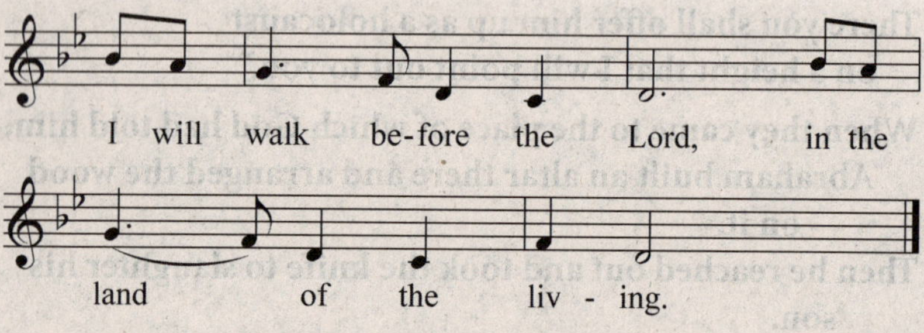

Psalm 116:10, 15, 16-17, 18-19

℟. (9) **I will walk before the Lord, in the land of the living.**

I believed, even when I said,
"I am greatly afflicted."
Precious in the eyes of the LORD
is the death of his faithful ones. ℟.

O LORD, I am your servant;
I am your servant, the son of your handmaid;
you have loosed my bonds.
To you will I offer sacrifice of thanksgiving,
and I will call upon the name of the LORD. ℟.

My vows to the LORD I will pay
in the presence of all his people,
In the courts of the house of the LORD,
in your midst, O Jerusalem. ℟.

READING II (Romans 8:31b-34)

A reading from the Letter of Saint Paul to the Romans

God did not spare his own Son.

Brothers and sisters:
If God is for us, who can be against us?
He who did not spare his own Son
but handed him over for us all,
how will he not also give us everything else along with him?

Who will bring a charge against God's chosen ones?
It is God who acquits us, who will condemn?
Christ Jesus it is who died—or, rather, was raised—
who also is at the right hand of God,
who indeed intercedes for us.

The word of the Lord. All: **Thanks be to God.**

GOSPEL (Mark 9:2-10)

VERSE BEFORE THE GOSPEL (See Matthew 17:5)

℣. Praise and honor to you, Lord Jesus Christ.
℟. **Praise and honor to you, Lord Jesus Christ.**
℣. From the shining cloud the Father's voice is heard:
This is my beloved Son, listen to him. ℟.

✠ **A reading from the holy Gospel according to Mark**

All: **Glory to you, O Lord.**

This is my beloved Son.

Jesus took Peter, James, and John
and led them up a high mountain apart by themselves.
And he was transfigured before them,
and his clothes became dazzling white,
such as no fuller on earth could bleach them.
Then Elijah appeared to them along with Moses,
and they were conversing with Jesus.
Then Peter said to Jesus in reply,
"Rabbi, it is good that we are here!
Let us make three tents:
one for you, one for Moses, and one for Elijah."
He hardly knew what to say, they were so terrified.
Then a cloud came, casting a shadow over them;
from the cloud came a voice,
"This is my beloved Son. Listen to him."
Suddenly, looking around, they no longer saw anyone
but Jesus alone with them.

As they were coming down from the mountain,
he charged them not to relate what they had seen to anyone,
except when the Son of Man had risen from the dead.
So they kept the matter to themselves,
questioning what rising from the dead meant.

The Gospel of the Lord. All: **Praise to you, Lord Jesus Christ.**

Prayer over the Offerings

May this sacrifice, O Lord, we pray,
cleanse us of our faults
and sanctify your faithful in body and mind
for the celebration of the paschal festivities.
Through Christ our Lord. All: **Amen.**

Communion Antiphon (Matthew 17:5)

This is my beloved Son, with whom I am well pleased;
listen to him.

Prayer after Communion

As we receive these glorious mysteries,
we make thanksgiving to you, O Lord,
for allowing us while still on earth
to be partakers even now of the things of heaven.
Through Christ our Lord. All: **Amen.**

Third Sunday of Lent

February 28, 2027

Reflection on the Gospel

In today's gospel, we see Jesus filled with righteous anger as he drives out the money changers from the temple. This image—zealous and forceful—can feel jarring when we're used to seeing Jesus as the Good Shepherd or the Prince of Peace. But it's an important reminder: God is more than any one image or role. If we only ever see God as distant Creator or Almighty Judge, we risk missing the fullness of God's identity. This fullness is made known in Jesus Christ, fully God and fully human.

—Living Liturgy™, *Third Sunday of Lent 2027*

ENTRANCE ANTIPHON (Cf. Psalm 25[24]:15-16)
My eyes are always on the Lord,
for he rescues my feet from the snare.
Turn to me and have mercy on me,
for I am alone and poor.

Or:

(Cf. Ezekiel 36:23-26)
When I prove my holiness among you,
I will gather you from all the foreign lands;
and I will pour clean water upon you
and cleanse you from all your impurities,
and I will give you a new spirit, says the Lord.

COLLECT
O God, author of every mercy and of all goodness,
who in fasting, prayer and almsgiving
have shown us a remedy for sin,
look graciously on this confession of our lowliness,
that we, who are bowed down by our conscience,
may always be lifted up by your mercy.
Through our Lord Jesus Christ, your Son,
who lives and reigns with you in the unity of the Holy Spirit,
God, for ever and ever. All: **Amen.**

The readings given for Year A, n. 28, may be used in place of these given here. *See pages 148–154.*

READING I (L 29-B) (Exodus 20:1-17) *or* Shorter Form [ ]
(Exodus 20:1-3, 7-8, 12-17)

A reading from the Book of Exodus

The law was given through Moses.

[In those days, God delivered all these commandments:
"I, the LORD, am your God,
who brought you out of the land of Egypt, that place of slavery.
You shall not have other gods besides me.]
You shall not carve idols for yourselves
in the shape of anything in the sky above
or on the earth below or in the waters beneath the earth;

you shall not bow down before them or worship them.
For I, the LORD, your God, am a jealous God,
inflicting punishment for their fathers' wickedness
on the children of those who hate me,
down to the third and fourth generation;
but bestowing mercy down to the thousandth generation
on the children of those who love me and keep my commandments.

[“You shall not take the name of the LORD, your God, in vain.
For the LORD will not leave unpunished
the one who takes his name in vain.

“Remember to keep holy the sabbath day.]
Six days you may labor and do all your work,
but the seventh day is the sabbath of the LORD, your God.
No work may be done then either by you, or your son or daughter,
or your male or female slave, or your beast,
or by the alien who lives with you.
In six days the LORD made the heavens and the earth,
the sea and all that is in them;
but on the seventh day he rested.
That is why the LORD has blessed the sabbath day and made it holy.

[“Honor your father and your mother,
that you may have a long life in the land
which the LORD, your God, is giving you.
You shall not kill.
You shall not commit adultery.
You shall not steal.
You shall not bear false witness against your neighbor.
You shall not covet your neighbor's house.

You shall not covet your neighbor's wife,
nor his male or female slave, nor his ox or ass,
nor anything else that belongs to him."]

The word of the Lord. All: **Thanks be to God.**

Responsorial Psalm 19

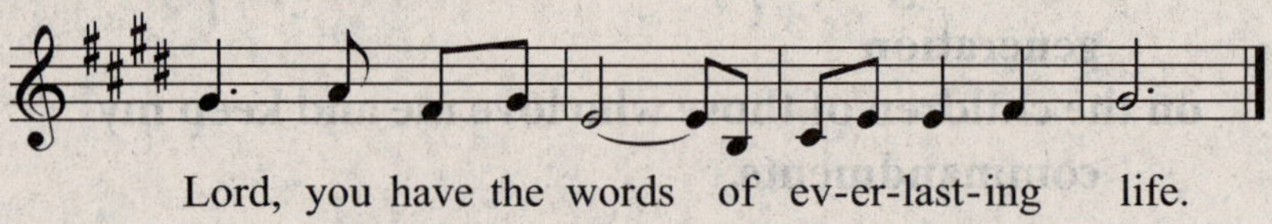

Psalm 19:8, 9, 10, 11

℟. (John 6:68c) **Lord, you have the words of everlasting life.**

The law of the LORD is perfect,
refreshing the soul;
The decree of the LORD is trustworthy,
giving wisdom to the simple. ℟.

The precepts of the LORD are right,
rejoicing the heart;
the command of the LORD is clear,
enlightening the eye. ℟.

The fear of the LORD is pure,
enduring forever;
the ordinances of the LORD are true,
all of them just. ℟.

They are more precious than gold,
than a heap of purest gold;
sweeter also than syrup
or honey from the comb. ℟.

Reading II (1 Corinthians 1:22-25)

A reading from the first Letter of Saint Paul to the Corinthians

We proclaim Christ crucified, a stumbling block to many, but to those who are called, the wisdom of God.

Brothers and sisters:
Jews demand signs and Greeks look for wisdom,
but we proclaim Christ crucified,
a stumbling block to Jews and foolishness to Gentiles,
but to those who are called, Jews and Greeks alike,
Christ the power of God and the wisdom of God.
For the foolishness of God is wiser than human wisdom,
and the weakness of God is stronger than human strength.

The word of the Lord. All: **Thanks be to God.**

GOSPEL (John 2:13-25)
VERSE BEFORE THE GOSPEL (John 3:16)

℣. Praise to you, Lord Jesus Christ, king of endless glory.
℟. **Praise to you, Lord Jesus Christ, king of endless glory.**
℣. God so loved the world that he gave his only Son,
so that everyone who believes in him might have eternal life. ℟.

✠ **A reading from the holy Gospel according to John**

All: **Glory to you, O Lord.**

Destroy this temple, and in three days I will raise it up.

Since the Passover of the Jews was near,
Jesus went up to Jerusalem.
He found in the temple area those who sold oxen, sheep, and doves,
as well as the money changers seated there.
He made a whip out of cords
and drove them all out of the temple area, with the sheep and oxen,
and spilled the coins of the money changers
and overturned their tables,
and to those who sold doves he said,
"Take these out of here,
and stop making my Father's house a marketplace."
His disciples recalled the words of Scripture,
Zeal for your house will consume me.

At this the Jews answered and said to him,
"What sign can you show us for doing this?"
Jesus answered and said to them,
"Destroy this temple and in three days I will raise it up."
The Jews said,
"This temple has been under construction for forty-six years,
and you will raise it up in three days?"
But he was speaking about the temple of his body.
Therefore, when he was raised from the dead,
his disciples remembered that he had said this,
and they came to believe the Scripture
and the word Jesus had spoken.
While he was in Jerusalem for the feast of Passover,
many began to believe in his name
when they saw the signs he was doing.
But Jesus would not trust himself to them because he knew them all,
and did not need anyone to testify about human nature.
He himself understood it well.

The Gospel of the Lord. All: **Praise to you, Lord Jesus Christ.**

Or:

Reading I (Exodus 17:3-7)

A reading from the Book of Exodus

Give us water, so that we may drink.

In those days, in their thirst for water,
the people grumbled against Moses,
saying, "Why did you ever make us leave Egypt?
Was it just to have us die here of thirst
with our children and our livestock?"
So Moses cried out to the Lord,

"What shall I do with this people?
A little more and they will stone me!"
The Lord answered Moses,
"Go over there in front of the people,
along with some of the elders of Israel,
holding in your hand, as you go,
the staff with which you struck the river.
I will be standing there in front of you on the rock in Horeb.
Strike the rock, and the water will flow from it
for the people to drink."
This Moses did, in the presence of the elders of Israel.
The place was called Massah and Meribah,
because the Israelites quarreled there
and tested the Lord, saying,
"Is the Lord in our midst or not?"

The word of the Lord. All: **Thanks be to God.**

Responsorial Psalm 95

The response is preferably sung twice after each verse

Psalm 95:1-2, 6-7, 8-9

℟. (8) **If today you hear his voice, harden not your hearts.**

Come, let us sing joyfully to the Lord;
let us acclaim the Rock of our salvation.
Let us come into his presence with thanksgiving;
let us joyfully sing psalms to him. ℟.

(continued)

Come, let us bow down in worship;
let us kneel before the LORD who made us.
For he is our God,
and we are the people he shepherds, the flock he guides. ℟.

Oh, that today you would hear his voice:
"Harden not your hearts as at Meribah,
as in the day of Massah in the desert.
Where your fathers tempted me;
they tested me though they had seen my works." ℟.

READING II (Romans 5:1-2, 5-8)

A reading from the Letter of Saint Paul to the Romans

The love of God has been poured into our hearts through the Holy Spirit that has been given to us.

Brothers and sisters:
Since we have been justified by faith,
we have peace with God through our Lord Jesus Christ,
through whom we have gained access by faith
to this grace in which we stand,
and we boast in hope of the glory of God.

And hope does not disappoint,
because the love of God has been poured out into our hearts
through the Holy Spirit who has been given to us.
For Christ, while we were still helpless,
died at the appointed time for the ungodly.
Indeed, only with difficulty does one die for a just person,
though perhaps for a good person one might even find courage to die.
But God proves his love for us
in that while we were still sinners Christ died for us.

The word of the Lord. All: **Thanks be to God.**

GOSPEL (John 4:5-42) *or* Shorter Form [ ] (John 4:5-15, 19b-26, 39a, 40-42)

VERSE BEFORE THE GOSPEL (*See* John 4:42, 15)

℣. Praise to you, Lord Jesus Christ, King of endless glory!
℟. **Praise to you, Lord Jesus Christ, King of endless glory!**
℣. Lord, you are truly the Savior of the world;
give me living water, that I may never thirst again. ℟.

✠ **A reading from the holy Gospel according to John**

All: **Glory to you, O Lord.**

The water that I shall give will become a spring of eternal life.

**[Jesus came to a town of Samaria called Sychar,
near the plot of land that Jacob had given to his son Joseph.
Jacob's well was there.
Jesus, tired from his journey, sat down there at the well.
It was about noon.**

**A woman of Samaria came to draw water.
Jesus said to her,
"Give me a drink."
His disciples had gone into the town to buy food.
The Samaritan woman said to him,
"How can you, a Jew, ask me, a Samaritan woman, for a drink?"
—For Jews use nothing in common with Samaritans.—
Jesus answered and said to her,
"If you knew the gift of God
and who is saying to you, 'Give me a drink,'
you would have asked him
and he would have given you living water."
The woman said to him,
"Sir, you do not even have a bucket and the cistern is deep;
where then can you get this living water?
Are you greater than our father Jacob,
who gave us this cistern and drank from it himself
with his children and his flocks?"**

Jesus answered and said to her,
"Everyone who drinks this water will be thirsty again;
but whoever drinks the water I shall give will never thirst;
the water I shall give will become in him
a spring of water welling up to eternal life."
The woman said to him,
"Sir, give me this water, so that I may not be thirsty
or have to keep coming here to draw water."]

Jesus said to her,
"Go call your husband and come back."
The woman answered and said to him,
"I do not have a husband."
Jesus answered her,
"You are right in saying, 'I do not have a husband.'
For you have had five husbands,
and the one you have now is not your husband.
What you have said is true."
The woman said to him,
["Sir, I can see that you are a prophet.
Our ancestors worshiped on this mountain;
but you people say that the place to worship is in Jerusalem."
Jesus said to her,
"Believe me, woman, the hour is coming
when you will worship the Father
neither on this mountain nor in Jerusalem.
You people worship what you do not understand;
we worship what we understand,
because salvation is from the Jews.
But the hour is coming, and is now here,
when true worshipers will worship the Father in Spirit and truth;
and indeed the Father seeks such people to worship him.

God is Spirit, and those who worship him
must worship in Spirit and truth."
The woman said to him,
"I know that the Messiah is coming, the one called the Christ;
when he comes, he will tell us everything."
Jesus said to her,
"I am he, the one* speaking with you."]

At that moment his disciples returned,
and were amazed that he was talking with a woman,
but still no one said, "What are you looking for?"
or "Why are you talking with her?"
The woman left her water jar
and went into the town and said to the people,
"Come see a man who told me everything I have done.
Could he possibly be the Christ?"
They went out of the town and came to him.
Meanwhile, the disciples urged him, "Rabbi, eat."
But he said to them,
"I have food to eat of which you do not know."
So the disciples said to one another,
"Could someone have brought him something to eat?"
Jesus said to them,
"My food is to do the will of the one who sent me
and to finish his work.
Do you not say, 'In four months the harvest will be here'?
I tell you, look up and see the fields ripe for the harvest.
The reaper is already receiving payment
and gathering crops for eternal life,
so that the sower and reaper can rejoice together.
For here the saying is verified that 'One sows and another reaps.'

* Short form: **the one who is**

I sent you to reap what you have not worked for;
others have done the work,
and you are sharing the fruits of their work."

[Many of the Samaritans of that town began to believe in him]
because of the word of the woman who testified,
"He told me everything I have done."
[When the Samaritans came to him,
they invited him to stay with them;
and he stayed there two days.
Many more began to believe in him because of his word,
and they said to the woman,
"We no longer believe because of your word;
for we have heard for ourselves,
and we know that this is truly the savior of the world."]

The Gospel of the Lord. All: **Praise to you, Lord Jesus Christ.**

Prayer over the Offerings

Be pleased, O Lord, with these sacrificial offerings,
and grant that we who beseech pardon for our own sins,
may take care to forgive our neighbor.
Through Christ our Lord. All: **Amen.**

Communion Antiphon (Cf. Psalm 84[83]:4-5)

The sparrow finds a home,
and the swallow a nest for her young:
by your altars, O Lord of hosts, my King and my God.
Blessed are they who dwell in your house,
for ever singing your praise.

Prayer after Communion

As we receive the pledge
of things yet hidden in heaven
and are nourished while still on earth
with the Bread that comes from on high,
we humbly entreat you, O Lord,
that what is being brought about in us in mystery
may come to true completion.
Through Christ our Lord. All: **Amen.**

Fourth Sunday of Lent

March 7, 2027

Reflection on the Gospel

John 3:16 is a familiar passage from today's gospel: "For God so loved the world that he gave his only Son, so that everyone who believes in him might not perish but might have eternal life." This eternal life is offered to us as a gift. It is nothing to be earned or bought; it can only be gratefully received. The immensity of God's love for us is represented both in what the gift is—eternal life with God—and by the gift of God sending his Son to us.

—Living Liturgy™, *Fourth Sunday of Lent 2027*

ENTRANCE ANTIPHON (Cf. Isaiah 66:10-11)

Rejoice, Jerusalem, and all who love her.
Be joyful, all who were in mourning;
exult and be satisfied at her consoling breast.

COLLECT

O God, who through your Word
reconcile the human race to yourself in a wonderful way,
grant, we pray,
that with prompt devotion and eager faith
the Christian people may hasten
toward the solemn celebrations to come.
Through our Lord Jesus Christ, your Son,
who lives and reigns with you in the unity of the Holy Spirit,
God, for ever and ever. All: **Amen.**

The readings given for Year A, n. 28, may be used in place of these given here. *See pages 159–166.*

READING I (L 32-B) (2 Chronicles 36:14-16, 19-23)

A reading from the second Book of Chronicles

The wrath and the mercy of the Lord are revealed in the exile and liberation of his people.

In those days, all the princes of Judah, the priests, and the people
added infidelity to infidelity,
practicing all the abominations of the nations
and polluting the LORD's temple
which he had consecrated in Jerusalem.

Early and often did the LORD, the God of their fathers,
send his messengers to them,
for he had compassion on his people and his dwelling place.
But they mocked the messengers of God,
despised his warnings, and scoffed at his prophets,
until the anger of the LORD against his people was so inflamed
that there was no remedy.
Their enemies burnt the house of God,
tore down the walls of Jerusalem,
set all its palaces afire,
and destroyed all its precious objects.
Those who escaped the sword were carried captive to Babylon,
where they became servants of the king of the Chaldeans and his sons
until the kingdom of the Persians came to power.
All this was to fulfill the word of the LORD spoken by Jeremiah:
"Until the land has retrieved its lost sabbaths,
during all the time it lies waste it shall have rest
while seventy years are fulfilled."

In the first year of Cyrus, king of Persia,
in order to fulfill the word of the LORD spoken by Jeremiah,
the LORD inspired King Cyrus of Persia
to issue this proclamation throughout his kingdom,
both by word of mouth and in writing:

"Thus says Cyrus, king of Persia:
All the kingdoms of the earth
the LORD, the God of heaven, has given to me,
and he has also charged me to build him a house
in Jerusalem, which is in Judah.
Whoever, therefore, among you belongs to any part of his people,
let him go up, and may his God be with him!"

The word of the Lord. All: **Thanks be to God.**

RESPONSORIAL PSALM 137

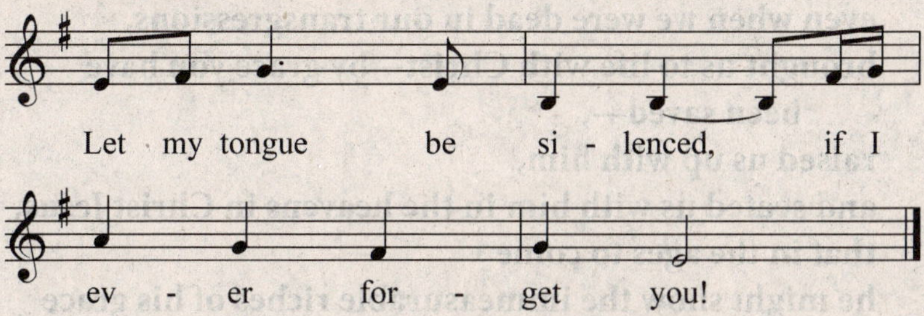

Text: Refrain, *Lectionary for Mass,* © 1969, 1981, 1997, ICEL
Music: *The Collegeville Psalter*, © 2017, Paul Inwood.

Psalm 137:1-2, 3, 4-5, 6

℟. (6ab) **Let my tongue be silenced, if I ever forget you!**

By the streams of Babylon
we sat and wept
when we remembered Zion.
On the aspens of that land
we hung up our harps. ℟.

For there our captors asked of us
the lyrics of our songs,
And our despoilers urged us to be joyous:
"Sing for us the songs of Zion!" ℟.

How could we sing a song of the LORD
in a foreign land?
If I forget you, Jerusalem,
may my right hand be forgotten! ℟.

(continued)

May my tongue cleave to my palate
if I remember you not,
If I place not Jerusalem
ahead of my joy. ℟.

READING II (Ephesians 2:4-10)

A reading from the Letter of Saint Paul to the Ephesians

Though dead in your transgressions, by grace you have been saved.

Brothers and sisters:
God, who is rich in mercy,
because of the great love he had for us,
even when we were dead in our transgressions,
brought us to life with Christ—by grace you have been saved—,
raised us up with him,
and seated us with him in the heavens in Christ Jesus,
that in the ages to come
he might show the immeasurable riches of his grace
in his kindness to us in Christ Jesus.
For by grace you have been saved through faith,
and this is not from you; it is the gift of God;
it is not from works, so no one may boast.
For we are his handiwork, created in Christ Jesus for the good works
that God has prepared in advance,
that we should live in them.

The word of the Lord. All: **Thanks be to God.**

GOSPEL (John 3:14-21)

VERSE BEFORE THE GOSPEL (John 3:16)

℣. Praise to you, Lord Jesus Christ, king of endless glory!
℟. **Praise to you, Lord Jesus Christ, king of endless glory!**
℣. God so loved the world that he gave his only Son,
so everyone who believes in him might have eternal life. ℟.

✠ **A reading from the holy Gospel according to John**

All: **Glory to you, O Lord.**

God sent his Son so that the world might be saved through him.

Jesus said to Nicodemus:
"Just as Moses lifted up the serpent in the desert,
so must the Son of Man be lifted up,
so that everyone who believes in him may have eternal life."

For God so loved the world that he gave his only Son,
so that everyone who believes in him might not perish
but might have eternal life.
For God did not send his Son into the world to condemn the world,
but that the world might be saved through him.
Whoever believes in him will not be condemned,
but whoever does not believe has already been condemned,
because he has not believed in the name of the only Son of God.
And this is the verdict,
that the light came into the world,
but people preferred darkness to light,
because their works were evil.
For everyone who does wicked things hates the light
and does not come toward the light,
so that his works might not be exposed.
But whoever lives the truth comes to the light,
so that his works may be clearly seen as done in God.

The Gospel of the Lord. All: **Praise to you, Lord Jesus Christ.**

Or:

READING I (L 31-A) (1 Samuel 16:1b, 6-7, 10-13a)

A reading from the first Book of Samuel

David is anointed as king of Israel.

The LORD said to Samuel:
"Fill your horn with oil, and be on your way.
I am sending you to Jesse of Bethlehem,
for I have chosen my king from among his sons."

As Jesse and his sons came to the sacrifice,
Samuel looked at Eliab and thought,
"Surely the LORD's anointed is here before him."
But the LORD said to Samuel:
"Do not judge from his appearance or from his lofty stature,
because I have rejected him.
Not as man sees does God see,
because man sees the appearance
but the LORD looks into the heart."
In the same way Jesse presented seven sons before Samuel,
but Samuel said to Jesse,
"The LORD has not chosen any one of these."
Then Samuel asked Jesse,
"Are these all the sons you have?"
Jesse replied,
"There is still the youngest, who is tending the sheep."
Samuel said to Jesse,
"Send for him;
we will not begin the sacrificial banquet until he arrives here."
Jesse sent and had the young man brought to them.
He was ruddy, a youth handsome to behold
and making a splendid appearance.
The LORD said,
"There—anoint him, for this is the one!"
Then Samuel, with the horn of oil in hand,
anointed David in the presence of his brothers;
and from that day on, the spirit of the LORD rushed upon David.

The word of the Lord. All: **Thanks be to God.**

Responsorial Psalm 23

Psalm 23:1-3a, 3b-4, 5, 6

℟. (1) **The Lord is my shepherd; there is nothing I shall want.**

The LORD is my shepherd; I shall not want.
 In verdant pastures he gives me repose;
beside restful waters he leads me;
 he refreshes my soul. ℟.

He guides me in right paths
 for his name's sake.
Even though I walk in the dark valley
 I fear no evil; for you are at my side
with your rod and your staff
 that give me courage. ℟.

You spread the table before me
 in the sight of my foes;
you anoint my head with oil;
 my cup overflows. ℟.

Only goodness and kindness follow me
 all the days of my life;
and I shall dwell in the house of the LORD
 for years to come. ℟.

Reading II (Ephesians 5:8-14)

A reading from the Letter of Saint Paul to the Ephesians

Arise from the dead, and Christ will give you light.

Brothers and sisters:
You were once darkness,
but now you are light in the Lord.
Live as children of light,
for light produces every kind of goodness
and righteousness and truth.
Try to learn what is pleasing to the Lord.
Take no part in the fruitless works of darkness;
rather expose them, for it is shameful even to mention
the things done by them in secret;
but everything exposed by the light becomes visible,
for everything that becomes visible is light.
Therefore, it says:
"Awake, O sleeper,
and arise from the dead,
and Christ will give you light."

The word of the Lord. All: **Thanks be to God.**

GOSPEL (John 9:1-41) *or* Shorter Form [ ] (John 9:1, 6-9, 13-17, 34-38)

VERSE BEFORE THE GOSPEL (John 8:12)

℣. Praise to you, Lord Jesus Christ, King of endless glory!
℟. **Praise to you, Lord Jesus Christ, King of endless glory!**
℣. I am the light of the world, says the Lord;
whoever follows me will have the light of life. ℟.

✠ **A reading from the holy Gospel according to John**

All: **Glory to you, O Lord.**

The man who was blind went off and washed himself and came back able to see.

[**As Jesus passed by he saw a man blind from birth.**]
His disciples asked him,
"Rabbi, who sinned, this man or his parents,
that he was born blind?"
Jesus answered,
"Neither he nor his parents sinned;

it is so that the works of God might be made visible through him.
We have to do the works of the one who sent me while it is day.
Night is coming when no one can work.
While I am in the world, I am the light of the world."
When he had said this, [he spat on the ground
and made clay with the saliva,
and smeared the clay on his eyes, and said to him,
"Go wash in the Pool of Siloam"—which means Sent—.
So he went and washed, and came back able to see.

His neighbors and those who had seen him earlier as a beggar said,
"Isn't this the one who used to sit and beg?"
Some said, "It is,"
but others said, "No, he just looks like him."
He said, "I am."]
So they said to him, "How were your eyes opened?"
He replied,
"The man called Jesus made clay and anointed my eyes
and told me, 'Go to Siloam and wash.'
So I went there and washed and was able to see."
And they said to him, "Where is he?"
He said, "I don't know."

[They brought the one who was once blind to the Pharisees.
Now Jesus had made clay and opened his eyes on a sabbath.
So then the Pharisees also asked him how he was able to see.
He said to them,
"He put clay on my eyes, and I washed, and now I can see."
So some of the Pharisees said,
"This man is not from God,
because he does not keep the sabbath."

But others said,
"How can a sinful man do such signs?"
And there was a division among them.
So they said to the blind man again,
"What do you have to say about him,
since he opened your eyes?"
He said, "He is a prophet."]

Now the Jews did not believe
that he had been blind and gained his sight
until they summoned the parents of the one who had gained his sight.
They asked them,
"Is this your son, who you say was born blind?
How does he now see?"
His parents answered and said,
"We know that this is our son and that he was born blind.
We do not know how he sees now,
nor do we know who opened his eyes.
Ask him, he is of age;
he can speak for himself."
His parents said this because they were afraid
of the Jews, for the Jews had already agreed
that if anyone acknowledged him as the Christ,
he would be expelled from the synagogue.
For this reason his parents said,
"He is of age; question him."

So a second time they called the man who had been blind
and said to him, "Give God the praise!
We know that this man is a sinner."
He replied,
"If he is a sinner, I do not know.
One thing I do know is that I was blind and now I see."
So they said to him,

"What did he do to you?
How did he open your eyes?"
He answered them,
"I told you already and you did not listen.
Why do you want to hear it again?
Do you want to become his disciples, too?"
They ridiculed him and said,
"You are that man's disciple;
we are disciples of Moses!
We know that God spoke to Moses,
but we do not know where this one is from."
The man answered and said to them,
"This is what is so amazing,
that you do not know where he is from, yet he opened my eyes.
We know that God does not listen to sinners,
but if one is devout and does his will, he listens to him.
It is unheard of that anyone ever opened the eyes of a person born blind.
If this man were not from God,
he would not be able to do anything."
[They answered and said to him,
"You were born totally in sin,
and are you trying to teach us?"
Then they threw him out.

When Jesus heard that they had thrown him out,
he found him and said, "Do you believe in the Son of Man?"
He answered and said,
"Who is he, sir, that I may believe in him?"
Jesus said to him,
"You have seen him,
and the one speaking with you is he."
He said,
"I do believe, Lord," and he worshiped him.]

Then Jesus said,
"I came into this world for judgment,
so that those who do not see might see,
and those who do see might become blind."

Some of the Pharisees who were with him heard this
and said to him, "Surely we are not also blind, are we?"
Jesus said to them,
"If you were blind, you would have no sin;
but now you are saying, 'We see,' so your sin remains."

The Gospel of the Lord. All: **Praise to you, Lord Jesus Christ.**

PRAYER OVER THE OFFERINGS

We place before you with joy these offerings,
which bring eternal remedy, O Lord,
praying that we may both faithfully revere them
and present them to you, as is fitting,
for the salvation of all the world.
Through Christ our Lord. All: **Amen.**

COMMUNION ANTIPHON (Cf. Psalm 122[121]:3-4)

Jerusalem is built as a city bonded as one together.
It is there that the tribes go up, the tribes of the Lord,
to praise the name of the Lord.

PRAYER AFTER COMMUNION

O God, who enlighten everyone who comes into this world,
illuminate our hearts, we pray,
with the splendor of your grace,
that we may always ponder
what is worthy and pleasing to your majesty
and love you in all sincerity.
Through Christ our Lord. All: **Amen.**

Fifth Sunday of Lent

March 14, 2027

Reflection on the Gospel

On this Sunday we hear that there are days coming when God will make a new covenant, where God's laws will not be handed on to us externally, like the Ten Commandments on tablets, but will be written on our hearts. In the gospel, we are told of God's thunderous voice, much like the voice at the transfiguration. Everything seems to return us to where the journey began: Jesus's proclamation that the kingdom of God is at hand.

—Living Liturgy™, *Fifth Sunday of Lent 2027*

ENTRANCE ANTIPHON (Cf. Psalm 43[42]:1-2)

Give me justice, O God,
and plead my cause against a nation that is faithless.
From the deceitful and cunning rescue me,
for you, O God, are my strength.

COLLECT

By your help, we beseech you, Lord our God,
may we walk eagerly in that same charity
with which, out of love for the world,
your Son handed himself over to death.
Through our Lord Jesus Christ, your Son,
who lives and reigns with you in the unity of the Holy Spirit,
God, for ever and ever. All: **Amen.**

The readings given for Year A, n. 28, may be used in place of these given here. *See pages 170–176.*

READING I (L 35-B) (Jeremiah 31:31-34)

A reading from the Book of the Prophet Jeremiah

I will make a new covenant and remember their sin no more.

The days are coming, says the LORD,
when I will make a new covenant with the house of Israel
and the house of Judah.

It will not be like the covenant I made with their fathers
the day I took them by the hand
to lead them forth from the land of Egypt;
for they broke my covenant,
and I had to show myself their master, says the Lord.
But this is the covenant that I will make
with the house of Israel after those days, says the Lord.
I will place my law within them and write it upon their hearts;
I will be their God, and they shall be my people.
No longer will they have need to teach their friends and relatives
how to know the Lord.
All, from least to greatest, shall know me, says the Lord,
for I will forgive their evildoing and remember their sin no more.

The word of the Lord. All: **Thanks be to God.**

Responsorial Psalm 51

Psalm 51:3-4, 12-13, 14-15

℟. (12a) **Create a clean heart in me, O God.**

Have mercy on me, O God, in your goodness;
in the greatness of your compassion wipe out my offense.
Thoroughly wash me from my guilt
and of my sin cleanse me. ℟.

A clean heart create for me, O God,
and a steadfast spirit renew within me.
Cast me not out from your presence,
and your Holy Spirit take not from me. ℟.

Give me back the joy of your salvation,
  and a willing spirit sustain in me.
I will teach transgressors your ways,
  and sinners shall return to you. ℟.

READING II (Hebrews 5:7-9)

A reading from the Letter to the Hebrews

Christ learned obedience and became the source of eternal salvation.

In the days when Christ Jesus was in the flesh,
he offered prayers and supplications with loud cries and tears
to the one who was able to save him from death,
and he was heard because of his reverence.
Son though he was, he learned obedience from what he suffered;
and when he was made perfect,
he became the source of eternal salvation for all who obey him.

The word of the Lord. All: **Thanks be to God.**

GOSPEL (John 12:20-33)

VERSE BEFORE THE GOSPEL (John 12:26)

℣. Glory to you, Word of God, Lord Jesus Christ!
℟. **Glory to you, Word of God, Lord Jesus Christ!**
℣. Whoever serves me must follow me, says the Lord;
and where I am, there also will my servant be. ℟.

✠ **A reading from the holy Gospel according to John**

All: **Glory to you, O Lord.**

If a grain of wheat falls to the ground and dies, it produces much fruit.

Some Greeks who had come to worship at the Passover Feast
came to Philip, who was from Bethsaida in Galilee,
and asked him, "Sir, we would like to see Jesus."
Philip went and told Andrew;
then Andrew and Philip went and told Jesus.

Jesus answered them,
"The hour has come for the Son of Man to be glorified.
Amen, amen, I say to you,
unless a grain of wheat falls to the ground and dies,
it remains just a grain of wheat;
but if it dies, it produces much fruit.
Whoever loves his life loses it,
and whoever hates his life in this world
will preserve it for eternal life.
Whoever serves me must follow me,
and where I am, there also will my servant be.
The Father will honor whoever serves me.

"I am troubled now. Yet what should I say?
'Father, save me from this hour'?
But it was for this purpose that I came to this hour.
Father, glorify your name."
Then a voice came from heaven,
"I have glorified it and will glorify it again."
The crowd there heard it and said it was thunder;
but others said, "An angel has spoken to him."
Jesus answered and said,
"This voice did not come for my sake but for yours.
Now is the time of judgment on this world;
now the ruler of this world will be driven out.
And when I am lifted up from the earth,
I will draw everyone to myself."
He said this indicating the kind of death he would die.

The Gospel of the Lord. All: **Praise to you, Lord Jesus Christ.**

Or:

READING I (L 34-A) (Ezekiel 37:12-14)

A reading from the Book of the Prophet Ezekiel

I will put my spirit in you that you may live.

Thus says the Lord GOD:
O my people, I will open your graves

and have you rise from them,
and bring you back to the land of Israel.
Then you shall know that I am the LORD,
when I open your graves and have you rise from them,
O my people!
I will put my spirit in you that you may live,
and I will settle you upon your land;
thus you shall know that I am the LORD.
I have promised, and I will do it, says the LORD.

The word of the Lord. All: **Thanks be to God.**

RESPONSORIAL PSALM 130

Text: Refrain, *Lectionary for Mass,* © 1969, 1981, 1997, ICEL
Music: *The Collegeville Psalter*, © 2017, Paul Inwood.

Psalm 130:1-2, 3-4, 5-6, 7-8

℟. (7) **With the Lord there is mercy and fullness of redemption.**

Out of the depths I cry to you, O LORD;
LORD, hear my voice!
Let your ears be attentive
to my voice in supplication. ℟.

If you, O LORD, mark iniquities,
LORD, who can stand?
But with you is forgiveness,
that you may be revered. ℟.

I trust in the LORD;
my soul trusts in his word.
More than sentinels wait for the dawn,
let Israel wait for the LORD. ℟.

(continued)

For with the LORD is kindness
and with him is plenteous redemption;
and he will redeem Israel
from all their iniquities. ℟.

READING II (Romans 8:8-11)

A reading from the Letter of Saint Paul to the Romans

The Spirit of the One who raised Jesus from the dead dwells in you.

Brothers and sisters:
Those who are in the flesh cannot please God.
But you are not in the flesh;
on the contrary, you are in the spirit,
if only the Spirit of God dwells in you.
Whoever does not have the Spirit of Christ does not belong to him.
But if Christ is in you,
although the body is dead because of sin,
the spirit is alive because of righteousness.
If the Spirit of the one who raised Jesus from the dead dwells in you,
the one who raised Christ from the dead
will give life to your mortal bodies also,
through his Spirit dwelling in you.

The word of the Lord. All: **Thanks be to God.**

GOSPEL (John 11:1-45) *or* Shorter Form [ ] (John 11:3-7, 17, 20-27, 33b-45)

VERSE BEFORE THE GOSPEL (John 11:25a, 26)

℣. Praise to you, Lord Jesus Christ, King of endless glory!
℟. **Praise to you, Lord Jesus Christ, King of endless glory!**
℣. I am the resurrection and the life, says the Lord;
whoever believes in me, even if he dies, will never die. ℟.

✠ **A reading from the holy Gospel according to John**

All: **Glory to you, O Lord.**

I am the resurrection and the life.

Now a man was ill, Lazarus from Bethany,
the village of Mary and her sister Martha.
Mary was the one who had anointed the Lord with perfumed oil
and dried his feet with her hair;
it was her brother Lazarus who was ill.
So [the sisters* sent word to Jesus saying,
"Master, the one you love is ill."
When Jesus heard this he said,
"This illness is not to end in death,
but is for the glory of God,
that the Son of God may be glorified through it."
Now Jesus loved Martha and her sister and Lazarus.
So when he heard that he was ill,
he remained for two days in the place where he was.
Then after this he said to his disciples,
"Let us go back to Judea."]
The disciples said to him,
"Rabbi, the Jews were just trying to stone you,
and you want to go back there?"
Jesus answered,
"Are there not twelve hours in a day?
If one walks during the day, he does not stumble,
because he sees the light of this world.
But if one walks at night, he stumbles,
because the light is not in him."
He said this, and then told them,
"Our friend Lazarus is asleep,
but I am going to awaken him."
So the disciples said to him,
"Master, if he is asleep, he will be saved."
But Jesus was talking about his death,
while they thought that he meant ordinary sleep.
So then Jesus said to them clearly,
"Lazarus has died.

* Shorter form: **The sisters of Lazarus**

And I am glad for you that I was not there,
that you may believe.
Let us go to him."
So Thomas, called Didymus, said to his fellow disciples,
"Let us also go to die with him."

[When Jesus arrived, he found that Lazarus
had already been in the tomb for four days.]
Now Bethany was near Jerusalem, only about two miles away.
And many of the Jews had come to Martha and Mary
to comfort them about their brother.
[When Martha heard that Jesus was coming,
she went to meet him;
but Mary sat at home.
Martha said to Jesus,
"Lord, if you had been here,
my brother would not have died.
But even now I know that whatever you ask of God,
God will give you."
Jesus said to her,
"Your brother will rise."
Martha said to him,
"I know he will rise,
in the resurrection on the last day."
Jesus told her,
"I am the resurrection and the life;
whoever believes in me, even if he dies, will live,
and everyone who lives and believes in me will never die.
Do you believe this?"
She said to him, "Yes, Lord.
I have come to believe that you are the Christ, the Son of God,
the one who is coming into the world."]

When she had said this,
she went and called her sister Mary secretly, saying,
"The teacher is here and is asking for you."
As soon as she heard this,
she rose quickly and went to him.
For Jesus had not yet come into the village,
but was still where Martha had met him.
So when the Jews who were with her in the house comforting her
saw Mary get up quickly and go out,
they followed her,
presuming that she was going to the tomb to weep there.
When Mary came to where Jesus was and saw him,
she fell at his feet and said to him,
"Lord, if you had been here,
my brother would not have died."
When Jesus saw her weeping and the Jews who had come with her weeping,
[he became perturbed and deeply troubled, and said,
"Where have you laid him?"
They said to him, "Sir, come and see."
And Jesus wept.
So the Jews said, "See how he loved him."
But some of them said,
"Could not the one who opened the eyes of the blind man
have done something so that this man would not have died?"
So Jesus, perturbed again, came to the tomb.
It was a cave, and a stone lay across it.
Jesus said, "Take away the stone."
Martha, the dead man's sister, said to him,
"Lord, by now there will be a stench;
he has been dead for four days."

Jesus said to her,
"Did I not tell you that if you believe
you will see the glory of God?"
So they took away the stone.
And Jesus raised his eyes and said,
"Father, I thank you for hearing me.
I know that you always hear me;
but because of the crowd here I have said this,
that they may believe that you sent me."
And when he had said this,
he cried out in a loud voice,
"Lazarus, come out!"
The dead man came out,
tied hand and foot with burial bands,
and his face was wrapped in a cloth.
So Jesus said to them,
"Untie him and let him go."

Now many of the Jews who had come to Mary
and seen what he had done began to believe in him.]

The Gospel of the Lord. All: **Praise to you, Lord Jesus Christ.**

PRAYER OVER THE OFFERINGS

Hear us, almighty God,
and, having instilled in your servants
the teachings of the Christian faith,
graciously purify them
by the working of this sacrifice.
Through Christ our Lord. All: **Amen.**

COMMUNION ANTIPHON (John 12:24)

Amen, Amen I say to you: Unless a grain of wheat
falls to the ground and dies, it remains a single grain.
But if it dies, it bears much fruit.

PRAYER AFTER COMMUNION

We pray, almighty God,
that we may always be counted among the members of Christ,
in whose Body and Blood we have communion.
Who lives and reigns for ever and ever. All: **Amen.**

Palm Sunday of the Lord's Passion

March 21, 2027

Reflection on the Gospel

It might be easily overlooked how often Jesus goes from place to place: the entrance into Jerusalem, to the Passover supper, the agony in the garden, the trial, to Pilate, to the stripping and mocking, to his crucifixion. Each of these is a procession. Jesus's many processions are linked to our own. Our earthly travels mirror his: visiting friends, dining, sharing good news, and more. Our spiritual travels mirror his: pilgrimages through both the joys and sorrows of life, with the goal of eternal unity with God and God's people.

—Living Liturgy™, *Palm Sunday 2027*

The Commemoration of the Lord's Entrance into Jerusalem

FIRST FORM: THE PROCESSION

The congregation assembles in a secondary church or chapel or in some other suitable place distinct from the church to which the procession will move. The faithful carry palm branches.

Antiphon

Hosanna to the Son of David;
blessed is he who comes in the name of the Lord, the King of Israel.
Hosanna in the highest.

Priest: In the name of the Father, and of the Son, and of the Holy Spirit.
All: **Amen.**

Then he greets the people in the usual way. A brief address is given, in which the faithful are invited to participate actively and consciously in the celebration of this day, in these or similar words:

Dear brethren (brothers and sisters),
since the beginning of Lent until now
we have prepared our hearts by penance and charitable works.

Today we gather together to herald with the whole Church
the beginning of the celebration
of our Lord's Paschal Mystery,
that is to say, of his Passion and Resurrection.
For it was to accomplish this mystery
that he entered his own city of Jerusalem.
Therefore, with all faith and devotion,
let us commemorate
the Lord's entry into the city for our salvation,
following in his footsteps,
so that, being made by his grace partakers of the Cross,
we may have a share also in his Resurrection and in his life.

Let us pray.

A Almighty ever-living God,
sanctify ✠ these branches with your blessing,
that we, who follow Christ the King in exultation,
may reach the eternal Jerusalem through him.
Who lives and reigns for ever and ever. All: **Amen.**

B Increase the faith of those who place their hope in you, O God,
and graciously hear the prayers of those who call on you,
that we, who today hold high these branches
to hail Christ in his triumph,
may bear fruit for you by good works accomplished in him.
Who lives and reigns for ever and ever. All: **Amen.**

The Reading of the Gospel

Gospel (L 37-B)

A (Mark 11:1-10)

✠ A reading from the holy Gospel according to Mark

All: **Glory to you, O Lord.**

Blessed is he who comes in the name of the Lord.

When Jesus and his disciples drew near to Jerusalem,
to Bethphage and Bethany at the Mount of Olives,
he sent two of his disciples and said to them,
"Go into the village opposite you,
and immediately on entering it,
you will find a colt tethered on which no one has ever sat.
Untie it and bring it here.

If anyone should say to you,
'Why are you doing this?' reply,
'The Master has need of it
and will send it back here at once.'"
So they went off
and found a colt tethered at a gate outside on the street,
and they untied it.
Some of the bystanders said to them,
"What are you doing, untying the colt?"
They answered them just as Jesus had told them to,
and they permitted them to do it.
So they brought the colt to Jesus
and put their cloaks over it.
And he sat on it.
Many people spread their cloaks on the road,
and others spread leafy branches
that they had cut from the fields.
Those preceding him as well as those following kept
crying out:
"Hosanna!
Blessed is he who comes in the name of the Lord!
Blessed is the kingdom of our father David that
is to come!
Hosanna in the highest!"

The Gospel of the Lord. All: **Praise to you, Lord Jesus Christ.**

Or:

B (John 12:12-16)

✠ **A reading from the holy Gospel according to John**

All: **Glory to you, O Lord.**

Blessed is he who comes in the name of the Lord.

When the great crowd that had come to the feast heard
that Jesus was coming to Jerusalem,
they took palm branches and went out to meet him,
and cried out:

"Hosanna!
Blessed is he who comes in the name of the Lord,
the king of Israel."

Jesus found an ass and sat upon it, as is written:
Fear no more, O daughter Zion;
see, your king comes, seated upon an ass's colt.
His disciples did not understand this at first,
but when Jesus had been glorified
they remembered that these things were written about him
and that they had done this for him.

The Gospel of the Lord. All: **Praise to you, Lord Jesus Christ.**

To begin the procession, an invitation may be given in these or similar words:

Dear brethren (brothers and sisters),
like the crowds who acclaimed Jesus in Jerusalem,
let us go forth in peace.

or:

Let us go forth in peace.

In this latter case, all respond:

In the name of Christ. Amen.

PROCESSION WITH THE BLESSED BRANCHES

SECOND FORM: THE SOLEMN ENTRANCE

When the First Form cannot take place, the commemoration of the Lord's entrance may be celebrated before the principal Mass with the solemn entrance, which takes place within the church.

THIRD FORM: THE SIMPLE ENTRANCE

At other Masses, the Lord's entrance is commemorated with the following simple entrance.

ENTRANCE ANTIPHON (Cf. John 12:1, 12-13; Psalm 24[23]:9-10)

Six days before the Passover,
when the Lord came into the city of Jerusalem,
the children ran to meet him;
in their hands they carried palm branches
and with a loud voice cried out:
*Hosanna in the highest!

Blessed are you, who have come in your abundant mercy!
O gates, lift high your heads;
grow higher, ancient doors.
Let him enter, the king of glory!
Who is this king of glory?
He, the Lord of hosts, he is the king of glory.
*Hosanna in the highest!

Blessed are you, who have come in your abundant mercy!

COLLECT

Almighty ever-living God,
who as an example of humility for the human race to follow
caused our Savior to take flesh and submit to the Cross,
graciously grant that we may heed his lesson of patient suffering
and so merit a share in his Resurrection.
Who lives and reigns with you in the unity of the Holy Spirit,
God, for ever and ever. All: **Amen.**

READING I (L 38-ABC) (Isaiah 50:4-7)

A reading from the Book of the Prophet Isaiah

My face I did not shield from buffets and spitting knowing that I shall not be put to shame.

The Lord GOD has given me
a well-trained tongue,
that I might know how to speak to the weary
a word that will rouse them.
Morning after morning
he opens my ear that I may hear;
and I have not rebelled,
have not turned back.
I gave my back to those who beat me,
my cheeks to those who plucked my beard;
my face I did not shield
from buffets and spitting.

The Lord GOD is my help,
therefore I am not disgraced;
I have set my face like flint,
knowing that I shall not be put to shame.

The word of the Lord. All: **Thanks be to God.**

Responsorial Psalm 22

Psalm 22:8-9, 17-18, 19-20, 23-24

℟. (2a) **My God, my God, why have you abandoned me?**

All who see me scoff at me;
they mock me with parted lips, they wag their heads:
"He relied on the Lord; let him deliver him,
let him rescue him, if he loves him." ℟.

Indeed, many dogs surround me,
a pack of evildoers closes in upon me;
they have pierced my hands and my feet;
I can count all my bones. ℟.

They divide my garments among them,
and for my vesture they cast lots.
But you, O Lord, be not far from me;
O my help, hasten to aid me. ℟.

I will proclaim your name to my brethren;
in the midst of the assembly I will praise you:
"You who fear the Lord, praise him;
all you descendants of Jacob, give glory to him;
revere him, all you descendants of Israel!" ℟.

Reading II (Philippians 2:6-11)

A reading from the Letter of Saint Paul to the Philippians

Christ humbled himself. Because of this God greatly exalted him.

**Christ Jesus, though he was in the form of God,
did not regard equality with God
something to be grasped.
Rather, he emptied himself,
taking the form of a slave,
coming in human likeness;**

and found human in appearance,
he humbled himself,
becoming obedient to the point of death,
even death on a cross.
Because of this, God greatly exalted him
and bestowed on him the name
which is above every name,
that at the name of Jesus
every knee should bend,
of those in heaven and on earth and under the earth,
and every tongue confess that
Jesus Christ is Lord,
to the glory of God the Father.

The word of the Lord. All: **Thanks be to God.**

GOSPEL (Mark 14:1—15:47) *or* Shorter Form [ ] (Mark 15:1-39)
VERSE BEFORE THE GOSPEL (Philippians 2:8-9)

℣. Praise to you, Lord Jesus Christ, King of endless glory!
℟. **Praise to you, Lord Jesus Christ, King of endless glory!**
℣. Christ became obedient to the point of death,
even death on a cross.
Because of this, God greatly exalted him
and bestowed on him the name which is above every name. ℟.

The symbols in the following passion narrative represent:

- C. Narrator;
- ✠ Christ;
- S. speakers other than Christ;
- SS. groups of speakers.

The Passion of our Lord Jesus Christ according to Mark

The Passion of our Lord Jesus Christ.

C. **The Passover and the Feast of Unleavened Bread**
were to take place in two days' time.
So the chief priests and the scribes were seeking a way
to arrest him by treachery and put him to death.
They said,

SS. "Not during the festival,
for fear that there may be a riot among the people."

C. When he was in Bethany reclining at table
in the house of Simon the leper,
a woman came with an alabaster jar of perfumed oil,
costly genuine spikenard.
She broke the alabaster jar and poured it on his head.
There were some who were indignant.

SS. "Why has there been this waste of perfumed oil?
It could have been sold for more than three hundred days' wages
and the money given to the poor."

C. They were infuriated with her.
Jesus said,

✠ "Let her alone.
Why do you make trouble for her?
She has done a good thing for me.
The poor you will always have with you,
and whenever you wish you can do good to them,
but you will not always have me.
She has done what she could.
She has anticipated anointing my body for burial.
Amen, I say to you,
wherever the gospel is proclaimed to the whole world,
what she has done will be told in memory of her."

C. Then Judas Iscariot, one of the Twelve,
went off to the chief priests to hand him over to them.
When they heard him they were pleased and promised to pay him money.
Then he looked for an opportunity to hand him over.

On the first day of the Feast of Unleavened Bread,
when they sacrificed the Passover lamb,
his disciples said to him,

SS. **"Where do you want us to go**
and prepare for you to eat the Passover?"
C. **He sent two of his disciples and said to them,**
✠ **"Go into the city and a man will meet you,**
carrying a jar of water.
Follow him.
Wherever he enters, say to the master of the house,
'The Teacher says, "Where is my guest room
where I may eat the Passover with my disciples?"'
Then he will show you a large upper room furnished and ready.
Make the preparations for us there."
C. **The disciples then went off, entered the city,**
and found it just as he had told them;
and they prepared the Passover.

When it was evening, he came with the Twelve.
And as they reclined at table and were eating,
Jesus said,
✠ **"Amen, I say to you, one of you will betray me,**
one who is eating with me."
C. **They began to be distressed and to say to him, one by one,**
S. **"Surely it is not I?"**
C. **He said to them,**
✠ **"One of the Twelve, the one who dips with me into the dish.**
For the Son of Man indeed goes, as it is written of him,
but woe to that man by whom the Son of Man is betrayed.
It would be better for that man if he had never been born."
C. **While they were eating,**
he took bread, said the blessing,
broke it, and gave it to them, and said,

✠ "Take it; this is my body."

C. Then he took a cup, gave thanks, and gave it to them,
and they all drank from it.
He said to them,

✠ "This is my blood of the covenant,
which will be shed for many.
Amen, I say to you,
I shall not drink again the fruit of the vine
until the day when I drink it new in the kingdom of God."

C. Then, after singing a hymn,
they went out to the Mount of Olives.

Then Jesus said to them,

✠ "All of you will have your faith shaken, for it is written:
I will strike the shepherd,
and the sheep will be dispersed.
But after I have been raised up,
I shall go before you to Galilee."

C. Peter said to him,

S. "Even though all should have their faith shaken,
mine will not be."

C. Then Jesus said to him,

✠ "Amen, I say to you,
this very night before the cock crows twice
you will deny me three times."

C. But he vehemently replied,

S. "Even though I should have to die with you,
I will not deny you."

C. And they all spoke similarly.

Then they came to a place named Gethsemane,
and he said to his disciples,

✠ "Sit here while I pray."

C. He took with him Peter, James, and John,
and began to be troubled and distressed.

Then he said to them,
✠ "My soul is sorrowful even to death.
Remain here and keep watch."
C. He advanced a little and fell to the ground and prayed
that if it were possible the hour might pass by him;
he said,
✠ "Abba, Father, all things are possible to you.
Take this cup away from me,
but not what I will but what you will."
C. When he returned he found them asleep.
He said to Peter,
✠ "Simon, are you asleep?
Could you not keep watch for one hour?
Watch and pray that you may not undergo the test.
The spirit is willing but the flesh is weak."
C. Withdrawing again, he prayed, saying the same thing.
Then he returned once more and found them asleep,
for they could not keep their eyes open
and did not know what to answer him.
He returned a third time and said to them,
✠ "Are you still sleeping and taking your rest?
It is enough. The hour has come.
Behold, the Son of Man is to be handed over to sinners.
Get up, let us go.
See, my betrayer is at hand."
C. Then, while he was still speaking,
Judas, one of the Twelve, arrived,
accompanied by a crowd with swords and clubs
who had come from the chief priests,
the scribes, and the elders.
His betrayer had arranged a signal with them, saying,
S. "The man I shall kiss is the one;
arrest him and lead him away securely."
C. He came and immediately went over to him and said,

S. **"Rabbi."**

C. **And he kissed him.**
At this they laid hands on him and arrested him.
One of the bystanders drew his sword,
struck the high priest's servant, and cut off his ear.
Jesus said to them in reply,

✠ **"Have you come out as against a robber,**
with swords and clubs, to seize me?
Day after day I was with you teaching in the temple area,
yet you did not arrest me;
but that the Scriptures may be fulfilled."

C. **And they all left him and fled.**
Now a young man followed him
wearing nothing but a linen cloth about his body.
They seized him,
but he left the cloth behind and ran off naked.

They led Jesus away to the high priest,
and all the chief priests and the elders and the scribes came together.
Peter followed him at a distance into the high priest's courtyard
and was seated with the guards, warming himself at the fire.
The chief priests and the entire Sanhedrin
kept trying to obtain testimony against Jesus
in order to put him to death, but they found none.
Many gave false witness against him,
but their testimony did not agree.
Some took the stand and testified falsely against him, alleging,

SS. **"We heard him say,**
'I will destroy this temple made with hands
and within three days I will build another
not made with hands.'"

C. **Even so their testimony did not agree.**
The high priest rose before the assembly and questioned Jesus, saying,
S. **"Have you no answer?**
What are these men testifying against you?"
C. **But he was silent and answered nothing.**
Again the high priest asked him and said to him,
S. **"Are you the Christ, the son of the Blessed One?"**
C. **Then Jesus answered,**
✠ **"I am;**
and 'you will see the Son of Man
seated at the right hand of the Power
and coming with the clouds of heaven.'"
C. **At that the high priest tore his garments and said,**
S. **"What further need have we of witnesses?**
You have heard the blasphemy.
What do you think?"
C. **They all condemned him as deserving to die.**
Some began to spit on him.
They blindfolded him and struck him and said to him,
SS. **"Prophesy!"**
C. **And the guards greeted him with blows.**

While Peter was below in the courtyard,
one of the high priest's maids came along.
Seeing Peter warming himself,
she looked intently at him and said,
S. **"You too were with the Nazarene, Jesus."**
C. **But he denied it saying,**
S. **"I neither know nor understand what you are talking about."**
C. **So he went out into the outer court.**
Then the cock crowed.
The maid saw him and began again to say to the bystanders,
S. **"This man is one of them."**

C. **Once again he denied it.**
A little later the bystanders said to Peter once more,
SS. **"Surely you are one of them; for you too are a Galilean."**
C. **He began to curse and to swear,**
S. **"I do not know this man about whom you are talking."**
C. **And immediately a cock crowed a second time.**
Then Peter remembered the word that Jesus had said to him,
✠ **"Before the cock crows twice you will deny me three times."**
C. **He broke down and wept.**

[**As soon as morning came,**
the chief priests with the elders and the scribes,
that is, the whole Sanhedrin, held a council.
They bound Jesus, led him away, and handed him over to Pilate.
Pilate questioned him,
S. **"Are you the king of the Jews?"**
C. **He said to him in reply,**
✠ **"You say so."**
C. **The chief priests accused him of many things.**
Again Pilate questioned him,
S. **"Have you no answer?**
See how many things they accuse you of."
C. **Jesus gave him no further answer, so that Pilate was amazed.**

Now on the occasion of the feast he used to release to them
one prisoner whom they requested.
A man called Barabbas was then in prison
along with the rebels who had committed murder in a rebellion.
The crowd came forward and began to ask him
to do for them as he was accustomed.

Pilate answered,

S. "Do you want me to release to you the king of the Jews?"

C. For he knew that it was out of envy
that the chief priests had handed him over.
But the chief priests stirred up the crowd
to have him release Barabbas for them instead.
Pilate again said to them in reply,

S. "Then what do you want me to do
with the man you call the king of the Jews?"

C. They shouted again,

SS. "Crucify him."

C. Pilate said to them,

S. "Why? What evil has he done?"

C. They only shouted the louder,

SS. "Crucify him."

C. So Pilate, wishing to satisfy the crowd,
released Barabbas to them and, after he had Jesus scourged,
handed him over to be crucified.
The soldiers led him away inside the palace,
that is, the praetorium, and assembled the whole cohort.
They clothed him in purple and,
weaving a crown of thorns, placed it on him.
They began to salute him with,

SS. "Hail, King of the Jews!"

C. and kept striking his head with a reed and spitting upon him.
They knelt before him in homage.
And when they had mocked him,
they stripped him of the purple cloak,
dressed him in his own clothes,
and led him out to crucify him.
They pressed into service a passer-by, Simon,
a Cyrenian, who was coming in from the country,

the father of Alexander and Rufus,
to carry his cross.

They brought him to the place of Golgotha
—which is translated Place of the Skull—.
They gave him wine drugged with myrrh,
but he did not take it.
Then they crucified him and divided his garments
by casting lots for them to see what each should take.
It was nine o'clock in the morning when they crucified him.
The inscription of the charge against him read,
"The King of the Jews."
With him they crucified two revolutionaries,
one on his right and one on his left.
Those passing by reviled him,
shaking their heads and saying,

SS. **"Aha! You who would destroy the temple**
and rebuild it in three days,
save yourself by coming down from the cross."

C. **Likewise the chief priests, with the scribes,**
mocked him among themselves and said,

SS. **"He saved others; he cannot save himself.**
Let the Christ, the King of Israel,
come down now from the cross
that we may see and believe."

C. **Those who were crucified with him also kept abusing him.**

At noon darkness came over the whole land
until three in the afternoon.
And at three o'clock Jesus cried out in a loud voice,

✠ ***"Eloi, Eloi, lema sabachthani?"***

C. **which is translated,**

✠ **"My God, my God, why have you forsaken me?"**

C. **Some of the bystanders who heard it said,**

SS. **"Look, he is calling Elijah."**

C. **One of them ran, soaked a sponge with wine, put it on a reed**
and gave it to him to drink saying,

S. **"Wait, let us see if Elijah comes to take him down."**

C. **Jesus gave a loud cry and breathed his last.**

Here all kneel and pause for a short time.

The veil of the sanctuary was torn in two from top to bottom.
When the centurion who stood facing him
saw how he breathed his last he said,

S. **"Truly this man was the Son of God!"]**

C. **There were also women looking on from a distance.**
Among them were Mary Magdalene,
Mary the mother of the younger James and of Joses, and Salome.
These women had followed him when he was in Galilee
and ministered to him.
There were also many other women
who had come up with him to Jerusalem.
When it was already evening,
since it was the day of preparation,
the day before the sabbath, Joseph of Arimathea,
a distinguished member of the council,
who was himself awaiting the kingdom of God,
came and courageously went to Pilate
and asked for the body of Jesus.
Pilate was amazed that he was already dead.
He summoned the centurion
and asked him if Jesus had already died.
And when he learned of it from the centurion,
he gave the body to Joseph.
Having bought a linen cloth, he took him down,
wrapped him in the linen cloth,

and laid him in a tomb that had been hewn out of the rock.
Then he rolled a stone against the entrance to the tomb.
Mary Magdalene and Mary the mother of Joses watched where he was laid.

The Gospel of the Lord. All: **Praise to you, Lord Jesus Christ.**

Prayer over the Offerings

Through the Passion of your Only Begotten Son, O Lord,
may our reconciliation with you be near at hand,
so that, though we do not merit it by our own deeds,
yet by this sacrifice made once for all,
we may feel already the effects of your mercy.
Through Christ our Lord. All: **Amen.**

Communion Antiphon (Matthew 26:42)

Father, if this chalice cannot pass without my drinking it,
your will be done.

Prayer after Communion

Nourished with these sacred gifts,
we humbly beseech you, O Lord,
that, just as through the death of your Son
you have brought us to hope for what we believe,
so by his Resurrection
you may lead us to where you call.
Through Christ our Lord. All: **Amen.**

The Sacred Paschal Triduum

The divine love we celebrate these days is so immeasurable that it reconciles all to itself in a supreme act of self-giving. It is so immense that the divine Son's arms open wide to embrace the world from the ignominy of a cross of human making. It is so impartial that sinners and outcasts, the poor and desperate, those alienated and forgotten all can receive without cost, without judgment, without losing dignity. Divine love is nothing less than the inner Life of the Trinity.

—Living Liturgy™, *Easter Triduum 2027*

Holy Thursday solemnly inaugurates "the triduum during which the Lord died, was buried and rose again" (St. Augustine). To these days Jesus referred when he prophesied: "Destroy this temple and in three days I will raise it up again" (John 2:14).

Thursday of the Lord's Supper (Holy Thursday)

AT THE EVENING MASS

March 25, 2027

Reflection on the Gospel

The liturgy itself links the eucharistic meal to that which those who partake in it must be and must do. The followers of Christ must be humble servants, giving of themselves as the least among their peers. This is what it means to be in Christian community: each member in Christ's body should be a humble, generous servant to one another. This is where unity is found—not in any uniformity of language or appearance, but in love, perfectly demonstrated by God's own Son.

—Living Liturgy™, *Holy Thursday 2027*

ENTRANCE ANTIPHON (Cf. Galatians 6:14)

We should glory in the Cross of our Lord Jesus Christ,
in whom is our salvation, life and resurrection,
through whom we are saved and delivered.

Collect

O God, who have called us to participate
in this most sacred Supper,
in which your Only Begotten Son,
when about to hand himself over to death,
entrusted to the Church a sacrifice new for all eternity,
the banquet of his love,
grant, we pray,
that we may draw from so great a mystery,
the fullness of charity and of life.
Through our Lord Jesus Christ, your Son,
who lives and reigns with you in the unity of the Holy Spirit,
God, for ever and ever. All: **Amen.**

Reading I (L 39-ABC) (Exodus 12:1-8, 11-14)

A reading from the Book of Exodus

The law regarding the Passover meal.

The Lord said to Moses and Aaron in the land of Egypt,
"This month shall stand at the head of your calendar;
you shall reckon it the first month of the year.
Tell the whole community of Israel:
On the tenth of this month every one of your families
must procure for itself a lamb, one apiece for each household.
If a family is too small for a whole lamb,
it shall join the nearest household in procuring one
and shall share in the lamb
in proportion to the number of persons who partake of it.
The lamb must be a year-old male and without blemish.
You may take it from either the sheep or the goats.
You shall keep it until the fourteenth day of this month,
and then, with the whole assembly of Israel present,
it shall be slaughtered during the evening twilight.
They shall take some of its blood
and apply it to the two doorposts and the lintel
of every house in which they partake of the lamb.
That same night they shall eat its roasted flesh
with unleavened bread and bitter herbs.

“This is how you are to eat it:
with your loins girt, sandals on your feet and your staff in hand,
you shall eat like those who are in flight.
It is the Passover of the Lord.
For on this same night I will go through Egypt,
striking down every firstborn of the land, both man and beast,
and executing judgment on all the gods of Egypt—
I, the Lord!
But the blood will mark the houses where you are.
Seeing the blood, I will pass over you;
thus, when I strike the land of Egypt,
no destructive blow will come upon you.

“This day shall be a memorial feast for you,
which all your generations shall celebrate
with pilgrimage to the Lord, as a perpetual institution.”

The word of the Lord. All: **Thanks be to God.**

Responsorial Psalm 116

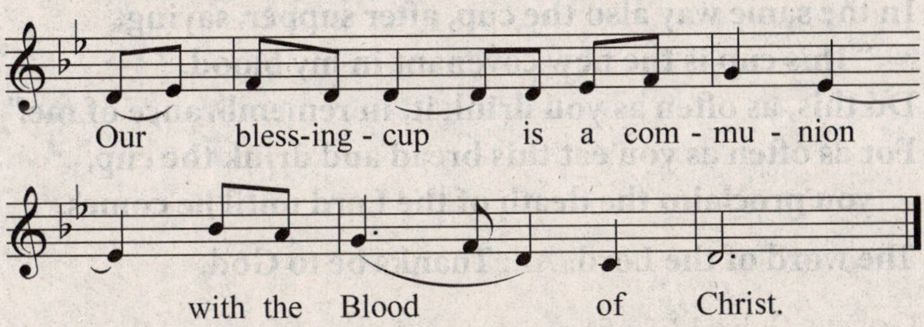

Psalm 116:12-13, 15-16bc, 17-18

℟. (*See* 1 Corinthians 10:16) **Our blessing-cup is a communion with the Blood of Christ.**

How shall I make a return to the Lord
for all the good he has done for me?
The cup of salvation I will take up,
and I will call upon the name of the Lord. ℟.

Precious in the eyes of the LORD
is the death of his faithful ones.
I am your servant, the son of your handmaid;
you have loosed my bonds. ℟.

To you will I offer sacrifice of thanksgiving,
and I will call upon the name of the LORD.
My vows to the LORD I will pay
in the presence of all his people. ℟.

READING II (1 Corinthians 11:23-26)

A reading from the first Letter of Saint Paul to the Corinthians

For as often as you eat this bread and drink the cup, you proclaim the death of the Lord.

Brothers and sisters:
I received from the Lord what I also handed on to you,
that the Lord Jesus, on the night he was handed over,
took bread, and, after he had given thanks,
broke it and said, "This is my body that is for you.
Do this in remembrance of me."
In the same way also the cup, after supper, saying,
"This cup is the new covenant in my blood.
Do this, as often as you drink it, in remembrance of me."
For as often as you eat this bread and drink the cup,
you proclaim the death of the Lord until he comes.

The word of the Lord. All: **Thanks be to God.**

GOSPEL (John 13:1-15)

VERSE BEFORE THE GOSPEL (John 13:34)

℣. Praise to you, Lord Jesus Christ, King of endless glory!
℟. **Praise to you, Lord Jesus Christ, King of endless glory!**
℣. I give you a new commandment, says the Lord:
love one another as I have loved you. ℟.

✠ **A reading from the holy Gospel according to John**

All: **Glory to you, O Lord.**

Jesus loved them to the end.

Before the feast of Passover, Jesus knew that his hour had come
to pass from this world to the Father.
He loved his own in the world and he loved them to the end.
The devil had already induced Judas, son of Simon the Iscariot, to hand him over.
So, during supper,
fully aware that the Father had put everything into his power
and that he had come from God and was returning to God,
he rose from supper and took off his outer garments.
He took a towel and tied it around his waist.
Then he poured water into a basin
and began to wash the disciples' feet
and dry them with the towel around his waist.
He came to Simon Peter, who said to him,
"Master, are you going to wash my feet?"
Jesus answered and said to him,
"What I am doing, you do not understand now,
but you will understand later."
Peter said to him, "You will never wash my feet."
Jesus answered him,
"Unless I wash you, you will have no inheritance with me."
Simon Peter said to him,
"Master, then not only my feet, but my hands and head as well."
Jesus said to him,
"Whoever has bathed has no need except to have his feet washed, for he is clean all over;
so you are clean, but not all."
For he knew who would betray him;
for this reason, he said, "Not all of you are clean."

So when he had washed their feet
and put his garments back on and reclined at table again,
he said to them, "Do you realize what I have done for you?
You call me 'teacher' and 'master,' and rightly so,
for indeed I am.
If I, therefore, the master and teacher, have washed your feet,
you ought to wash one another's feet.
I have given you a model to follow,
so that as I have done for you, you should also do."

The Gospel of the Lord. All: **Praise to you, Lord Jesus Christ.**

THE WASHING OF FEET

Antiphons or other appropriate songs are sung.

PRAYER OVER THE OFFERINGS

Grant us, O Lord, we pray,
that we may participate worthily in these mysteries,
for whenever the memorial of this sacrifice is celebrated
the work of our redemption is accomplished.
Through Christ our Lord. All: **Amen.**

COMMUNION ANTIPHON (1 Corinthians 11:24-25)

This is the Body that will be given up for you;
this is the Chalice of the new covenant in my Blood,
says the Lord;
do this, whenever you receive it, in memory of me.

PRAYER AFTER COMMUNION

Grant, almighty God,
that, just as we are renewed
by the Supper of your Son in this present age,
so we may enjoy his banquet for all eternity.
Who lives and reigns for ever and ever. All: **Amen.**

THE TRANSFER OF THE MOST BLESSED SACRAMENT

Friday of the Passion of the Lord (Good Friday)

March 26, 2027

Reflection on the Gospel

The passion narratives say very little about the cross itself. The authors apparently presume that their readers know what it is without any elaboration. In today's gospel, John does take time to observe that Jesus carried the cross himself and makes no reference to Simon of Cyrene as the three Synoptics do. Perhaps it alludes to Isaac (Gen 22:6-8), who carried the wood for the holocaust on his own shoulders. The difference may also be to emphasize Jesus's conscious, willing, and intentional fulfillment of prophecy and his divine mission.

—Living Liturgy™, *Good Friday 2027*

The Celebration of the Passion of the Lord

Prayer (Let us pray is not said)

Remember your mercies, O Lord,
and with your eternal protection sanctify your servants,
for whom Christ your Son,
by the shedding of his Blood,
established the Paschal Mystery.
Who lives and reigns for ever and ever. All: **Amen.**

Or:

O God, who by the Passion of Christ your Son, our Lord,
abolished the death inherited from ancient sin
by every succeeding generation,
grant that just as, being conformed to him,
we have borne by the law of nature
the image of the man of earth,
so by the sanctification of grace
we may bear the image of the Man of heaven.
Through Christ our Lord. All: **Amen.**

FIRST PART: LITURGY OF THE WORD

READING I (L 40-ABC) (Isaiah 52:13—53:12)

A reading from the Book of the Prophet Isaiah

He himself was wounded for our sins.
(Fourth oracle of the Servant of the Lord.)

See, my servant shall prosper,
he shall be raised high and greatly exalted.
Even as many were amazed at him—
so marred was his look beyond human semblance
and his appearance beyond that of the sons of man—
so shall he startle many nations,
because of him kings shall stand speechless;
for those who have not been told shall see,
those who have not heard shall ponder it.

Who would believe what we have heard?
To whom has the arm of the LORD been revealed?
He grew up like a sapling before him,
like a shoot from the parched earth;
there was in him no stately bearing to make us look at him,
nor appearance that would attract us to him.
He was spurned and avoided by people,
a man of suffering, accustomed to infirmity,
one of those from whom people hide their faces,
spurned, and we held him in no esteem.

Yet it was our infirmities that he bore,
our sufferings that he endured,
while we thought of him as stricken,
as one smitten by God and afflicted.
But he was pierced for our offenses,
crushed for our sins;
upon him was the chastisement that makes us whole,
by his stripes we were healed.
We had all gone astray like sheep,
each following his own way;

but the LORD laid upon him
the guilt of us all.

Though he was harshly treated, he submitted
and opened not his mouth;
like a lamb led to the slaughter
or a sheep before the shearers,
he was silent and opened not his mouth.
Oppressed and condemned, he was taken away,
and who would have thought any more of his destiny?
When he was cut off from the land of the living,
and smitten for the sin of his people,
a grave was assigned him among the wicked
and a burial place with evildoers,
though he had done no wrong
nor spoken any falsehood.
But the LORD was pleased
to crush him in infirmity.

If he gives his life as an offering for sin,
he shall see his descendants in a long life,
and the will of the LORD shall be accomplished through him.

Because of his affliction
he shall see the light in fullness of days;
through his suffering, my servant shall justify many,
and their guilt he shall bear.
Therefore I will give him his portion among the great,
and he shall divide the spoils with the mighty,
because he surrendered himself to death
and was counted among the wicked;
and he shall take away the sins of many,
and win pardon for their offenses.

The word of the Lord. All: Thanks be to God.

Responsorial Psalm 31

Psalm 31:2, 6, 12-13, 15-16, 17, 25

℟. (Luke 23:46) **Father, into your hands I commend my spirit.**

In you, O Lord, I take refuge;
let me never be put to shame.
In your justice rescue me.
Into your hands I commend my spirit;
you will redeem me, O Lord, O faithful God. ℟.

For all my foes I am an object of reproach,
a laughingstock to my neighbors, and a dread to my friends;
they who see me abroad flee from me.
I am forgotten like the unremembered dead;
I am like a dish that is broken. ℟.

But my trust is in you, O Lord;
I say, "You are my God.
In your hands is my destiny; rescue me
from the clutches of my enemies and my persecutors." ℟.

Let your face shine upon your servant;
save me in your kindness.
Take courage and be stouthearted,
all you who hope in the Lord. ℟.

Reading II (Hebrews 4:14-16; 5:7-9)

A reading from the Letter to the Hebrews

Jesus learned obedience and became the source of salvation for all who obey him.

Brothers and sisters:
Since we have a great high priest who has passed through the heavens,
Jesus, the Son of God,
let us hold fast to our confession.
For we do not have a high priest
who is unable to sympathize with our weaknesses,
but one who has similarly been tested in every way,
yet without sin.
So let us confidently approach the throne of grace
to receive mercy and to find grace for timely help.

In the days when Christ was in the flesh,
he offered prayers and supplications with loud cries and tears
to the one who was able to save him from death,
and he was heard because of his reverence.
Son though he was, he learned obedience from what he suffered;
and when he was made perfect,
he became the source of eternal salvation for all who obey him.

The word of the Lord. All: **Thanks be to God.**

* The passion narratives are proclaimed in full so that all see vividly the love of Christ for each person. In light of this, the crimes during the Passion of Christ cannot be attributed, in either preaching or catechesis, indiscriminately to all Jews of that time, nor to Jews today. The Jewish people should not be referred to as though rejected or cursed, as if this view followed from Scripture. The Church ever keeps in mind that Jesus, his mother Mary, and the apostles all were Jewish. As the Church has always held, Christ freely suffered his passion and death because of the sins of all, that all might be saved.

Gospel (John 18:1—19:42)

Verse before the Gospel (Philippians 2:8-9)

℣. Praise to you, Lord Jesus Christ, King of endless glory!
℟. Praise to you, Lord Jesus Christ, King of endless glory!
℣. Christ became obedient to the point of death,
even death on a cross.
Because of this, God greatly exalted him
and bestowed on him the name which is above every other name. ℟.

The symbols in the following passion narrative represent:

C. Narrator;
✠ Christ;
S. speakers other than Christ;
SS. groups of speakers.

The Passion of our Lord Jesus Christ according to John

The Passion of our Lord Jesus Christ.

C. **Jesus went out with his disciples across the Kidron valley**
to where there was a garden,
into which he and his disciples entered.
Judas his betrayer also knew the place,
because Jesus had often met there with his disciples.
So Judas got a band of soldiers and guards
from the chief priests and the Pharisees
and went there with lanterns, torches, and weapons.
Jesus, knowing everything that was going to happen to him,
went out and said to them,
✠ **"Whom are you looking for?"**
C. **They answered him,**
SS. **"Jesus the Nazorean."**
C. **He said to them,**
✠ **"I AM."**
C. **Judas his betrayer was also with them.**
When he said to them, "I AM,"
they turned away and fell to the ground.
So he again asked them,

✠ “Whom are you looking for?”
C. They said,
SS. “Jesus the Nazorean.”
C. Jesus answered,
✠ “I told you that I AM.
So if you are looking for me, let these men go.”
C. This was to fulfill what he had said,
“I have not lost any of those you gave me.”
Then Simon Peter, who had a sword, drew it,
struck the high priest’s slave, and cut off his right ear.
The slave’s name was Malchus.
Jesus said to Peter,
✠ “Put your sword into its scabbard.
Shall I not drink the cup that the Father gave me?”

C. So the band of soldiers, the tribune, and the Jewish guards seized Jesus,
bound him, and brought him to Annas first.
He was the father-in-law of Caiaphas,
who was high priest that year.
It was Caiaphas who had counseled the Jews
that it was better that one man should die rather than the people.

Simon Peter and another disciple followed Jesus.
Now the other disciple was known to the high priest,
and he entered the courtyard of the high priest with Jesus.
But Peter stood at the gate outside.
So the other disciple, the acquaintance of the high priest,
went out and spoke to the gatekeeper and brought Peter in.
Then the maid who was the gatekeeper said to Peter,
S. “You are not one of this man’s disciples, are you?”
C. He said,

S. "I am not."

C. Now the slaves and the guards were standing around a charcoal fire
that they had made, because it was cold,
and were warming themselves.
Peter was also standing there keeping warm.

The high priest questioned Jesus
about his disciples and about his doctrine.
Jesus answered him,

✠ "I have spoken publicly to the world.
I have always taught in a synagogue
or in the temple area where all the Jews gather,
and in secret I have said nothing. Why ask me?
Ask those who heard me what I said to them.
They know what I said."

C. When he had said this,
one of the temple guards standing there struck Jesus and said,

S. "Is this the way you answer the high priest?"

C. Jesus answered him,

✠ "If I have spoken wrongly, testify to the wrong;
but if I have spoken rightly, why do you strike me?"

C. Then Annas sent him bound to Caiaphas the high priest.

Now Simon Peter was standing there keeping warm.
And they said to him,

SS. "You are not one of his disciples, are you?"

C. He denied it and said,

S. "I am not."

C. One of the slaves of the high priest,
a relative of the one whose ear Peter had cut off, said,

S. "Didn't I see you in the garden with him?"

C. Again Peter denied it.
And immediately the cock crowed.

Then they brought Jesus from Caiaphas to the
praetorium.
It was morning.
And they themselves did not enter the praetorium,
in order not to be defiled so that they could eat
the Passover.
So Pilate came out to them and said,
S. "What charge do you bring against this man?"
C. They answered and said to him,
SS. "If he were not a criminal,
we would not have handed him over to you."
C. At this, Pilate said to them,
S. "Take him yourselves, and judge him according
to your law."
C. The Jews answered him,
SS. "We do not have the right to execute anyone,"
C. in order that the word of Jesus might be fulfilled
that he said indicating the kind of death he would
die.
So Pilate went back into the praetorium
and summoned Jesus and said to him,
S. "Are you the King of the Jews?"
C. Jesus answered,
✠ "Do you say this on your own
or have others told you about me?"
C. Pilate answered,
S. "I am not a Jew, am I?
Your own nation and the chief priests handed you
over to me.
What have you done?"
C. Jesus answered,
✠ "My kingdom does not belong to this world.
If my kingdom did belong to this world,
my attendants would be fighting
to keep me from being handed over to the Jews.
But as it is, my kingdom is not here."

C. **So Pilate said to him,**
S. **"Then you are a king?"**
C. **Jesus answered,**
✠ **"You say I am a king.**
For this I was born and for this I came into the world,
to testify to the truth.
Everyone who belongs to the truth listens to my voice."
C. **Pilate said to him,**
S. **"What is truth?"**

C. **When he had said this,**
he again went out to the Jews and said to them,
S. **"I find no guilt in him.**
But you have a custom that I release one prisoner to you at Passover.
Do you want me to release to you the King of the Jews?"
C. **They cried out again,**
SS. **"Not this one but Barabbas!"**
C. **Now Barabbas was a revolutionary.**

Then Pilate took Jesus and had him scourged.
And the soldiers wove a crown out of thorns and placed it on his head,
and clothed him in a purple cloak,
and they came to him and said,
SS. **"Hail, King of the Jews!"**
C. **And they struck him repeatedly.**
Once more Pilate went out and said to them,
S. **"Look, I am bringing him out to you,**
so that you may know that I find no guilt in him."
C. **So Jesus came out,**
wearing the crown of thorns and the purple cloak.
And he said to them,
S. **"Behold, the man!"**

C. **When the chief priests and the guards saw him they cried out,**

SS. **"Crucify him, crucify him!"**

C. **Pilate said to them,**

S. **"Take him yourselves and crucify him.**
I find no guilt in him."

C. **The Jews answered,**

SS. **"We have a law, and according to that law he ought to die,**
because he made himself the Son of God."

C. **Now when Pilate heard this statement,**
he became even more afraid,
and went back into the praetorium and said to Jesus,

S. **"Where are you from?"**

C. **Jesus did not answer him.**
So Pilate said to him,

S. **"Do you not speak to me?**
Do you not know that I have power to release you and I have power to crucify you?"

C. **Jesus answered him,**

✠ **"You would have no power over me**
if it had not been given to you from above.
For this reason the one who handed me over to you has the greater sin."

C. **Consequently, Pilate tried to release him; but the Jews cried out,**

SS. **"If you release him, you are not a Friend of Caesar.**
Everyone who makes himself a king opposes Caesar."

C. **When Pilate heard these words he brought Jesus out**
and seated him on the judge's bench
in the place called Stone Pavement, in Hebrew, Gabbatha.
It was preparation day for Passover, and it was about noon.
And he said to the Jews,

S. **"Behold, your king!"**
C. **They cried out,**
SS. **"Take him away, take him away! Crucify him!"**
C. **Pilate said to them,**
S. **"Shall I crucify your king?"**
C. **The chief priests answered,**
SS. **"We have no king but Caesar."**
C. **Then he handed him over to them to be crucified.**

So they took Jesus, and, carrying the cross himself,
he went out to what is called the Place of the Skull,
in Hebrew, Golgotha.
There they crucified him, and with him two others,
one on either side, with Jesus in the middle.
Pilate also had an inscription written and put on the cross.
It read,
"Jesus the Nazorean, the King of the Jews."
Now many of the Jews read this inscription,
because the place where Jesus was crucified was near the city;
and it was written in Hebrew, Latin, and Greek.
So the chief priests of the Jews said to Pilate,
SS. **"Do not write 'The King of the Jews,'**
but that he said, 'I am the King of the Jews.'"
C. **Pilate answered,**
S. **"What I have written, I have written."**

C. **When the soldiers had crucified Jesus,**
they took his clothes and divided them into four shares,
a share for each soldier.
They also took his tunic, but the tunic was seamless,
woven in one piece from the top down.
So they said to one another,
SS. **"Let's not tear it, but cast lots for it to see whose it will be,"**

C. **in order that the passage of Scripture might be**
fulfilled that says:
They divided my garments among them,
and for my vesture they cast lots.
This is what the soldiers did.
Standing by the cross of Jesus were his mother
and his mother's sister, Mary the wife of Clopas,
and Mary of Magdala.
When Jesus saw his mother and the disciple there
whom he loved
he said to his mother,
✠ **"Woman, behold, your son."**
C. **Then he said to the disciple,**
✠ **"Behold, your mother."**
C. **And from that hour the disciple took her into his**
home.

After this, aware that everything was now finished,
in order that the Scripture might be fulfilled,
Jesus said,
✠ **"I thirst."**
C. **There was a vessel filled with common wine.**
So they put a sponge soaked in wine on a sprig of
hyssop
and put it up to his mouth.
When Jesus had taken the wine, he said,
✠ **"It is finished."**
C. **And bowing his head, he handed over the spirit.**

Here all kneel and pause for a short time.

Now since it was preparation day,
in order that the bodies might not remain
on the cross on the sabbath,
for the sabbath day of that week was a solemn one,
the Jews asked Pilate that their legs be broken
and that they be taken down.

So the soldiers came and broke the legs of the first
and then of the other one who was crucified with
Jesus.
But when they came to Jesus and saw that he was
already dead,
they did not break his legs,
but one soldier thrust his lance into his side,
and immediately blood and water flowed out.
An eyewitness has testified, and his testimony is true;
he knows that he is speaking the truth,
so that you also may come to believe.
For this happened so that the Scripture passage
might be fulfilled:
Not a bone of it will be broken.
And again another passage says:
They will look upon him whom they have pierced.

After this, Joseph of Arimathea,
secretly a disciple of Jesus for fear of the Jews,
asked Pilate if he could remove the body of Jesus.
And Pilate permitted it.
So he came and took his body.
Nicodemus, the one who had first come to him at
night,
also came bringing a mixture of myrrh and aloes
weighing about one hundred pounds.
They took the body of Jesus
and bound it with burial cloths along with the
spices,
according to the Jewish burial custom.
Now in the place where he had been crucified there
was a garden,
and in the garden a new tomb, in which no one
had yet been buried.

So they laid Jesus there because of the Jewish preparation day;
for the tomb was close by.

The Gospel of the Lord. All: **Praise to you, Lord Jesus Christ.**

The Solemn Intercessions

I. For Holy Church

Let us pray, dearly beloved, for the holy Church of God,
that our God and Lord be pleased to give her peace,
to guard her and to unite her throughout the whole world
and grant that, leading our life in tranquility and quiet,
we may glorify God the Father almighty.

Prayer in silence. Then the Priest sings or says:

Almighty ever-living God,
who in Christ revealed your glory to all the nations,
watch over the works of your mercy,
that your Church, spread throughout all the world,
may persevere with steadfast faith in confessing your name.
Through Christ our Lord. All: **Amen.**

II. For the Pope

Let us pray also for our most Holy Father Pope N.,
that our God and Lord,
who chose him for the Order of Bishops,
may keep him safe and unharmed for the Lord's holy Church,
to govern the holy People of God.

Prayer in silence. Then the Priest sings or says:

Almighty ever-living God,
by whose decree all things are founded,
look with favor on our prayers
and in your kindness protect the Pope chosen for us,
that, under him, the Christian people,
governed by you their maker,
may grow in merit by reason of their faith.
Through Christ our Lord. All: **Amen.**

III. For All Orders and Degrees of the Faithful

Let us pray also for our Bishop N.,*
for all Bishops, Priests, and Deacons of the Church
and for the whole of the faithful people.

* Mention may be made here of the Coadjutor Bishop, or Auxiliary Bishops, as noted in the *General Instruction of the Roman Missal*, no. 149.

Prayer in silence. Then the Priest sings or says:

Almighty ever-living God,
by whose Spirit the whole body of the Church
is sanctified and governed,
hear our humble prayer for your ministers,
that, by the gift of your grace,
all may serve you faithfully.
Through Christ our Lord. All: **Amen.**

IV. For Catechumens

Let us pray also for (our) catechumens,
that our God and Lord
may open wide the ears of their inmost hearts
and unlock the gates of his mercy,
that, having received forgiveness of all their sins
through the waters of rebirth,
they, too, may be one with Christ Jesus our Lord.

Prayer in silence. Then the Priest sings or says:

Almighty ever-living God,
who make your Church ever fruitful with new offspring,
increase the faith and understanding of (our) catechumens,
that, reborn in the font of Baptism,
they may be added to the number of your adopted children.
Through Christ our Lord. All: **Amen.**

V. For the Unity of Christians

Let us pray also for all our brothers and sisters who believe in Christ,
that our God and Lord may be pleased,
as they live the truth,
to gather them together and keep them in his one Church.

Prayer in silence. Then the Priest sings or says:

Almighty ever-living God,
who gather what is scattered
and keep together what you have gathered,
look kindly on the flock of your Son,
that those whom one Baptism has consecrated
may be joined together by integrity of faith
and united in the bond of charity.
Through Christ our Lord. All: **Amen.**

VI. For the Jewish People

Let us pray also for the Jewish people,
to whom the Lord our God spoke first,
that he may grant them to advance in love of his name
and in faithfulness to his covenant.

Prayer in silence. Then the Priest sings or says:

Almighty ever-living God,
who bestowed your promises on Abraham and his descendants,
graciously hear the prayers of your Church,
that the people you first made your own
may attain the fullness of redemption.
Through Christ our Lord. All: **Amen.**

VII. For Those Who Do Not Believe in Christ

Let us pray also for those who do not believe in Christ,
that, enlightened by the Holy Spirit,
they, too, may enter on the way of salvation.

Prayer in silence. Then the Priest sings or says:

Almighty ever-living God,
grant to those who do not confess Christ
that, by walking before you with a sincere heart,
they may find the truth
and that we ourselves, being constant in mutual love
and striving to understand more fully the mystery of your life,
may be made more perfect witnesses to your love in the world.
Through Christ our Lord. All: **Amen.**

VIII. For Those Who Do Not Believe in God

Let us pray also for those who do not acknowledge God,
that, following what is right in sincerity of heart,
they may find the way to God himself.

Prayer in silence. Then the Priest sings or says:

Almighty ever-living God,
who created all people
to seek you always by desiring you
and, by finding you, come to rest,
grant, we pray,
that, despite every harmful obstacle,
all may recognize the signs of your fatherly love
and the witness of the good works
done by those who believe in you,
and so in gladness confess you,
the one true God and Father of our human race.
Through Christ our Lord. All: **Amen.**

IX. For Those in Public Office

Let us pray also for those in public office,
that our God and Lord
may direct their minds and hearts according to his will
for the true peace and freedom of all.

Prayer in silence. Then the Priest sings or says:

Almighty ever-living God,
in whose hand lies every human heart
and the rights of peoples,
look with favor, we pray,
on those who govern with authority over us,
that throughout the whole world,
the prosperity of peoples,
the assurance of peace,
and freedom of religion
may through your gift be made secure.
Through Christ our Lord. All: **Amen.**

X. For Those in Tribulation

Let us pray, dearly beloved,
to God the Father almighty,
that he may cleanse the world of all errors,
banish disease, drive out hunger,
unlock prisons, loosen fetters,
granting to travelers safety, to pilgrims return,
health to the sick, and salvation to the dying.

Prayer in silence. Then the Priest sings or says:

Almighty ever-living God,
comfort of mourners, strength of all who toil,
may the prayers of those who cry out in any tribulation
come before you,
that all may rejoice,
because in their hour of need
your mercy was at hand.
Through Christ our Lord. All: **Amen.**

SECOND PART: THE ADORATION OF THE HOLY CROSS

The Showing of the Holy Cross

The Cross is shown to the congregation in one of two ways:

First Form: through the gradual uncovering with a veil in the sanctuary
Second Form: by means of a procession through the church

In either form, either of the following is chanted three times:

A ℣. Ecce lignum Crucis,
in quo salus mundi pependit.
All respond: **Venite adoremus.**

B ℣. Behold the wood of the Cross,
on which hung the salvation of the world.
All respond: **Come, let us adore.**

The Adoration of the Holy Cross

The Priest, clergy, and faithful approach to venerate the cross in a kind of procession.

THIRD PART: HOLY COMMUNION

At the Savior's command
and formed by divine teaching,
we dare to say:

The Priest, with hands extended says, and all present continue:

**Our Father, who art in heaven,
hallowed be thy name;
thy kingdom come,
thy will be done
on earth as it is in heaven.
Give us this day our daily bread,
and forgive us our trespasses,
as we forgive those who trespass against us;
and lead us not into temptation,
but deliver us from evil.**

With hands extended, the Priest continues alone:

Deliver us, Lord, we pray, from every evil,
graciously grant peace in our days,
that, by the help of your mercy,
we may be always free from sin
and safe from all distress,
as we await the blessed hope
and the coming of our Savior, Jesus Christ.

He joins his hands. The people conclude the prayer, acclaiming:

For the kingdom, the power and the glory are yours
now and for ever.

Then the Priest, with hands joined, says quietly:

May the receiving of your Body and Blood,
Lord Jesus Christ,
not bring me to judgment and condemnation,
but through your loving mercy
be for me protection in mind and body
and a healing remedy.

The Priest then genuflects, takes a particle, and, holding it slightly raised over the ciborium, while facing the people, says aloud:

Behold the Lamb of God,
behold him who takes away the sins of the world.
Blessed are those called to the supper of the Lamb.

And together with the people he adds once:

Lord, I am not worthy
that you should enter under my roof,
but only say the word
and my soul shall be healed.

Prayer after Communion

Almighty ever-living God,
who have restored us to life
by the blessed Death and Resurrection of your Christ,
preserve in us the work of your mercy,
that, by partaking of this mystery,
we may have a life unceasingly devoted to you.
Through Christ our Lord. All: **Amen.**

Prayer over the People

May abundant blessing, O Lord, we pray,
descend upon your people,
who have honored the Death of your Son
in the hope of their resurrection:
may pardon come,
comfort be given,
holy faith increase,
and everlasting redemption be made secure.
Through Christ our Lord. All: **Amen.**

After genuflecting to the Cross, all depart in silence. The altar is stripped; the Cross remains, however, with two or four candles.

Holy Saturday

The Easter Vigil in the Holy Night

March 27, 2027

Reflection on the Gospel
There is something quite magical about witnessing a sunrise. Being outside before dawn and then experiencing the gradual transition from darkness to light, looking for the first sign of the rising sun appearing on the horizon, seeing how the growing rays paint the sky and clouds hues of oranges and reds—these are moments like no other. A sunrise takes its own time to achieve its purpose of bringing light and warmth to a waiting world. How appropriate, then, that the discovery of Jesus's resurrection should occur at sunrise.

—Living Liturgy™, *At the Easter Vigil in the Holy Night of Easter 2027*

FIRST PART: THE SOLEMN BEGINNING OF THE VIGIL OR LUCERNARIUM

The Blessing of the Fire

Priest: In the name of the Father, and of the Son, and of the Holy Spirit.
All: **Amen.**

Then he greets the assembled people in the usual way and briefly instructs them about the night vigil in these or similar words:

Dear brethren (brothers and sisters),
on this most sacred night,
in which our Lord Jesus Christ
passed over from death to life,
the Church calls upon her sons and daughters,
scattered throughout the world,
to come together to watch and pray.
If we keep the memorial
of the Lord's paschal solemnity in this way,
listening to his word and celebrating his mysteries,
then we shall have the sure hope
of sharing his triumph over death
and living with him in God.

Let us pray.
O God, who through your Son
bestowed upon the faithful the fire of your glory,
sanctify ✠ this new fire, we pray,
and grant that,
by these paschal celebrations,
we may be so inflamed with heavenly desires,
that with minds made pure
we may attain festivities of unending splendor.
Through Christ our Lord. All: **Amen.**

THE PREPARATION OF THE CANDLE

(1) CHRIST YESTERDAY AND TODAY (he cuts a vertical line);
(2) THE BEGINNING AND THE END (he cuts a horizontal line);
(3) THE ALPHA (he cuts the letter Alpha above the vertical line);
(4) AND THE OMEGA (he cuts the letter Omega below the vertical line).
(5) ALL TIME BELONGS TO HIM (he cuts the first numeral of the current year in the upper left corner of the cross);
(6) AND ALL THE AGES (he cuts the second numeral of the current year in the upper right corner of the cross).
(7) TO HIM BE GLORY AND POWER (he cuts the third numeral of the current year in the lower left corner of the cross);
(8) THROUGH EVERY AGE AND FOR EVER. AMEN. (he cuts the fourth numeral of the current year in the lower right corner of the cross).

A
2 | 0
2 | 7
Ω

(1) BY HIS HOLY — 1
(2) AND GLORIOUS WOUNDS,
(3) MAY CHRIST THE LORD — 4 2 5
(4) GUARD US
(5) AND PROTECT US. AMEN. — 3

May the light of Christ rising in glory
dispel the darkness of our hearts and minds.

PROCESSION

℣. The Light of Christ. *or* ℣. Lumen Christi.
℟. **Thanks be to God.** ℟. **Deo Gratias.**

℣. The Light of Christ. *or* ℣. Lumen Christi.
℟. **Thanks be to God.** ℟. **Deo Gratias.**

℣. The Light of Christ. *or* ℣. Lumen Christi.
℟. **Thanks be to God.** ℟. **Deo Gratias.**

or

or

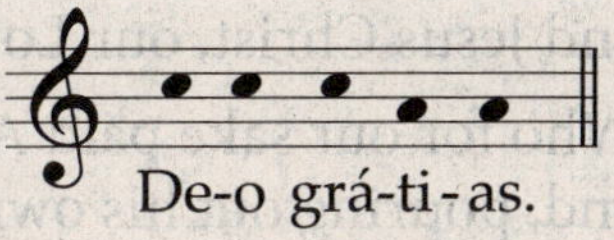

THE EASTER PROCLAMATION (EXSULTET)
Longer Form
(*Sung only by an ordained minister)

Exult, let them exult, the hosts of heaven,
exult, let Angel ministers of God exult,
let the trumpet of salvation
sound aloud our mighty King's triumph!
Be glad, let earth be glad, as glory floods her,
ablaze with light from her eternal King,
let all corners of the earth be glad,
knowing an end to gloom and darkness.
Rejoice, let Mother Church also rejoice,
arrayed with the lightning of his glory,
let this holy building shake with joy,
filled with the mighty voices of the peoples.

(*Therefore, dearest friends,
standing in the awesome glory of this holy light,
invoke with me, I ask you,
the mercy of God almighty,
that he, who has been pleased to number me,
though unworthy, among the Levites,
may pour into me his light unshadowed,
that I may sing this candle's perfect praises.)

(*℣. The Lord be with you.
℟. **And with your spirit.**)

℣. Lift up your hearts.
℟. **We lift them up to the Lord.**

℣. Let us give thanks to the Lord our God.
℟. **It is right and just.**

It is truly right and just,
with ardent love of mind and heart
and with devoted service of our voice,
to acclaim our God invisible, the almighty Father,
and Jesus Christ, our Lord, his Son, his Only Begotten.

Who for our sake paid Adam's debt to the eternal Father,
and, pouring out his own dear Blood,
wiped clean the record of our ancient sinfulness.

These, then, are the feasts of Passover,
in which is slain the Lamb, the one true Lamb,
whose Blood anoints the doorposts of believers.

This is the night,
when once you led our forebears, Israel's children,
from slavery in Egypt
and made them pass dry-shod through the Red Sea.

This is the night
that with a pillar of fire
banished the darkness of sin.

This is the night
that even now, throughout the world,
sets Christian believers apart from worldly vices
and from the gloom of sin,
leading them to grace
and joining them to his holy ones.

This is the night,
when Christ broke the prison-bars of death
and rose victorious from the underworld.

Our birth would have been no gain,
had we not been redeemed.
O wonder of your humble care for us!
O love, O charity beyond all telling,
to ransom a slave you gave away your Son!

O truly necessary sin of Adam,
destroyed completely by the Death of Christ!

O happy fault
that earned so great, so glorious a Redeemer!

O truly blessed night,
worthy alone to know the time and hour
when Christ rose from the underworld!

This is the night
of which it is written:
The night shall be as bright as day,
dazzling is the night for me,
and full of gladness.

The sanctifying power of this night
dispels wickedness, washes faults away,
restores innocence to the fallen, and joy to mourners,
drives out hatred, fosters concord, and brings down the
mighty.

On this, your night of grace, O holy Father,
accept this candle, a solemn offering,
the work of bees and of your servants' hands,
an evening sacrifice of praise,
this gift from your most holy Church.

But now we know the praises of this pillar,
which glowing fire ignites for God's honor,
a fire into many flames divided,
yet never dimmed by sharing of its light,
for it is fed by melting wax,
drawn out by mother bees
to build a torch so precious.

O truly blessed night,
when things of heaven are wed to those of earth,
and divine to the human.

Therefore, O Lord,
we pray you that this candle,
hallowed to the honor of your name,
may persevere undimmed,
to overcome the darkness of this night.
Receive it as a pleasing fragrance,
and let it mingle with the lights of heaven.
May this flame be found still burning

by the Morning Star:
the one Morning Star who never sets,
Christ your Son,
who, coming back from death's domain,
has shed his peaceful light on humanity,
and lives and reigns for ever and ever. All: **Amen.**

THE EASTER PROCLAMATION (EXSULTET)
Shorter Form
(*Sung only by an ordained minister)

Exult, let them exult, the hosts of heaven,
exult, let Angel ministers of God exult,
let the trumpet of salvation
sound aloud our mighty King's triumph!
Be glad, let earth be glad, as glory floods her,
ablaze with light from her eternal King,
let all corners of the earth be glad,
knowing an end to gloom and darkness.
Rejoice, let Mother Church also rejoice,
arrayed with the lightning of his glory,
let this holy building shake with joy,
filled with the mighty voices of the peoples.

(*℣. The Lord be with you.
℟. **And with your spirit.**)

℣. Lift up your hearts.
℟. **We lift them up to the Lord.**

℣. Let us give thanks to the Lord our God.
℟. **It is right and just.**

It is truly right and just,
with ardent love of mind and heart
and with devoted service of our voice,
to acclaim our God invisible, the almighty Father,
and Jesus Christ, our Lord, his Son, his Only Begotten.

Who for our sake paid Adam's debt to the eternal Father,
and, pouring out his own dear Blood,
wiped clean the record of our ancient sinfulness.

These, then, are the feasts of Passover,
in which is slain the Lamb, the one true Lamb,
whose Blood anoints the doorposts of believers.

This is the night,
when once you led our forebears, Israel's children,
from slavery in Egypt
and made them pass dry-shod through the Red Sea.

This is the night
that with a pillar of fire
banished the darkness of sin.

This is the night
that even now, throughout the world,
sets Christian believers apart from worldly vices
and from the gloom of sin,
leading them to grace
and joining them to his holy ones.

This is the night,
when Christ broke the prison-bars of death
and rose victorious from the underworld.

O wonder of your humble care for us!
O love, O charity beyond all telling,
to ransom a slave you gave away your Son!

O truly necessary sin of Adam,
destroyed completely by the Death of Christ!

O happy fault
that earned so great, so glorious a Redeemer!
The sanctifying power of this night
dispels wickedness, washes faults away,
restores innocence to the fallen, and joy to mourners.

O truly blessed night,
when things of heaven are wed to those of earth,
and divine to the human.

On this, your night of grace, O holy Father,
accept this candle, a solemn offering,
the work of bees and of your servants' hands,

an evening sacrifice of praise,
this gift from your most holy Church.

Therefore, O Lord,
we pray you that this candle,
hallowed to the honor of your name,
may persevere undimmed,
to overcome the darkness of this night.
Receive it as a pleasing fragrance,
and let it mingle with the lights of heaven.
May this flame be found still burning
by the Morning Star:
the one Morning Star who never sets,
Christ your Son,
who, coming back from death's domain,
has shed his peaceful light on humanity,
and lives and reigns for ever and ever. All: **Amen.**

SECOND PART: THE LITURGY OF THE WORD

Dear brethren (brothers and sisters),
now that we have begun our solemn Vigil,
let us listen with quiet hearts to the Word of God.
Let us meditate on how God in times past saved his people
and in these, the last days, has sent us his Son as our Redeemer.
Let us pray that our God may complete this paschal work of salvation
by the fullness of redemption.

READING I (L 41-ABC) (Genesis 1:1—2:2) *or* Shorter Form [ ] (Genesis 1:1, 26-31a)

A reading from the Book of Genesis

God looked at everything he had made, and he found it very good.

[**In the beginning, when God created the heavens and the earth,**]
the earth was a formless wasteland, and darkness covered the abyss,
while a mighty wind swept over the waters.

Then God said,
"Let there be light," and there was light.
God saw how good the light was.

God then separated the light from the darkness.
God called the light "day," and the darkness he called "night."
Thus evening came, and morning followed—the first day.

Then God said,
"Let there be a dome in the middle of the waters,
to separate one body of water from the other."
And so it happened:
God made the dome,
and it separated the water above the dome from the water below it.
God called the dome "the sky."
Evening came, and morning followed—the second day.

Then God said,
"Let the water under the sky be gathered into a single basin,
so that the dry land may appear."
And so it happened:
the water under the sky was gathered into its basin,
and the dry land appeared.
God called the dry land "the earth,"
and the basin of the water he called "the sea."
God saw how good it was.
Then God said,
"Let the earth bring forth vegetation:
every kind of plant that bears seed
and every kind of fruit tree on earth
that bears fruit with its seed in it."
And so it happened:
the earth brought forth every kind of plant that bears seed
and every kind of fruit tree on earth
that bears fruit with its seed in it.
God saw how good it was.
Evening came, and morning followed—the third day.

Then God said:
"Let there be lights in the dome of the sky,
to separate day from night.
Let them mark the fixed times, the days and the years,
and serve as luminaries in the dome of the sky,
to shed light upon the earth."
And so it happened:
God made the two great lights,
the greater one to govern the day,
and the lesser one to govern the night;
and he made the stars.
God set them in the dome of the sky,
to shed light upon the earth,
to govern the day and the night,
and to separate the light from the darkness.
God saw how good it was.
Evening came, and morning followed—the fourth day.

Then God said,
"Let the water teem with an abundance of living creatures,
and on the earth let birds fly beneath the dome of the sky."
And so it happened:
God created the great sea monsters
and all kinds of swimming creatures with which the water teems,
and all kinds of winged birds.
God saw how good it was, and God blessed them, saying,
"Be fertile, multiply, and fill the water of the seas;
and let the birds multiply on the earth."
Evening came, and morning followed—the fifth day.

Then God said,
"Let the earth bring forth all kinds of living creatures:
cattle, creeping things, and wild animals of all kinds."

And so it happened:
God made all kinds of wild animals, all kinds of cattle,
and all kinds of creeping things of the earth.
God saw how good it was.
Then [God said:
"Let us make man in our image, after our likeness.
Let them have dominion over the fish of the sea,
the birds of the air, and the cattle,
and over all the wild animals
and all the creatures that crawl on the ground."
God created man in his image;
in the image of God he created him;
male and female he created them.
God blessed them, saying:
"Be fertile and multiply;
fill the earth and subdue it.
Have dominion over the fish of the sea, the birds of the air,
and all the living things that move on the earth."
God also said:
"See, I give you every seed-bearing plant all over the earth
and every tree that has seed-bearing fruit on it to be your food;
and to all the animals of the land, all the birds of the air,
and all the living creatures that crawl on the ground,
I give all the green plants for food."
And so it happened.
God looked at everything he had made, and he found it very good.]
Evening came, and morning followed—the sixth day.

Thus the heavens and the earth and all their array were completed.
Since on the seventh day God was finished
with the work he had been doing,

he rested on the seventh day from all the work he had undertaken.

The word of the Lord.

Responsorial Psalm 104 or 33

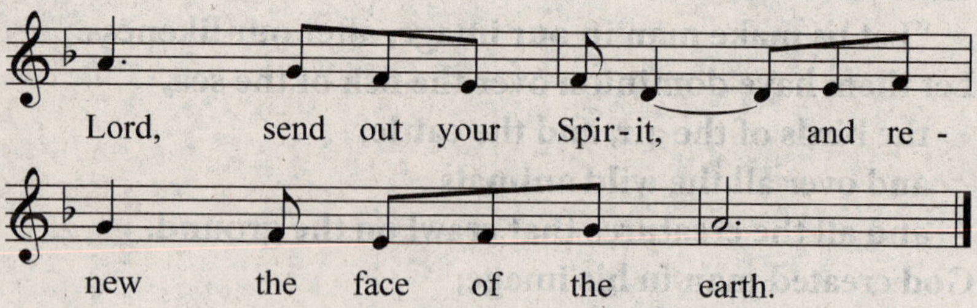

A Psalm 104:1-2, 5-6, 10, 12, 13-14, 24, 35

℟. (30) **Lord, send out your Spirit, and renew the face of the earth.**

Bless the Lord, O my soul!
  O Lord, my God, you are great indeed!
You are clothed with majesty and glory,
  robed in light as with a cloak. ℟.

You fixed the earth upon its foundation,
  not to be moved forever;
with the ocean, as with a garment, you covered it;
  above the mountains the waters stood. ℟.

You send forth springs into the watercourses
  that wind among the mountains.
Beside them the birds of heaven dwell;
  from among the branches they send forth their song. ℟.

You water the mountains from your palace;
  the earth is replete with the fruit of your works.
You raise grass for the cattle,
  and vegetation for man's use,
producing bread from the earth. ℟.

How manifold are your works, O Lord!
  In wisdom you have wrought them all—

the earth is full of your creatures.
Bless the LORD, O my soul! ℟.

Or:

B Psalm 33:4-5, 6-7, 12-13, 20 and 22

℟. (5b) **The earth is full of the goodness of the Lord.**

Upright is the word of the LORD,
and all his works are trustworthy.
He loves justice and right;
of the kindness of the LORD the earth is full. ℟.

By the word of the LORD the heavens were made;
by the breath of his mouth all their host.
He gathers the waters of the sea as in a flask;
in cellars he confines the deep. ℟.

Blessed the nation whose God is the LORD,
the people he has chosen for his own inheritance.
From heaven the LORD looks down;
he sees all mankind. ℟.

Our soul waits for the LORD,
who is our help and our shield.
May your kindness, O LORD, be upon us
who have put our hope in you. ℟.

PRAYER

Let us pray.

Almighty ever-living God,
who are wonderful in the ordering of all your works,
may those you have redeemed understand
that there exists nothing more marvelous
than the world's creation in the beginning
except that, at the end of the ages,
Christ our Passover has been sacrificed.
Who lives and reigns for ever and ever. All: **Amen.**

Or:

On the creation of man:
O God, who wonderfully created human nature
and still more wonderfully redeemed it,
grant us, we pray,
to set our minds against the enticements of sin,
that we may merit to attain eternal joys.
Through Christ our Lord. All: **Amen.**

READING II (Genesis 22:1-18) *or* Shorter Form [ ]
(Genesis 22:1-2, 9a, 10-13, 15-18)

A reading from the Book of Genesis

The sacrifice of Abraham, our father in faith.

[God put Abraham to the test.
He called to him, "Abraham!"
"Here I am," he replied.
Then God said:
"Take your son Isaac, your only one, whom you love,
and go to the land of Moriah.
There you shall offer him up as a holocaust
on a height that I will point out to you."]
Early the next morning Abraham saddled his donkey,
took with him his son Isaac and two of his servants as well,
and with the wood that he had cut for the holocaust,
set out for the place of which God had told him.

On the third day Abraham got sight of the place from afar.
Then he said to his servants:
"Both of you stay here with the donkey,
while the boy and I go on over yonder.
We will worship and then come back to you."
Thereupon Abraham took the wood for the holocaust
and laid it on his son Isaac's shoulders,
while he himself carried the fire and the knife.
As the two walked on together, Isaac spoke to his father Abraham:
"Father!" Isaac said.

"Yes, son," he replied.
Isaac continued, "Here are the fire and the wood,
but where is the sheep for the holocaust?"
"Son," Abraham answered,
"God himself will provide the sheep for the holocaust."
Then the two continued going forward.

[When they came to the place of which God had told him,
Abraham built an altar there and arranged the wood
on it.]
Next he tied up his son Isaac,
and put him on top of the wood on the altar.
[Then he reached out and took the knife to slaughter
his son.
But the LORD's messenger called to him from heaven,
"Abraham, Abraham!"
"Here I am!" he answered.
"Do not lay your hand on the boy," said the messenger.
"Do not do the least thing to him.
I know now how devoted you are to God,
since you did not withhold from me your own
beloved son."
As Abraham looked about,
he spied a ram caught by its horns in the thicket.
So he went and took the ram
and offered it up as a holocaust in place of his son.]
Abraham named the site Yahweh-yireh;
hence people now say, "On the mountain the LORD
will see."

[Again the LORD's messenger called to Abraham from
heaven and said:
"I swear by myself, declares the LORD,
that because you acted as you did
in not withholding from me your beloved son,
I will bless you abundantly
and make your descendants as countless

as the stars of the sky and the sands of the seashore;
your descendants shall take possession
of the gates of their enemies,
and in your descendants all the nations of the earth
shall find blessing—
all this because you obeyed my command."]

The word of the Lord.

RESPONSORIAL PSALM 16

Text: Refrain, *Lectionary for Mass,* © 1969, 1981, 1997, ICEL
Music: *The Collegeville Psalter*, © 2017, Paul Inwood.

Psalm 16:5, 8, 9-10, 11

℟. (1) **You are my inheritance, O Lord.**

O LORD, my allotted portion and my cup,
you it is who hold fast my lot.
I set the LORD ever before me;
with him at my right hand I shall not be disturbed. ℟.

Therefore my heart is glad and my soul rejoices,
my body, too, abides in confidence;
because you will not abandon my soul to the netherworld,
nor will you suffer your faithful one to undergo
corruption. ℟.

You will show me the path to life,
fullness of joys in your presence,
the delights at your right hand forever. ℟.

PRAYER

Let us pray.

O God, supreme Father of the faithful,
who increase the children of your promise

by pouring out the grace of adoption
throughout the whole world
and who through the Paschal Mystery
make your servant Abraham father of nations,
as once you swore,
grant, we pray,
that your peoples may enter worthily
into the grace to which you call them.
Through Christ our Lord. All: **Amen.**

READING III (Exodus 14:15—15:1)

A reading from the Book of Exodus

The Israelites marched on dry land through the midst of the sea.

The LORD said to Moses, "Why are you crying out to me?
Tell the Israelites to go forward.
And you, lift up your staff and, with hand outstretched over the sea,
split the sea in two,
that the Israelites may pass through it on dry land.
But I will make the Egyptians so obstinate
that they will go in after them.
Then I will receive glory through Pharaoh and all his army,
his chariots and charioteers.
The Egyptians shall know that I am the LORD,
when I receive glory through Pharaoh
and his chariots and charioteers."

The angel of God, who had been leading Israel's camp,
now moved and went around behind them.
The column of cloud also, leaving the front,
took up its place behind them,
so that it came between the camp of the Egyptians
and that of Israel.
But the cloud now became dark, and thus the night passed
without the rival camps coming any closer together all night long.
Then Moses stretched out his hand over the sea,
and the LORD swept the sea

with a strong east wind throughout the night
and so turned it into dry land.
When the water was thus divided,
the Israelites marched into the midst of the sea on dry land,
with the water like a wall to their right and to their left.

The Egyptians followed in pursuit;
all Pharaoh's horses and chariots and charioteers went after them
right into the midst of the sea.
In the night watch just before dawn
the LORD cast through the column of the fiery cloud
upon the Egyptian force a glance that threw it into a panic;
and he so clogged their chariot wheels
that they could hardly drive.
With that the Egyptians sounded the retreat before Israel,
because the LORD was fighting for them against the Egyptians.

Then the LORD told Moses, "Stretch out your hand over the sea,
that the water may flow back upon the Egyptians,
upon their chariots and their charioteers."
So Moses stretched out his hand over the sea,
and at dawn the sea flowed back to its normal depth.
The Egyptians were fleeing head on toward the sea,
when the LORD hurled them into its midst.
As the water flowed back,
it covered the chariots and the charioteers of Pharaoh's whole army
which had followed the Israelites into the sea.
Not a single one of them escaped.
But the Israelites had marched on dry land
through the midst of the sea,
with the water like a wall to their right and to their left.

Thus the Lord saved Israel on that day
from the power of the Egyptians.
When Israel saw the Egyptians lying dead on the seashore
and beheld the great power that the Lord
had shown against the Egyptians,
they feared the Lord and believed in him and in his servant Moses.

Then Moses and the Israelites sang this song to the Lord:
I will sing to the Lord, for he is gloriously triumphant;
horse and chariot he has cast into the sea.

The word of the Lord.

Responsorial Psalm (Exodus 15)

Text: Refrain, *Lectionary for Mass,* © 1969, 1981, 1997, ICEL
Music: *The Collegeville Psalter,* © 2017, Paul Inwood.

Exodus 15:1-2, 3-4, 5-6, 17-18

℟. (1b) **Let us sing to the Lord; he has covered himself in glory.**

I will sing to the Lord, for he is gloriously triumphant;
horse and chariot he has cast into the sea.
My strength and my courage is the Lord,
and he has been my savior.
He is my God, I praise him;
the God of my father, I extol him. ℟.

The Lord is a warrior,
Lord is his name!
Pharaoh's chariots and army he hurled into the sea;
the elite of his officers were submerged in the Red Sea. ℟.

(continued)

The flood waters covered them,
they sank into the depths like a stone.
Your right hand, O LORD, magnificent in power,
your right hand, O LORD, has shattered the enemy. ℟.

You brought in the people you redeemed
and planted them on the mountain of your
inheritance—
the place where you made your seat, O LORD,
the sanctuary, LORD, which your hands established.
The LORD shall reign forever and ever. ℟.

PRAYER

Let us pray.

O God, whose ancient wonders
remain undimmed in splendor even in our day,
for what you once bestowed on a single people,
freeing them from Pharaoh's persecution
by the power of your right hand,
now you bring about as the salvation of the nations
through the waters of rebirth,
grant, we pray, that the whole world
may become children of Abraham
and inherit the dignity of Israel's birthright.
Through Christ our Lord. All: **Amen.**

Or:

O God, who by the light of the New Testament
have unlocked the meaning
of wonders worked in former times,
so that the Red Sea prefigures the sacred font
and the nation delivered from slavery
foreshadows the Christian people,
grant, we pray, that all nations,
obtaining the privilege of Israel by merit of faith,
may be reborn by partaking of your Spirit.
Through Christ our Lord. All: **Amen.**

READING IV (Isaiah 54:5-14)

A reading from the Book of the Prophet Isaiah

With enduring love, the Lord your redeemer takes pity on you.

The One who has become your husband is your Maker;
his name is the LORD of hosts;
your redeemer is the Holy One of Israel,
called God of all the earth.
The LORD calls you back,
like a wife forsaken and grieved in spirit,
a wife married in youth and then cast off,
says your God.
For a brief moment I abandoned you,
but with great tenderness I will take you back.
In an outburst of wrath, for a moment
I hid my face from you;
but with enduring love I take pity on you,
says the LORD, your redeemer.
This is for me like the days of Noah,
when I swore that the waters of Noah
should never again deluge the earth;
so I have sworn not to be angry with you,
or to rebuke you.
Though the mountains leave their place
and the hills be shaken,
my love shall never leave you
nor my covenant of peace be shaken,
says the LORD, who has mercy on you.
O afflicted one, storm-battered and unconsoled,
I lay your pavements in carnelians,
and your foundations in sapphires;
I will make your battlements of rubies,
your gates of carbuncles,
and all your walls of precious stones.
All your children shall be taught by the LORD,
and great shall be the peace of your children.
In justice shall you be established,
far from the fear of oppression,
where destruction cannot come near you.

The word of the Lord.

Responsorial Psalm 30

Psalm 30:2, 4, 5-6, 11-12, 13

℟. (2a) **I will praise you, Lord, for you have rescued me.**

I will extol you, O Lord, for you drew me clear
and did not let my enemies rejoice over me.
O Lord, you brought me up from the netherworld;
you preserved me from among those going down into the pit. ℟.

Sing praise to the Lord, you his faithful ones,
and give thanks to his holy name.
For his anger lasts but a moment;
a lifetime, his good will.
At nightfall, weeping enters in,
but with the dawn, rejoicing. ℟.

Hear, O Lord, and have pity on me;
O Lord, be my helper.
You changed my mourning into dancing;
O Lord, my God, forever will I give you thanks. ℟.

Prayer

Let us pray.

Almighty ever-living God,
surpass, for the honor of your name,
what you pledged to the Patriarchs by reason of their faith,
and through sacred adoption increase the children of your promise,
so that what the Saints of old never doubted would come to pass
your Church may now see in great part fulfilled.
Through Christ our Lord. All: **Amen.**

Reading V (Isaiah 55:1-11)

A reading from the Book of the Prophet Isaiah

Come to me that you may have life. I will renew with you an everlasting covenant.

Thus says the Lord:
All you who are thirsty,
come to the water!
You who have no money,
come, receive grain and eat;
come, without paying and without cost,
drink wine and milk!
Why spend your money for what is not bread,
your wages for what fails to satisfy?
Heed me, and you shall eat well,
you shall delight in rich fare.
Come to me heedfully,
listen, that you may have life.
I will renew with you the everlasting covenant,
the benefits assured to David.
As I made him a witness to the peoples,
a leader and commander of nations,
so shall you summon a nation you knew not,
and nations that knew you not shall run to you,
because of the Lord, your God,
the Holy One of Israel, who has glorified you.

Seek the Lord while he may be found,
call him while he is near.
Let the scoundrel forsake his way,
and the wicked man his thoughts;
let him turn to the Lord for mercy;
to our God, who is generous in forgiving.
For my thoughts are not your thoughts,
nor are your ways my ways, says the Lord.
As high as the heavens are above the earth,
so high are my ways above your ways
and my thoughts above your thoughts.

For just as from the heavens
the rain and snow come down
and do not return there
till they have watered the earth,
making it fertile and fruitful,
giving seed to the one who sows
and bread to the one who eats,
so shall my word be
that goes forth from my mouth;
my word shall not return to me void,
but shall do my will,
achieving the end for which I sent it.

The word of the Lord.

RESPONSORIAL PSALM (Isaiah 12)

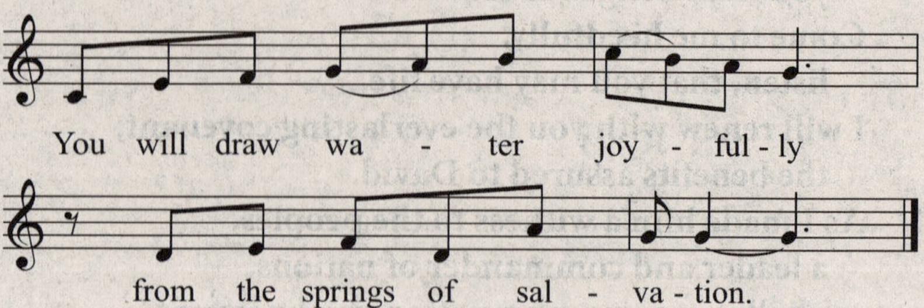

Isaiah 12:2-3, 4, 5-6

℟. (3) **You will draw water joyfully from the springs of salvation.**

God indeed is my savior;
I am confident and unafraid.
My strength and my courage is the LORD,
and he has been my savior.
With joy you will draw water
at the fountain of salvation. ℟.

Give thanks to the LORD, acclaim his name;
among the nations make known his deeds,
proclaim how exalted is his name. ℟.

Sing praise to the LORD for his glorious achievement;
 let this be known throughout all the earth.
Shout with exultation, O city of Zion,
 for great in your midst
 is the Holy One of Israel! ℟.

PRAYER

Let us pray.

Almighty ever-living God,
sole hope of the world,
who by the preaching of your Prophets
unveiled the mysteries of this present age,
graciously increase the longing of your people,
for only at the prompting of your grace
do the faithful progress in any kind of virtue.
Through Christ our Lord. All: **Amen.**

READING VI (Baruch 3:9-15, 32—4:4)

A reading from the Book of the Prophet Baruch

Walk toward the splendor of the Lord.

Hear, O Israel, the commandments of life:
 listen, and know prudence!
How is it, Israel,
 that you are in the land of your foes,
 grown old in a foreign land,
defiled with the dead,
 accounted with those destined for the netherworld?
You have forsaken the fountain of wisdom!
 Had you walked in the way of God,
 you would have dwelt in enduring peace.
Learn where prudence is,
 where strength, where understanding;
that you may know also
 where are length of days, and life,
 where light of the eyes, and peace.
Who has found the place of wisdom,
 who has entered into her treasuries?

The One who knows all things knows her;
he has probed her by his knowledge—
the One who established the earth for all time,
and filled it with four-footed beasts;
he who dismisses the light, and it departs,
calls it, and it obeys him trembling;
before whom the stars at their posts
shine and rejoice;
when he calls them, they answer, "Here we are!"
shining with joy for their Maker.
Such is our God;
no other is to be compared to him:
he has traced out the whole way of understanding,
and has given her to Jacob, his servant,
to Israel, his beloved son.

Since then she has appeared on earth,
and moved among people.
She is the book of the precepts of God,
the law that endures forever;
all who cling to her will live,
but those will die who forsake her.
Turn, O Jacob, and receive her:
walk by her light toward splendor.
Give not your glory to another,
your privileges to an alien race.
Blessed are we, O Israel;
for what pleases God is known to us!

The word of the Lord.

Responsorial Psalm 19

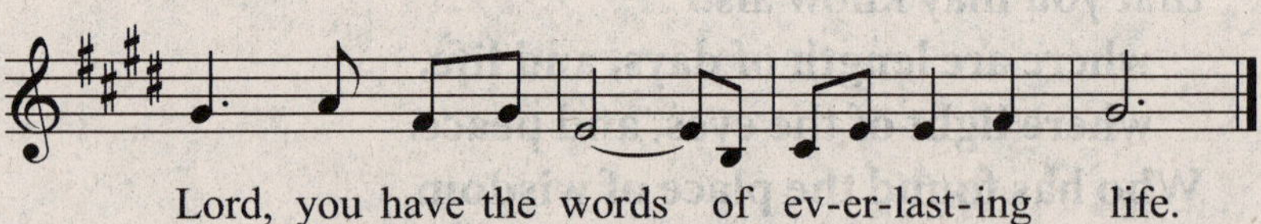

Psalm 19:8, 9, 10, 11

℟. (John 6:68c) **Lord, you have the words of everlasting life.**

The law of the LORD is perfect,
refreshing the soul;
the decree of the LORD is trustworthy,
giving wisdom to the simple. ℟.

The precepts of the LORD are right,
rejoicing the heart;
the command of the LORD is clear,
enlightening the eye. ℟.

The fear of the LORD is pure,
enduring forever;
the ordinances of the LORD are true,
all of them just. ℟.

They are more precious than gold,
than a heap of purest gold;
sweeter also than syrup
or honey from the comb. ℟.

PRAYER

Let us pray.

O God, who constantly increase your Church
by your call to the nations,
graciously grant
to those you wash clean in the waters of Baptism
the assurance of your unfailing protection.
Through Christ our Lord. All: **Amen.**

READING VII (Ezekiel 36:16-17a, 18-28)

A reading from the Book of the Prophet Ezekiel

I shall sprinkle clean water upon you and I shall give you a new heart.

The word of the LORD came to me, saying:
Son of man, when the house of Israel lived in their land,
they defiled it by their conduct and deeds.
Therefore I poured out my fury upon them
because of the blood that they poured out on the ground,

and because they defiled it with idols.
I scattered them among the nations,
dispersing them over foreign lands;
according to their conduct and deeds I judged them.
But when they came among the nations wherever they came,
they served to profane my holy name,
because it was said of them: "These are the people of the LORD,
yet they had to leave their land."
So I have relented because of my holy name
which the house of Israel profaned
among the nations where they came.
Therefore say to the house of Israel: Thus says the Lord GOD:
Not for your sakes do I act, house of Israel,
but for the sake of my holy name,
which you profaned among the nations to which you came.
I will prove the holiness of my great name, profaned among the nations,
in whose midst you have profaned it.
Thus the nations shall know that I am the LORD, says the Lord GOD,
when in their sight I prove my holiness through you.
For I will take you away from among the nations,
gather you from all the foreign lands,
and bring you back to your own land.
I will sprinkle clean water upon you
to cleanse you from all your impurities,
and from all your idols I will cleanse you.
I will give you a new heart and place a new spirit within you,
taking from your bodies your stony hearts
and giving you natural hearts.

I will put my spirit within you and make you live by my statutes,
careful to observe my decrees.
You shall live in the land I gave your fathers;
you shall be my people, and I will be your God.

The word of the Lord.

Responsorial Psalm

A *When baptism is celebrated*

Psalms 42:3, 5; 43:3, 4

℟. (42:2) **Like a deer that longs for running streams,**
my soul longs for you, my God.

Athirst is my soul for God, the living God.
When shall I go and behold the face of God? ℟.

I went with the throng
and led them in procession to the house of God,
amid loud cries of joy and thanksgiving,
with the multitude keeping festival. ℟.

Send forth your light and your fidelity;
they shall lead me on
and bring me to your holy mountain,
to your dwelling-place. ℟.

Then will I go in to the altar of God,
the God of my gladness and joy;
then will I give you thanks upon the harp,
O God, my God! ℟.

B *When baptism is not celebrated*

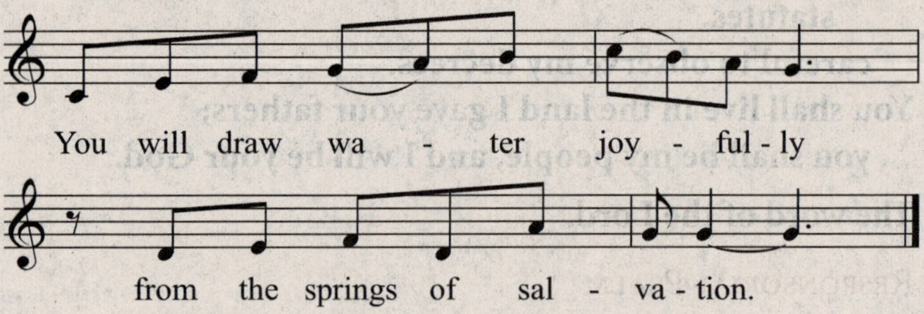

Isaiah 12:2-3, 4bcd, 5-6

℟. (3) **You will draw water joyfully from the springs of salvation.**

God indeed is my savior;
I am confident and unafraid.
My strength and my courage is the Lord,
and he has been my savior.
With joy you will draw water
at the fountain of salvation. ℟.

Give thanks to the Lord, acclaim his name;
among the nations make known his deeds,
proclaim how exalted is his name. ℟.

Sing praise to the Lord for his glorious achievement;
let this be known throughout all the earth.
Shout with exultation, O city of Zion,
for great in your midst
is the Holy One of Israel! ℟.

C *When baptism is not celebrated*

Psalm 51:12-13, 14-15, 18-19

℟. (12a) **Create a clean heart in me, O God.**

A clean heart create for me, O God,
and a steadfast spirit renew within me.
Cast me not out from your presence,
and your Holy Spirit take not from me. ℟.

Give me back the joy of your salvation,
and a willing spirit sustain in me.
I will teach transgressors your ways,
and sinners shall return to you. ℟.

For you are not pleased with sacrifices;
should I offer a holocaust, you would not accept it.
My sacrifice, O God, is a contrite spirit;
a heart contrite and humbled, O God, you will not
spurn. ℟.

PRAYER

Let us pray.

O God of unchanging power and eternal light,
look with favor on the wondrous mystery of the whole Church
and serenely accomplish the work of human salvation,
which you planned from all eternity;
may the whole world know and see
that what was cast down is raised up,
what had become old is made new,
and all things are restored to integrity through Christ,
just as by him they came into being.
Who lives and reigns for ever and ever. All: **Amen.**

Or:

O God, who by the pages of both Testaments
instruct and prepare us to celebrate the Paschal Mystery,
grant that we may comprehend your mercy,
so that the gifts we receive from you this night
may confirm our hope of the gifts to come.
Through Christ our Lord. All: **Amen.**

GLORIA (*See* page 4).

COLLECT

Let us pray.

O God, who make this most sacred night radiant
with the glory of the Lord's Resurrection,
stir up in your Church a spirit of adoption,
so that, renewed in body and mind,
we may render you undivided service.
Through our Lord Jesus Christ, your Son,
who lives and reigns with you in the unity of the Holy Spirit,
God, for ever and ever. All: **Amen.**

EPISTLE (Romans 6:3-11)

A reading from the Letter of Saint Paul to the Romans

Christ, raised from the dead, dies no more.

Brothers and sisters:
Are you unaware that we who were baptized into Christ Jesus
were baptized into his death?
We were indeed buried with him through baptism into death,
so that, just as Christ was raised from the dead
by the glory of the Father,
we too might live in newness of life.

For if we have grown into union with him through a death like his,
we shall also be united with him in the resurrection.
We know that our old self was crucified with him,
so that our sinful body might be done away with,
that we might no longer be in slavery to sin.
For a dead person has been absolved from sin.
If, then, we have died with Christ,
we believe that we shall also live with him.
We know that Christ, raised from the dead, dies no more;
death no longer has power over him.
As to his death, he died to sin once and for all;
as to his life, he lives for God.

Consequently, you too must think of yourselves as being dead to sin
and living for God in Christ Jesus.

The word of the Lord.

The Priest solemnly intones the Alleluia three times, raising his voice by a step each time, with all repeating it.

Responsorial Psalm 118

Psalm 118:1-2, 16-17, 22-23

℟. **Alleluia, alleluia, alleluia.**

Give thanks to the LORD, for he is good,
for his mercy endures forever.
Let the house of Israel say,
"His mercy endures forever." ℟.

The right hand of the LORD has struck with power;
the right hand of the LORD is exalted.
I shall not die, but live,
and declare the works of the LORD. ℟.

The stone which the builders rejected
has become the cornerstone.
By the LORD has this been done;
it is wonderful in our eyes. ℟.

Gospel B (Mark 16:1-7)

✠ **A reading from the holy Gospel according to Mark**

All: **Glory to you, O Lord.**

Jesus of Nazareth, the crucified, has been raised.

When the sabbath was over,
Mary Magdalene, Mary, the mother of James, and Salome

bought spices so that they might go and anoint him.
Very early when the sun had risen,
on the first day of the week, they came to the tomb.
They were saying to one another,
"Who will roll back the stone for us
from the entrance to the tomb?"
When they looked up,
they saw that the stone had been rolled back;
it was very large.
On entering the tomb they saw a young man
sitting on the right side, clothed in a white robe,
and they were utterly amazed.
He said to them, "Do not be amazed!
You seek Jesus of Nazareth, the crucified.
He has been raised; he is not here.
Behold the place where they laid him.
But go and tell his disciples and Peter,
'He is going before you to Galilee;
there you will see him, as he told you.'"

The Gospel of the Lord. All: **Praise to you, Lord Jesus Christ.**

THIRD PART: BAPTISMAL LITURGY

If there are candidates to be baptized:

Dearly beloved,
with one heart and one soul, let us by our prayers
come to the aid of these our brothers and sisters in their blessed hope,
so that, as they approach the font of rebirth,
the almighty Father may bestow on them
all his merciful help.

If the font is to be blessed, but there is no one to be baptized:

Dearly beloved,
let us humbly invoke upon this font
the grace of God the almighty Father,
that those who from it are born anew
may be numbered among the children of adoption in Christ.

THE LITANY OF THE SAINTS

The Litany is sung by two cantors, with all standing (because it is Easter Time) and responding. (If no one is to be baptized and the font is not to be blessed, the Litany is omitted, and the Blessing of Baptismal Water [pp. 255–256] takes place at once.)

Lord, have mercy.	**Lord, have mercy.**
Christ, have mercy.	**Christ, have mercy.**
Lord, have mercy.	**Lord, have mercy.**
Holy Mary, Mother of God,	**pray for us.**
[. . .]	
Lord, be merciful,	**Lord, deliver us we pray.**
[. . .]	
Be merciful to us sinners,	**Lord, we ask you, hear our prayer.**
[. . .]	
Christ, hear us.	**Christ, hear us.**
Christ, graciously hear us.	**Christ, graciously hear us.**

If there are candidates to be baptized, the Priest says the following prayer:

Almighty ever-living God,
be present by the mysteries of your great love
and send forth the spirit of adoption
to create the new peoples
brought to birth for you in the font of Baptism,
so that what is to be carried out by our humble service
may be brought to fulfillment by your mighty power.
Through Christ our Lord. All: **Amen.**

BLESSING OF BAPTISMAL WATER

O God, who by invisible power
accomplish a wondrous effect
through sacramental signs
and who in many ways have prepared water, your creation,
to show forth the grace of Baptism;

O God, whose Spirit
in the first moments of the world's creation
hovered over the waters,
so that the very substance of water
would even then take to itself the power to sanctify;

O God, who by the outpouring of the flood
foreshadowed regeneration,
so that from the mystery of one and the same element of water
would come an end to vice and a beginning of virtue;

O God, who caused the children of Abraham
to pass dry-shod through the Red Sea,
so that the chosen people,
set free from slavery to Pharaoh,
would prefigure the people of the baptized;

O God, whose Son,
baptized by John in the waters of the Jordan,
was anointed with the Holy Spirit,
and, as he hung upon the Cross,
gave forth water from his side along with blood,
and after his Resurrection, commanded his disciples:
"Go forth, teach all nations, baptizing them
in the name of the Father and of the Son and of the Holy Spirit,"
look now, we pray, upon the face of your Church
and graciously unseal for her the fountain of Baptism.

May this water receive by the Holy Spirit
the grace of your Only Begotten Son,
so that human nature, created in your image
and washed clean through the Sacrament of Baptism
from all the squalor of the life of old,
may be found worthy to rise to the life of newborn children
through water and the Holy Spirit.

May the power of the Holy Spirit,
O Lord, we pray,
come down through your Son
into the fullness of this font,
so that all who have been buried with Christ
by Baptism into death
may rise again to life with him.
Who lives and reigns with you in the unity of the Holy Spirit,
God, for ever and ever. All: **Amen.**

Celebration of Baptism

Renunciation of Sin and Profession of Faith

The celebrant in a series of questions to which the elect (or the parents and godparents of infants to be baptized) reply **I DO**, asks the elect (or parents and godparents) to renounce sin and profess their faith.

BAPTISM OF ADULTS

The celebrant baptizes the elect, saying:

N., I BAPTIZE YOU IN THE NAME OF THE FATHER,

He immerses the elect or pours water the first time.

AND OF THE SON,

He immerses the elect or pours water the second time.

AND OF THE HOLY SPIRIT.

He immerses the elect or pours water the third time.

After each Baptism, it is appropriate for the people to sing a short acclamation, such as:

Blessed be God, who chose you in Christ.

or

Holy Church, stretch out your hands
to welcome those brought to new birth from the waters
by the Holy Spirit of God.

or another appropriate acclamation.

BAPTISM OF CHILDREN

Celebrant: Is it your will, therefore, that N. should receive Baptism in the faith of the Church?

Parents and godparents: **It is.**

He baptizes the child, saying:

N., I BAPTIZE YOU IN THE NAME OF THE FATHER,

He immerses the child or pours water the first time.

AND OF THE SON,

He immerses the child or pours water the second time.

AND OF THE HOLY SPIRIT.

He immerses the child or pours water the third time.

After each Baptism, it is appropriate for the people to sing a short acclamation, such as:

You are God's work of art, created in Christ Jesus.

ANOINTING AFTER BAPTISM

Almighty God, the Father of our Lord Jesus Christ,
has freed you from sin,
given you new birth by water and the Holy Spirit,
and joined you to his people.
He now anoints you with the Chrism of salvation,

so that you may remain members of Christ, Priest, Prophet and King,
unto eternal life.
All: **Amen.**

CLOTHING WITH A WHITE GARMENT

N. and N., you have become a new creation
and have clothed yourselves in Christ.
Receive, therefore, the white garment
and bring it unstained
before the judgment seat of our Lord Jesus Christ,
that you may have eternal life.
All: **Amen.**

HANDING ON OF A LIGHTED CANDLE

You have been made light in Christ.
Walk always as children of light,
that persevering in faith
you may run to meet the Lord when he comes
with all the Saints in the heavenly court.
All: **Amen.**

RENEWAL OF BAPTISMAL PROMISES AND PROFESSION OF FAITH

Dear brethren (brothers and sisters), through the Paschal Mystery
we have been buried with Christ in Baptism,
so that we may walk with him in newness of life.
And so, now that our Lenten observance is concluded,
let us renew the promises of Holy Baptism,
by which we once renounced Satan and his works
and promised to serve God in the holy Catholic Church.

And so I ask you:

A Celebrant: Do you renounce Satan? All: **I do.**
Celebrant: And all his works? All: **I do.**
Celebrant: And all his empty show? All: **I do.**

Or:

B Celebrant: Do you renounce sin,
so as to live in the freedom of the children of God?
All: **I do.**

Celebrant: Do you renounce the lure of evil,
so that sin may have no mastery over you?
All: **I do.**

Celebrant: Do you renounce Satan,
the author and prince of sin?
All: **I do.**

Then the celebrant continues:

Celebrant: Do you believe in God,
the Father almighty,
Creator of heaven and earth?

All: **I do.**

Celebrant: Do you believe in Jesus Christ, his only Son, our Lord,
who was born of the Virgin Mary,
suffered death and was buried,
rose again from the dead
and is seated at the right hand of the Father?

All: **I do.**

Celebrant: Do you believe in the Holy Spirit,
the holy catholic Church,
the communion of saints,
the forgiveness of sins,
the resurrection of the body,
and life everlasting?

All: **I do.**

And may almighty God, the Father of our Lord Jesus Christ,
who has given us new birth by water and the Holy Spirit
and bestowed on us forgiveness of our sins,
keep us by his grace,
in Christ Jesus our Lord,
for eternal life. All: **Amen.**

The celebrant sprinkles the people with the blessed water, while all sing the following or another chant that is baptismal in character:

I saw water flowing from the Temple,
from its right-hand side, alleluia;
and all to whom this water came were saved
and shall say: Alleluia, alleluia. (Cf. Ezekiel 47:1-2, 9)

Celebration of Reception

The celebrant invites the candidates for Reception, along with their sponsors, to come into the sanctuary, and before the community to make the following Profession of Faith:

I believe and profess
all that the holy Catholic Church
believes, teaches, and proclaims as revealed by God.

Then the candidates with their sponsors go individually to the celebrant, who says to each candidate:

N., the Lord receives you into the Catholic Church.
In his mercy he has led you here,
so that in the Holy Spirit
you may have full communion with us
in the faith you have professed before this his family.

Celebration of Confirmation*

If the Bishop has conferred Baptism, he should now also confer Confirmation. If the Bishop is not present, the Priest who conferred Baptism and received the candidates into full communion is authorized to confirm. The infants who were baptized during this celebration are not confirmed. However, the newly baptized children who have gone through the OCIA process are confirmed.

Invitation

Dearly beloved,
let us pray to God the almighty Father,
that he will graciously pour out the Holy Spirit
upon these neophytes
to confirm them with his abundant gifts,
and through his anointing
conform them more fully to Christ, the Son of God.

The Laying On of Hands

Almighty God, Father of our Lord Jesus Christ,
who brought these your servants to new birth
by water and the Holy Spirit,
freeing them from sin:
send upon them, O Lord, the Holy Spirit, the Paraclete;
give them the spirit of wisdom and understanding,
the spirit of counsel and fortitude,
the spirit of knowledge and piety;
fill them with the spirit of the fear of the Lord.
Through Christ our Lord. All: **Amen.**

The Anointing with Chrism

N., be sealed with the Gift of the Holy Spirit.
The newly confirmed: **Amen.**

The celebrant adds: Peace be with you.
The newly confirmed: **And with your Spirit.**

Prayer of the Faithful

*From the OCIA, nos. 232–235.

FOURTH PART: THE LITURGY OF THE EUCHARIST

Prayer over the Offerings

Accept, we ask, O Lord,
the prayers of your people
with the sacrificial offerings,
that what has begun in the paschal mysteries
may, by the working of your power,
bring us to the healing of eternity.
Through Christ our Lord. All: **Amen.**

Communion Antiphon (1 Corinthians 5:7-8)

Christ our Passover has been sacrificed;
therefore let us keep the feast
with the unleavened bread of purity and truth, alleluia.

Prayer after Communion

Pour out on us, O Lord, the Spirit of your love,
and in your kindness make those you have nourished
by this paschal Sacrament
one in mind and heart.
Through Christ our Lord. All: **Amen.**

Dismissal

To dismiss the people the Deacon or, if there is no Deacon, the Priest himself sings or says:

Go forth, the Mass is ended, alleluia, alleluia.

Or:

Go in peace, alleluia, alleluia.

All reply: **Thanks be to God, alleluia, alleluia.**

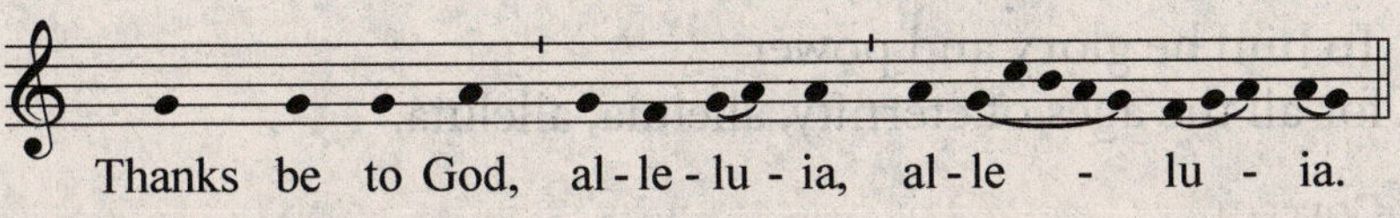

This practice is observed throughout the Octave of Easter.

Easter Sunday

THE RESURRECTION OF THE LORD

MASS DURING THE DAY

March 28, 2027

Reflection on the Gospel

In John's telling of the discovery of the resurrection he points out that "the other disciple whom Jesus loved" ran faster than Peter to the tomb. While John arrives at the tomb first, he does not enter. Rather, it is the typically impetuous Peter who enters to examine the scene. All of this happens, though, because Mary of Magdala runs to them first, having been the first to see the stone rolled away. As Apostle to the Apostles, the first kerygma belongs to her.

—Living Liturgy™, *Easter Sunday 2027*

ENTRANCE ANTIPHON (Cf. Psalm 139[138]:18, 5-6)

I have risen, and I am with you still, alleluia.
You have laid your hand upon me, alleluia.
Too wonderful for me, this knowledge, alleluia, alleluia.

Or:

(Luke 24:34; cf. Revelation 1:6)

The Lord is truly risen, alleluia.
To him be glory and power
for all the ages of eternity, alleluia, alleluia.

COLLECT

O God, who on this day,
through your Only Begotten Son,
have conquered death
and unlocked for us the path to eternity,
grant, we pray, that we who keep
the solemnity of the Lord's Resurrection
may, through the renewal brought by your Spirit,
rise up in the light of life.

Through our Lord Jesus Christ, your Son,
who lives and reigns with you in the unity of the Holy Spirit,
God, for ever and ever. All: **Amen.**

READING I (L 42) (Acts of the Apostles 10:34a, 37-43)

A reading from the Acts of the Apostles

We ate and drank with him after he rose from the dead.

Peter proceeded to speak and said:
"You know what has happened all over Judea,
beginning in Galilee after the baptism
that John preached,
how God anointed Jesus of Nazareth
with the Holy Spirit and power.
He went about doing good
and healing all those oppressed by the devil,
for God was with him.
We are witnesses of all that he did
both in the country of the Jews and in Jerusalem.
They put him to death by hanging him on a tree.
This man God raised on the third day and granted that he be visible,
not to all the people, but to us,
the witnesses chosen by God in advance,
who ate and drank with him after he rose from the dead.
He commissioned us to preach to the people
and testify that he is the one appointed by God
as judge of the living and the dead.
To him all the prophets bear witness,
that everyone who believes in him
will receive forgiveness of sins through his name."

The word of the Lord. All: **Thanks be to God.**

Responsorial Psalm 118

Psalm 118:1-2, 16-17, 22-23

℟. (24) **This is the day the Lord has made; let us rejoice and be glad.** *or:* ℟. **Alleluia.**

Give thanks to the Lord, for he is good,
for his mercy endures forever.
Let the house of Israel say,
"His mercy endures forever." ℟.

"The right hand of the Lord has struck with power;
the right hand of the Lord is exalted.
I shall not die, but live,
and declare the works of the Lord." ℟.

The stone which the builders rejected
has become the cornerstone.
By the Lord has this been done;
it is wonderful in our eyes. ℟.

Reading II

A (Colossians 3:1-4)

A reading from the Letter of Saint Paul to the Colossians

Seek what is above, where Christ is.

Brothers and sisters:
If then you were raised with Christ, seek what is above,
where Christ is seated at the right hand of God.
Think of what is above, not of what is on earth.
For you have died, and your life is hidden with Christ
in God.

When Christ your life appears,
then you too will appear with him in glory.

The word of the Lord. All: **Thanks be to God.**

Or:

B (1 Corinthians 5:6b-8)

A reading from the first Letter of Saint Paul to the Corinthians

Clear out the old yeast, so that you may become a fresh batch of dough.

Brothers and sisters:
Do you not know that a little yeast leavens all the dough?
Clear out the old yeast,
so that you may become a fresh batch of dough,
inasmuch as you are unleavened.
For our paschal lamb, Christ, has been sacrificed.
Therefore, let us celebrate the feast,
not with the old yeast, the yeast of malice and wickedness,
but with the unleavened bread of sincerity and truth.

The word of the Lord. All: **Thanks be to God.**

Sequence

Victimae paschali laudes

Christians, to the Paschal Victim
Offer your thankful praises!
A Lamb the sheep redeems;
Christ, who only is sinless,
Reconciles sinners to the Father.
Death and life have contended in that combat stupendous:
The Prince of life, who died, reigns immortal.
Speak, Mary, declaring
What you saw, wayfaring.
"The tomb of Christ, who is living,
The glory of Jesus' resurrection;

Bright angels attesting,
The shroud and napkin resting.
Yes, Christ my hope is arisen;
To Galilee he goes before you."
Christ indeed from death is risen, our new life obtaining.
Have mercy, victor King, ever reigning!
Amen. Alleluia.

GOSPEL (John 20:1-9, below)
or (Mark 16:1-7)
Jesus of Nazareth, the crucified, has been raised.
or afternoon (Luke 24:13-35)
Stay with us since it is almost evening.

ALLELUIA (*See* 1 Corinthians 5:7b-8a)
℣. Alleluia, alleluia. ℟. **Alleluia, alleluia.**
℣. Christ, our paschal lamb, has been sacrificed;
let us then feast with joy in the Lord. ℟.

✠ **A reading from the holy Gospel according to John**

All: **Glory to you, O Lord.**

He had to rise from the dead.

On the first day of the week,
Mary of Magdala came to the tomb early in the morning,
while it was still dark,
and saw the stone removed from the tomb.
So she ran and went to Simon Peter
and to the other disciple whom Jesus loved, and told them,
"They have taken the Lord from the tomb,
and we don't know where they put him."
So Peter and the other disciple went out and came to the tomb.
They both ran, but the other disciple ran faster than Peter
and arrived at the tomb first;
he bent down and saw the burial cloths there, but did not go in.

When Simon Peter arrived after him,
he went into the tomb and saw the burial cloths there,
and the cloth that had covered his head,
not with the burial cloths but rolled up in a separate place.
Then the other disciple also went in,
the one who had arrived at the tomb first,
and he saw and believed.
For they did not yet understand the Scripture
that he had to rise from the dead.

The Gospel of the Lord. All: **Praise to you, Lord Jesus Christ.**

RENEWAL OF BAPTISMAL PROMISES

The renewal of baptismal promises may take place at all Masses today. The form followed is the same as at the Easter Vigil, pages 258–259.

PRAYER OVER THE OFFERINGS

Exultant with paschal gladness, O Lord,
we offer the sacrifice
by which your Church
is wondrously reborn and nourished.
Through Christ our Lord. All: **Amen.**

COMMUNION ANTIPHON (1 Corinthians 5:7-8)

Christ our Passover has been sacrificed, alleluia;
therefore let us keep the feast with the unleavened bread
of purity and truth, alleluia, alleluia.

PRAYER AFTER COMMUNION

Look upon your Church, O God,
with unfailing love and favor,
so that, renewed by the paschal mysteries,
she may come to the glory of the resurrection.
Through Christ our Lord. All: **Amen.**

Second Sunday of Easter
(or SUNDAY OF DIVINE MERCY)

April 4, 2027

Reflection on the Gospel

It is on this Second Sunday of Easter each year when we hear about the apostle Thomas and his first encounter with the risen Lord. Christ's resurrected and glorified body certainly could have been made completely whole again, yet the wounds of the nails and spear persist, and Thomas is able to touch and feel them. "My Lord and my God!" he cries. Here Christ is truly a wounded healer—and beyond that, a teacher, a friend, and a brother.

—Living Liturgy™, *Second Sunday of Easter 2027*

ENTRANCE ANTIPHON (1 Peter 2:2)

Like newborn infants, you must long for the pure, spiritual
milk,
that in him you may grow to salvation, alleluia.

Or:

(4 Esdras 2:36-37)

Receive the joy of your glory, giving thanks to God,
who has called you into the heavenly kingdom, alleluia.

COLLECT

God of everlasting mercy,
who in the very recurrence of the paschal feast
kindle the faith of the people you have made your own,
increase, we pray, the grace you have bestowed,
that all may grasp and rightly understand
in what font they have been washed,
by whose Spirit they have been reborn,
by whose Blood they have been redeemed.
Through our Lord Jesus Christ, your Son,

who lives and reigns with you in the unity of the Holy Spirit,
God, for ever and ever. All: **Amen.**

Reading I (L 44-B) (Acts of the Apostles 4:32-35)

A reading from the Acts of the Apostles

They were of one heart and mind.

The community of believers was of one heart and mind,
and no one claimed that any of his possessions was his own,
but they had everything in common.
With great power the apostles bore witness
to the resurrection of the Lord Jesus,
and great favor was accorded them all.
There was no needy person among them,
for those who owned property or houses would sell them,
bring the proceeds of the sale,
and put them at the feet of the apostles,
and they were distributed to each according to need.

The word of the Lord. All: **Thanks be to God.**

Responsorial Psalm 118

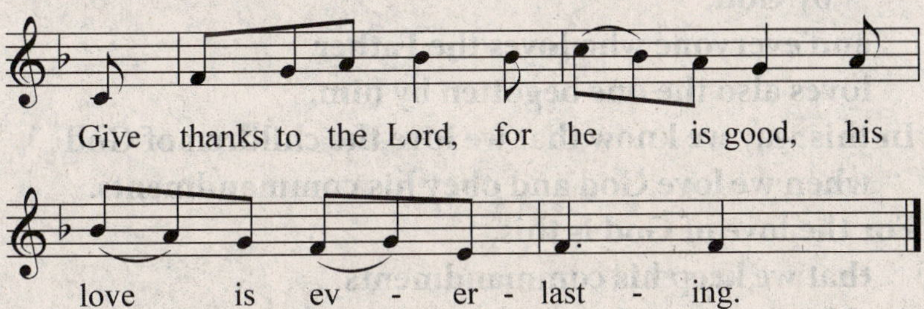

Psalm 118:2-4, 13-15, 22-24

℟. (1) **Give thanks to the Lord for he is good, his love is everlasting.** *or:* ℟. **Alleluia.**

Let the house of Israel say,
"His mercy endures forever."

(continued)

Let the house of Aaron say,
"His mercy endures forever."
Let those who fear the LORD say,
"His mercy endures forever." ℟.

I was hard pressed and was falling,
but the LORD helped me.
My strength and my courage is the LORD,
and he has been my savior.
The joyful shout of victory
in the tents of the just. ℟.

The stone which the builders rejected
has become the cornerstone.
By the LORD has this been done;
it is wonderful in our eyes.
This is the day the LORD has made;
let us be glad and rejoice in it. ℟.

READING II (1 John 5:1-6)

A reading from the first Letter of Saint John

Whoever is begotten by God conquers the world.

Beloved:
Everyone who believes that Jesus is the Christ is begotten by God,
and everyone who loves the Father
loves also the one begotten by him.
In this way we know that we love the children of God
when we love God and obey his commandments.
For the love of God is this,
that we keep his commandments.
And his commandments are not burdensome,
for whoever is begotten by God conquers the world.
And the victory that conquers the world is our faith.
Who indeed is the victor over the world
but the one who believes that Jesus is the Son of God?

This is the one who came through water and blood, Jesus Christ,
not by water alone, but by water and blood.

The Spirit is the one that testifies,
and the Spirit is truth.

The word of the Lord. All: **Thanks be to God.**

SEQUENCE (optional, see pp. 265–266)

GOSPEL (John 20:19-31)

ALLELUIA (John 20:29)

℣. Alleluia, alleluia. ℟. **Alleluia, alleluia.**

℣. You believe in me, Thomas, because you have seen me, says the Lord;
blessed are those who have not seen me, but still believe! ℟.

✠ **A reading from the holy Gospel according to John**

All: **Glory to you, O Lord.**

Eight days later Jesus came and stood in their midst.

On the evening of that first day of the week,
when the doors were locked, where the disciples were,
for fear of the Jews,
Jesus came and stood in their midst
and said to them, "Peace be with you."
When he had said this, he showed them his hands and his side.
The disciples rejoiced when they saw the Lord.
Jesus said to them again, "Peace be with you.
As the Father has sent me, so I send you."
And when he had said this, he breathed on them and said to them,
"Receive the Holy Spirit.
Whose sins you forgive are forgiven them,
and whose sins you retain are retained."

Thomas, called Didymus, one of the Twelve,
was not with them when Jesus came.
So the other disciples said to him, "We have seen the Lord."

But he said to them,
"Unless I see the mark of the nails in his hands
and put my finger into the nailmarks
and put my hand into his side, I will not believe."

Now a week later his disciples were again inside
and Thomas was with them.
Jesus came, although the doors were locked,
and stood in their midst and said, "Peace be with you."
Then he said to Thomas, "Put your finger here and see my hands,
and bring your hand and put it into my side,
and do not be unbelieving, but believe."
Thomas answered and said to him, "My Lord and my God!"
Jesus said to him, "Have you come to believe because you have seen me?
Blessed are those who have not seen and have believed."

Now Jesus did many other signs in the presence of his disciples
that are not written in this book.
But these are written that you may come to believe
that Jesus is the Christ, the Son of God,
and that through this belief you may have life in his name.

The Gospel of the Lord. All: **Praise to you, Lord Jesus Christ.**

Prayer over the Offerings

Accept, O Lord, we pray,
the oblations of your people
(and of those you have brought to new birth),
that, renewed by confession of your name and by Baptism,
they may attain unending happiness.
Through Christ our Lord. All: **Amen.**

Communion Antiphon (Cf. John 20:27)

Bring your hand and feel the place of the nails,
and do not be unbelieving but believing, alleluia.

Prayer after Communion
Grant, we pray, almighty God,
that our reception of this paschal Sacrament
may have a continuing effect
in our minds and hearts.
Through Christ our Lord. All: **Amen.**

Third Sunday of Easter

April 11, 2027

Reflection on the Gospel
Up until now, the good news of Christ's resurrection was primarily shared among friends and relatives, a very close circle of those who surrounded Jesus himself during his three years of ministry. We are at a "hinge" moment of the narrative, and of our Easter season, when Christ, in the last line of the gospel, reminds the apostles that it is their ministry, foretold by the prophets, to share the joy of the resurrection and forgiveness of sins with all nations. We too must consider how we do that ourselves.
—Living Liturgy™, *Third Sunday of Easter 2027*

Entrance Antiphon (Cf. Psalm 66[65]:1-2)
Cry out with joy to God, all the earth;
O sing to the glory of his name.
O render him glorious praise, alleluia.

Collect
May your people exult for ever, O God,
in renewed youthfulness of spirit,
so that, rejoicing now in the restored glory of our adoption,
we may look forward in confident hope
to the rejoicing of the day of resurrection.
Through our Lord Jesus Christ, your Son,

who lives and reigns with you in the unity of the Holy Spirit,
God, for ever and ever. All: **Amen.**

Reading I (L 47-B) (Acts of the Apostles 3:13-15, 17-19)

A reading from the Acts of the Apostles

The author of life you put to death, but God raised him from the dead.

Peter said to the people:
"The God of Abraham,
the God of Isaac, and the God of Jacob,
the God of our fathers, has glorified his servant Jesus,
whom you handed over and denied in Pilate's presence
when he had decided to release him.
You denied the Holy and Righteous One
and asked that a murderer be released to you.
The author of life you put to death,
but God raised him from the dead; of this we are witnesses.
Now I know, brothers,
that you acted out of ignorance, just as your leaders did;
but God has thus brought to fulfillment
what he had announced beforehand
through the mouth of all the prophets,
that his Christ would suffer.
Repent, therefore, and be converted, that your sins may be wiped away."

The word of the Lord. All: **Thanks be to God.**

Responsorial Psalm 4

Psalm 4:2, 4, 7-8, 9

℟. (7a) **Lord, let your face shine on us.** *or:* ℟. **Alleluia.**

When I call, answer me, O my just God,
you who relieve me when I am in distress;
have pity on me, and hear my prayer! ℟.

Know that the LORD does wonders for his faithful one;
the LORD will hear me when I call upon him. ℟.

O LORD, let the light of your countenance shine upon us!
You put gladness into my heart. ℟.

As soon as I lie down, I fall peacefully asleep,
for you alone, O LORD,
bring security to my dwelling. ℟.

READING II (1 John 2:1-5a)

A reading from the first Letter of Saint John

Jesus Christ is expiation not for our sins only but for those of the whole world.

My children, I am writing this to you
so that you may not commit sin.
But if anyone does sin, we have an Advocate with the Father,
Jesus Christ the righteous one.
He is expiation for our sins,
and not for our sins only but for those of the whole world.
The way we may be sure that we know him is to keep his commandments.
Those who say, "I know him," but do not keep his commandments
are liars, and the truth is not in them.
But whoever keeps his word,
the love of God is truly perfected in him.

The word of the Lord. All: **Thanks be to God.**

Gospel (Luke 24:35-48)

Alleluia (*See* Luke 24:32)

℣. Alleluia, alleluia. ℟. **Alleluia, alleluia.**
℣. Lord Jesus, open the Scriptures to us;
make our hearts burn while you speak to us. ℟.

✠ **A reading from the holy Gospel according to Luke**

All: **Glory to you, O Lord.**

Thus it was written that the Christ would suffer and rise from the dead on the third day.

The two disciples recounted what had taken place on the way,
and how Jesus was made known to them
in the breaking of bread.

While they were still speaking about this,
he stood in their midst and said to them,
"Peace be with you."
But they were startled and terrified
and thought that they were seeing a ghost.
Then he said to them, "Why are you troubled?
And why do questions arise in your hearts?
Look at my hands and my feet, that it is I myself.
Touch me and see, because a ghost does not have flesh and bones
as you can see I have."
And as he said this,
he showed them his hands and his feet.
While they were still incredulous for joy and were amazed,
he asked them, "Have you anything here to eat?"
They gave him a piece of baked fish;
he took it and ate it in front of them.

He said to them,
"These are my words that I spoke to you while I was still with you,

that everything written about me in the law of Moses
and in the prophets and psalms must be fulfilled."
Then he opened their minds to understand the Scriptures.
And he said to them,
"Thus it is written that the Christ would suffer
and rise from the dead on the third day
and that repentance, for the forgiveness of sins,
would be preached in his name
to all the nations, beginning from Jerusalem.
You are witnesses of these things."

The Gospel of the Lord. All: **Praise to you, Lord Jesus Christ.**

Prayer over the Offerings

Receive, O Lord, we pray,
these offerings of your exultant Church,
and, as you have given her cause for such great gladness,
grant also that the gifts we bring
may bear fruit in perpetual happiness.
Through Christ our Lord. All: **Amen.**

Communion Antiphon Year B (Luke 24:46-47)

The Christ had to suffer and on the third day rise from the dead;
in his name repentance and remission of sins
must be preached to all the nations, alleluia.

Prayer after Communion

Look with kindness upon your people, O Lord,
and grant, we pray,
that those you were pleased to renew by eternal mysteries
may attain in their flesh
the incorruptible glory of the resurrection.
Through Christ our Lord. All: **Amen.**

Fourth Sunday of Easter

April 18, 2027

Reflection on the Gospel

Though the imagery is not as prevalent in this cycle of readings, it is still Good Shepherd Sunday, the gospel reminds us. While we might wish to imagine the good shepherd as the one who, upon finding the lost sheep, lovingly hoists it over his shoulders to bring it back to the other ninety-nine, this is not the shepherd Jesus speaks of today. This good shepherd has to protect the flock from wolves—and lays down his life to do so.

—Living Liturgy™, *Fourth Sunday of Easter 2027*

Entrance Antiphon (Cf. Psalm 33[32]:5-6)

The merciful love of the Lord fills the earth;
by the word of the Lord the heavens were made, alleluia.

Collect

Almighty ever-living God,
lead us to a share in the joys of heaven,
so that the humble flock may reach
where the brave Shepherd has gone before.
Who lives and reigns with you in the unity of the Holy Spirit,
God, for ever and ever. All: **Amen.**

Reading I (L 50-B) (Acts of the Apostles 4:8-12)

A reading from the Acts of the Apostles

There is no salvation through anyone else.

Peter, filled with the Holy Spirit, said:
"Leaders of the people and elders:
If we are being examined today
about a good deed done to a cripple,
namely, by what means he was saved,
then all of you and all the people of Israel should know

that it was in the name of Jesus Christ the Nazorean
whom you crucified, whom God raised from the dead;
in his name this man stands before you healed.
He is *the stone rejected by you, the builders,*
which has become the cornerstone.
There is no salvation through anyone else,
nor is there any other name under heaven
given to the human race by which we are to be saved."

The word of the Lord. All: **Thanks be to God.**

Responsorial Psalm 118

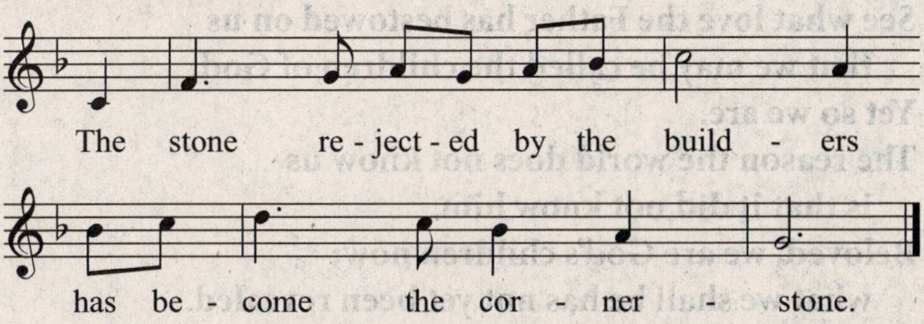

Psalm 118:1, 8-9, 21-23, 26, 28, 29

℟. (22) **The stone rejected by the builders has become the cornerstone.** *or:* ℟. **Alleluia.**

Give thanks to the Lord, for he is good,
for his mercy endures forever.
It is better to take refuge in the Lord
than to trust in man.
It is better to take refuge in the Lord
than to trust in princes. ℟.

I will give thanks to you, for you have answered me
and have been my savior.
The stone which the builders rejected
has become the cornerstone.
By the Lord has this been done;
it is wonderful in our eyes. ℟.

Blessed is he who comes in the name of the LORD;
  we bless you from the house of the LORD.
I will give thanks to you, for you have answered me
  and have been my savior.
Give thanks to the LORD, for he is good;
  for his kindness endures forever. ℟.

READING II (1 John 3:1-2)

A reading from the first Letter of Saint John

We shall see God as he really is.

Beloved:
See what love the Father has bestowed on us
that we may be called the children of God.
Yet so we are.
The reason the world does not know us
is that it did not know him.
Beloved, we are God's children now;
what we shall be has not yet been revealed.
We do know that when it is revealed we shall be like him,
for we shall see him as he is.

The word of the Lord. All: **Thanks be to God.**

GOSPEL (John 10:11-18)

ALLELUIA (John 10:14)

℣. Alleluia, alleluia. ℟. **Alleluia, alleluia.**
℣. I am the good shepherd, says the Lord;
I know my sheep, and mine know me. ℟.

✠ **A reading from the holy Gospel according to John**

All: **Glory to you, O Lord.**

The good shepherd lays down his life for the sheep.

Jesus said:
"I am the good shepherd.
A good shepherd lays down his life for the sheep.
A hired man, who is not a shepherd
and whose sheep are not his own,

sees a wolf coming and leaves the sheep and runs away,
and the wolf catches and scatters them.
This is because he works for pay and has no concern for the sheep.
I am the good shepherd,
and I know mine and mine know me,
just as the Father knows me and I know the Father;
and I will lay down my life for the sheep.
I have other sheep that do not belong to this fold.
These also I must lead, and they will hear my voice,
and there will be one flock, one shepherd.
This is why the Father loves me,
because I lay down my life in order to take it up again.
No one takes it from me, but I lay it down on my own.
I have power to lay it down, and power to take it up again.
This command I have received from my Father."

The Gospel of the Lord. All: **Praise to you, Lord Jesus Christ.**

Prayer over the Offerings

Grant, we pray, O Lord,
that we may always find delight in these paschal mysteries,
so that the renewal constantly at work within us
may be the cause of our unending joy.
Through Christ our Lord. All: **Amen.**

Communion Antiphon

The Good Shepherd has risen,
who laid down his life for his sheep
and willingly died for his flock, alleluia.

Prayer after Communion

Look upon your flock, kind Shepherd,
and be pleased to settle in eternal pastures
the sheep you have redeemed
by the Precious Blood of your Son.
Who lives and reigns for ever and ever. All: **Amen.**

Fifth Sunday of Easter

April 25, 2027

Reflection on the Gospel

In today's gospel, Jesus reminds us that sometimes his Father prunes the vine so that it may bear more fruit. If you are feeling particularly stretched this year, it may be time for some pruning. Consider starting a list of the various responsibilities and tasks you have to do each day. In a month or two, look at that list and see where opportunities may exist to prune the vine. Be prepared for some initial pain amid the pruning, trusting the Lord that more abundant fruit lies ahead.

—Living Liturgy™, *Fifth Sunday of Easter 2027*

ENTRANCE ANTIPHON (Cf. Psalm 98[97]:1-2)

O sing a new song to the Lord,
for he has worked wonders;
in the sight of the nations
he has shown his deliverance, alleluia.

COLLECT

Almighty ever-living God,
constantly accomplish the Paschal Mystery within us,
that those you were pleased to make new in Holy Baptism
may, under your protective care, bear much fruit
and come to the joys of life eternal.
Through our Lord Jesus Christ, your Son,
who lives and reigns with you in the unity of the Holy Spirit,
God, for ever and ever. All: **Amen.**

READING I (L 53-B) (Acts of the Apostles 9:26-31)

A reading from the Acts of the Apostles

Barnabas reported to the Apostles how Saul had seen the Lord on the way.

When Saul arrived in Jerusalem he tried to join the disciples,
but they were all afraid of him,
not believing that he was a disciple.
Then Barnabas took charge of him and brought him to the apostles,
and he reported to them how he had seen the Lord,
and that he had spoken to him,
and how in Damascus he had spoken out boldly in the name of Jesus.
He moved about freely with them in Jerusalem,
and spoke out boldly in the name of the Lord.
He also spoke and debated with the Hellenists,
but they tried to kill him.
And when the brothers learned of this,
they took him down to Caesarea
and sent him on his way to Tarsus.

The church throughout all Judea, Galilee, and Samaria was at peace.
It was being built up and walked in the fear of the Lord,
and with the consolation of the Holy Spirit it grew in numbers.

The word of the Lord. All: **Thanks be to God.**

Responsorial Psalm 22

Psalm 22:26-27, 28, 30, 31-32

℟. (26a) **I will praise you, Lord, in the assembly of your people.** *or:* ℟. **Alleluia.**

I will fulfill my vows before those who fear the LORD.

The lowly shall eat their fill;
they who seek the Lord shall praise him:
"May your hearts live forever!" ℟.

All the ends of the earth
shall remember and turn to the Lord;
all the families of the nations
shall bow down before him. ℟.

To him alone shall bow down
all who sleep in the earth;
before him shall bend
all who go down into the dust. ℟.

And to him my soul shall live;
my descendants shall serve him.
Let the coming generation be told of the Lord
that they may proclaim to a people yet to be born
the justice he has shown. ℟.

Reading II (1 John 3:18-24)

A reading from the first Letter of Saint John

This is his commandment: that we may believe and love.

Children, let us love not in word or speech
but in deed and truth.

Now this is how we shall know that we belong to the truth
and reassure our hearts before him
in whatever our hearts condemn,
for God is greater than our hearts and knows everything.
Beloved, if our hearts do not condemn us,
we have confidence in God
and receive from him whatever we ask,
because we keep his commandments and do what pleases him.
And his commandment is this:
we should believe in the name of his Son, Jesus Christ,
and love one another just as he commanded us.

Those who keep his commandments remain in him, and
he in them,
and the way we know that he remains in us
is from the Spirit he gave us.

The word of the Lord. All: **Thanks be to God.**

GOSPEL (John 15:1-8)

ALLELUIA (John 15:4a, 5b)

℣. Alleluia, alleluia. ℟. **Alleluia, alleluia.**
℣. Remain in me as I remain in you, says the Lord.
Whoever remains in me will bear much fruit. ℟.

✠ **A reading from the holy Gospel according to John**

All: **Glory to you, O Lord.**

Whoever remains in me and I in him will bear much fruit.

Jesus said to his disciples:
"I am the true vine, and my Father is the vine grower.
He takes away every branch in me that does not bear
fruit,
and every one that does he prunes so that it bears
more fruit.
You are already pruned because of the word that I spoke
to you.
Remain in me, as I remain in you.
Just as a branch cannot bear fruit on its own
unless it remains on the vine,
so neither can you unless you remain in me.
I am the vine, you are the branches.
Whoever remains in me and I in him will bear much
fruit,
because without me you can do nothing.
Anyone who does not remain in me
will be thrown out like a branch and wither;
people will gather them and throw them into a fire
and they will be burned.
If you remain in me and my words remain in you,
ask for whatever you want and it will be done for you.

**By this is my Father glorified,
that you bear much fruit and become my disciples."**

The Gospel of the Lord. All: **Praise to you, Lord Jesus Christ.**

Prayer over the Offerings

O God, who by the wonderful exchange effected in this sacrifice
have made us partakers of the one supreme Godhead,
grant, we pray,
that, as we have come to know your truth,
we may make it ours by a worthy way of life.
Through Christ our Lord. All: **Amen.**

Communion Antiphon (Cf. John 15:1, 5)

I am the true vine and you are the branches, says the Lord.
Whoever remains in me, and I in him, bears fruit in plenty,
alleluia.

Prayer after Communion

Graciously be present to your people, we pray, O Lord,
and lead those you have imbued with heavenly mysteries
to pass from former ways to newness of life.
Through Christ our Lord. All: **Amen.**

Sixth Sunday of Easter

May 2, 2027

Reflection on the Gospel

To be called a friend of Jesus is to be drawn into the very heart of divine love. Yet it also carries responsibility. Jesus immediately connects this new friendship with the commandment to love one another as he has loved us. Friendship with Christ is not a private privilege; it is the soil from which self-giving love must grow. We are chosen and appointed to bear fruit—fruit that will last—by living out that same sacrificial love that defined Jesus's life and death.

—Living Liturgy™, *Sixth Sunday of Easter 2027*

ENTRANCE ANTIPHON (Cf. Isaiah 48:20)

Proclaim a joyful sound and let it be heard;
proclaim to the ends of the earth:
The Lord has freed his people, alleluia.

COLLECT

Grant, almighty God,
that we may celebrate with heartfelt devotion these days of joy,
which we keep in honor of the risen Lord,
and that what we relive in remembrance
we may always hold to in what we do.
Through our Lord Jesus Christ, your Son,
who lives and reigns with you in the unity of the Holy Spirit,
God, for ever and ever. All: **Amen.**

When the Ascension of the Lord is celebrated the following Sunday, the second reading and Gospel from the Seventh Sunday of Easter (*see* nos. 59–61) may be read on the Sixth Sunday of Easter.

READING I (L 56-B)
(Acts of the Apostles 10:25-26, 34-35, 44-48)

A reading from the Acts of the Apostles

The gift of the Holy Spirit was poured out on the Gentiles also.

When Peter entered, Cornelius met him
and, falling at his feet, paid him homage.
Peter, however, raised him up, saying,
"Get up. I myself am also a human being."

Then Peter proceeded to speak and said,
"In truth, I see that God shows no partiality.
Rather, in every nation whoever fears him and acts uprightly
is acceptable to him."

While Peter was still speaking these things,
the Holy Spirit fell upon all who were listening to the word.
The circumcised believers who had accompanied Peter
were astounded that the gift of the Holy Spirit
should have been poured out on the Gentiles also,

for they could hear them speaking in tongues and glorifying God.
Then Peter responded,
"Can anyone withhold the water for baptizing these people,
who have received the Holy Spirit even as we have?"
He ordered them to be baptized in the name of Jesus Christ.

The word of the Lord. All: **Thanks be to God.**

Responsorial Psalm 98

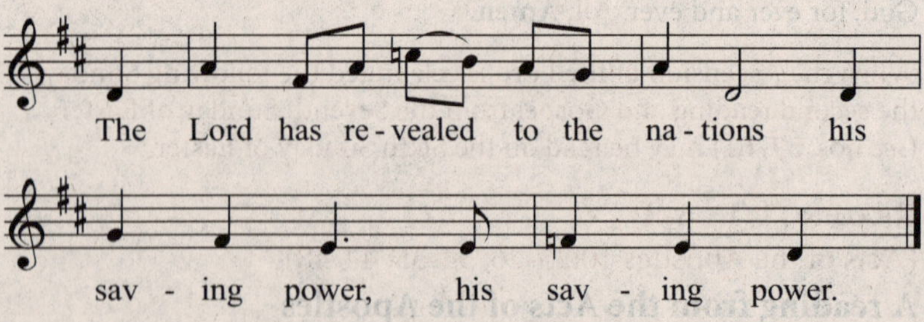

Psalm 98:1, 2-3, 3-4

℟. (cf. 2b) **The Lord has revealed to the nations his saving power.** *or:* ℟. **Alleluia.**

Sing to the LORD a new song,
for he has done wondrous deeds;
His right hand has won victory for him,
his holy arm. ℟.

The LORD has made his salvation known:
in the sight of the nations he has revealed his justice.
He has remembered his kindness and his faithfulness
toward the house of Israel. ℟.

All the ends of the earth have seen
the salvation by our God.
Sing joyfully to the LORD, all you lands;
break into song; sing praise. ℟.

READING II (1 John 4:7-10)

A reading from the first Letter of Saint John

God is love.

Beloved, let us love one another,
because love is of God;
everyone who loves is begotten by God and knows God.
Whoever is without love does not know God, for God is love.
In this way the love of God was revealed to us:
God sent his only Son into the world
so that we might have life through him.
In this is love:
not that we have loved God, but that he loved us
and sent his Son as expiation for our sins.

The word of the Lord. All: **Thanks be to God.**

GOSPEL (John 15:9-17)

ALLELUIA (John 14:23)

℣. Alleluia, alleluia. ℟. **Alleluia, alleluia.**
℣. Whoever loves me will keep my word, says the Lord,
and my Father will love him and we will come to him. ℟.

✠ **A reading from the holy Gospel according to John**

All: **Glory to you, O Lord.**

No one has greater love than this: to lay down one's life for one's friends.

Jesus said to his disciples:
"As the Father loves me, so I also love you.
Remain in my love.
If you keep my commandments, you will remain in my love,
just as I have kept my Father's commandments
and remain in his love.

"I have told you this so that my joy may be in you
and your joy might be complete.

This is my commandment: love one another as I love you.
No one has greater love than this,
to lay down one's life for one's friends.
You are my friends if you do what I command you.
I no longer call you slaves,
because a slave does not know what his master is doing.
I have called you friends,
because I have told you everything I have heard from my Father.
It was not you who chose me, but I who chose you
and appointed you to go and bear fruit that will remain,
so that whatever you ask the Father in my name he may give you.
This I command you: love one another."

The Gospel of the Lord. All: **Praise to you, Lord Jesus Christ.**

Prayer over the Offerings

May our prayers rise up to you, O Lord,
together with the sacrificial offerings,
so that, purified by your graciousness,
we may be conformed to the mysteries of your mighty love.
Through Christ our Lord. All: **Amen.**

Communion Antiphon (John 14:15-16)

If you love me, keep my commandments, says the Lord,
and I will ask the Father and he will send you another Paraclete,
to abide with you for ever, alleluia.

Prayer after Communion

Almighty ever-living God,
who restore us to eternal life in the Resurrection of Christ,
increase in us, we pray, the fruits of this paschal Sacrament
and pour into our hearts the strength of this saving food.
Through Christ our Lord. All: **Amen.**

The Ascension of the Lord

AT THE VIGIL MASS

May 5 or 8, 2027

This Mass is used on the evening of the day before the Solemnity, either before or after First Vespers (Evening Prayer I) of the Ascension.

Reflection on the Gospel

Jesus's death and resurrection earned for us a new life, but we're not there yet. His ascension shows us that where he has gone, we one day hope to follow—but not yet. "Already, not yet" is one of the often-overlooked paradoxes of our Christian faith. This odd in-between time can be hard to wrap our heads around. But isn't that the ultimate goal, as recited in the Creed every Sunday: the resurrection of the dead *and* the life of the world to come?

—Living Liturgy™, *The Ascension of the Lord 2027*

Entrance Antiphon (Psalm 68[67]:33, 35)

You kingdoms of the earth, sing to God;
praise the Lord, who ascends above the highest heavens;
his majesty and might are in the skies, alleluia.

Collect

O God, whose Son today ascended to the heavens
as the Apostles looked on,
grant, we pray, that, in accordance with his promise,
we may be worthy for him to live with us always on earth,
and we with him in heaven.
Who lives and reigns with you in the unity of the Holy Spirit,
God, for ever and ever. All: **Amen.**

(Readings are those of the day.)

Prayer over the Offerings

O God, whose Only Begotten Son, our High Priest,
is seated ever-living at your right hand to intercede for us,

grant that we may approach with confidence the throne of grace
and there obtain your mercy.
Through Christ our Lord. All: **Amen.**

Communion Antiphon (Cf. Hebrews 10:12)

Christ, offering a single sacrifice for sins,
is seated for ever at God's right hand, alleluia.

Prayer after Communion

May the gifts we have received from your altar, Lord,
kindle in our hearts a longing for the heavenly homeland
and cause us to press forward, following in the Savior's footsteps,
to the place where for our sake he entered before us.
Who lives and reigns for ever and ever. All: **Amen.**

May 6 or 9

AT THE MASS DURING THE DAY

If the feast of the Ascension is celebrated on the Seventh Sunday of Easter in your diocese, please turn to page 298 for the texts for today.

Entrance Antiphon (Acts of the Apostles 1:11)

Men of Galilee, why gaze in wonder at the heavens?
This Jesus whom you saw ascending into heaven
will return as you saw him go, alleluia.

Collect

Gladden us with holy joys, almighty God,
and make us rejoice with devout thanksgiving,
for the Ascension of Christ your Son
is our exaltation,
and, where the Head has gone before in glory,
the Body is called to follow in hope.
Through our Lord Jesus Christ, your Son,
who lives and reigns with you in the unity of the Holy Spirit,
God, for ever and ever. All: **Amen.**

Or:

Grant, we pray, almighty God,
that we, who believe that your Only Begotten Son, our Redeemer,
ascended this day to the heavens,
may in spirit dwell already in heavenly realms.
Who lives and reigns with you in the unity of the Holy Spirit,
God, for ever and ever. All: **Amen.**

Reading I (L 58-B) (Acts of the Apostles 1:1-11)

A reading from the beginning of the Acts of the Apostles

As the Apostles were looking on, Jesus was lifted up.

In the first book, Theophilus,
I dealt with all that Jesus did and taught
until the day he was taken up,
after giving instructions through the Holy Spirit
to the apostles whom he had chosen.
He presented himself alive to them
by many proofs after he had suffered,
appearing to them during forty days
and speaking about the kingdom of God.
While meeting with them,
he enjoined them not to depart from Jerusalem,
but to wait for "the promise of the Father
about which you have heard me speak;
for John baptized with water,
but in a few days you will be baptized with the Holy Spirit."

When they had gathered together they asked him,
"Lord, are you at this time going to restore the kingdom to Israel?"
He answered them, "It is not for you to know the times or seasons
that the Father has established by his own authority.
But you will receive power when the Holy Spirit comes upon you,
and you will be my witnesses in Jerusalem,
throughout Judea and Samaria,
and to the ends of the earth."
When he had said this, as they were looking on,
he was lifted up, and a cloud took him from their sight.
While they were looking intently at the sky as he was going,
suddenly two men dressed in white garments stood beside them.

They said, "Men of Galilee,
why are you standing there looking at the sky?
This Jesus who has been taken up from you into heaven
will return in the same way as you have seen him
going into heaven."

The word of the Lord. All: **Thanks be to God.**

Responsorial Psalm 47

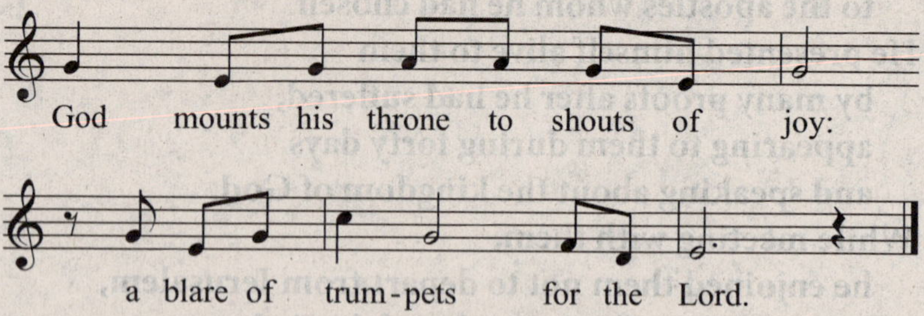

Psalm 47:2-3, 6-7, 8-9

℟. (6) **God mounts his throne to shouts of joy: a blare of trumpets for the Lord.** *or:* ℟. **Alleluia.**

All you peoples, clap your hands,
shout to God with cries of gladness.
For the Lord, the Most High, the awesome,
is the great king over all the earth. ℟.

God mounts his throne amid shouts of joy;
the Lord, amid trumpet blasts.
Sing praise to God, sing praise;
sing praise to our king, sing praise. ℟.

For king of all the earth is God;
sing hymns of praise.
God reigns over the nations,
God sits upon his holy throne. ℟.

READING II

A (Ephesians 1:17-23)

A reading from the Letter of Saint Paul to the Ephesians

God seated Jesus at his right hand in the heavens.

Brothers and sisters:
May the God of our Lord Jesus Christ, the Father of glory,
give you a Spirit of wisdom and revelation
resulting in knowledge of him.
May the eyes of your hearts be enlightened,
that you may know what is the hope that belongs to his call,
what are the riches of glory
in his inheritance among the holy ones,
and what is the surpassing greatness of his power
for us who believe,
in accord with the exercise of his great might,
which he worked in Christ,
raising him from the dead
and seating him at his right hand in the heavens,
far above every principality, authority, power, and dominion,
and every name that is named
not only in this age but also in the one to come.
And he put all things beneath his feet
and gave him as head over all things to the church,
which is his body,
the fullness of the one who fills all things in every way.

The word of the Lord. All: **Thanks be to God.**

Or:

B Longer Form (Ephesians 4:1-13) or *C* Shorter Form [ ] (Ephesians 4:1-7, 11-13)

A reading from the Letter of Saint Paul to the Ephesians

To the extent of the full stature of Christ.

[Brothers and sisters,
I, a prisoner for the Lord,
urge you to live in a manner worthy of the call
you have received,
with all humility and gentleness, with patience,
bearing with one another through love,
striving to preserve the unity of the Spirit
through the bond of peace:
one body and one Spirit,
as you were also called to the one hope of your call;
one Lord, one faith, one baptism;
one God and Father of all,
who is over all and through all and in all.

But grace was given to each of us
according to the measure of Christ's gift.]
Therefore, it says:
He ascended on high and took prisoners captive;
he gave gifts to men.
What does "he ascended" mean except that he also
descended
into the lower regions of the earth?
The one who descended is also the one who ascended
far above all the heavens,
that he might fill all things.

[And he gave some as apostles, others as prophets,
others as evangelists, others as pastors and teachers,
to equip the holy ones for the work of ministry,
for building up the body of Christ,
until we all attain to the unity of faith
and knowledge of the Son of God, to mature manhood,
to the extent of the full stature of Christ.]

The word of the Lord. All: **Thanks be to God.**

GOSPEL (Mark 16:15-20)

ALLELUIA (Matthew 28:19a, 20b)

℣. Alleluia, alleluia. ℟. **Alleluia, alleluia.**

℣. Go and teach all nations, says the Lord;
I am with you always, until the end of the world. ℟.

✠ **A reading from the holy Gospel according to Mark**

All: **Glory to you, O Lord.**

The Lord Jesus was taken up into heaven and took his seat at the right hand of God.

Jesus said to his disciples:
"Go into the whole world
and proclaim the gospel to every creature.
Whoever believes and is baptized will be saved;
whoever does not believe will be condemned.
These signs will accompany those who believe:
in my name they will drive out demons,
they will speak new languages.
They will pick up serpents with their hands,
and if they drink any deadly thing, it will not harm them.
They will lay hands on the sick, and they will recover."

So then the Lord Jesus, after he spoke to them,
was taken up into heaven
and took his seat at the right hand of God.
But they went forth and preached everywhere,
while the Lord worked with them
and confirmed the word through accompanying signs.

The Gospel of the Lord. All: **Praise to you, Lord Jesus Christ.**

PRAYER OVER THE OFFERINGS

We offer sacrifice now in supplication, O Lord,
to honor the wondrous Ascension of your Son:
grant, we pray,
that through this most holy exchange
we, too, may rise up to the heavenly realms.
Through Christ our Lord. All: **Amen.**

Communion Antiphon (Matthew 28:20)

Behold, I am with you always,
even to the end of the age, alleluia.

Prayer after Communion

Almighty ever-living God,
who allow those on earth to celebrate divine mysteries,
grant, we pray,
that Christian hope may draw us onward
to where our nature is united with you.
Through Christ our Lord. All: **Amen.**

Seventh Sunday of Easter

May 9, 2027

Reflection on the Gospel

The gospel today is indeed Jesus praying, as if a presider over his community. He asks his Father that "they may share my joy completely" and that he "keep them from the evil one." Not invoked by name in this pericope, Jesus had just spoken of the coming Advocate, and we may safely link the Holy Spirit to these prayers for joy, security, and unity. If we are to pray what we believe and believe what we pray, let us all give these orations the attention and intelligibility they need.

—Living Liturgy™, *Seventh Sunday of Easter 2027*

Entrance Antiphon (Cf. Psalm 27[26]:7-9)

O Lord, hear my voice, for I have called to you;
of you my heart has spoken: Seek his face;
hide not your face from me, alleluia.

Collect

Graciously hear our supplications, O Lord,
so that we, who believe that the Savior of the human race
is with you in your glory,
may experience, as he promised,

until the end of the world,
his abiding presence among us.
Who lives and reigns with you in the unity of the Holy Spirit,
God, for ever and ever. All: **Amen.**

In those places where the solemnity of the Ascension of the Lord has been transferred to the Seventh Sunday of Easter, the Mass and readings of the Ascension are used. *See* page 292.

READING I (L 60-B) (Acts of the Apostles 1:15-17, 20a, 20c-26)

A reading from the Acts of the Apostles

It is necessary that one of the men who accompanied us become with us a witness to the resurrection.

Peter stood up in the midst of the brothers
—there was a group of about one hundred and twenty persons
in the one place—.
He said, "My brothers,
the Scripture had to be fulfilled
which the Holy Spirit spoke beforehand
through the mouth of David, concerning Judas,
who was the guide for those who arrested Jesus.
He was numbered among us
and was allotted a share in this ministry.
"For it is written in the Book of Psalms:
May another take his office.

"Therefore, it is necessary that one of the men
who accompanied us the whole time
the Lord Jesus came and went among us,
beginning from the baptism of John
until the day on which he was taken up from us,
become with us a witness to his resurrection."
So they proposed two, Judas called Barsabbas,
who was also known as Justus, and Matthias.
Then they prayed,
"You, Lord, who know the hearts of all,
show which one of these two you have chosen

to take the place in this apostolic ministry
from which Judas turned away to go to his own place."
Then they gave lots to them, and the lot fell upon
Matthias,
and he was counted with the eleven apostles.

The word of the Lord. All: **Thanks be to God.**

RESPONSORIAL PSALM 103

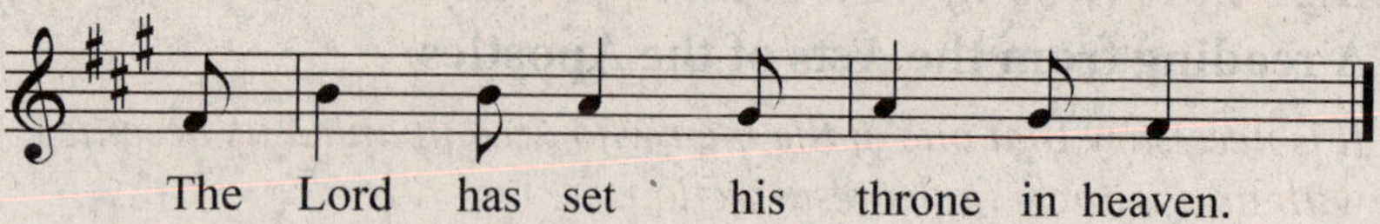

Psalm 103:1-2, 11-12, 19-20

℟. (19a) **The Lord has set his throne in heaven.**
or: ℟. **Alleluia.**

Bless the LORD, O my soul;
and all my being, bless his holy name.
Bless the LORD, O my soul,
and forget not all his benefits. ℟.

For as the heavens are high above the earth,
so surpassing is his kindness toward those who fear
him.
As far as the east is from the west,
so far has he put our transgressions from us. ℟.

The LORD has established his throne in heaven,
and his kingdom rules over all.
Bless the LORD, all you his angels,
you mighty in strength, who do his bidding. ℟.

READING II (1 John 4:11-16)

A reading from the first Letter of Saint John

Whoever remains in love, remains in God, and God in them.

Beloved, if God so loved us,
we also must love one another.
No one has ever seen God.

Yet, if we love one another, God remains in us,
and his love is brought to perfection in us.

This is how we know that we remain in him and he in us,
that he has given us of his Spirit.
Moreover, we have seen and testify
that the Father sent his Son as savior of the world.
Whoever acknowledges that Jesus is the Son of God,
God remains in him and he in God.
We have come to know and to believe in the love God has for us.

God is love, and whoever remains in love
remains in God and God in him.

The word of the Lord. All: **Thanks be to God.**

GOSPEL (John 17:11b-19)
ALLELUIA (*See* John 14:18)

℣. Alleluia, alleluia. ℟. **Alleluia, alleluia.**
℣. I will not leave you orphans, says the Lord.
I will come back to you, and your hearts will rejoice. ℟.

✠ **A reading from the holy Gospel according to John**

All: **Glory to you, O Lord.**

That they may be one just as we are one!

Lifting up his eyes to heaven, Jesus prayed, saying:
"Holy Father, keep them in your name that you have given me,
so that they may be one just as we are one.
When I was with them I protected them in your name that you gave me,
and I guarded them, and none of them was lost
except the son of destruction,
in order that the Scripture might be fulfilled.
But now I am coming to you.
I speak this in the world
so that they may share my joy completely.

I gave them your word, and the world hated them,
because they do not belong to the world
any more than I belong to the world.
I do not ask that you take them out of the world
but that you keep them from the evil one.
They do not belong to the world
any more than I belong to the world.
Consecrate them in the truth. Your word is truth.
As you sent me into the world,
so I sent them into the world.
And I consecrate myself for them,
so that they also may be consecrated in truth."

The Gospel of the Lord. All: **Praise to you, Lord Jesus Christ.**

Prayer over the Offerings

Accept, O Lord, the prayers of your faithful
with the sacrificial offerings,
that through these acts of devotedness
we may pass over to the glory of heaven.
Through Christ our Lord. All: **Amen.**

Communion Antiphon (John 17:22)

Father, I pray that they may be one
as we also are one, alleluia.

Prayer after Communion

Hear us, O God our Savior,
and grant us confidence,
that through these sacred mysteries
there will be accomplished in the body of the whole Church
what has already come to pass in Christ her Head.
Who lives and reigns for ever and ever. All: **Amen.**

Pentecost Sunday

VIGIL MASS Extended Form

May 15, 2027

Reflection on the Gospel

In this gospel for the Pentecost Vigil, we find not tongues of flame nor driving winds, but rather, "Rivers of living water" as the dominant image for the coming of the Holy Spirit. The image of flowing water is abundant across Scripture and uses water as a symbol of new life. The gift of the Holy Spirit, poured out upon the faithful, brings new life as well. It's intriguing, isn't it, that seemingly oppositional imagery, fire and water, can be used to embody the same Spirit!

—Living Liturgy™, *Vigil of Pentecost 2027*

The Mass of the Vigil of Pentecost is used on Saturday evening.

ENTRANCE ANTIPHON (Romans 5:5; cf. 8:11)

The love of God has been poured into our hearts
through the Spirit of God dwelling within us, alleluia.

COLLECT

Almighty ever-living God,
who willed the Paschal Mystery
to be encompassed as a sign in fifty days,
grant that from out of the scattered nations
the confusion of many tongues
may be gathered by heavenly grace
into one great confession of your name.
Through our Lord Jesus Christ, your Son,
who lives and reigns with you in the unity of the Holy Spirit,
God, for ever and ever. All: **Amen.**

Or:

Grant, we pray, almighty God,
that the splendor of your glory
may shine forth upon us
and that, by the bright rays of the Holy Spirit,
the light of your light may confirm the hearts
of those born again by your grace.

Through our Lord Jesus Christ, your Son,
who lives and reigns with you in the unity of the Holy Spirit,
God, for ever and ever. All: **Amen.**

In churches where the Simple Form of the Vigil Mass is celebrated one of the following first readings is used at Saturday Evening Mass celebrated either before or after Evening Prayer I of Pentecost Sunday. The Mass continues with Psalm 104 on page 313.

In churches where the Vigil Mass is celebrated in an Extended Form, before the Gloria the prayer *Grant, we pray, almighty God* above is said, followed by four readings from the Old Testament. Each reading may be followed with a psalm or a period of silence, after which all stand for a prayer led by the Priest. The Mass continues as usual with the Gloria, followed by the Collect *Almighty ever-living God* above. The readings with their proper Psalms are proclaimed in the following order:

Before the readings:

Dear brethren (brothers and sisters),
we have now begun our Pentecost Vigil,
after the example of the Apostles and disciples,
who with Mary, the Mother of Jesus, persevered in prayer,
awaiting the Spirit promised by the Lord;
like them, let us, too, listen with quiet hearts to the Word of God.
Let us meditate on how many great deeds
God in times past did for his people
and let us pray that the Holy Spirit,
whom the Father sent as the first fruits for those who believe,
may bring to perfection his work in the world.

READING I (L 62) *A* (Genesis 11:1-9)

A reading from the Book of Genesis

It was called Babel because there the LORD confused the speech of all the world.

The whole world spoke the same language, using the same words.
While the people were migrating in the east,
they came upon a valley in the land of Shinar and settled there.
They said to one another,
"Come, let us mold bricks and harden them with fire."

They used bricks for stone, and bitumen for mortar.
Then they said, "Come, let us build ourselves a city
and a tower with its top in the sky,
and so make a name for ourselves;
otherwise we shall be scattered all over the earth."

The Lord came down to see the city and the tower
that the people had built.
Then the Lord said: "If now, while they are one people,
all speaking the same language,
they have started to do this,
nothing will later stop them from doing whatever
they presume to do.
Let us then go down there and confuse their language,
so that one will not understand what another says."
Thus the Lord scattered them from there all over the
earth,
and they stopped building the city.
That is why it was called Babel,
because there the Lord confused the speech of all the
world.
It was from that place that he scattered them all over the
earth.

The word of the Lord. All: Thanks be to God.

Responsorial Psalm 33

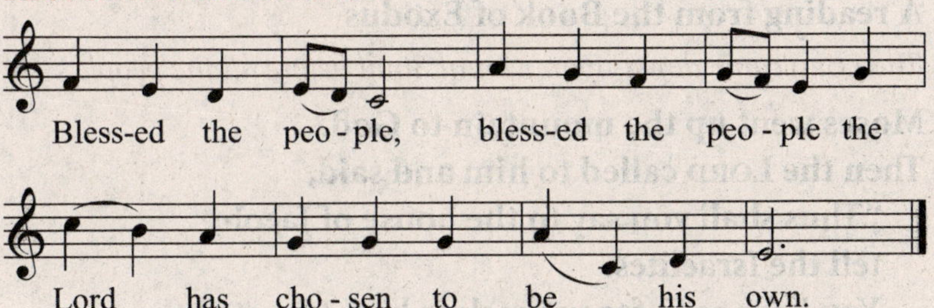

Psalm 33:10-11, 12-13, 14-15

℟. (12) **Blessed the people the Lord has chosen to be his own.**

The LORD brings to nought the plans of nations;
he foils the designs of peoples.
But the plan of the LORD stands forever;
the design of his heart, through all generations. ℟.

Blessed the nation whose God is the LORD,
the people he has chosen for his own inheritance.
From heaven the LORD looks down;
he sees all mankind. ℟.

From his fixed throne he beholds
all who dwell on the earth,
He who fashioned the heart of each,
he who knows all their works. ℟.

PRAYER

Let us pray.

Grant, we pray, almighty God,
that your Church may always remain that holy people,
formed as one by the unity of Father, Son and Holy Spirit,
which manifests to the world
the Sacrament of your holiness and unity
and leads it to the perfection of your charity.
Through Christ our Lord. All: **Amen.**

READING II (Exodus 19:3-8a, 16-20b)

A reading from the Book of Exodus

The LORD came down upon Mount Sinai before all the people.

Moses went up the mountain to God.
Then the LORD called to him and said,
"Thus shall you say to the house of Jacob;
tell the Israelites:
You have seen for yourselves how I treated the Egyptians
and how I bore you up on eagle wings
and brought you here to myself.

Therefore, if you hearken to my voice and keep my covenant,
you shall be my special possession,
dearer to me than all other people,
though all the earth is mine.
You shall be to me a kingdom of priests, a holy nation.
That is what you must tell the Israelites."
So Moses went and summoned the elders of the people.
When he set before them
all that the LORD had ordered him to tell them,
the people all answered together,
"Everything the LORD has said, we will do."

On the morning of the third day
there were peals of thunder and lightning,
and a heavy cloud over the mountain,
and a very loud trumpet blast,
so that all the people in the camp trembled.
But Moses led the people out of the camp to meet God,
and they stationed themselves at the foot of the mountain.
Mount Sinai was all wrapped in smoke,
for the LORD came down upon it in fire.
The smoke rose from it as though from a furnace,
and the whole mountain trembled violently.
The trumpet blast grew louder and louder, while Moses was speaking,
and God answering him with thunder.

When the LORD came down to the top of Mount Sinai,
he summoned Moses to the top of the mountain.

The word of the Lord. All: **Thanks be to God.**

Responsorial Psalm

Daniel 3:52, 53, 54, 55, 56

℟. (52b) **Glory and praise for ever!**

"Blessed are you, O Lord, the God of our fathers,
praiseworthy and exalted above all forever;
And blessed is your holy and glorious name,
praiseworthy and exalted above all for all ages." ℟.

"Blessed are you in the temple of your holy glory,
praiseworthy and glorious above all forever." ℟.

"Blessed are you on the throne of your Kingdom,
praiseworthy and exalted above all forever." ℟.

"Blessed are you who look into the depths
from your throne upon the cherubim,
praiseworthy and exalted above all forever." ℟.

"Blessed are you in the firmament of heaven,
praiseworthy and glorious forever." ℟.

Or:

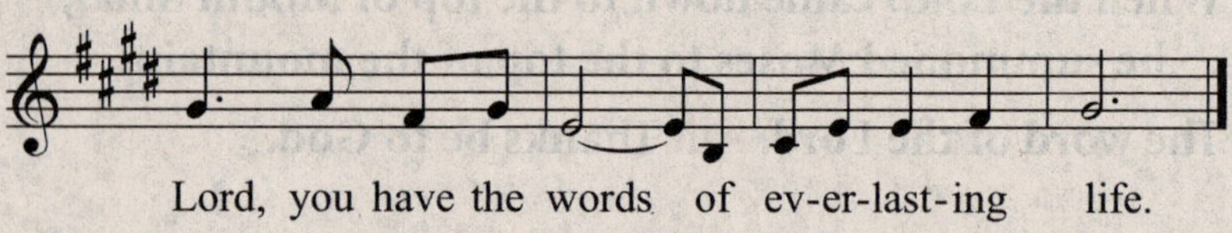

Psalm 19:8, 9, 10, 11

℟. (John 6:68c) **Lord, you have the words of everlasting life.**

The law of the LORD is perfect,
refreshing the soul;
The decree of the LORD is trustworthy,
giving wisdom to the simple. ℟.

The precepts of the LORD are right,
rejoicing the heart;
The command of the LORD is clear,
enlightening the eye. ℟.

The fear of the LORD is pure,
enduring forever;
The ordinances of the LORD are true,
all of them just. ℟.

They are more precious than gold,
than a heap of purest gold;
Sweeter also than syrup
or honey from the comb. ℟.

PRAYER

Let us pray.

O God, who in fire and lightning
gave the ancient Law to Moses on Mount Sinai
and on this day manifested the new covenant
in the fire of the Spirit,
grant, we pray,
that we may always be aflame with that same Spirit
whom you wondrously poured out on your Apostles,
and that the new Israel,
gathered from every people,
may receive with rejoicing
the eternal commandment of your love.
Through Christ our Lord. All: **Amen.**

READING III (Ezekiel 37:1-14)

A reading from the Book of the Prophet Ezekiel

Dry bones of Israel, I will bring spirit into you, that you may come to life.

The hand of the LORD came upon me,
and he led me out in the spirit of the LORD
and set me in the center of the plain,
which was now filled with bones.
He made me walk among the bones in every direction
so that I saw how many they were on the surface of the plain.
How dry they were!
He asked me:
Son of man, can these bones come to life?
I answered, "Lord GOD, you alone know that."
Then he said to me:
Prophesy over these bones, and say to them:
Dry bones, hear the word of the LORD!
Thus says the Lord GOD to these bones:
See! I will bring spirit into you, that you may come to life.
I will put sinews upon you, make flesh grow over you,
cover you with skin, and put spirit in you
so that you may come to life and know that I am the LORD.
I, Ezekiel, prophesied as I had been told,
and even as I was prophesying I heard a noise;
it was a rattling as the bones came together, bone joining bone.
I saw the sinews and the flesh come upon them,
and the skin cover them, but there was no spirit in them.
Then the LORD said to me:
Prophesy to the spirit, prophesy, son of man,
and say to the spirit: Thus says the Lord GOD:
From the four winds come, O spirit,
and breathe into these slain that they may come to life.
I prophesied as he told me, and the spirit came into them;
they came alive and stood upright, a vast army.

Then he said to me:
Son of man, these bones are the whole house of Israel.
They have been saying,
"Our bones are dried up,
our hope is lost, and we are cut off."
Therefore, prophesy and say to them: Thus says the Lord God:
O my people, I will open your graves
and have you rise from them,
and bring you back to the land of Israel.
Then you shall know that I am the Lord,
when I open your graves and have you rise from them,
O my people!
I will put my spirit in you that you may live,
and I will settle you upon your land;
thus you shall know that I am the Lord.
I have promised, and I will do it, says the Lord.

The word of the Lord. All: **Thanks be to God.**

Responsorial Psalm 107

The response is preferably sung twice each time.

Psalm 107:2-3, 4-5, 6-7, 8-9

℟. (1) **Give thanks to the Lord; his love is everlasting.**
or: ℟. **Alleluia.**

Let the redeemed of the Lord say,
those whom he has redeemed from the hand of the foe
And gathered from the lands,
from the east and the west, from the north and the south. ℟.

(continued)

They went astray in the desert wilderness;
the way to an inhabited city they did not find.
Hungry and thirsty,
their life was wasting away within them. ℟.

They cried to the Lord in their distress;
from their straits he rescued them.
And he led them by a direct way
to reach an inhabited city. ℟.

Let them give thanks to the Lord for his mercy
and his wondrous deeds to the children of men,
Because he satisfied the longing soul
and filled the hungry soul with good things. ℟.

Prayer

Let us pray.

Lord, God of power,
who restore what has fallen
and preserve what you have restored,
increase, we pray, the peoples
to be renewed by the sanctification of your name,
that all who are washed clean by holy Baptism
may always be directed by your prompting.
Through Christ our Lord. All: **Amen.**

Or:

O God, who have brought us to rebirth by the word of life,
pour out upon us your Holy Spirit,
that, walking in oneness of faith,
we may attain in our flesh
the incorruptible glory of the resurrection.
Through Christ our Lord. All: **Amen.**

Or:

May your people exult for ever, O God,
in renewed youthfulness of spirit,
so that, rejoicing now in the restored glory of our adoption,
we may look forward in confident hope
to the rejoicing of the day of resurrection.
Through Christ our Lord. All: **Amen.**

Reading IV (Joel 3:1-5)

A reading from the Book of the Prophet Joel

I will pour out my spirit upon the servants and handmaids.

Thus says the Lord:
I will pour out my spirit upon all flesh.
Your sons and daughters shall prophesy,
your old men shall dream dreams,
your young men shall see visions;
even upon the servants and the handmaids,
in those days, I will pour out my spirit.
And I will work wonders in the heavens and on the earth,
blood, fire, and columns of smoke;
the sun will be turned to darkness,
and the moon to blood,
at the coming of the day of the Lord,
the great and terrible day.
Then everyone shall be rescued
who calls on the name of the Lord;
for on Mount Zion there shall be a remnant,
as the Lord has said,
and in Jerusalem survivors
whom the Lord shall call.

The word of the Lord. All: **Thanks be to God.**

Responsorial Psalm 104

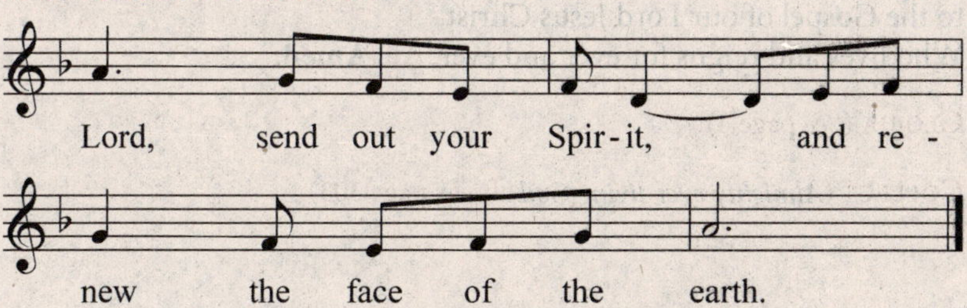

Psalm 104:1-2, 24, 35, 27-28, 29, 30

℟. (*See* 30) **Lord, send out your Spirit, and renew the face of the earth.** *or:* ℟. **Alleluia.**

Bless the LORD, O my soul!
O LORD, my God, you are great indeed!
You are clothed with majesty and glory,
robed in light as with a cloak. ℟.

How manifold are your works, O LORD!
In wisdom you have wrought them all—
the earth is full of your creatures;
bless the LORD, O my soul! Alleluia. ℟.

Creatures all look to you
to give them food in due time.
When you give it to them, they gather it;
when you open your hand, they are filled with good things. ℟.

If you take away their breath, they perish
and return to their dust.
When you send forth your spirit, they are created,
and you renew the face of the earth. ℟.

PRAYER

Let us pray.

Fulfill for us your gracious promise,
O Lord, we pray, so that by his coming
the Holy Spirit may make us witnesses before the world
to the Gospel of our Lord Jesus Christ.
Who lives and reigns for ever and ever. All: **Amen.**

GLORIA (*See* page 4).

COLLECT (*Almighty ever-living God* above, page 303).

EPISTLE (Romans 8:22-27)

A reading from the Letter of Saint Paul to the Romans

The Spirit intercedes with inexpressible groanings.

Brothers and sisters:
We know that all creation is groaning in labor pains
even until now;
and not only that, but we ourselves,
who have the firstfruits of the Spirit,
we also groan within ourselves
as we wait for adoption, the redemption of our bodies.
For in hope we were saved.
Now hope that sees is not hope.
For who hopes for what one sees?
But if we hope for what we do not see, we wait with
endurance.

In the same way, the Spirit too comes to the aid of our
weakness;
for we do not know how to pray as we ought,
but the Spirit himself intercedes with inexpressible
groanings.
And the one who searches hearts
knows what is the intention of the Spirit,
because he intercedes for the holy ones
according to God's will.

The word of the Lord. All: **Thanks be to God.**

GOSPEL (John 7:37-39)

ALLELUIA

℣. Alleluia, alleluia. ℟. **Alleluia, alleluia.**
℣. Come, Holy Spirit, fill the hearts of your faithful
and kindle in them the fire of your love. ℟.

✠ **A reading from the holy Gospel according to John**

All: **Glory to you, O Lord.**

Rivers of living water will flow.

On the last and greatest day of the feast,
Jesus stood up and exclaimed,
"Let anyone who thirsts come to me and drink.
As Scripture says:
***Rivers of living water will flow from within him* who believes in me."**

He said this in reference to the Spirit
that those who came to believe in him were to receive.
There was, of course, no Spirit yet,
because Jesus had not yet been glorified.

The Gospel of the Lord. All: **Praise to you, Lord Jesus Christ.**

Prayer over the Offerings

Pour out upon these gifts the blessing of your Spirit,
we pray, O Lord,
so that through them your Church may be imbued with such love
that the truth of your saving mystery
may shine forth for the whole world.
Through Christ our Lord. All: **Amen.**

Communion Antiphon (John 7:37)

On the last day of the festival, Jesus stood and cried out:
If anyone is thirsty, let him come to me and drink, alleluia.

Prayer after Communion

May these gifts we have consumed
benefit us, O Lord,
that we may always be aflame with the same Spirit,
whom you wondrously poured out on your Apostles.
Through Christ our Lord. All: **Amen.**

Pentecost

MASS DURING THE DAY

May 16, 2027

Reflection on the Gospel

Just before receiving the Spirit, those who have until then been hiding in the Upper Room are sent on mission. The first specific directive is about the forgiveness of sins—or alternatively, the withholding of that forgiveness. This is the start of a new way of life for humanity. That new life begins with reconciliation, the healing of broken relationships, and the Holy Spirit empowers the disciples to extend resurrection life by offering forgiveness. Just as Jesus's resurrection overcomes death, the Spirit overcomes sin.

—Living Liturgy™, *Pentecost Sunday 2027*

ENTRANCE ANTIPHON (Wisdom 1:7)

The Spirit of the Lord has filled the whole world
and that which contains all things
understands what is said, alleluia.

Or:

(Romans 5:5; cf. 8:11)

The love of God has been poured into our hearts
through the Spirit of God dwelling within us, alleluia.

COLLECT

O God, who by the mystery of today's great feast
sanctify your whole Church in every people and nation,
pour out, we pray, the gifts of the Holy Spirit
across the face of the earth
and, with the divine grace that was at work
when the Gospel was first proclaimed,
fill now once more the hearts of believers.
Through our Lord Jesus Christ, your Son,
who lives and reigns with you in the unity of the Holy Spirit,
God, for ever and ever. All: **Amen.**

READING I (L 63) (Acts of the Apostles 2:1-11)

A reading from the Acts of the Apostles

They were all filled with the Holy Spirit and began to speak.

When the time for Pentecost was fulfilled,
they were all in one place together.
And suddenly there came from the sky
a noise like a strong driving wind,
and it filled the entire house in which they were.
Then there appeared to them tongues as of fire,
which parted and came to rest on each one of them.
And they were all filled with the Holy Spirit
and began to speak in different tongues,
as the Spirit enabled them to proclaim.

Now there were devout Jews from every nation under heaven staying in Jerusalem.
At this sound, they gathered in a large crowd,
but they were confused
because each one heard them speaking in his own language.
They were astounded, and in amazement they asked,
"Are not all these people who are speaking Galileans?
Then how does each of us hear them in his native language?
We are Parthians, Medes, and Elamites,
inhabitants of Mesopotamia, Judea and Cappadocia,
Pontus and Asia, Phrygia and Pamphylia,
Egypt and the districts of Libya near Cyrene,
as well as travelers from Rome,
both Jews and converts to Judaism, Cretans and Arabs,
yet we hear them speaking in our own tongues
of the mighty acts of God."

The word of the Lord. All: **Thanks be to God.**

Responsorial Psalm 104

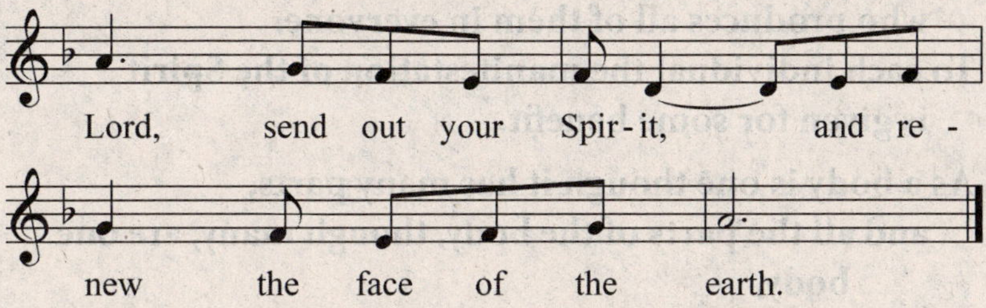

Psalm 104:1, 24, 29-30, 31, 34

℟. (*See* 30) **Lord, send out your Spirit, and renew the face of the earth.** *or:* ℟. **Alleluia.**

Bless the Lord, O my soul!
O Lord, my God, you are great indeed!
How manifold are your works, O Lord!
The earth is full of your creatures. ℟.

If you take away their breath, they perish
and return to their dust.
When you send forth your spirit, they are created,
and you renew the face of the earth. ℟.

May the glory of the Lord endure forever;
may the Lord be glad in his works!
Pleasing to him be my theme;
I will be glad in the Lord. ℟.

Reading II

A (1 Corinthians 12:3b-7, 12-13)

A reading from the first Letter of Saint Paul to the Corinthians

In one Spirit we were all baptized into one body.

Brothers and sisters:
No one can say, "Jesus is Lord," except by the Holy Spirit.

There are different kinds of spiritual gifts but the same Spirit;
there are different forms of service but the same Lord;

there are different workings but the same God
who produces all of them in everyone.
To each individual the manifestation of the Spirit
is given for some benefit.

As a body is one though it has many parts,
and all the parts of the body, though many, are one body,
so also Christ.
For in one Spirit we were all baptized into one body,
whether Jews or Greeks, slaves or free persons,
and we were all given to drink of one Spirit.

The word of the Lord. All: **Thanks be to God.**

Or:

B (Galatians 5:16-25)

A reading from the Letter of Saint Paul to the Galatians

The fruit of the Spirit.

Brothers and sisters, live by the Spirit
and you will certainly not gratify the desire of the flesh.
For the flesh has desires against the Spirit,
and the Spirit against the flesh;
these are opposed to each other,
so that you may not do what you want.
But if you are guided by the Spirit, you are not under the law.
Now the works of the flesh are obvious:
immorality, impurity, lust, idolatry,
sorcery, hatreds, rivalry, jealousy,
outbursts of fury, acts of selfishness,
dissensions, factions, occasions of envy,
drinking bouts, orgies, and the like.
I warn you, as I warned you before,
that those who do such things will not inherit the kingdom of God.

In contrast, the fruit of the Spirit is love, joy, peace,
patience, kindness, generosity,
faithfulness, gentleness, self-control.
Against such there is no law.
Now those who belong to Christ Jesus have crucified
their flesh
with its passions and desires.
If we live in the Spirit, let us also follow the Spirit.

The word of the Lord. All: **Thanks be to God.**

SEQUENCE
Veni, Sancte Spiritus

Come, Holy Spirit, come!
And from your celestial home
Shed a ray of light divine!
Come, Father of the poor!
Come, source of all our store!
Come, within our bosoms shine.
You, of comforters the best;
You, the soul's most welcome guest;
Sweet refreshment here below;
In our labor, rest most sweet;
Grateful coolness in the heat;
Solace in the midst of woe.
O most blessed Light divine,
Shine within these hearts of yours,
And our inmost being fill!
Where you are not, we have naught,
Nothing good in deed or thought,
Nothing free from taint of ill.
Heal our wounds, our strength renew;
On our dryness pour your dew;
Wash the stains of guilt away:
Bend the stubborn heart and will;
Melt the frozen, warm the chill;
Guide the steps that go astray.

On the faithful, who adore
And confess you, evermore
In your sevenfold gift descend;
Give them virtue's sure reward;
Give them your salvation, Lord;
Give them joys that never end. Amen.
Alleluia.

Gospel

Alleluia

℣. Alleluia, alleluia. ℟. **Alleluia, alleluia.**
℣. Come, Holy Spirit, fill the hearts of your faithful
and kindle in them the fire of your love. ℟.

A (John 20:19-23)

✠ **A reading from the holy Gospel according to John**

All: **Glory to you, O Lord.**

As the Father sent me, so I send you: Receive the Holy Spirit.

On the evening of that first day of the week,
when the doors were locked, where the disciples were,
for fear of the Jews,
Jesus came and stood in their midst
and said to them, "Peace be with you."
When he had said this, he showed them his hands and his side.
The disciples rejoiced when they saw the Lord.
Jesus said to them again, "Peace be with you.
As the Father has sent me, so I send you."
And when he had said this, he breathed on them and said to them,
"Receive the Holy Spirit.
Whose sins you forgive are forgiven them,
and whose sins you retain are retained."

The Gospel of the Lord. All: **Praise to you, Lord Jesus Christ.**

Or:

B (John 15:26-27; 16:12-15)

✠ A reading from the holy Gospel according to John

All: **Glory to you, O Lord.**

The Spirit of truth will guide you to all the truth.

Jesus said to his disciples:
"When the Advocate comes whom I will send you
from the Father,
the Spirit of truth that proceeds from the Father,
he will testify to me.
And you also testify,
because you have been with me from the beginning.

"I have much more to tell you, but you cannot bear it now.
But when he comes, the Spirit of truth,
he will guide you to all truth.
He will not speak on his own,
but he will speak what he hears,
and will declare to you the things that are coming.
He will glorify me,
because he will take from what is mine and declare it
to you.
Everything that the Father has is mine;
for this reason I told you that he will take from what
is mine
and declare it to you."

The Gospel of the Lord. All: **Praise to you, Lord Jesus Christ.**

If it is customary or obligatory for the faithful to attend Mass on the Monday or even the Tuesday after Pentecost, the readings from the Mass of Pentecost Sunday may be repeated or the readings of the Ritual Mass for Confirmation, nos. 764–768, may be used in its place.

Prayer over the Offerings

Grant, we pray, O Lord,
that, as promised by your Son,
the Holy Spirit may reveal to us more abundantly
the hidden mystery of this sacrifice
and graciously lead us into all truth.
Through Christ our Lord. All: **Amen.**

Communion Antiphon (Acts of the Apostles 2:4, 11)

They were all filled with the Holy Spirit
and spoke of the marvels of God, alleluia.

Prayer after Communion

O God, who bestow heavenly gifts upon your Church,
safeguard, we pray, the grace you have given,
that the gift of the Holy Spirit poured out upon her
may retain all its force
and that this spiritual food
may gain her abundance of eternal redemption.
Through Christ our Lord. All: **Amen.**

Dismissal

To dismiss the people the Deacon or, if there is no Deacon, the Priest himself sings or says:

Go forth, the Mass is ended, alleluia, alleluia.

Or:

Go in peace, alleluia, alleluia.

All reply: **Thanks be to God, alleluia, alleluia.**

The Most Holy Trinity

May 23, 2027

Reflection on the Gospel

Today's solemnity, in a way, could be seen as the "Solemnity of Who God Is, Not What God Does." Of course, what God has accomplished for us across salvation history is important, to dramatically understate things. We would be wise, however, to avoid naming God, especially the three persons, by titles of actions or accomplishments. We must rather recall that the persons of the Trinity are not defined by what they do, but only who they are: each God, related to but not the other two persons.

—Living Liturgy™, *The Most Holy Trinity 2027*

Entrance Antiphon

Blest be God the Father,
and the Only Begotten Son of God,
and also the Holy Spirit,
for he has shown us his merciful love.

Collect

God our Father, who by sending into the world
the Word of truth and the Spirit of sanctification
made known to the human race your wondrous mystery,
grant us, we pray, that in professing the true faith,
we may acknowledge the Trinity of eternal glory
and adore your Unity, powerful in majesty.
Through our Lord Jesus Christ, your Son,
who lives and reigns with you in the unity of the Holy Spirit,
God, for ever and ever. All: **Amen.**

Reading I (L 165-B) (Deuteronomy 4:32-34, 39-40)

A reading from the Book of Deuteronomy

The Lord is God in the heavens above and on earth below and there is no other.

Moses said to the people:
"Ask now of the days of old, before your time,
ever since God created man upon the earth;
ask from one end of the sky to the other:
Did anything so great ever happen before?
Was it ever heard of?
Did a people ever hear the voice of God
speaking from the midst of fire, as you did, and live?
Or did any god venture to go and take a nation for himself
from the midst of another nation,
by testings, by signs and wonders, by war,
with strong hand and outstretched arm, and by great terrors,
all of which the Lord, your God,
did for you in Egypt before your very eyes?
This is why you must now know,
and fix in your heart, that the Lord is God
in the heavens above and on earth below,
and that there is no other.
You must keep his statutes and commandments that I enjoin on you today,
that you and your children after you may prosper,
and that you may have long life on the land
which the Lord, your God, is giving you forever."
The word of the Lord. All: **Thanks be to God.**

Responsorial Psalm 33

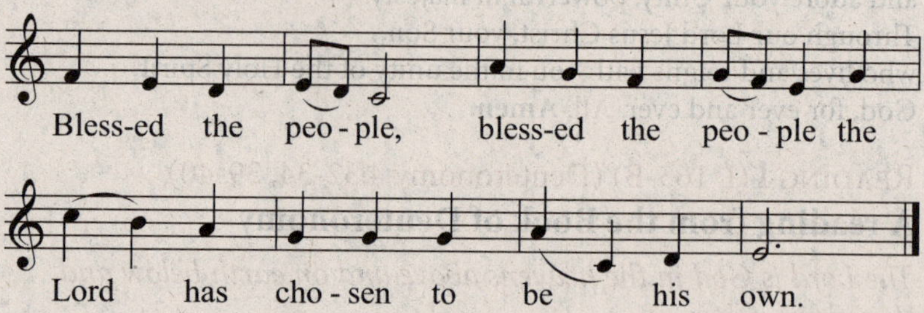

Psalm 33:4-5, 6, 9, 18-19, 20, 22

℟. (12b) **Blessed the people the Lord has chosen to be his own.**

Upright is the word of the Lord,
and all his works are trustworthy.
He loves justice and right;
of the kindness of the Lord the earth is full. ℟.

By the word of the Lord the heavens were made;
by the breath of his mouth all their host.
For he spoke, and it was made;
he commanded, and it stood forth. ℟.

See, the eyes of the Lord are upon those who fear him,
upon those who hope for his kindness,
to deliver them from death
and preserve them in spite of famine. ℟.

Our soul waits for the Lord,
who is our help and our shield.
May your kindness, O Lord, be upon us
who have put our hope in you. ℟.

Reading II (Romans 8:14-17)

A reading from the Letter of Saint Paul to the Romans

You received a Spirit of adoption, through whom we cry, "Abba, Father!"

Brothers and sisters:
Those who are led by the Spirit of God are sons of God.
For you did not receive a spirit of slavery to fall back into fear,
but you received a Spirit of adoption,
through whom we cry, "Abba, Father!"
The Spirit himself bears witness with our spirit
that we are children of God,
and if children, then heirs,
heirs of God and joint heirs with Christ,
if only we suffer with him
so that we may also be glorified with him.

The word of the Lord. All: **Thanks be to God.**

Gospel (Matthew 28:16-20)

Alleluia (Revelation 1:8)

℣. Alleluia, alleluia. ℟. **Alleluia, alleluia.**

℣. Glory to the Father, the Son, and the Holy Spirit;
to God who is, who was, and who is to come. ℟.

✠ **A reading from the holy Gospel according to Matthew**

All: **Glory to you, O Lord.**

Baptizing them in the name of the Father, and of the Son, and of the Holy Spirit.

The eleven disciples went to Galilee,
to the mountain to which Jesus had ordered them.
When they all saw him, they worshiped, but they doubted.
Then Jesus approached and said to them,
"All power in heaven and on earth has been given to me.
Go, therefore, and make disciples of all nations,
baptizing them in the name of the Father,
and of the Son, and of the Holy Spirit,
teaching them to observe all that I have commanded you.
And behold, I am with you always, until the end of the age."

The Gospel of the Lord. All: **Praise to you, Lord Jesus Christ.**

Prayer over the Offerings

Sanctify by the invocation of your name,
we pray, O Lord our God,
this oblation of our service,
and by it make of us an eternal offering to you.
Through Christ our Lord. All: **Amen.**

Communion Antiphon (Galatians 4:6)

Since you are children of God,
God has sent into your hearts the Spirit of his Son,
the Spirit who cries out: Abba, Father.

Prayer after Communion

May receiving this Sacrament, O Lord our God,
bring us health of body and soul,
as we confess your eternal holy Trinity and undivided Unity.
Through Christ our Lord. All: **Amen.**

The Most Holy Body and Blood of Christ (Corpus Christi)

May 30, 2027

Reflection on the Gospel

*Many of us are familiar with the expression "source and summit of our faith." This expression draws from the Vatican II Constitution on the Church, notably regarding the faithful: "Taking part in the Eucharistic sacrifice, the source and summit of the Christian life, [the faithful] offer the divine victim to God and themselves along with him" (*Lumen Gentium *11). This quote refers specifically to taking part in the eucharistic sacrifice—that is, the whole of Mass, not just the consumption of the host.*

—Living Liturgy™, *The Most Holy Body and Blood of Christ 2027*

ENTRANCE ANTIPHON (Cf. Psalm 81[80]:17)

He fed them with the finest wheat
and satisfied them with honey from the rock.

COLLECT

O God, who in this wonderful Sacrament
have left us a memorial of your Passion,
grant us, we pray,
so to revere the sacred mysteries of your Body and Blood
that we may always experience in ourselves
the fruits of your redemption.
Who live and reign with God the Father
in the unity of the Holy Spirit,
God, for ever and ever. All: **Amen.**

READING I (L 168-B) (Exodus 24:3-8)

A reading from the Book of Exodus

This is the blood of the covenant that the Lord has made with you.

When Moses came to the people
and related all the words and ordinances of the LORD,
they all answered with one voice,
"We will do everything that the LORD has told us."
Moses then wrote down all the words of the LORD and,
rising early the next day,
he erected at the foot of the mountain an altar
and twelve pillars for the twelve tribes of Israel.
Then, having sent certain young men of the Israelites
to offer holocausts and sacrifice young bulls
as peace offerings to the LORD,
Moses took half of the blood and put it in large bowls;
the other half he splashed on the altar.
Taking the book of the covenant, he read it aloud to the people,
who answered, "All that the LORD has said, we will heed and do."
Then he took the blood and sprinkled it on the people, saying,
"This is the blood of the covenant
that the LORD has made with you
in accordance with all these words of his."

The word of the Lord. All: **Thanks be to God.**

RESPONSORIAL PSALM 116

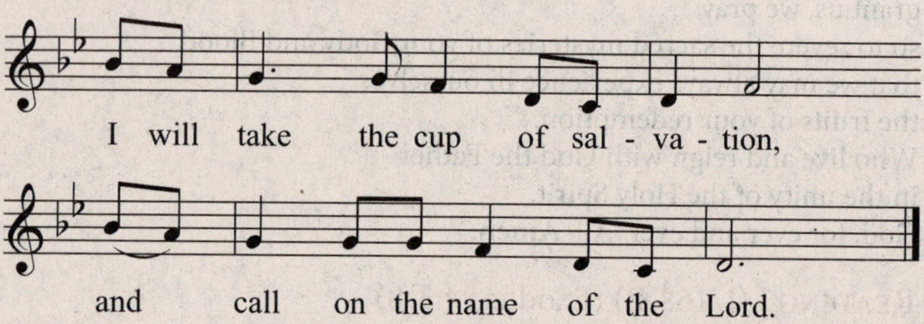

Psalm 116:12-13, 15-16, 17-18

℟. (13) **I will take the cup of salvation, and call on the name of the Lord.** *or:* ℟. **Alleluia.**

How shall I make a return to the LORD
for all the good he has done for me?
The cup of salvation I will take up,
and I will call upon the name of the LORD. ℟.

Precious in the eyes of the LORD
is the death of his faithful ones.
I am your servant, the son of your handmaid;
you have loosed my bonds. ℟.

To you will I offer sacrifice of thanksgiving,
and I will call upon the name of the LORD.
My vows to the LORD I will pay
in the presence of all his people. ℟.

READING II (Hebrews 9:11-15)

A reading from the Letter to the Hebrews

The blood of Christ will cleanse our consciences.

Brothers and sisters:
When Christ came as high priest
of the good things that have come to be,
passing through the greater and more perfect tabernacle
not made by hands, that is, not belonging to this creation,
he entered once for all into the sanctuary,
not with the blood of goats and calves
but with his own blood, thus obtaining eternal redemption.
For if the blood of goats and bulls
and the sprinkling of a heifer's ashes
can sanctify those who are defiled
so that their flesh is cleansed,
how much more will the blood of Christ,

who through the eternal Spirit offered himself
unblemished to God,
cleanse our consciences from dead works
to worship the living God.

For this reason he is mediator of a new covenant:
since a death has taken place for deliverance
from transgressions under the first covenant,
those who are called may receive the promised eternal
inheritance.

The word of the Lord. All: **Thanks be to God.**

SEQUENCE
Lauda Sion

The sequence *Laud, O Zion (Lauda Sion),* or the shorter form beginning with the verse *Lo! the angel's food is given,* may be sung optionally before the Alleluia.

Laud, O Zion, your salvation,
Laud with hymns of exultation,
Christ, your king and shepherd true:

Bring him all the praise you know,
He is more than you bestow.
Never can you reach his due.

Special theme for glad thanksgiving
Is the quick'ning and the living
Bread today before you set:

From his hands of old partaken,
As we know, by faith unshaken,
Where the Twelve at supper met.

Full and clear ring out your chanting,
Joy nor sweetest grace be wanting,
From your heart let praises burst:

For today the feast is holden,
When the institution olden
Of that supper was rehearsed.

Here the new law's new oblation,
By the new king's revelation,
Ends the form of ancient rite:

Now the new the old effaces,
Truth away the shadow chases,
Light dispels the gloom of night.

What he did at supper seated,
Christ ordained to be repeated,
His memorial ne'er to cease:

And his rule for guidance taking,
Bread and wine we hallow, making
Thus our sacrifice of peace.

This the truth each Christian learns,
Bread into his flesh he turns,
To his precious blood the wine:

Sight has fail'd, nor thought conceives,
But a dauntless faith believes,
Resting on a pow'r divine.

Here beneath these signs are hidden
Priceless things to sense forbidden;
Signs, not things are all we see:

Blood is poured and flesh is broken,
Yet in either wondrous token
Christ entire we know to be.

Whoso of this food partakes,
Does not rend the Lord nor breaks;
Christ is whole to all that taste:

Thousands are, as one, receivers,
One, as thousands of believers,
Eats of him who cannot waste.

Bad and good the feast are sharing,
Of what divers dooms preparing,
Endless death, or endless life.

Life to these, to those damnation,
See how like participation
Is with unlike issues rife.

When the sacrament is broken,
Doubt not, but believe 'tis spoken,
That each sever'd outward token
doth the very whole contain.

Nought the precious gift divides,
Breaking but the sign betides
Jesus still the same abides,
still unbroken does remain.

The shorter form of the sequence begins here.

Lo! the angel's food is given
To the pilgrim who has striven;
See the children's bread from heaven,
which on dogs may not be spent.

Truth the ancient types fulfilling,
Isaac bound, a victim willing,
Paschal lamb, its lifeblood spilling,
manna to the fathers sent.

Very bread, good shepherd, tend us,
Jesu, of your love befriend us,
You refresh us, you defend us,
Your eternal goodness send us
In the land of life to see.

You who all things can and know,
Who on earth such food bestow,
Grant us with your saints, though lowest,
Where the heav'nly feast you show,
Fellow heirs and guests to be. Amen. Alleluia.

GOSPEL (Mark 14:12-16, 22-26)

ALLELUIA (John 6:51)

℣. Alleluia, alleluia. ℟. **Alleluia, alleluia.**

℣. I am the living bread that came down from heaven,
says the Lord;
whoever eats this bread will live forever. ℟.

✠ **A reading from the holy Gospel according to Mark**

All: **Glory to you, O Lord.**

This is my body. This is my blood.

On the first day of the Feast of Unleavened Bread,
when they sacrificed the Passover lamb,
Jesus' disciples said to him,
"Where do you want us to go
and prepare for you to eat the Passover?"
He sent two of his disciples and said to them,
"Go into the city and a man will meet you,
carrying a jar of water.
Follow him.
Wherever he enters, say to the master of the house,
'The Teacher says, "Where is my guest room
where I may eat the Passover with my disciples?"'
Then he will show you a large upper room furnished and ready.
Make the preparations for us there."
The disciples then went off, entered the city,
and found it just as he had told them;
and they prepared the Passover.

While they were eating,
he took bread, said the blessing,
broke it, gave it to them, and said,
"Take it; this is my body."
Then he took a cup, gave thanks, and gave it to them,
and they all drank from it.

He said to them,
"This is my blood of the covenant,
which will be shed for many.
Amen, I say to you,
I shall not drink again the fruit of the vine
until the day when I drink it new in the kingdom of God."
Then, after singing a hymn,
they went out to the Mount of Olives.

The Gospel of the Lord. All: **Praise to you, Lord Jesus Christ.**

PRAYER OVER THE OFFERINGS

Grant your Church, O Lord, we pray,
the gifts of unity and peace,
whose signs are to be seen in mystery
in the offerings we here present.
Through Christ our Lord. All: **Amen.**

COMMUNION ANTIPHON (John 6:57)

Whoever eats my flesh and drinks my blood
remains in me and I in him, says the Lord.

PRAYER AFTER COMMUNION

Grant, O Lord, we pray,
that we may delight for all eternity
in that share in your divine life,
which is foreshadowed in the present age
by our reception of your precious Body and Blood.
Who live and reign for ever and ever. All: **Amen.**

Tenth Sunday in Ordinary Time

June 6, 2027

Reflection on the Gospel

It's noteworthy that in this gospel, Jesus is redefining what it means to be family. Especially in our modern context, what constitutes a family continues to evolve, expand, and account for a myriad of circumstances. Jesus teaches that to him, family is "whoever does the will of God." Would that every parish family be bold enough to embrace that definition! No follower of Jesus is perfect, and this Sunday is a good time for each of us to check ourselves, both as individuals and as part of a Christian community.

—Living Liturgy™, *Tenth Sunday in Ordinary Time 2027*

Entrance Antiphon (Cf. Ps 27 (26): 1-2)

The Lord is my light and my salvation; whom shall I fear?
The Lord is the stronghold of my life; whom should I dread?
When those who do evil draw near, they stumble and fall.

Collect

O God, from whom all good things come,
grant that we, who call on you in our need,
may at your prompting discern what is right,
and by your guidance do it.
Through our Lord Jesus Christ, your Son,
who lives and reigns with you in the unity of the Holy Spirit,
God, for ever and ever. All: **Amen.**

Reading I (L 89) (Genesis 3:9-15)

A reading from the Book of Genesis

I will put enmity between your offspring and her offspring.

After the man, Adam, had eaten of the tree,
the Lord God called to the man and asked him,
"Where are you?"

He answered, "I heard you in the garden;
but I was afraid, because I was naked,
so I hid myself."
Then he asked, "Who told you that you were naked?
You have eaten, then,
from the tree of which I had forbidden you to eat!"
The man replied, "The woman whom you put here with me—
she gave me fruit from the tree, and so I ate it."
The LORD God then asked the woman,
"Why did you do such a thing?"
The woman answered, "The serpent tricked me into it, so I ate it."
Then the LORD God said to the serpent:
"Because you have done this, you shall be banned
from all the animals
and from all the wild creatures;
on your belly shall you crawl,
and dirt shall you eat
all the days of your life.
I will put enmity between you and the woman,
and between your offspring and hers;
he will strike at your head,
while you strike at his heel."

The word of the Lord. All: **Thanks be to God.**

RESPONSORIAL PSALM 130

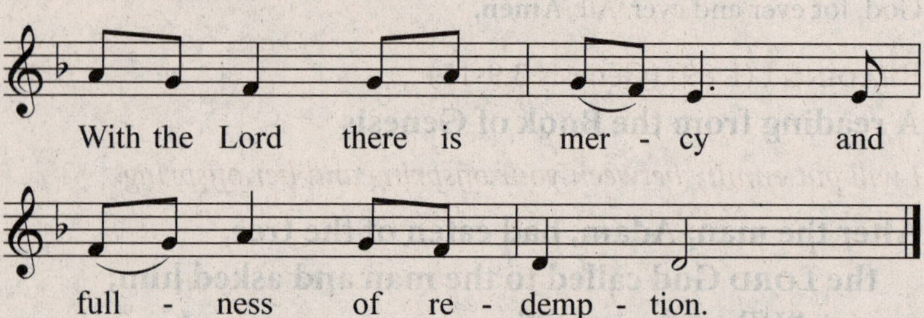

Psalm 130:1-2, 3-4, 5-6, 7-8

℟. (7bc) **With the Lord there is mercy, and fullness of redemption.**

Out of the depths I cry to you, O LORD;
LORD, hear my voice!
Let your ears be attentive
to my voice in supplication. ℟.

If you, O LORD, mark iniquities,
LORD, who can stand?
But with you is forgiveness,
that you may be revered. ℟.

I trust in the LORD;
my soul trusts in his word.
More than sentinels wait for the dawn,
let Israel wait for the LORD. ℟.

For with the LORD is kindness
and with him is plenteous redemption;
and he will redeem Israel
from all their iniquities. ℟.

READING II (1 Corinthians 4:13—5:1)

A reading from the second Letter of Saint Paul to the Corinthians

We too believe and therefore we speak.

Brothers and sisters:
Since we have the same spirit of faith,
according to what is written, I believed, therefore I spoke,
we too believe and therefore we speak,
knowing that the one who raised the Lord Jesus
will raise us also with Jesus
and place us with you in his presence.
Everything indeed is for you,
so that the grace bestowed in abundance on more and more people
may cause the thanksgiving to overflow for the glory of God.

Therefore, we are not discouraged;
rather, although our outer self is wasting away,
our inner self is being renewed day by day.
For this momentary light affliction
is producing for us an eternal weight of glory
beyond all comparison,
as we look not to what is seen but to what is unseen;
for what is seen is transitory, but what is unseen is eternal.
For we know that if our earthly dwelling, a tent,
should be destroyed,
we have a building from God,
a dwelling not made with hands, eternal in heaven.

The word of the Lord. All: **Thanks be to God.**

GOSPEL (Mark 3:20-35)

ALLELUIA (John 12:31b-32)

℣. Alleluia, alleluia. ℟. **Alleluia, alleluia.**

℣. Now the ruler of this world will be driven out, says the Lord;
and when I am lifted up from the earth, I will draw everyone to myself. ℟.

✠ **A reading from the holy Gospel according to Mark**

All: **Glory to you, O Lord.**

It is the end of Satan.

Jesus came home with his disciples.
Again the crowd gathered,
making it impossible for them even to eat.
When his relatives heard of this they set out to seize him,
for they said, "He is out of his mind."
The scribes who had come from Jerusalem said,
"He is possessed by Beelzebul, "
and "By the prince of demons he drives out demons."
Summoning them, he began to speak to them in parables,
"How can Satan drive out Satan?

If a kingdom is divided against itself,
that kingdom cannot stand.
And if a house is divided against itself,
that house will not be able to stand.
And if Satan has risen up against himself
and is divided, he cannot stand;
that is the end of him.
But no one can enter a strong man's house to plunder his property
unless he first ties up the strong man.
Then he can plunder the house.
Amen, I say to you,
all sins and all blasphemies that people utter will be forgiven them.
But whoever blasphemes against the Holy Spirit
will never have forgiveness,
but is guilty of an everlasting sin."
For they had said, "He has an unclean spirit."

His mother and his brothers arrived.
Standing outside they sent word to him and called him.
A crowd seated around him told him,
"Your mother and your brothers and your sisters
are outside asking for you."
But he said to them in reply,
"Who are my mother and my brothers?"
And looking around at those seated in the circle he said,
"Here are my mother and my brothers.
For whoever does the will of God
is my brother and sister and mother."

The Gospel of the Lord. All: **Praise to you, Lord Jesus Christ.**

Prayer over the Offerings

Look kindly upon our service, O Lord, we pray,
that what we offer
may be an acceptable oblation to you
and lead us to grow in charity.
Through Christ our Lord. All: **Amen.**

Communion Antiphon (Psalm 18[17]:3)

The Lord is my rock, my fortress, and my deliverer;
my God is my saving strength.

Or:

(1 John 4:16)

God is love, and whoever abides in love
abides in God, and God in him.

Prayer after Communion

May your healing work, O Lord,
free us, we pray, from doing evil
and lead us to what is right.
Through Christ our Lord. All: **Amen.**

Eleventh Sunday in Ordinary Time

June 13, 2027

Reflection on the Gospel

The mustard seed in Jesus's parable today is small, unassuming, and ordinary. Yet God can take the ordinary and from it, if hearts are receptive and willing, bring about holiness, devotion, and even saintliness. Consider the posture of sitting. It may not look like action or power, but it is the posture of growth—the fertile stillness where something begins to take root. Just as the mustard seed holds potential for astonishing growth, sitting attentively before the Word allows the seed of faith to be planted and nurtured in us.

—Living Liturgy™, *Eleventh Sunday in Ordinary Time 2027*

Entrance Antiphon (Cf. Ps 27[26]:7, 9)

O Lord, hear my voice, for I have called to you; be my help.
Do not abandon or forsake me, O God, my Savior!

Collect

O God, strength of those who hope in you,
graciously hear our pleas,
and, since without you mortal frailty can do nothing,

grant us always the help of your grace,
that in following your commands
we may please you by our resolve and our deeds.
Through our Lord Jesus Christ, your Son,
who lives and reigns with you in the unity of the Holy Spirit,
God, for ever and ever. All: **Amen.**

Reading I (L 92-B) (Ezekiel 17:22-24)

A reading from the Book of the Prophet Ezekiel

I have lifted high the lowly tree.

Thus says the Lord God:
I, too, will take from the crest of the cedar,
from its topmost branches tear off a tender shoot,
and plant it on a high and lofty mountain;
on the mountain heights of Israel I will plant it.
It shall put forth branches and bear fruit,
and become a majestic cedar.
Birds of every kind shall dwell beneath it,
every winged thing in the shade of its boughs.
And all the trees of the field shall know
that I, the Lord,
bring low the high tree,
lift high the lowly tree,
wither up the green tree,
and make the withered tree bloom.
As I, the Lord, have spoken, so will I do.

The word of the Lord. All: **Thanks be to God.**

Responsorial Psalm 92

Psalm 92:2-3, 13-14, 15-16

R. (*See* 2a) **Lord, it is good to give thanks to you.**

It is good to give thanks to the LORD,
to sing praise to your name, Most High,
To proclaim your kindness at dawn
and your faithfulness throughout the night. **℟.**

The just one shall flourish like the palm tree,
like a cedar of Lebanon shall he grow.
They that are planted in the house of the LORD
shall flourish in the courts of our God. **℟.**

They shall bear fruit even in old age;
vigorous and sturdy shall they be,
Declaring how just is the LORD,
my rock, in whom there is no wrong. **℟.**

READING II (2 Corinthians 5:6-10)

A reading from the second Letter of Saint Paul to the Corinthians

Whether we are at home or away, we aspire to please the Lord.

Brothers and sisters:
We are always courageous,
although we know that while we are at home in the body
we are away from the Lord,
for we walk by faith, not by sight.
Yet we are courageous,
and we would rather leave the body and go home to the Lord.
Therefore, we aspire to please him,
whether we are at home or away.
For we must all appear before the judgment seat of Christ,
so that each may receive recompense,
according to what he did in the body, whether good or evil.

The word of the Lord. All: **Thanks be to God.**

Gospel (Mark 4:26-34)

Alleluia

℣. Alleluia, alleluia. ℟. **Alleluia, alleluia.**

℣. The seed is the word of God, Christ is the sower.
All who come to him will live for ever. ℟.

✠ **A reading from the holy Gospel according to Mark**

All: **Glory to you, O Lord.**

It is the smallest of all seeds, and becomes the largest of plants.

Jesus said to the crowds:
"This is how it is with the kingdom of God;
it is as if a man were to scatter seed on the land
and would sleep and rise night and day
and through it all the seed would sprout and grow,
he knows not how.
Of its own accord the land yields fruit,
first the blade, then the ear, then the full grain in the ear.
And when the grain is ripe, he wields the sickle at once,
for the harvest has come."

He said,
"To what shall we compare the kingdom of God,
or what parable can we use for it?
It is like a mustard seed that, when it is sown in the ground,
is the smallest of all the seeds on the earth.
But once it is sown, it springs up and becomes the largest of plants
and puts forth large branches,
so that the birds of the sky can dwell in its shade."
With many such parables
he spoke the word to them as they were able to understand it.
Without parables he did not speak to them,
but to his own disciples he explained everything in private.

The Gospel of the Lord. All: **Praise to you, Lord Jesus Christ.**

PRAYER OVER THE OFFERINGS

O God, who in the offerings presented here
provide for the twofold needs of human nature,
nourishing us with food
and renewing us with your Sacrament,
grant, we pray,
that the sustenance they provide
may not fail us in body or in spirit.
Through Christ our Lord. All: **Amen.**

COMMUNION ANTIPHON (Psalm 27[26]:4)

There is one thing I ask of the Lord, only this do I seek:
to live in the house of the Lord all the days of my life.

Or:

(John 17:11)

Holy Father, keep in your name those you have given me,
that they may be one as we are one, says the Lord.

PRAYER AFTER COMMUNION

As this reception of your Holy Communion, O Lord,
foreshadows the union of the faithful in you,
so may it bring about unity in your Church.
Through Christ our Lord. All: **Amen.**

Twelfth Sunday in Ordinary Time

June 20, 2027

Reflection on the Gospel

Very few of us experience God in such an obvious, tangible way as do the disciples in today's gospel. Inasmuch as we might experience individually God's voice in communal prayer, the whole of the community also experiences God: Christ sharing himself by his presence in word, Eucharist, the priest-celebrant, and the assembly itself. The answer to our prayers at liturgy then, whatever they are, is always relationship with God (word, sacrifice, meal) and with one another (priest and assembly), all underpinned by faith and trust.

—Living Liturgy™, *Twelfth Sunday in Ordinary Time 2027*

Entrance Antiphon (Cf. Psalm 28[27]:8-9)

The Lord is the strength of his people,
a saving refuge for the one he has anointed.
Save your people, Lord, and bless your heritage,
and govern them for ever.

Collect

Grant, O Lord,
that we may always revere and love your holy name,
for you never deprive of your guidance
those you set firm on the foundation of your love.
Through our Lord Jesus Christ, your Son,
who lives and reigns with you in the unity of the Holy Spirit,
God, for ever and ever. All: **Amen.**

Reading I (L 95-B) (Job 38:1, 8-11)

A reading from the Book of Job

Here shall your proud waves be stilled!

The Lord addressed Job out of the storm and said:
Who shut within doors the sea,
when it burst forth from the womb;

when I made the clouds its garment
and thick darkness its swaddling bands?
When I set limits for it
and fastened the bar of its door,
and said: Thus far shall you come but no farther,
and here shall your proud waves be stilled!

The word of the Lord. All: **Thanks be to God.**

Responsorial Psalm 107

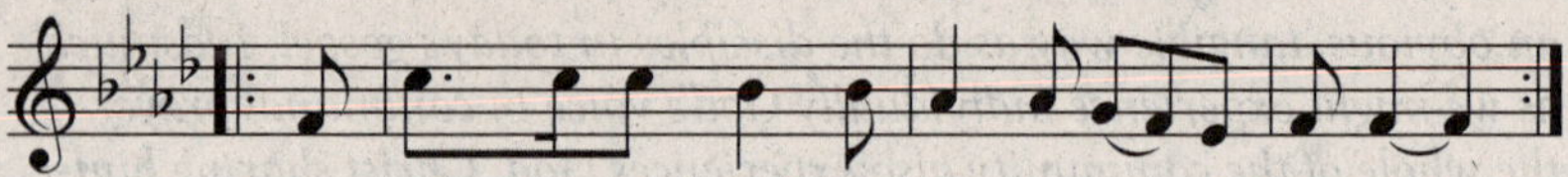

The response is preferably sung twice each time.

Psalm 107:23-24, 25-26, 28-29, 30-31

℟. (1b) **Give thanks to the Lord, his love is everlasting.**
or: ℟. **Alleluia.**

They who sailed the sea in ships,
trading on the deep waters,
these saw the works of the Lord
and his wonders in the abyss. ℟.

His command raised up a storm wind
which tossed its waves on high.
They mounted up to heaven; they sank to the depths;
their hearts melted away in their plight. ℟.

They cried to the Lord in their distress;
from their straits he rescued them,
He hushed the storm to a gentle breeze,
and the billows of the sea were stilled. ℟.

They rejoiced that they were calmed,
and he brought them to their desired haven.
Let them give thanks to the Lord for his kindness
and his wondrous deeds to the children of men. ℟.

READING II (2 Corinthians 5:14-17)

A reading from the second Letter of Saint Paul to the Corinthians

Behold, new things have come.

Brothers and sisters:
The love of Christ impels us,
once we have come to the conviction that one died for all;
therefore, all have died.
He indeed died for all,
so that those who live might no longer live for themselves
but for him who for their sake died and was raised.
Consequently, from now on we regard no one according to the flesh;
even if we once knew Christ according to the flesh,
yet now we know him so no longer.
So whoever is in Christ is a new creation:
the old things have passed away;
behold, new things have come.

The word of the Lord. All: **Thanks be to God.**

GOSPEL (Mark 4:35-41)

ALLELUIA (Luke 7:16)

℣. Alleluia, alleluia. ℟. **Alleluia, alleluia.**
℣. A great prophet has risen in our midst.
God has visited his people. ℟.

✠ **A reading from the holy Gospel according to Mark**

All: **Glory to you, O Lord.**

Who is this whom even wind and sea obey?

On that day, as evening drew on, Jesus said to his disciples:
"Let us cross to the other side."
Leaving the crowd, they took Jesus with them in the boat just as he was.

And other boats were with him.
A violent squall came up and waves were breaking over the boat,
so that it was already filling up.
Jesus was in the stern, asleep on a cushion.
They woke him and said to him,
"Teacher, do you not care that we are perishing?"
He woke up,
rebuked the wind, and said to the sea, "Quiet! Be still!"
The wind ceased and there was great calm.
Then he asked them, "Why are you terrified?
Do you not yet have faith?"
They were filled with great awe and said to one another,
"Who then is this whom even wind and sea obey?"

The Gospel of the Lord. All: **Praise to you, Lord Jesus Christ.**

Prayer over the Offerings

Receive, O Lord, the sacrifice of conciliation and praise
and grant that, cleansed by its action,
we may make offering of a heart pleasing to you.
Through Christ our Lord. All: **Amen.**

Communion Antiphon (Psalm 145[144]:15)

The eyes of all look to you, Lord,
and you give them their food in due season.

Or:

(John 10:11, 15)
I am the Good Shepherd,
and I lay down my life for my sheep, says the Lord.

Prayer after Communion

Renewed and nourished
by the Sacred Body and Precious Blood of your Son,
we ask of your mercy, O Lord,
that what we celebrate with constant devotion
may be our sure pledge of redemption.
Through Christ our Lord. All: **Amen.**

Thirteenth Sunday in Ordinary Time

June 27, 2027

Reflection on the Gospel
There are very few Aramaic words of Jesus quoted directly in Scripture. So when we do encounter them—like "Talitha koum," *spoken to Jairus's daughter—we should recognize their deep importance. In our call to share the good news with others, the words we choose are of utmost importance, and we must consider what we wish the response to be. We must approach each person with specific care and attention, that our kerygma elicit in them the new life that Jesus's* "Talitha koum" *did for Jairus's daughter.*

—Living Liturgy™, *Thirteenth Sunday in Ordinary Time 2027*

Entrance Antiphon (Psalm 47[46]:2)

All peoples, clap your hands.
Cry to God with shouts of joy!

Collect

O God, who through the grace of adoption
chose us to be children of light,
grant, we pray,
that we may not be wrapped in the darkness of error
but always be seen to stand in the bright light of truth.
Through our Lord Jesus Christ, your Son,
who lives and reigns with you in the unity of the Holy Spirit,
God, for ever and ever. All: **Amen.**

Reading I (L 98-B) (Wisdom 1:13-15; 2:23-24)

A reading from the Book of Wisdom

By the envy of the devil, death entered the world.

God did not make death,
nor does he rejoice in the destruction of the living.

For he fashioned all things that they might have being;
and the creatures of the world are wholesome,
and there is not a destructive drug among them
nor any domain of the netherworld on earth,
for justice is undying.
For God formed man to be imperishable;
the image of his own nature he made him.
But by the envy of the devil, death entered the world,
and they who belong to his company experience it.

The word of the Lord. All: **Thanks be to God.**

Responsorial Psalm 30

Psalm 30:2, 4, 5-6, 11, 12, 13

℟. (2a) **I will praise you, Lord, for you have rescued me.**

I will extol you, O LORD, for you drew me clear
and did not let my enemies rejoice over me.
O LORD, you brought me up from the netherworld;
you preserved me from among those going down into the pit. ℟.

Sing praise to the LORD, you his faithful ones,
and give thanks to his holy name.
For his anger lasts but a moment;
a lifetime, his good will.
At nightfall, weeping enters in,
but with the dawn, rejoicing. ℟.

Hear, O LORD, and have pity on me;
O LORD, be my helper.

You changed my mourning into dancing;
O LORD, my God, forever will I give you thanks. ℟.

READING II (2 Corinthians 8:7, 9, 13-15)

A reading from the second Letter of Saint Paul to the Corinthians

Your abundance should supply the needs of the poor.

Brothers and sisters:
As you excel in every respect, in faith, discourse,
knowledge, all earnestness, and in the love we have
for you,
may you excel in this gracious act also.

For you know the gracious act of our Lord Jesus Christ,
that though he was rich, for your sake he became poor,
so that by his poverty you might become rich.
Not that others should have relief while you are burdened,
but that as a matter of equality
your abundance at the present time should supply
their needs,
so that their abundance may also supply your needs,
that there may be equality.
As it is written:
Whoever had much did not have more,
and whoever had little did not have less.

The word of the Lord. All: **Thanks be to God.**

GOSPEL (Mark 5:21-43) *or* Shorter Form [ ]
(Mark 5:21-24, 35b-43)

ALLELUIA (*See* 2 Timothy 1:10)

℣. Alleluia, alleluia. ℟. **Alleluia, alleluia.**
℣. Our Savior Jesus Christ destroyed death
and brought life to light through the Gospel. ℟.

✠ **A reading from the holy Gospel according to Mark**

All: **Glory to you, O Lord.**

Little girl, I say to you, arise!

[When Jesus had crossed again in the boat
to the other side,
a large crowd gathered around him, and he stayed close to the sea.
One of the synagogue officials, named Jairus, came forward.
Seeing him he fell at his feet and pleaded earnestly with him, saying,
"My daughter is at the point of death.
Please, come lay your hands on her
that she may get well and live."
He went off with him,
and a large crowd followed him and pressed upon him.]

There was a woman afflicted with hemorrhages for twelve years.
She had suffered greatly at the hands of many doctors
and had spent all that she had.
Yet she was not helped but only grew worse.
She had heard about Jesus and came up behind him in the crowd
and touched his cloak.
She said, "If I but touch his clothes, I shall be cured."
Immediately her flow of blood dried up.
She felt in her body that she was healed of her affliction.
Jesus, aware at once that power had gone out from him,
turned around in the crowd and asked, "Who has touched my clothes?"
But his disciples said to Jesus,
"You see how the crowd is pressing upon you,
and yet you ask, 'Who touched me?'"
And he looked around to see who had done it.
The woman, realizing what had happened to her,
approached in fear and trembling.
She fell down before Jesus and told him the whole truth.

He said to her, "Daughter, your faith has saved you.
Go in peace and be cured of your affliction."

[**While he was still speaking,**
people from the synagogue official's house arrived and said,
"Your daughter has died; why trouble the teacher any longer?"
Disregarding the message that was reported,
Jesus said to the synagogue official,
"Do not be afraid; just have faith."
He did not allow anyone to accompany him inside
except Peter, James, and John, the brother of James.
When they arrived at the house of the synagogue official,
he caught sight of a commotion,
people weeping and wailing loudly.
So he went in and said to them,
"Why this commotion and weeping?
The child is not dead but asleep."
And they ridiculed him.
Then he put them all out.
He took along the child's father and mother
and those who were with him
and entered the room where the child was.
He took the child by the hand and said to her,
"*Talitha koum*,"
which means, "Little girl, I say to you, arise!"
The girl, a child of twelve, arose immediately and walked around.
At that they were utterly astounded.
He gave strict orders that no one should know this
and said that she should be given something to eat.]

The Gospel of the Lord. All: **Praise to you, Lord Jesus Christ.**

Prayer over the Offerings

O God, who graciously accomplish
the effects of your mysteries,
grant, we pray,
that the deeds by which we serve you
may be worthy of these sacred gifts.
Through Christ our Lord. All: **Amen.**

Communion Antiphon (Cf. Psalm 103[102]:1)

Bless the Lord, O my soul,
and all within me, his holy name.

Or:

(John 17:20-21)

O Father, I pray for them, that they may be one in us,
that the world may believe that you have sent me, says the Lord.

Prayer after Communion

May this divine sacrifice we have offered and received
fill us with life, O Lord, we pray,
so that, bound to you in lasting charity,
we may bear fruit that lasts for ever.
Through Christ our Lord. All: **Amen.**

Fourteenth Sunday in Ordinary Time

July 4, 2027

Reflection on the Gospel

Communication always carries risk. No matter the medium—spoken, written, or digital—listeners and readers interpret through their own lens, drawing from tone, context, or cultural background, often mishearing or misunderstanding, even when intentions are good. Perhaps this is a main reason that even Jesus was received in his native place—as we hear in today's gospel—without honor. On civic holidays like today, we must be mindful of the universal nature of the church and the diverse people gathered in Christ's name in how we communicate with each other.

—Living Liturgy™, *Fourteenth Sunday in Ordinary Time 2027*

Entrance Antiphon (Cf. Psalm 48[47]:10-11)

Your merciful love, O God,
we have received in the midst of your temple.
Your praise, O God, like your name,
reaches the ends of the earth;
your right hand is filled with saving justice.

Collect

O God, who in the abasement of your Son
have raised up a fallen world,
fill your faithful with holy joy,
for on those you have rescued from slavery to sin
you bestow eternal gladness.
Through our Lord Jesus Christ, your Son,
who lives and reigns with you in the unity of the Holy Spirit,
God, for ever and ever. All: **Amen.**

Reading I (L 101-B) (Ezekiel 2:2-5)

A reading from the Book of the Prophet Ezekiel

They are a rebellious house but shall know that a prophet has been among them.

As the LORD spoke to me, the spirit entered into me
and set me on my feet,
and I heard the one who was speaking say to me:
Son of man, I am sending you to the Israelites,
rebels who have rebelled against me;
they and their ancestors have revolted against me to this very day.
Hard of face and obstinate of heart
are they to whom I am sending you.
But you shall say to them: Thus says the Lord GOD!
And whether they heed or resist—for they are a rebellious house—
they shall know that a prophet has been among them.

The word of the Lord. All: **Thanks be to God.**

RESPONSORIAL PSALM 123

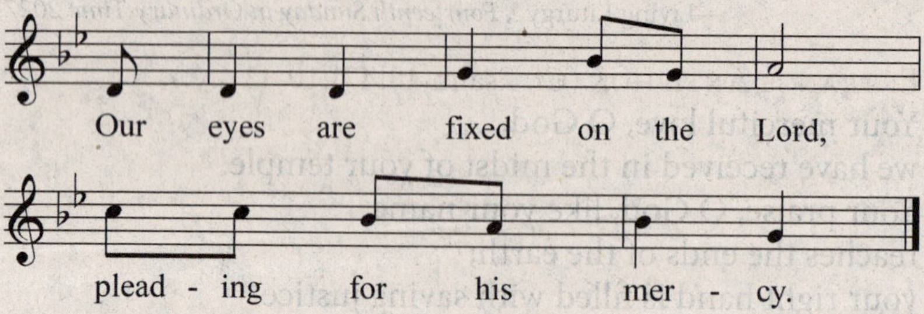

Psalm 123:1-2, 2, 3-4

℟. (2cd) **Our eyes are fixed on the Lord, pleading for his mercy.**

To you I lift up my eyes
who are enthroned in heaven—
As the eyes of servants
are on the hands of their masters. ℟.

As the eyes of a maid
are on the hands of her mistress,
So are our eyes on the LORD, our God,
till he have pity on us. ℟.

Have pity on us, O LORD, have pity on us,
for we are more than sated with contempt;
our souls are more than sated
with the mockery of the arrogant,
with the contempt of the proud. ℟.

READING II (2 Corinthians 12:7-10)

A reading from the second Letter of Saint Paul to the Corinthians

I will boast in my weaknesses, in order that the power of Christ may dwell in me.

Brothers and sisters:
That I, Paul, might not become too elated,
because of the abundance of the revelations,
a thorn in the flesh was given to me, an angel of Satan,
to beat me, to keep me from being too elated.
Three times I begged the Lord about this, that it might leave me,
but he said to me, "My grace is sufficient for you,
for power is made perfect in weakness."
I will rather boast most gladly of my weaknesses,
in order that the power of Christ may dwell with me.
Therefore, I am content with weaknesses, insults,
hardships, persecutions, and constraints,
for the sake of Christ;
for when I am weak, then I am strong.

The word of the Lord. All: **Thanks be to God.**

GOSPEL (Mark 6:1-6)

ALLELUIA (*See* Luke 4:18)

℣. Alleluia, alleluia. ℟. **Alleluia, alleluia.**
℣. The Spirit of the Lord is upon me
for he sent me to bring glad tidings to the poor. ℟.

✠ **A reading from the holy Gospel according to Mark**

All: **Glory to you, O Lord.**

A prophet is not without honor except in his native place.

Jesus departed from there and came to his native place,
accompanied by his disciples.
When the sabbath came he began to teach in the synagogue,
and many who heard him were astonished.
They said, "Where did this man get all this?
What kind of wisdom has been given him?
What mighty deeds are wrought by his hands!
Is he not the carpenter, the son of Mary,
and the brother of James and Joses and Judas and Simon?
And are not his sisters here with us?"
And they took offense at him.
Jesus said to them,
"A prophet is not without honor except in his native place
and among his own kin and in his own house."
So he was not able to perform any mighty deed there,
apart from curing a few sick people by laying his hands on them.
He was amazed at their lack of faith.

The Gospel of the Lord. All: **Praise to you, Lord Jesus Christ.**

PRAYER OVER THE OFFERINGS

May this oblation dedicated to your name
purify us, O Lord,
and day by day bring our conduct
closer to the life of heaven.
Through Christ our Lord. All: **Amen.**

COMMUNION ANTIPHON (Psalm 34[33]:9)

Taste and see that the Lord is good;
blessed the man who seeks refuge in him.

Or:

(Matthew 11:28)

Come to me, all who labor and are burdened,
and I will refresh you, says the Lord.

PRAYER AFTER COMMUNION
Grant, we pray, O Lord,
that, having been replenished by such great gifts,
we may gain the prize of salvation
and never cease to praise you.
Through Christ our Lord. All: **Amen.**

Fifteenth Sunday in Ordinary Time

July 11, 2027

Reflection on the Gospel

Jesus sends his apostles to proclaim the reign of God. He tells them to stay once they have entered a house through which one must past through the door. The door to the church is a gateway to heaven itself, or at least a foretaste of it. Candidates in OCIA are met at those doors, as is a casket, holding the remains of a loved one. As we enter the church by such a door, we too are sent out to be Christ's hands and feet in the world.

—Living Liturgy™, *Fifteenth Sunday in Ordinary Time 2027*

ENTRANCE ANTIPHON (Cf. Psalm 17[16]:15)
As for me, in justice I shall behold your face;
I shall be filled with the vision of your glory.

COLLECT
O God, who show the light of your truth
to those who go astray,
so that they may return to the right path,
give all who for the faith they profess
are accounted Christians
the grace to reject whatever is contrary to the name of Christ
and to strive after all that does it honor.
Through our Lord Jesus Christ, your Son,
who lives and reigns with you in the unity of the Holy Spirit,
God, for ever and ever. All: **Amen.**

Reading I (L 104-B) (Amos 7:12-15)

A reading from the Book of the Prophet Amos

Go, prophesy to my people.

Amaziah, priest of Bethel, said to Amos,
"Off with you, visionary, flee to the land of Judah!
There earn your bread by prophesying,
but never again prophesy in Bethel;
for it is the king's sanctuary and a royal temple."
Amos answered Amaziah, "I was no prophet,
nor have I belonged to a company of prophets;
I was a shepherd and a dresser of sycamores.
The Lord took me from following the flock, and said to me,
Go, prophesy to my people Israel."

The word of the Lord. All: **Thanks be to God.**

Responsorial Psalm 85

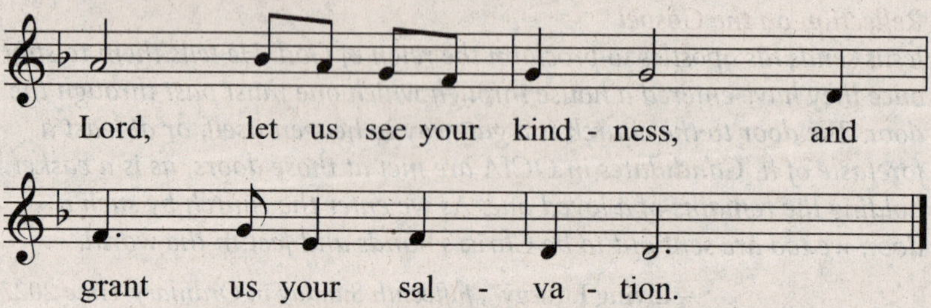

Psalm 85:9-10, 11-12, 13-14

℟. (8) **Lord, let us see your kindness, and grant us your salvation.**

I will hear what God proclaims;
the Lord—for he proclaims peace.
Near indeed is his salvation to those who fear him,
glory dwelling in our land. ℟.

Kindness and truth shall meet;
justice and peace shall kiss.

Truth shall spring out of the earth,
and justice shall look down from heaven. ℟.

The Lord himself will give his benefits;
our land shall yield its increase.
Justice shall walk before him,
and prepare the way of his steps. ℟.

Reading II (Ephesians 1:3-14) *or* Shorter Form [ ]
(Ephesians 1:3-10)

A reading from the Letter of Saint Paul to the Ephesians

God chose us in Christ, before the foundation of the world.

[Blessed be the God and Father of our Lord Jesus Christ,
who has blessed us in Christ
with every spiritual blessing in the heavens,
as he chose us in him, before the foundation of the world,
to be holy and without blemish before him.
In love he destined us for adoption to himself through Jesus Christ,
in accord with the favor of his will,
for the praise of the glory of his grace
that he granted us in the beloved.

In him we have redemption by his blood,
the forgiveness of transgressions,
in accord with the riches of his grace that he lavished upon us.
In all wisdom and insight, he has made known to us
the mystery of his will in accord with his favor
that he set forth in him as a plan for the fullness of times,
to sum up all things in Christ, in heaven and on earth.]

In him we were also chosen,
destined in accord with the purpose of the One
who accomplishes all things according to the intention of his will,

so that we might exist for the praise of his glory,
we who first hoped in Christ.
In him you also, who have heard the word of truth,
the gospel of your salvation, and have believed in him,
were sealed with the promised holy Spirit,
which is the first installment of our inheritance
toward redemption as God's possession, to the praise of his glory.

The word of the Lord. All: **Thanks be to God.**

GOSPEL (Mark 6:7-13)

ALLELUIA (*See* Ephesians 1:17-18)

℣. Alleluia, alleluia. ℟. **Alleluia, alleluia.**
℣. May the Father of our Lord Jesus Christ
enlighten the eyes of our hearts,
that we may know what is the hope that
belongs to our call. ℟.

✠ **A reading from the holy Gospel according to Mark**

All: **Glory to you, O Lord.**

He began to send them out.

Jesus summoned the Twelve and began to send them out two by two
and gave them authority over unclean spirits.
He instructed them to take nothing for the journey
but a walking stick—
no food, no sack, no money in their belts.
They were, however, to wear sandals
but not a second tunic.
He said to them,
"Wherever you enter a house, stay there until you leave.
Whatever place does not welcome you or listen to you,
leave there and shake the dust off your feet
in testimony against them."
So they went off and preached repentance.

The Twelve drove out many demons,
and they anointed with oil many who were sick and cured them.

The Gospel of the Lord. All: **Praise to you, Lord Jesus Christ.**

PRAYER OVER THE OFFERINGS

Look upon the offerings of the Church, O Lord,
as she makes her prayer to you,
and grant that, when consumed by those who believe,
they may bring ever greater holiness.
Through Christ our Lord. All: **Amen.**

COMMUNION ANTIPHON (Cf. Psalm 84[83]:4-5)

The sparrow finds a home,
and the swallow a nest for her young:
by your altars, O Lord of hosts, my King and my God.
Blessed are they who dwell in your house,
for ever singing your praise.

Or:

(John 6:57)

Whoever eats my flesh and drinks my blood
remains in me and I in him, says the Lord.

PRAYER AFTER COMMUNION

Having consumed these gifts, we pray, O Lord,
that, by our participation in this mystery,
its saving effects upon us may grow.
Through Christ our Lord. All: **Amen.**

Sixteenth Sunday in Ordinary Time

July 18, 2027

Reflection on the Gospel

In the gospel today, Jesus invites the apostles to "Come away by yourselves." Forming smaller Christian communities within a larger whole has immense value in this regard. Small, faith-sharing groups intensify a sense of belonging in a world where the number of close friendships is shrinking, and people yearn for any connection and "fitting in." We can also do our part to make every liturgy a place where all feel welcome, valued, and engaged. Thus, the whole community can grow together in holiness and unity.

—Living Liturgy™, *Sixteenth Sunday in Ordinary Time 2027*

Entrance Antiphon (Psalm 54[53]:6, 8)

See, I have God for my help.
The Lord sustains my soul.
I will sacrifice to you with willing heart,
and praise your name, O Lord, for it is good.

Collect

Show favor, O Lord, to your servants
and mercifully increase the gifts of your grace,
that, made fervent in hope, faith and charity,
they may be ever watchful in keeping your commands.
Through our Lord Jesus Christ, your Son,
who lives and reigns with you in the unity of the Holy Spirit,
God, for ever and ever. All: **Amen.**

Reading I (L 107-B) (Jeremiah 23:1-6)

A reading from the Book of the Prophet Jeremiah

I will gather the remnant of my flock and appoint shepherds for them.

Woe to the shepherds
who mislead and scatter the flock of my pasture,
says the LORD.
Therefore, thus says the LORD, the God of Israel,
against the shepherds who shepherd my people:
You have scattered my sheep and driven them away.
You have not cared for them,
but I will take care to punish your evil deeds.
I myself will gather the remnant of my flock
from all the lands to which I have driven them
and bring them back to their meadow;
there they shall increase and multiply.
I will appoint shepherds for them who will shepherd them
so that they need no longer fear and tremble;
and none shall be missing, says the LORD.

Behold, the days are coming, says the LORD,
when I will raise up a righteous shoot to David;
as king he shall reign and govern wisely,
he shall do what is just and right in the land.
In his days Judah shall be saved,
Israel shall dwell in security.
This is the name they give him:
"The LORD our justice."

The word of the Lord. All: **Thanks be to God.**

RESPONSORIAL PSALM 23

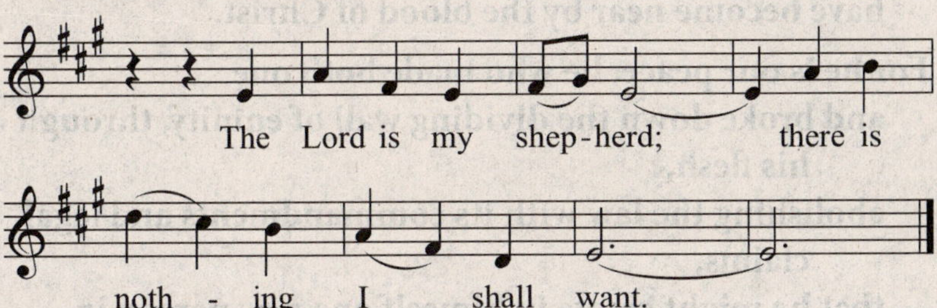

Psalm 23:1-3, 3-4, 5, 6

℟. (1) **The Lord is my shepherd; there is nothing I shall want.**

The LORD is my shepherd; I shall not want.
In verdant pastures he gives me repose;
beside restful waters he leads me;
he refreshes my soul. ℟.

He guides me in right paths
for his name's sake.
Even though I walk in the dark valley
I fear no evil; for you are at my side
with your rod and your staff
that give me courage. ℟.

You spread the table before me
in the sight of my foes;
you anoint my head with oil;
my cup overflows. ℟.

Only goodness and kindness follow me
all the days of my life;
and I shall dwell in the house of the LORD
for years to come. ℟.

READING II (Ephesians 2:13-18)

A reading from the Letter of Saint Paul to the Ephesians

Christ is our peace who made both one.

Brothers and sisters:
In Christ Jesus you who once were far off
have become near by the blood of Christ.

For he is our peace, he who made both one
and broke down the dividing wall of enmity, through his flesh,
abolishing the law with its commandments and legal claims,
that he might create in himself one new person in place of the two,
thus establishing peace,

and might reconcile both with God,
in one body, through the cross,
putting that enmity to death by it.
He came and preached peace to you who were far off
and peace to those who were near,
for through him we both have access in one Spirit to the Father.

The word of the Lord. All: **Thanks be to God.**

GOSPEL (Mark 6:30-34)
ALLELUIA (John 10:27)
℣. Alleluia, alleluia. ℟. **Alleluia, alleluia.**
℣. My sheep hear my voice, says the Lord;
I know them, and they follow me. ℟.

✠ **A reading from the holy Gospel according to Mark**
All: **Glory to you, O Lord.**

They were like sheep without a shepherd.

The apostles gathered together with Jesus
and reported all they had done and taught.
He said to them,
"Come away by yourselves to a deserted place and rest a while."
People were coming and going in great numbers,
and they had no opportunity even to eat.
So they went off in the boat by themselves to a deserted place.
People saw them leaving and many came to know about it.
They hastened there on foot from all the towns
and arrived at the place before them.

When he disembarked and saw the vast crowd,
his heart was moved with pity for them,
for they were like sheep without a shepherd;
and he began to teach them many things.

The Gospel of the Lord. All: **Praise to you, Lord Jesus Christ.**

Prayer over the Offerings

O God, who in the one perfect sacrifice
brought to completion varied offerings of the law,
accept, we pray, this sacrifice from your faithful servants
and make it holy, as you blessed the gifts of Abel,
so that what each has offered to the honor of your majesty
may benefit the salvation of all.
Through Christ our Lord. All: **Amen.**

Communion Antiphon (Psalm 111[110]:4-5)

The Lord, the gracious, the merciful,
has made a memorial of his wonders;
he gives food to those who fear him.

Or:

(Revelation 3:20)

Behold, I stand at the door and knock, says the Lord.
If anyone hears my voice and opens the door to me,
I will enter his house and dine with him, and he with me.

Prayer after Communion

Graciously be present to your people, we pray, O Lord,
and lead those you have imbued with heavenly mysteries
to pass from former ways to newness of life.
Through Christ our Lord. All: **Amen.**

Seventeenth Sunday in Ordinary Time

July 25, 2027

Reflection on the Gospel

It is seemingly no accident that in our rites the assembly is sent forth almost immediately upon reception of the Eucharist. Within mere moments, the presider pronounces the dismissal: "Ite, missa est"*—which roughly translates to "Go, you are sent." "Go" is what we're told, not "but wait, adore for a minute what is literally now inside you." Our mission work as faithful disciples, the Christian activity we are all called to, begins immediately while we are still literally filled with Christ's Real Presence, which a waiting world sorely needs.*

—Living Liturgy™, *Seventeenth Sunday in Ordinary Time 2027*

Entrance Antiphon (Cf. Psalm 68[67]:6-7, 36)

God is in his holy place,
God who unites those who dwell in his house;
he himself gives might and strength to his people.

Collect

O God, protector of those who hope in you,
without whom nothing has firm foundation, nothing is holy,
bestow in abundance your mercy upon us
and grant that, with you as our ruler and guide,
we may use the good things that pass
in such a way as to hold fast even now
to those that ever endure.
Through our Lord Jesus Christ, your Son,
who lives and reigns with you in the unity of the Holy Spirit,
God, for ever and ever. All: **Amen.**

Reading I (L 110-B) (2 Kings 4:42-44)

A reading from the second Book of Kings

They shall eat and there shall be some left over.

A man came from Baal-shalishah bringing to Elisha,
the man of God,
twenty barley loaves made from the firstfruits,
and fresh grain in the ear.
Elisha said, "Give it to the people to eat."
But his servant objected,
"How can I set this before a hundred people?"
Elisha insisted, "Give it to the people to eat.
For thus says the LORD,
'They shall eat and there shall be some left over.' "
And when they had eaten, there was some left over,
as the LORD had said.

The word of the Lord. All: **Thanks be to God.**

RESPONSORIAL PSALM 145

Psalm 145:10-11, 15-16, 17-18

℟. (*See* 16) **The hand of the Lord feeds us; he answers all our needs.**

Let all your works give you thanks, O LORD,
and let your faithful ones bless you.
Let them discourse of the glory of your kingdom
and speak of your might. ℟.

The eyes of all look hopefully to you,
and you give them their food in due season;
you open your hand
and satisfy the desire of every living thing. ℟.

The LORD is just in all his ways
and holy in all his works.
The LORD is near to all who call upon him,
to all who call upon him in truth. ℟.

READING II (Ephesians 4:1-6)

A reading from the Letter of Saint Paul to the Ephesians

One body, one Lord, one faith, one baptism.

Brothers and sisters:
I, a prisoner for the Lord,
urge you to live in a manner worthy of the call you have received,
with all humility and gentleness, with patience,
bearing with one another through love,
striving to preserve the unity of the spirit through the bond of peace:
one body and one Spirit,
as you were also called to the one hope of your call;
one Lord, one faith, one baptism;
one God and Father of all,
who is over all and through all and in all.

The word of the Lord. All: **Thanks be to God.**

GOSPEL (John 6:1-15)

ALLELUIA (Luke 7:16)

℣. Alleluia, alleluia. ℟. **Alleluia, alleluia.**
℣. A great prophet has risen in our midst.
God has visited his people. ℟.

✠ **A reading from the holy Gospel according to John**

All: **Glory to you, O Lord.**

He distributed as much as they wanted to those who were reclining.

Jesus went across the Sea of Galilee.
A large crowd followed him,
because they saw the signs he was performing on the sick.

Jesus went up on the mountain,
and there he sat down with his disciples.
The Jewish feast of Passover was near.
When Jesus raised his eyes
and saw that a large crowd was coming to him,
he said to Philip,
"Where can we buy enough food for them to eat?"
He said this to test him,
because he himself knew what he was going to do.
Philip answered him,
"Two hundred days' wages worth of food would not be enough
for each of them to have a little."
One of his disciples,
Andrew, the brother of Simon Peter, said to him,
"There is a boy here who has five barley loaves and two fish;
but what good are these for so many?"
Jesus said, "Have the people recline."
Now there was a great deal of grass in that place.
So the men reclined, about five thousand in number.
Then Jesus took the loaves, gave thanks,
and distributed them to those who were reclining,
and also as much of the fish as they wanted.
When they had had their fill, he said to his disciples,
"Gather the fragments left over,
so that nothing will be wasted."
So they collected them,
and filled twelve wicker baskets with fragments
from the five barley loaves
that had been more than they could eat.
When the people saw the sign he had done, they said,
"This is truly the Prophet, the one who is to come into the world."

Since Jesus knew that they were going to come and carry him off
to make him king,
he withdrew again to the mountain alone.

The Gospel of the Lord. All: **Praise to you, Lord Jesus Christ.**

Prayer over the Offerings

Accept, O Lord, we pray, the offerings
which we bring from the abundance of your gifts,
that through the powerful working of your grace
these most sacred mysteries may sanctify our present way of life
and lead us to eternal gladness.
Through Christ our Lord. All: **Amen.**

Communion Antiphon (Psalm 103[102]:2)

Bless the Lord, O my soul,
and never forget all his benefits.

Or:

(Matthew 5:7-8)
Blessed are the merciful, for they shall receive mercy.
Blessed are the clean of heart, for they shall see God.

Prayer after Communion

We have consumed, O Lord, this divine Sacrament,
the perpetual memorial of the Passion of your Son;
grant, we pray, that this gift,
which he himself gave us with love beyond all telling,
may profit us for salvation.
Through Christ our Lord. All: **Amen.**

Eighteenth Sunday in Ordinary Time

August 1, 2027

Reflection on the Gospel

The theme of today's readings is one of dependence, relying on God completely for sustenance. This is elaborated in the words of the Lord's Prayer: "Give us this day our daily bread." This prayer asks for only what is needed today and petitions the Lord to provide it. This complete dependence is something most of us are not well versed in or willing to accept. Dependence isn't something that can be faked. It must be lived by example, by prayer into action, or even inaction, if you will.

—Living Liturgy™, *Eighteenth Sunday in Ordinary Time 2027*

Entrance Antiphon (Psalm 70[69]:2, 6)

O God, come to my assistance;
O Lord, make haste to help me!
You are my rescuer, my help;
O Lord, do not delay.

Collect

Draw near to your servants, O Lord,
and answer their prayers with unceasing kindness,
that, for those who glory in you as their Creator and guide,
you may restore what you have created
and keep safe what you have restored.
Through our Lord Jesus Christ, your Son,
who lives and reigns with you in the unity of the Holy Spirit,
God, for ever and ever. All: **Amen.**

Reading I (L 113-B) (Exodus 16:2-4, 12-15)

A reading from the Book of Exodus

I will rain down bread from heaven for you.

The whole Israelite community grumbled against Moses and Aaron.
The Israelites said to them,

"Would that we had died at the LORD's hand in the land of Egypt,
as we sat by our fleshpots and ate our fill of bread!
But you had to lead us into this desert
to make the whole community die of famine!"

Then the LORD said to Moses,
"I will now rain down bread from heaven for you.
Each day the people are to go out and gather their daily portion;
thus will I test them,
to see whether they follow my instructions or not.

"I have heard the grumbling of the Israelites.
Tell them: In the evening twilight you shall eat flesh,
and in the morning you shall have your fill of bread,
so that you may know that I, the LORD, am your God."

In the evening quail came up and covered the camp.
In the morning a dew lay all about the camp,
and when the dew evaporated, there on the surface of the desert
were fine flakes like hoarfrost on the ground.
On seeing it, the Israelites asked one another, "What is this?"
for they did not know what it was.
But Moses told them,
"This is the bread that the LORD has given you to eat."

The word of the Lord. All: **Thanks be to God.**

RESPONSORIAL PSALM 78

Text: Refrain, *Lectionary for Mass*, © 1969, 1981, 1997, ICEL
Music: *The Collegeville Psalter*, © 2017, Paul Inwood.

Psalm 78:3-4, 23-24, 25, 54

℟. (24b) **The Lord gave them bread from heaven.**

What we have heard and know,
and what our fathers have declared to us,
We will declare to the generation to come
the glorious deeds of the Lord and his strength
and the wonders that he wrought. ℟.

He commanded the skies above
and opened the doors of heaven;
he rained manna upon them for food
and gave them heavenly bread. ℟.

Man ate the bread of angels,
food he sent them in abundance.
And he brought them to his holy land,
to the mountains his right hand had won. ℟.

Reading II (Ephesians 4:17, 20-24)

A reading from the Letter of Saint Paul to the Ephesians

Put on the new self that has been created in God's way.

Brothers and sisters:
I declare and testify in the Lord
that you must no longer live as the Gentiles do,
in the futility of their minds;
that is not how you learned Christ,
assuming that you have heard of him and were taught in him,
as truth is in Jesus,
that you should put away the old self of your former way of life,
corrupted through deceitful desires,
and be renewed in the spirit of your minds,
and put on the new self,
created in God's way in righteousness and holiness of truth.

The word of the Lord. All: **Thanks be to God.**

Gospel (John 6:24-35)

Alleluia (Matthew 4:4b)

℣. Alleluia, alleluia. ℟. **Alleluia, alleluia.**
℣. One does not live on bread alone, but by every word that comes forth from the mouth of God. ℟.

✠ **A reading from the holy Gospel according to John**

All: **Glory to you, O Lord.**

Whoever comes to me will never hunger, and whoever believes in me will never thirst.

When the crowd saw that neither Jesus nor his disciples were there,
they themselves got into boats
and came to Capernaum looking for Jesus.
And when they found him across the sea they said to him,
"Rabbi, when did you get here?"
Jesus answered them and said,
"Amen, amen, I say to you,
you are looking for me not because you saw signs
but because you ate the loaves and were filled.
Do not work for food that perishes
but for the food that endures for eternal life,
which the Son of Man will give you.
For on him the Father, God, has set his seal."
So they said to him,
"What can we do to accomplish the works of God?"
Jesus answered and said to them,
"This is the work of God, that you believe in the one he sent."
So they said to him,
"What sign can you do, that we may see and believe in you?
What can you do?
Our ancestors ate manna in the desert, as it is written:
***He gave them bread from heaven to eat.*"**

So Jesus said to them,
"Amen, amen, I say to you,
it was not Moses who gave the bread from heaven;
my Father gives you the true bread from heaven.
For the bread of God is that which comes down from heaven
and gives life to the world."

So they said to him,
"Sir, give us this bread always."
Jesus said to them,
"I am the bread of life;
whoever comes to me will never hunger,
and whoever believes in me will never thirst."

The Gospel of the Lord. All: **Praise to you, Lord Jesus Christ.**

Prayer over the Offerings

Graciously sanctify these gifts, O Lord, we pray,
and, accepting the oblation of this spiritual sacrifice,
make of us an eternal offering to you.
Through Christ our Lord. All: **Amen.**

Communion Antiphon (Wisdom 16:20)

You have given us, O Lord, bread from heaven,
endowed with all delights and sweetness in every taste.

Or:

(John 6:35)
I am the bread of life, says the Lord;
whoever comes to me will not hunger
and whoever believes in me will not thirst.

Prayer after Communion

Accompany with constant protection, O Lord,
those you renew with these heavenly gifts
and, in your never-failing care for them,
make them worthy of eternal redemption.
Through Christ our Lord. All: **Amen.**

Ninteenth Sunday in Ordinary Time

August 8, 2027

Reflection on the Gospel

In the gospel today, we can note the emphasis on the Bread of Life sustaining us, and in a way different than other foods—like the manna we pondered a week ago. This bread not only sustains us physically until tomorrow, but "whoever eats this bread will live forever." Some choose to attend Mass daily to partake in such sustenance. Whether daily or only on Sundays, the church's liturgy is our prescribed, corporate prayer; the liturgy is our source and summit, our opportunity to partake in the Bread of Life.

—Living Liturgy™, *Nineteenth Sunday in Ordinary Time 2027*

Entrance Antiphon (Cf. Ps 74[73]:20, 19, 22, 23)

Look to your covenant, O Lord,
and forget not the life of your poor ones for ever.
Arise, O God, and defend your cause,
and forget not the cries of those who seek you.

Collect

Almighty ever-living God,
whom, taught by the Holy Spirit,
we dare to call our Father,
bring, we pray, to perfection in our hearts
the spirit of adoption as your sons and daughters,
that we may merit to enter into the inheritance
which you have promised.
Through our Lord Jesus Christ, your Son,
who lives and reigns with you in the unity of the Holy Spirit,
God, for ever and ever. All: **Amen.**

Reading I (L 116-B) (1 Kings 19:4-8)

A reading from the first Book of Kings

Strengthened by that food, he walked to the mountain of God.

Elijah went a day's journey into the desert,
until he came to a broom tree and sat beneath it.
He prayed for death, saying:
"This is enough, O LORD!
Take my life, for I am no better than my fathers."
He lay down and fell asleep under the broom tree,
but then an angel touched him and ordered him to get up and eat.
Elijah looked and there at his head was a hearth cake and a jug of water.
After he ate and drank, he lay down again,
but the angel of the LORD came back a second time,
touched him, and ordered,
"Get up and eat, else the journey will be too long for you!"
He got up, ate, and drank;
then strengthened by that food,
he walked forty days and forty nights to the mountain of God, Horeb.

The word of the Lord. All: **Thanks be to God.**

RESPONSORIAL PSALM 34

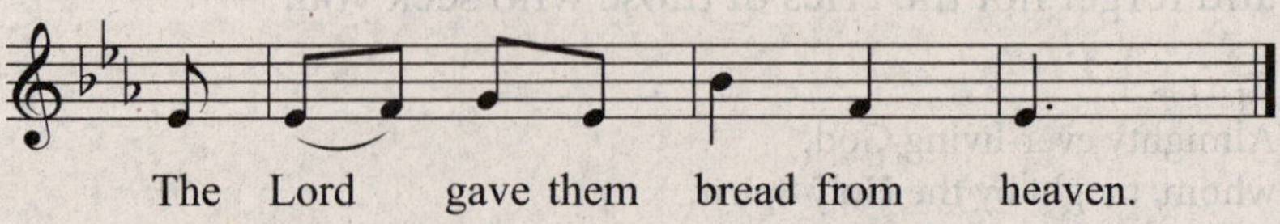

Text: Refrain, *Lectionary for Mass,* © 1969, 1981, 1997, ICEL
Music: *The Collegeville Psalter*, © 2017, Paul Inwood.

Psalm 34:2-3, 4-5, 6-7, 8-9

℟. (9a) **Taste and see the goodness of the Lord.**

I will bless the LORD at all times;
his praise shall be ever in my mouth.
Let my soul glory in the LORD;
the lowly will hear me and be glad. ℟.

Glorify the LORD with me,
let us together extol his name.

I sought the LORD, and he answered me
and delivered me from all my fears. ℟.

Look to him that you may be radiant with joy,
and your faces may not blush with shame.
When the afflicted man called out, the LORD heard,
and from all his distress he saved him. ℟.

The angel of the LORD encamps
around those who fear him and delivers them.
Taste and see how good the LORD is;
blessed the man who takes refuge in him. ℟.

READING II (Ephesians 4:30—5:2)

A reading from the Letter of Saint Paul to the Ephesians

Walk in love, just like Christ.

Brothers and sisters:
Do not grieve the Holy Spirit of God,
with which you were sealed for the day of redemption.
All bitterness, fury, anger, shouting, and reviling
must be removed from you, along with all malice.
And be kind to one another, compassionate,
forgiving one another as God has forgiven you in Christ.

So be imitators of God, as beloved children, and live in love,
as Christ loved us and handed himself over for us
as a sacrificial offering to God for a fragrant aroma.

The word of the Lord. All: **Thanks be to God.**

GOSPEL (John 6:41-51)

ALLELUIA (John 6:51)

℣. Alleluia, alleluia. ℟. **Alleluia, alleluia.**
℣. I am the living bread that came down from heaven, says the Lord;
whoever eats this bread will live forever. ℟.

✠ **A reading from the holy Gospel according to John**

All: **Glory to you, O Lord.**

I am the living bread that came down from heaven.

The Jews murmured about Jesus because he said,
"I am the bread that came down from heaven,"
and they said,
"Is this not Jesus, the son of Joseph?
Do we not know his father and mother?
Then how can he say,
'I have come down from heaven'?"
Jesus answered and said to them,
"Stop murmuring among yourselves.
No one can come to me unless the Father who sent me draw him,
and I will raise him on the last day.
It is written in the prophets:
They shall all be taught by God.
Everyone who listens to my Father and learns from him comes to me.
Not that anyone has seen the Father
except the one who is from God;
he has seen the Father.
Amen, amen, I say to you,
whoever believes has eternal life.
I am the bread of life.
Your ancestors ate the manna in the desert, but they died;
this is the bread that comes down from heaven
so that one may eat it and not die.
I am the living bread that came down from heaven;
whoever eats this bread will live forever;
and the bread that I will give is my flesh for the life of the world."

The Gospel of the Lord. All: **Praise to you, Lord Jesus Christ.**

Prayer over the Offerings

Be pleased, O Lord, to accept the offerings of your Church,
for in your mercy you have given them to be offered
and by your power you transform them
into the mystery of our salvation.
Through Christ our Lord. All: **Amen.**

COMMUNION ANTIPHON (Psalm 147:12, 14)

O Jerusalem, glorify the Lord,
who gives you your fill of finest wheat.

Or:

(Cf. John 6:51)

The bread that I will give, says the Lord,
is my flesh for the life of the world.

PRAYER AFTER COMMUNION

May the communion in your Sacrament
that we have consumed, save us, O Lord,
and confirm us in the light of your truth.
Through Christ our Lord. All: **Amen.**

The Assumption of the Blessed Virgin Mary

AT THE VIGIL MASS

August 14, 2027

The Mass of the Vigil of the Assumption is to be used at evening Masses.

Reflection on the Gospel

On the solemnity of the Assumption, we encounter the Magnificat *(Luke 1:46-55), Mary's own canticle of praise. Her words are deeply Christocentric, proclaiming the greatness of God, his mercy, and his justice. In singing Mary's song, the church echoes not just her devotion but her prophetic joy in the saving power of God. The* Magnificat *isn't only Mary's hymn, it is ours as well. Far from detracting from the eucharistic celebration, the* Magnificat *can focus us more fully on the mystery of Christ's presence, as Mary herself always does.*

—Living Liturgy™, *The Assumption of the Blessed Virgin Mary 2027*

ENTRANCE ANTIPHON

Glorious things are spoken of you, O Mary,
who today were exalted above the choirs of Angels
into eternal triumph with Christ.

COLLECT

O God, who, looking on the lowliness of the Blessed Virgin Mary,
raised her to this grace,
that your Only Begotten Son was born of her according to the flesh
and that she was crowned this day with surpassing glory,
grant through her prayers,
that, saved by the mystery of your redemption,
we may merit to be exalted by you on high.
Through our Lord Jesus Christ, your Son,
who lives and reigns with you in the unity of the Holy Spirit,
God, for ever and ever. All: **Amen.**

READING I (L 621) (1 Chronicles 15:3-4, 15-16; 16:1-2)

A reading from the first Book of Chronicles

They brought in the ark of God and set it within the tent which David had pitched for it.

David assembled all Israel in Jerusalem to bring the ark of the LORD
to the place which he had prepared for it.
David also called together the sons of Aaron and the Levites.

The Levites bore the ark of God on their shoulders with poles,
as Moses had ordained according to the word of the LORD.

David commanded the chiefs of the Levites
to appoint their kinsmen as chanters,
to play on musical instruments, harps, lyres, and cymbals,
to make a loud sound of rejoicing.

They brought in the ark of God and set it within the tent which David had pitched for it.
Then they offered up burnt offerings and peace offerings to God.
When David had finished offering up the burnt offerings and peace offerings,
he blessed the people in the name of the LORD.

The word of the Lord. All: **Thanks be to God.**

Responsorial Psalm 132

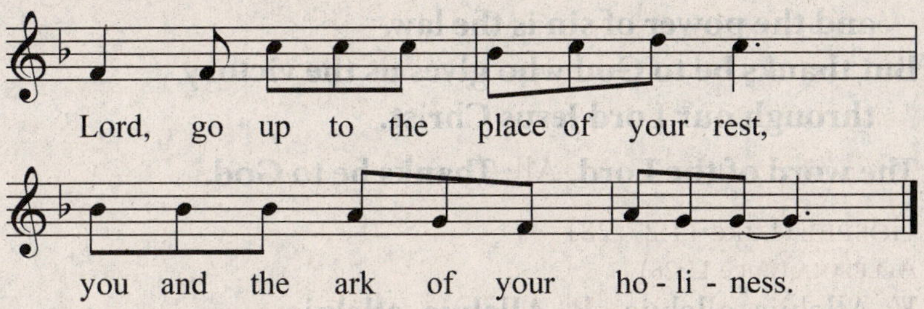

Psalm 132:6-7, 9-10, 13-14

℟. (8) **Lord, go up to the place of your rest, you and the ark of your holiness.**

Behold, we heard of it in Ephrathah;
we found it in the fields of Jaar.
Let us enter his dwelling,
let us worship at his footstool. ℟.

May your priests be clothed with justice;
let your faithful ones shout merrily for joy.
For the sake of David your servant,
reject not the plea of your anointed. ℟.

For the LORD has chosen Zion;
he prefers her for his dwelling.
"Zion is my resting place forever;
in her will I dwell, for I prefer her." ℟.

Reading II (1 Corinthians 15:54b-57)

A reading from the first Letter of Saint Paul to the Corinthians

God gave us victory through Jesus Christ.

Brothers and sisters:
When that which is mortal clothes itself with immortality,
then the word that is written shall come about:

Death is swallowed up in victory.
Where, O death, is your victory?
Where, O death, is your sting?

The sting of death is sin,
and the power of sin is the law.
But thanks be to God who gives us the victory
through our Lord Jesus Christ.

The word of the Lord. All: **Thanks be to God.**

GOSPEL (Luke 11:27-28)

ALLELUIA (Luke 11:28)

℣. Alleluia, alleluia. ℟. **Alleluia, alleluia.**
℣. Blessed are they who hear the word of God
and observe it. ℟.

✠ **A reading from the holy Gospel according to Luke**

All: **Glory to you, O Lord.**

Blessed is the womb that carried you!

While Jesus was speaking,
a woman from the crowd called out and said to him,
"Blessed is the womb that carried you
and the breasts at which you nursed."
He replied,
"Rather, blessed are those
who hear the word of God and observe it."

The Gospel of the Lord. All: **Praise to you, Lord Jesus Christ.**

PRAYER OVER THE OFFERINGS

Receive, we pray, O Lord,
the sacrifice of conciliation and praise,
which we celebrate on the Assumption of the holy Mother of God,
that it may lead us to your pardon
and confirm us in perpetual thanksgiving.
Through Christ our Lord. All: **Amen.**

COMMUNION ANTIPHON (Cf. Luke 11:27)

Blessed is the womb of the Virgin Mary,
which bore the Son of the eternal Father.

PRAYER AFTER COMMUNION

Having partaken of this heavenly table,
we beseech your mercy, Lord our God,
that we, who honor the Assumption of the Mother of God,
may be freed from every threat of harm.
Through Christ our Lord. All: **Amen.**

Sunday, August 15

AT THE MASS DURING THE DAY

ENTRANCE ANTIPHON (Cf. Revelation 12:1)

A great sign appeared in heaven:
a woman clothed with the sun, and the moon beneath her feet,
and on her head a crown of twelve stars.

Or:

Let us all rejoice in the Lord,
as we celebrate the feast day in honor of the Virgin Mary,
at whose Assumption the Angels rejoice
and praise the Son of God.

COLLECT

Almighty ever-living God,
who assumed the Immaculate Virgin Mary, the Mother of your Son,
body and soul into heavenly glory,
grant, we pray,
that, always attentive to the things that are above,
we may merit to be sharers of her glory.
Through our Lord Jesus Christ, your Son,
who lives and reigns with you in the unity of the Holy Spirit,
God, for ever and ever. All: **Amen.**

READING I (L 622) (Revelation 11:19a; 12:1-6a, 10ab)

A reading from the Book of Revelation

A woman clothed with the sun, with the moon beneath her feet.

God's temple in heaven was opened,
and the ark of his covenant could be seen in the temple.

A great sign appeared in the sky, a woman clothed with the sun,
with the moon under her feet,
and on her head a crown of twelve stars.
She was with child and wailed aloud in pain as she labored to give birth.

Then another sign appeared in the sky;
it was a huge red dragon, with seven heads and ten horns,
and on its heads were seven diadems.
Its tail swept away a third of the stars in the sky
and hurled them down to the earth.
Then the dragon stood before the woman about to give birth,
to devour her child when she gave birth.
She gave birth to a son, a male child,
destined to rule all the nations with an iron rod.
Her child was caught up to God and his throne.
The woman herself fled into the desert
where she had a place prepared by God.

Then I heard a loud voice in heaven say:
"Now have salvation and power come,
and the Kingdom of our God
and the authority of his Anointed One."

The word of the Lord. All: **Thanks be to God.**

Responsorial Psalm 45

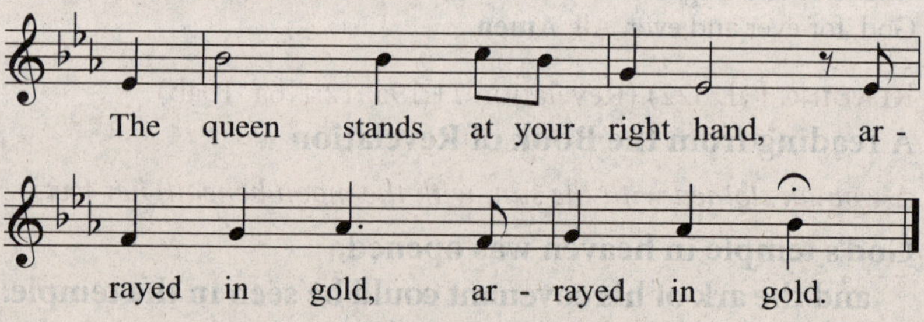

Psalm 45:10bc, 11, 12ab, 16

℟. (10bc) **The queen stands at your right hand, arrayed in gold.**

The queen takes her place at your right hand in gold of Ophir. ℟.

Hear, O daughter, and see; turn your ear,
  forget your people and your father's house. ℟.

So shall the king desire your beauty;
  for he is your lord. ℟.

They are borne in with gladness and joy;
  they enter the palace of the king. ℟.

READING II (1 Corinthians 15:20-27)

A reading from the first Letter of Saint Paul to the Corinthians

Christ, the firstfruits; then those who belong to him.

Brothers and sisters:
Christ has been raised from the dead,
the firstfruits of those who have fallen asleep.
For since death came through man,
the resurrection of the dead came also through man.
For just as in Adam all die,
so too in Christ shall all be brought to life,
but each one in proper order:
Christ the firstfruits;
then, at his coming, those who belong to Christ;
then comes the end,
when he hands over the Kingdom to his God and Father,
when he has destroyed every sovereignty
and every authority and power.
For he must reign until he has put all his enemies under his feet.
The last enemy to be destroyed is death,
for "he subjected everything under his feet."
The word of the Lord. All: **Thanks be to God.**

GOSPEL (Luke 1:39-56)

ALLELUIA

℣. Alleluia, alleluia. ℟. **Alleluia, alleluia.**
℣. Mary is taken up to heaven;
a chorus of angels exults. ℟.

✠ **A reading from the holy Gospel according to Luke**

All: **Glory to you, O Lord.**

The Almighty has done great things for me; he has raised up the lowly.

Mary set out
and traveled to the hill country in haste
to a town of Judah,
where she entered the house of Zechariah
and greeted Elizabeth.
When Elizabeth heard Mary's greeting,
the infant leaped in her womb,
and Elizabeth, filled with the Holy Spirit,
cried out in a loud voice and said,
"Blessed are you among women,
and blessed is the fruit of your womb.
And how does this happen to me,
that the mother of my Lord should come to me?
For at the moment the sound of your greeting reached my ears,
the infant in my womb leaped for joy.
Blessed are you who believed
that what was spoken to you by the Lord
would be fulfilled."

And Mary said:
"My soul proclaims the greatness of the Lord;
my spirit rejoices in God my Savior
for he has looked with favor on his lowly servant.
From this day all generations will call me blessed:
the Almighty has done great things for me,
and holy is his Name.

He has mercy on those who fear him
in every generation.
He has shown the strength of his arm,
and has scattered the proud in their conceit.
He has cast down the mighty from their thrones,
and has lifted up the lowly.
He has filled the hungry with good things,
and the rich he has sent away empty.
He has come to the help of his servant Israel
for he has remembered his promise of mercy,
the promise he made to our fathers,
to Abraham and his children forever."

Mary remained with her about three months
and then returned to her home.

The Gospel of the Lord. All: **Praise to you, Lord Jesus Christ.**

PRAYER OVER THE OFFERINGS

May this oblation, our tribute of homage,
rise up to you, O Lord,
and, through the intercession of the most Blessed Virgin Mary,
whom you assumed into heaven,
may our hearts, aflame with the fire of love,
constantly long for you.
Through Christ our Lord. All: **Amen.**

COMMUNION ANTIPHON (Luke 1:48-49)

All generations will call me blessed,
for he who is mighty has done great things for me.

PRAYER AFTER COMMUNION

Having received the Sacrament of salvation,
we ask you to grant, O Lord,
that, through the intercession of the Blessed Virgin Mary,
whom you assumed into heaven,
we may be brought to the glory of the resurrection.
Through Christ our Lord. All: **Amen.**

Twenty-First Sunday in Ordinary Time

August 22, 2027

Reflection on the Gospel

In the preceding verses to this week's gospel, Jesus tells the quarreling crowd, "Unless you eat the flesh of the Son of Man and drink his blood, you do not have life within you" (John 6:53). This shocking catechesis sets up today's passage, the conclusion of our weeks-long retreat on Jesus, the Bread of Life. Today's readings present our response to Christ's difficult teachings and the abundance, reliance, sustenance, and union given to us: belief. "Master, to whom shall we go? You have the words of eternal life."

—Living Liturgy™, *Twenty-First Sunday in Ordinary Time 2027*

Entrance Antiphon (Cf. Psalm 86[85]:1-3)

Turn your ear, O Lord, and answer me;
save the servant who trusts in you, my God.
Have mercy on me, O Lord, for I cry to you all the day long.

Collect

O God, who cause the minds of the faithful
to unite in a single purpose,
grant your people to love what you command
and to desire what you promise,
that, amid the uncertainties of this world,
our hearts may be fixed on that place
where true gladness is found.
Through our Lord Jesus Christ, your Son,
who lives and reigns with you in the unity of the Holy Spirit,
God, for ever and ever. All: **Amen.**

Reading I (L 122-B) (Joshua 24:1-2a, 15-17, 18b)

A reading from the Book of Joshua

We will serve the Lord, for he is our God.

Joshua gathered together all the tribes of Israel at Shechem,
summoning their elders, their leaders,
their judges, and their officers.
When they stood in ranks before God,
Joshua addressed all the people:
"If it does not please you to serve the LORD,
decide today whom you will serve,
the gods your fathers served beyond the River
or the gods of the Amorites in whose country you are now dwelling.
As for me and my household, we will serve the LORD."

But the people answered,
"Far be it from us to forsake the LORD
for the service of other gods.
For it was the LORD, our God,
who brought us and our fathers up out of the land of Egypt,
out of a state of slavery.
He performed those great miracles before our very eyes
and protected us along our entire journey
and among the peoples through whom we passed.
Therefore we also will serve the LORD, for he is our God."

The word of the Lord. All: **Thanks be to God.**

RESPONSORIAL PSALM 34

Psalm 34:2-3, 16-17, 18-19, 20-21

℟. (9a) **Taste and see the goodness of the Lord.**

I will bless the LORD at all times;
his praise shall be ever in my mouth.

Let my soul glory in the LORD;
the lowly will hear me and be glad. ℟.

The LORD has eyes for the just,
and ears for their cry.
The LORD confronts the evildoers,
to destroy remembrance of them from the earth. ℟.

When the just cry out, the LORD hears them,
and from all their distress he rescues them.
The LORD is close to the brokenhearted;
and those who are crushed in spirit he saves. ℟.

Many are the troubles of the just one,
but out of them all the LORD delivers him;
he watches over all his bones;
not one of them shall be broken. ℟.

READING II

A Longer Form (Ephesians 5:21-32)

A reading from the Letter of Saint Paul to the Ephesians

This is a great mystery, regarding Christ and the Church.

Brothers and sisters:
Be subordinate to one another out of reverence for Christ.
Wives should be subordinate to their husbands as to the Lord.
For the husband is head of his wife
just as Christ is head of the church,
he himself the savior of the body.
As the church is subordinate to Christ,
so wives should be subordinate to their husbands in everything.
Husbands, love your wives,
even as Christ loved the church
and handed himself over for her to sanctify her,
cleansing her by the bath of water with the word,
that he might present to himself the church in splendor,
without spot or wrinkle or any such thing,
that she might be holy and without blemish.

So also husbands should love their wives as their own bodies.
He who loves his wife loves himself.
For no one hates his own flesh
but rather nourishes and cherishes it,
even as Christ does the church,
because we are members of his body.
For this reason a man shall leave his father and his mother
and be joined to his wife,
and the two shall become one flesh.
This is a great mystery,
but I speak in reference to Christ and the church.
The word of the Lord. All: **Thanks be to God.**

Or:

B Shorter Form (Ephesians 5:2a, 25-32)

A reading from the Letter of Saint Paul to the Ephesians

This is a great mystery, regarding Christ and the Church.

Brothers and sisters:
Live in love, as Christ loved us.
Husbands, love your wives,
even as Christ loved the church
and handed himself over for her to sanctify her,
cleansing her by the bath of water with the word,
that he might present to himself the church in splendor,
without spot or wrinkle or any such thing,
that she might be holy and without blemish.
So also husbands should love their wives as their own bodies.
He who loves his wife loves himself.
For no one hates his own flesh
but rather nourishes and cherishes it,
even as Christ does the church,
because we are members of his body.

For this reason a man shall leave his father and his mother
and be joined to his wife,
and the two shall become one flesh.
This is a great mystery,
but I speak in reference to Christ and the church.

The word of the Lord. All: **Thanks be to God.**

GOSPEL (John 6:60-69)
ALLELUIA (John 6:63c, 68c)

℣. Alleluia, alleluia. ℟. **Alleluia, alleluia.**
℣. Your words, Lord, are Spirit and life;
you have the words of everlasting life. ℟.

✠ **A reading from the holy Gospel according to John**

All: **Glory to you, O Lord.**

To whom shall we go? You have the words of eternal life.

Many of Jesus' disciples who were listening said,
"This saying is hard; who can accept it?"
Since Jesus knew that his disciples were murmuring about this,
he said to them, "Does this shock you?
What if you were to see the Son of Man ascending
to where he was before?
It is the spirit that gives life,
while the flesh is of no avail.
The words I have spoken to you are Spirit and life.
But there are some of you who do not believe."
Jesus knew from the beginning the ones who would not believe
and the one who would betray him.
And he said,
"For this reason I have told you that no one can come to me
unless it is granted him by my Father."

As a result of this,
many of his disciples returned to their former way of life
and no longer accompanied him.
Jesus then said to the Twelve, "Do you also want to leave?"
Simon Peter answered him, "Master, to whom shall we go?
You have the words of eternal life.
We have come to believe
and are convinced that you are the Holy One of God."

The Gospel of the Lord. All: **Praise to you, Lord Jesus Christ.**

PRAYER OVER THE OFFERINGS
O Lord, who gained for yourself a people by adoption
through the one sacrifice offered once for all,
bestow graciously on us, we pray,
the gifts of unity and peace in your Church.
Through Christ our Lord. All: **Amen.**

COMMUNION ANTIPHON (Cf. Psalm 104[103]:13-15)
The earth is replete with the fruits of your work, O Lord;
you bring forth bread from the earth
and wine to cheer the heart.

Or:

(Cf. John 6:54)
Whoever eats my flesh and drinks my blood
has eternal life, says the Lord,
and I will raise him up on the last day.

PRAYER AFTER COMMUNION
Complete within us, O Lord, we pray,
the healing work of your mercy
and graciously perfect and sustain us,
so that in all things we may please you.
Through Christ our Lord. All: **Amen.**

Twenty-Second Sunday in Ordinary Time

August 29, 2027

Reflection on the Gospel

If those with whom we hope to share the good news don't know us and trust us as friends, any words we share will be hollow and distrusted. If those with whom we hope to share the good news are hungry, poorly clothed, or need shelter, these basic human needs will preclude them from hearing any other message. It's likely that the "needs" of those many of us meet are not needs relating to hunger or housing insecurity, but rather needs of relationship: belonging, being understood, sensing one's own belonging.

—Living Liturgy™, *Twenty-Second Sunday in Ordinary Time 2027*

Entrance Antiphon (Cf. Psalm 86[85]:3, 5)

Have mercy on me, O Lord, for I cry to you all the day long.
O Lord, you are good and forgiving,
full of mercy to all who call to you.

Collect

God of might, giver of every good gift,
put into our hearts the love of your name,
so that, by deepening our sense of reverence,
you may nurture in us what is good
and, by your watchful care,
keep safe what you have nurtured.
Through our Lord Jesus Christ, your Son,
who lives and reigns with you in the unity of the Holy Spirit,
God, for ever and ever. All: **Amen.**

Reading I (L 125-B) (Deuteronomy 4:1-2, 6-8)

A reading from the Book of Deuteronomy

You shall not add to what I command you . . . keep the commands of the Lord.

Moses said to the people:
"Now, Israel, hear the statutes and decrees
which I am teaching you to observe,

that you may live, and may enter in and take
possession of the land
which the LORD, the God of your fathers, is giving you.
In your observance of the commandments of the LORD,
your God,
which I enjoin upon you,
you shall not add to what I command you nor subtract
from it.
Observe them carefully,
for thus will you give evidence
of your wisdom and intelligence to the nations,
who will hear of all these statutes and say,
'This great nation is truly a wise and intelligent
people.'
For what great nation is there
that has gods so close to it as the LORD, our God,
is to us
whenever we call upon him?
Or what great nation has statutes and decrees
that are as just as this whole law
which I am setting before you today?"

The word of the Lord. All: Thanks be to God.

RESPONSORIAL PSALM 15

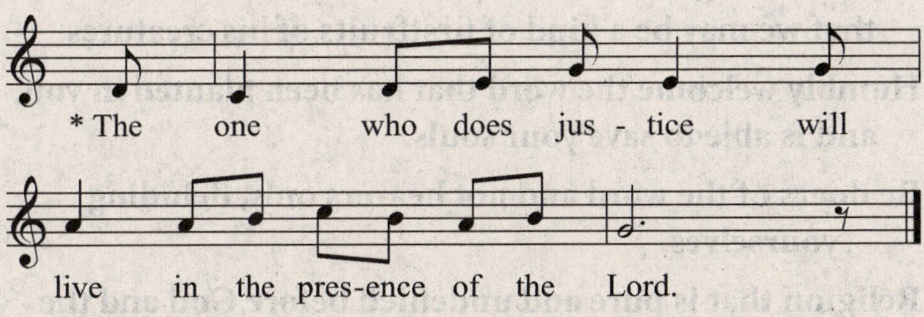

* *Some lectionaries omit the word* The *at the beginning of the response*

Psalm 15:2-3, 3-4, 4-5

℟. (1a) **The one who does justice will live in the presence of the Lord.**

Whoever walks blamelessly and does justice;
who thinks the truth in his heart
and slanders not with his tongue. ℟.

Who harms not his fellow man,
nor takes up a reproach against his neighbor;
by whom the reprobate is despised,
while he honors those who fear the LORD. ℟.

Who lends not his money at usury
and accepts no bribe against the innocent.
Whoever does these things
shall never be disturbed. ℟.

READING II (James 1:17-18, 21b-22, 27)

A reading from the Letter of Saint James

Be doers of the word.

Dearest brothers and sisters:
All good giving and every perfect gift is from above,
coming down from the Father of lights,
with whom there is no alteration or shadow caused by change.
He willed to give us birth by the word of truth
that we may be a kind of firstfruits of his creatures.

Humbly welcome the word that has been planted in you
and is able to save your souls.

Be doers of the word and not hearers only, deluding yourselves.

Religion that is pure and undefiled before God and the Father is this:
to care for orphans and widows in their affliction
and to keep oneself unstained by the world.

The word of the Lord. All: **Thanks be to God.**

Gospel (Mark 7:1-8, 14-15, 21-23)

Alleluia (James 1:18)

℣. Alleluia, alleluia. ℟. **Alleluia, alleluia.**
℣. The Father willed to give us birth by the word of truth
that we may be a kind of firstfruits of his creatures. ℟.

✠ **A reading from the holy Gospel according to Mark**

All: **Glory to you, O Lord.**

You disregard God's commandment but cling to human tradition.

When the Pharisees with some scribes who had come from Jerusalem
gathered around Jesus,
they observed that some of his disciples ate their meals
with unclean, that is, unwashed, hands.
—For the Pharisees and, in fact, all Jews,
do not eat without carefully washing their hands,
keeping the tradition of the elders.
And on coming from the marketplace
they do not eat without purifying themselves.
And there are many other things that they have traditionally observed,
the purification of cups and jugs and kettles and beds.—
So the Pharisees and scribes questioned him,
"Why do your disciples not follow the tradition of the elders
but instead eat a meal with unclean hands?"
He responded,
"Well did Isaiah prophesy about you hypocrites, as it is written:
This people honors me with their lips,
but their hearts are far from me;
in vain do they worship me,
teaching as doctrines human precepts.
You disregard God's commandment but cling to human tradition."

He summoned the crowd again and said to them,
"Hear me, all of you, and understand.
Nothing that enters one from outside can defile that person;
but the things that come out from within are what defile.

"From within people, from their hearts,
come evil thoughts, unchastity, theft, murder,
adultery, greed, malice, deceit,
licentiousness, envy, blasphemy, arrogance, folly.
All these evils come from within and they defile."

The Gospel of the Lord. All: **Praise to you, Lord Jesus Christ.**

PRAYER OVER THE OFFERINGS

May this sacred offering, O Lord,
confer on us always the blessing of salvation,
that what it celebrates in mystery
it may accomplish in power.
Through Christ our Lord. All: **Amen.**

COMMUNION ANTIPHON (Psalm 31[30]:20)

How great is the goodness, Lord,
that you keep for those who fear you.

Or:

(Matthew 5:9-10)

Blessed are the peacemakers,
for they shall be called children of God.
Blessed are they who are persecuted for the sake of righteousness,
for theirs is the kingdom of heaven.

PRAYER AFTER COMMUNION

Renewed by this bread from the heavenly table,
we beseech you, Lord,
that, being the food of charity,
it may confirm our hearts
and stir us to serve you in our neighbor.
Through Christ our Lord. All: **Amen.**

Twenty-Third Sunday in Ordinary Time

September 5, 2027

Reflection on the Gospel

Today's gospel, as did one earlier this year, includes Aramaic words: "Ephphatha!" *"Be opened!" The church continues to wrestle with questions of openness, especially around the Eucharist. Pope Francis, in* Evangelii Gaudium *(The Joy of the Gospel), reminded us that the Eucharist is "not a prize for the perfect but a powerful medicine and nourishment for the weak" (EG 47). Let us be vigilant in being open to all who seek Christ—especially in the liturgy—without placing artificial restrictions on who may pray, serve, or be nourished by grace.*

—Living Liturgy™, *Twenty-Third Sunday in Ordinary Time 2027*

Entrance Antiphon (Psalm 119[118]:137, 124)

You are just, O Lord, and your judgment is right;
treat your servant in accord with your merciful love.

Collect

O God, by whom we are redeemed and receive adoption,
look graciously upon your beloved sons and daughters,
that those who believe in Christ
may receive true freedom
and an everlasting inheritance.
Through our Lord Jesus Christ, your Son,
who lives and reigns with you in the unity of the Holy Spirit,
God, for ever and ever. All: **Amen.**

Reading I (L 128-B) (Isaiah 35:4-7a)

A reading from the Book of the Prophet Isaiah

The ears of those who are deaf will be cleared; and the tongue of those who are mute will sing.

Thus says the Lord:
Say to those whose hearts are frightened:
Be strong, fear not!

Here is your God,
he comes with vindication;
with divine recompense
he comes to save you.
Then will the eyes of the blind be opened,
the ears of the deaf be cleared;
then will the lame leap like a stag,
then the tongue of the mute will sing.
Streams will burst forth in the desert,
and rivers in the steppe.
The burning sands will become pools,
and the thirsty ground, springs of water.

The word of the Lord. All: **Thanks be to God.**

RESPONSORIAL PSALM 146

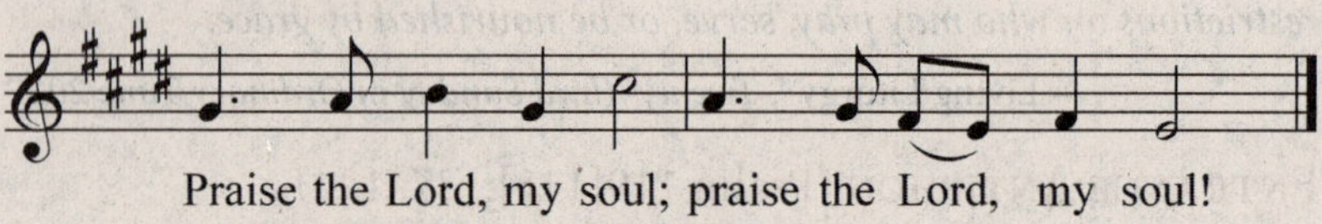

Psalm 146:6-7, 8-9a, 9bc-10

℟. (1b) **Praise the Lord, my soul!** *or:* ℟. **Alleluia.**

The God of Jacob keeps faith forever,
secures justice for the oppressed,
gives food to the hungry.
The LORD sets captives free. ℟.

The LORD gives sight to the blind;
the LORD raises up those who were bowed down.
The LORD loves the just;
the LORD protects strangers. ℟.

The fatherless and the widow the LORD sustains,
but the way of the wicked he thwarts.
The LORD shall reign forever;
your God, O Zion, through all generations. Alleluia. ℟.

READING II (James 2:1-5)

A reading from the Letter of Saint James

Did not God choose the poor to be heirs of the kingdom?

My brothers and sisters, show no partiality
as you adhere to the faith in our glorious Lord Jesus Christ.
For if a man with gold rings and fine clothes
comes into your assembly,
and a poor person in shabby clothes also comes in,
and you pay attention to the one wearing the fine clothes
and say, "Sit here, please,"
while you say to the poor one, "Stand there," or "Sit at my feet,"
have you not made distinctions among yourselves
and become judges with evil designs?

Listen, my beloved brothers and sisters.
Did not God choose those who are poor in the world
to be rich in faith and heirs of the kingdom
that he promised to those who love him?

The word of the Lord. All: **Thanks be to God.**

GOSPEL (Mark 7:31-37)

ALLELUIA (*See* Matthew 4:23)

℣. Alleluia, alleluia. ℟. **Alleluia, alleluia.**
℣. Jesus proclaimed the Gospel of the kingdom
and cured every disease among the people. ℟.

✠ **A reading from the holy Gospel according to Mark**

All: **Glory to you, O Lord.**

He makes the deaf hear and the mute speak.

Again Jesus left the district of Tyre
and went by way of Sidon to the Sea of Galilee,
into the district of the Decapolis.

And people brought to him a deaf man who had a speech impediment
and begged him to lay his hand on him.
He took him off by himself away from the crowd.
He put his finger into the man's ears
and, spitting, touched his tongue;
then he looked up to heaven and groaned, and said to him,
***"Ephphatha!"*—that is, "Be opened!"—**
And immediately the man's ears were opened,
his speech impediment was removed,
and he spoke plainly.
He ordered them not to tell anyone.
But the more he ordered them not to,
the more they proclaimed it.
They were exceedingly astonished and they said,
"He has done all things well.
He makes the deaf hear and the mute speak."

The Gospel of the Lord. All: **Praise to you, Lord Jesus Christ.**

Prayer over the Offerings

O God, who give us the gift of true prayer and of peace,
graciously grant that, through this offering,
we may do fitting homage to your divine majesty
and, by partaking of the sacred mystery,
we may be faithfully united in mind and heart.
Through Christ our Lord. All: **Amen.**

Communion Antiphon (Cf. Psalm 42[41]:2-3)

Like the deer that yearns for running streams,
so my soul is yearning for you, my God;
my soul is thirsting for God, the living God.

Or:

(John 8:12)
I am the light of the world, says the Lord;
whoever follows me will not walk in darkness,
but will have the light of life.

PRAYER AFTER COMMUNION

Grant that your faithful, O Lord,
whom you nourish and endow with life
through the food of your Word and heavenly Sacrament,
may so benefit from your beloved Son's great gifts
that we may merit an eternal share in his life.
Who lives and reigns for ever and ever. All: **Amen.**

Twenty-Fourth Sunday in Ordinary Time

September 12, 2027

Reflection on the Gospel

Jesus asks his disciples, "But who do you say that I am?" We might imagine a parallel question from Christ: "Where do you say that I am?" While Christ is not bound by time or space, the Vatican II Constitution on the Sacred Liturgy teaches that Christ is truly present in the liturgy in four ways: in the assembly, the word, the presiding minister, and uniquely so in the Eucharist. So, when we gather around the altar, Christ is in our midst: in each other, in the altar, and in the Eucharist we share.

—Living Liturgy™, *Twenty-Fourth Sunday in Ordinary Time 2027*

ENTRANCE ANTIPHON (Cf. Sirach 36:18)

Give peace, O Lord, to those who wait for you,
that your prophets be found true.
Hear the prayers of your servant,
and of your people Israel.

COLLECT

Look upon us, O God,
Creator and ruler of all things,
and, that we may feel the working of your mercy,
grant that we may serve you with all our heart.
Through our Lord Jesus Christ, your Son,
who lives and reigns with you in the unity of the Holy Spirit,
God, for ever and ever. All: **Amen.**

Reading I (L 131-B) (Isaiah 50:5-9a)

A reading from the Book of the Prophet Isaiah

I gave my back to those who beat me.

The Lord God opens my ear that I may hear;
and I have not rebelled,
have not turned back.
I gave my back to those who beat me,
my cheeks to those who plucked my beard;
my face I did not shield
from buffets and spitting.

The Lord God is my help,
therefore I am not disgraced;
I have set my face like flint,
knowing that I shall not be put to shame.
He is near who upholds my right;
if anyone wishes to oppose me,
let us appear together.
Who disputes my right?
Let that man confront me.
See, the Lord God is my help;
who will prove me wrong?

The word of the Lord. All: **Thanks be to God.**

Responsorial Psalm 116

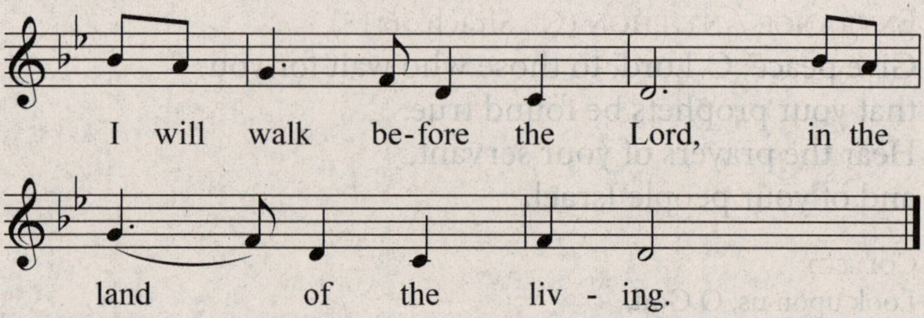

Psalm 116:1-2, 3-4, 5-6, 8-9

℟. (9) **I will walk before the Lord, in the land of the living.** *or:* ℟. **Alleluia.**

I love the LORD because he has heard
my voice in supplication,
because he has inclined his ear to me
the day I called. ℟.

The cords of death encompassed me;
the snares of the netherworld seized upon me;
I fell into distress and sorrow,
and I called upon the name of the LORD,
"O LORD, save my life!" ℟.

Gracious is the LORD and just;
yes, our God is merciful.
The LORD keeps the little ones;
I was brought low, and he saved me. ℟.

For he has freed my soul from death,
my eyes from tears, my feet from stumbling.
I shall walk before the LORD
in the land of the living. ℟.

READING II (James 2:14-18)

A reading from the Letter of Saint James

Faith, if it does not have works, is dead.

What good is it, my brothers and sisters,
if someone says he has faith but does not have works?
Can that faith save him?
If a brother or sister has nothing to wear
and has no food for the day,
and one of you says to them,
"Go in peace, keep warm, and eat well,"
but you do not give them the necessities of the body,
what good is it?
So also faith of itself,
if it does not have works, is dead.

Indeed someone might say,
"You have faith and I have works."
Demonstrate your faith to me without works,
and I will demonstrate my faith to you from my works.

The word of the Lord. All: **Thanks be to God.**

GOSPEL (Mark 8:27-35)
ALLELUIA (Galatians 6:14)

℣. Alleluia, alleluia. ℟. **Alleluia, alleluia.**
℣. May I never boast except in the cross of our Lord
through which the world has been crucified to me and
I to the world. ℟.

✠ **A reading from the holy Gospel according to Mark**

All: **Glory to you, O Lord.**

You are the Christ . . . the Son of Man must suffer greatly.

Jesus and his disciples set out
for the villages of Caesarea Philippi.
Along the way he asked his disciples,
"Who do people say that I am?"
They said in reply,
"John the Baptist, others Elijah,
still others one of the prophets."
And he asked them,
"But who do you say that I am?"
Peter said to him in reply,
"You are the Christ."
Then he warned them not to tell anyone about him.

He began to teach them
that the Son of Man must suffer greatly
and be rejected by the elders, the chief priests, and the scribes,
and be killed, and rise after three days.
He spoke this openly.
Then Peter took him aside and began to rebuke him.

At this he turned around and, looking at his disciples,
rebuked Peter and said, "Get behind me, Satan.
You are thinking not as God does, but as human beings do."

He summoned the crowd with his disciples and said to them,
"Whoever wishes to come after me must deny himself,
take up his cross, and follow me.
For whoever wishes to save his life will lose it,
but whoever loses his life for my sake
and that of the gospel will save it."

The Gospel of the Lord. All: **Praise to you, Lord Jesus Christ.**

PRAYER OVER THE OFFERINGS

Look with favor on our supplications, O Lord,
and in your kindness accept these, your servants' offerings,
that what each has offered to the honor of your name
may serve the salvation of all.
Through Christ our Lord. All: **Amen.**

COMMUNION ANTIPHON (Cf. Psalm 36[35]:8)

How precious is your mercy, O God!
The children of men seek shelter in the shadow of your wings.

Or:

(Cf. 1 Corinthians 10:16)

The chalice of blessing that we bless
is a communion in the Blood of Christ;
and the bread that we break
is a sharing in the Body of the Lord.

PRAYER AFTER COMMUNION

May the working of this heavenly gift, O Lord, we pray,
take possession of our minds and bodies,
so that its effects, and not our own desires,
may always prevail in us.
Through Christ our Lord. All: **Amen.**

Twenty-Fifth Sunday in Ordinary Time

September 19, 2027

Reflection on the Gospel

Disorder, wars, conflict, envy, passions: all words from the second reading this Sunday, culminating in the gospel, with the disciples arguing with one another. Where do these troubles come from, and why do they seem so persistent? Imagine if we took to heart the words of Jesus in the gospel, "If anyone wishes to be first, he shall be the last of all and the servant of all." As much as it is thanksgiving, our celebration and reception of the Eucharist is also service, solidarity, and our freedom.

—Living Liturgy™, *Twenty-Fifth Sunday in Ordinary Time 2027*

Entrance Antiphon

I am the salvation of the people, says the Lord.
Should they cry to me in any distress,
I will hear them, and I will be their Lord for ever.

Collect

O God, who founded all the commands of your sacred Law
upon love of you and of our neighbor,
grant that, by keeping your precepts,
we may merit to attain eternal life.
Through our Lord Jesus Christ, your Son,
who lives and reigns with you in the unity of the Holy Spirit,
God, for ever and ever. All: **Amen.**

Reading I (L 134-B) (Wisdom 2:12, 17-20)

A reading from the Book of Wisdom

Let us condemn him to a shameful death.

The wicked say:
Let us beset the just one, because he is obnoxious to us;
he sets himself against our doings,
reproaches us for transgressions of the law
and charges us with violations of our training.

Let us see whether his words be true;
let us find out what will happen to him.
For if the just one be the son of God, God will defend him
and deliver him from the hand of his foes.
With revilement and torture let us put the just one to the test
that we may have proof of his gentleness
and try his patience.
Let us condemn him to a shameful death;
for according to his own words, God will take care of him.

The word of the Lord. All: **Thanks be to God.**

Responsorial Psalm 54

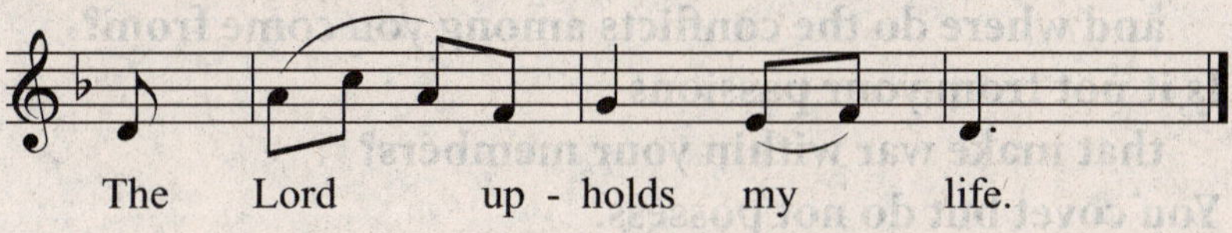

Psalm 54:3-4, 5, 6-8

℟. (6b) **The Lord upholds my life.**

O God, by your name save me,
and by your might defend my cause.
O God, hear my prayer;
hearken to the words of my mouth. ℟.

For the haughty have risen up against me,
the ruthless seek my life;
they set not God before their eyes. ℟.

Behold, God is my helper;
the Lord sustains my life.
Freely will I offer you sacrifice;
I will praise your name, O Lord, for its goodness. ℟.

READING II (James 3:16—4:3)

A reading from the Letter of Saint James

The fruit of righteousness is sown in peace for those who cultivate peace.

Beloved:
Where jealousy and selfish ambition exist,
there is disorder and every foul practice.
But the wisdom from above is first of all pure,
then peaceable, gentle, compliant,
full of mercy and good fruits,
without inconstancy or insincerity.
And the fruit of righteousness is sown in peace
for those who cultivate peace.

Where do the wars
and where do the conflicts among you come from?
Is it not from your passions
that make war within your members?
You covet but do not possess.
You kill and envy but you cannot obtain;
you fight and wage war.
You do not possess because you do not ask.
You ask but do not receive,
because you ask wrongly, to spend it on your passions.

The word of the Lord. All: **Thanks be to God.**

GOSPEL (Mark 9:30-37)

ALLELUIA (*See* 2 Thessalonians 2:14)

℣. Alleluia, alleluia. ℟. **Alleluia, alleluia.**
℣. God has called us through the Gospel
to possess the glory of our Lord Jesus Christ. ℟.

✠ **A reading from the holy Gospel according to Mark**

All: **Glory to you, O Lord.**

The Son of Man is to be handed over. . . .Whoever wishes to be first will be the servant of all.

Jesus and his disciples left from there and began a journey through Galilee,
but he did not wish anyone to know about it.
He was teaching his disciples and telling them,
"The Son of Man is to be handed over to men
and they will kill him,
and three days after his death the Son of Man will rise."
But they did not understand the saying,
and they were afraid to question him.

They came to Capernaum and, once inside the house,
he began to ask them,
"What were you arguing about on the way?"
But they remained silent.
They had been discussing among themselves on the way
who was the greatest.
Then he sat down, called the Twelve, and said to them,
"If anyone wishes to be first,
he shall be the last of all and the servant of all."
Taking a child, he placed it in their midst,
and putting his arms around it, he said to them,
"Whoever receives one child such as this in my name, receives me;
and whoever receives me,
receives not me but the One who sent me."

The Gospel of the Lord. All: **Praise to you, Lord Jesus Christ.**

Prayer over the Offerings

Receive with favor, O Lord, we pray,
the offerings of your people,
that what they profess with devotion and faith
may be theirs through these heavenly mysteries.
Through Christ our Lord. All: **Amen.**

Communion Antiphon (Psalm 119[118]:4-5)

You have laid down your precepts to be carefully kept;
may my ways be firm in keeping your statutes.

Or:

(John 10:14)
I am the Good Shepherd, says the Lord;
I know my sheep, and mine know me.

PRAYER AFTER COMMUNION
Graciously raise up, O Lord,
those you renew with this Sacrament,
that we may come to possess your redemption
both in mystery and in the manner of our life.
Through Christ our Lord. All: **Amen.**

Twenty-Sixth Sunday in Ordinary Time

September 26, 2027

Reflection on the Gospel
In today's readings, we hear of people preaching, healing, and leading even without formal authorization. In the gospel, Jesus tells John to let a stranger continue driving out demons in his name, because "whoever is not against us is for us." The church affirms that by baptism, all are priest, prophet, and king. Laypeople lead, teach, and evangelize in many important ways. Imagine what our liturgy could be if it included a broader range of voices—especially those that have been historically silenced or marginalized.

—Living Liturgy™, *Twenty-Sixth Sunday in Ordinary Time 2027*

ENTRANCE ANTIPHON (Daniel 3:31, 29, 30, 43, 42)
All that you have done to us, O Lord,
you have done with true judgment,
for we have sinned against you
and not obeyed your commandments.
But give glory to your name
and deal with us according to the bounty of your mercy.

COLLECT

O God, who manifest your almighty power
above all by pardoning and showing mercy,
bestow, we pray, your grace abundantly upon us
and make those hastening to attain your promises
heirs to the treasures of heaven.
Through our Lord Jesus Christ, your Son,
who lives and reigns with you in the unity of the Holy Spirit,
God, for ever and ever. All: **Amen.**

READING I (L 137-B) (Numbers 11:25-29)

A reading from the Book of Numbers

Are you jealous for my sake? Would that all the people of the Lord were prophets!

The LORD came down in the cloud and spoke to Moses.
Taking some of the spirit that was on Moses,
the LORD bestowed it on the seventy elders;
and as the spirit came to rest on them, they prophesied.

Now two men, one named Eldad and the other Medad,
were not in the gathering but had been left in the camp.
They too had been on the list, but had not gone out to the tent;
yet the spirit came to rest on them also,
and they prophesied in the camp.
So, when a young man quickly told Moses,
"Eldad and Medad are prophesying in the camp,"
Joshua, son of Nun, who from his youth had been Moses' aide, said,
"Moses, my lord, stop them."
But Moses answered him,
"Are you jealous for my sake?
Would that all the people of the LORD were prophets!
Would that the LORD might bestow his spirit on them all!"

The word of the Lord. All: **Thanks be to God.**

Responsorial Psalm 19

Psalm 19:8, 10, 12-13, 14

℟. (9a) **The precepts of the Lord give joy to the heart.**

The law of the LORD is perfect,
refreshing the soul;
the decree of the LORD is trustworthy,
giving wisdom to the simple. ℟.

The fear of the LORD is pure,
enduring forever;
the ordinances of the LORD are true,
all of them just. ℟.

Though your servant is careful of them,
very diligent in keeping them,
yet who can detect failings?
Cleanse me from my unknown faults! ℟.

From wanton sin especially, restrain your servant;
let it not rule over me.
Then shall I be blameless and innocent
of serious sin. ℟.

Reading II (James 5:1-6)

A reading from the Letter of Saint James

Your wealth has rotted away.

Come now, you rich, weep and wail over your impending miseries.
Your wealth has rotted away, your clothes have become moth-eaten,
your gold and silver have corroded,
and that corrosion will be a testimony against you;
it will devour your flesh like a fire.

You have stored up treasure for the last days.
Behold, the wages you withheld from the workers
who harvested your fields are crying aloud;
and the cries of the harvesters
have reached the ears of the Lord of hosts.
You have lived on earth in luxury and pleasure;
you have fattened your hearts for the day of slaughter.
You have condemned;
you have murdered the righteous one;
he offers you no resistance.

The word of the Lord. All: **Thanks be to God.**

GOSPEL (Mark 9:38-43, 45, 47-48)
ALLELUIA (*See* John 17:17b, 17a)

℣. Alleluia, alleluia. ℟. **Alleluia, alleluia.**
℣. Your word, O Lord, is truth;
consecrate us in the truth. ℟.

✠ **A reading from the holy Gospel according to Mark**

All: **Glory to you, O Lord.**

Whoever is not against us is for us. If your hand causes you to sin, cut it off.

At that time, John said to Jesus,
"Teacher, we saw someone driving out demons in your name,
and we tried to prevent him because he does not follow us."
Jesus replied, "Do not prevent him.
There is no one who performs a mighty deed in my name
who can at the same time speak ill of me.
For whoever is not against us is for us.
Anyone who gives you a cup of water to drink
because you belong to Christ,
amen, I say to you, will surely not lose his reward.

"Whoever causes one of these little ones who believe in me to sin,
it would be better for him if a great millstone

were put around his neck
and he were thrown into the sea.
If your hand causes you to sin, cut it off.
It is better for you to enter into life maimed
than with two hands to go into Gehenna,
into the unquenchable fire.
And if your foot causes you to sin, cut it off.
It is better for you to enter into life crippled
than with two feet to be thrown into Gehenna.
And if your eye causes you to sin, pluck it out.
Better for you to enter into the kingdom of God with one eye
than with two eyes to be thrown into Gehenna,
where 'their worm does not die, and the fire is not quenched.'"

The Gospel of the Lord. All: **Praise to you, Lord Jesus Christ.**

Prayer over the Offerings

Grant us, O merciful God,
that this our offering may find acceptance with you
and that through it the wellspring of all blessing
may be laid open before us.
Through Christ our Lord. All: **Amen.**

Communion Antiphon (Cf. Psalm 119[118]:49-50)

Remember your word to your servant, O Lord,
by which you have given me hope.
This is my comfort when I am brought low.

Or:

(1 John 3:16)

By this we came to know the love of God:
that Christ laid down his life for us;
so we ought to lay down our lives for one another.

Prayer after Communion

May this heavenly mystery, O Lord,
restore us in mind and body,
that we may be coheirs in glory with Christ,
to whose suffering we are united

whenever we proclaim his Death.
Who lives and reigns for ever and ever. All: **Amen.**

Twenty-Seventh Sunday in Ordinary Time

October 3, 2027

Reflection on the Gospel

Many long for their children to be touched by Jesus, and he welcomes them, embraces them, saying that the kingdom of God belongs to such as these. Jesus is probably not speaking about children who are pure or simplistic, but rather children who are powerless and rely on their parents for everything—shelter, food, love, and more. So too the kingdom of God belongs to those who rely on God, our adopted Father, for everything. As a loving parent, God always reaches out to embrace us.

—Living Liturgy™, *Twenty-Seventh Sunday in Ordinary Time 2027*

Entrance Antiphon (Cf. Esther 4:17)

Within your will, O Lord, all things are established,
and there is none that can resist your will.
For you have made all things, the heaven and the earth,
and all that is held within the circle of heaven;
you are the Lord of all.

Collect

Almighty ever-living God,
who in the abundance of your kindness
surpass the merits and the desires of those who entreat you,
pour out your mercy upon us
to pardon what conscience dreads
and to give what prayer does not dare to ask.

Through our Lord Jesus Christ, your Son,
who lives and reigns with you in the unity of the Holy Spirit,
God, for ever and ever. All: **Amen.**

Reading I (L 140-B) (Genesis 2:18-24)

A reading from the Book of Genesis

The two of them become one flesh.

The Lord God said: "It is not good for the man to be alone.
I will make a suitable partner for him."
So the Lord God formed out of the ground
various wild animals and various birds of the air,
and he brought them to the man to see what he would call them;
whatever the man called each of them would be its name.
The man gave names to all the cattle,
all the birds of the air, and all wild animals;
but none proved to be the suitable partner for the man.

So the Lord God cast a deep sleep on the man,
and while he was asleep,
he took out one of his ribs and closed up its place with flesh.
The Lord God then built up into a woman the rib
that he had taken from the man.
When he brought her to the man, the man said:
"This one, at last, is bone of my bones
and flesh of my flesh;
this one shall be called 'woman,'
for out of 'her man' this one has been taken."
That is why a man leaves his father and mother
and clings to his wife,
and the two of them become one flesh.

The word of the Lord. All: **Thanks be to God.**

Responsorial Psalm 128

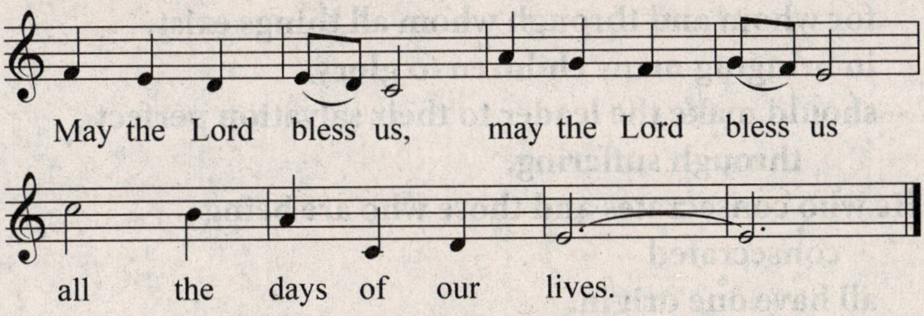

Psalm 128:1-2, 3, 4-5, 6

℟. (*See* 5) **May the Lord bless us all the days of our lives.**

Blessed are you who fear the LORD,
who walk in his ways!
For you shall eat the fruit of your handiwork;
blessed shall you be, and favored. ℟.

Your wife shall be like a fruitful vine
in the recesses of your home;
your children like olive plants
around your table. ℟.

Behold, thus is the man blessed
who fears the LORD.
The LORD bless you from Zion:
may you see the prosperity of Jerusalem
all the days of your life. ℟.

May you see your children's children.
Peace be upon Israel! ℟.

Reading II (Hebrews 2:9-11)

A reading from the Letter to the Hebrews

He who consecrates and those who are being consecrated all have one origin.

Brothers and sisters:
He "for a little while" was made "lower than the angels,"
that by the grace of God he might taste death for everyone.

For it was fitting that he,
for whom and through whom all things exist,
in bringing many children to glory,
should make the leader to their salvation perfect through suffering.
He who consecrates and those who are being consecrated
all have one origin.
Therefore, he is not ashamed to call them "brothers."

The word of the Lord. All: **Thanks be to God.**

GOSPEL (Mark 10:2-16) *or* Shorter Form [ ] (Mark 10:2-12)
ALLELUIA (1 John 4:12)

℣. Alleluia, alleluia. ℟. **Alleluia, alleluia.**
℣. If we love one another, God remains in us
and his love is brought to perfection in us. ℟.

✠ **A reading from the holy Gospel according to Mark**

All: **Glory to you, O Lord.**

Therefore what God has joined together, let no human being separate.

[The Pharisees approached Jesus and asked,
"Is it lawful for a husband to divorce his wife?"
They were testing him.
He said to them in reply, "What did Moses command you?"
They replied,
"Moses permitted a husband to write a bill of divorce
and dismiss her."
But Jesus told them,
"Because of the hardness of your hearts
he wrote you this commandment.
But from the beginning of creation, *God made them male and female.*
For this reason a man shall leave his father and mother
and be joined to his wife,
and the two shall become one flesh.

So they are no longer two but one flesh.
Therefore what God has joined together,
no human being must separate."
In the house the disciples again questioned Jesus about this.
He said to them,
"Whoever divorces his wife and marries another
commits adultery against her;
and if she divorces her husband and marries another,
she commits adultery."]

And people were bringing children to him that he might touch them,
but the disciples rebuked them.
When Jesus saw this he became indignant and said to them,
"Let the children come to me;
do not prevent them, for the kingdom of God belongs to such as these.
Amen, I say to you,
whoever does not accept the kingdom of God like a child
will not enter it."
Then he embraced them and blessed them,
placing his hands on them.

The Gospel of the Lord. All: **Praise to you, Lord Jesus Christ.**

PRAYER OVER THE OFFERINGS
Accept, O Lord, we pray,
the sacrifices instituted by your commands
and, through the sacred mysteries,
which we celebrate with dutiful service,
graciously complete the sanctifying work
by which you are pleased to redeem us.
Through Christ our Lord. All: **Amen.**

COMMUNION ANTIPHON (Lamentations 3:25)
The Lord is good to those who hope in him,
to the soul that seeks him.

Or:

(Cf. 1 Corinthians 10:17)
Though many, we are one bread, one body,
for we all partake of the one Bread and one Chalice.

PRAYER AFTER COMMUNION
Grant us, almighty God,
that we may be refreshed and nourished
by the Sacrament which we have received,
so as to be transformed into what we consume.
Through Christ our Lord. All: **Amen.**

Twenty-Eighth Sunday in Ordinary Time

October 10, 2027

Reflection on the Gospel

A king asked each of his three sons to completely fill an empty room. The eldest son was minister of war and filled the room with boulders; the second son, minister of finance, filled the room with money. The youngest son lived as a hermit and had only his own prayer. At the end of the test the king said to the youngest son, "Your two brothers tried to fill this room with power, with wealth—and they failed. You filled this room with light. You will be my successor."

—Living Liturgy™, *Twenty-Eighth Sunday in Ordinary Time 2027*

ENTRANCE ANTIPHON (Psalm 130[129]:3-4)
If you, O Lord, should mark iniquities,
Lord, who could stand?
But with you is found forgiveness,
O God of Israel.

Collect

May your grace, O Lord, we pray,
at all times go before us and follow after
and make us always determined
to carry out good works.
Through our Lord Jesus Christ, your Son,
who lives and reigns with you in the unity of the Holy Spirit,
God, for ever and ever. All: **Amen.**

Reading I (L 143-B) (Wisdom 7:7-11)

A reading from the Book of Wisdom

I deemed riches nothing in comparison to wisdom.

I prayed, and prudence was given me;
I pleaded, and the spirit of wisdom came to me.
I preferred her to scepter and throne,
and deemed riches nothing in comparison with her,
nor did I liken any priceless gem to her;
because all gold, in view of her, is a little sand,
and before her, silver is to be accounted mire.
Beyond health and comeliness I loved her,
and I chose to have her rather than the light,
because the splendor of her never yields to sleep.
Yet all good things together came to me in her company,
and countless riches at her hands.

The word of the Lord. All: **Thanks be to God.**

Responsorial Psalm 90

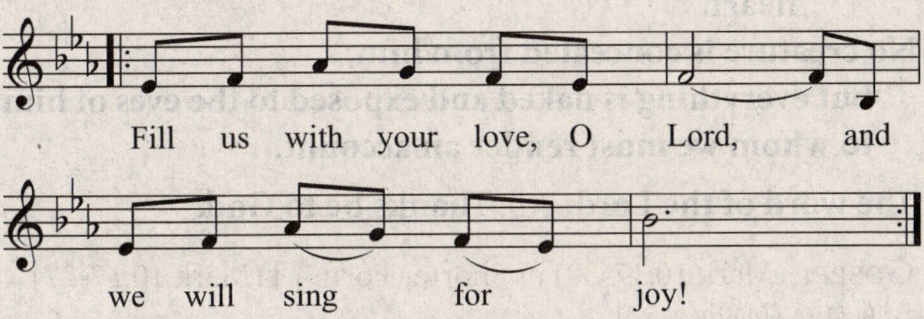

The response is preferably sung twice after each verse

Psalm 90:12-13, 14-15, 16-17

℟. (14) **Fill us with your love, O Lord, and we will sing for joy!**

Teach us to number our days aright,
that we may gain wisdom of heart.
Return, O LORD! How long?
Have pity on your servants! ℟.

Fill us at daybreak with your kindness,
that we may shout for joy and gladness all our days.
Make us glad, for the days when you afflicted us,
for the years when we saw evil. ℟.

Let your work be seen by your servants
and your glory by their children;
and may the gracious care of the Lord our God be ours;
prosper the work of our hands for us!
Prosper the work of our hands! ℟.

READING II (Hebrews 4:12-13)

A reading from the Letter to the Hebrews

The word of God discerns reflections and thoughts of the heart.

Brothers and sisters:
Indeed the word of God is living and effective,
sharper than any two-edged sword,
penetrating even between soul and spirit, joints and marrow,
and able to discern reflections and thoughts of the heart.
No creature is concealed from him,
but everything is naked and exposed to the eyes of him
to whom we must render an account.

The word of the Lord. All: **Thanks be to God.**

GOSPEL (Mark 10:17-30) *or* Shorter Form [ ] (Mark 10:17-27)

ALLELUIA (Matthew 5:3)

℣. Alleluia, alleluia. ℟. **Alleluia, alleluia.**
℣. Blessed are the poor in spirit,
for theirs is the kingdom of heaven. ℟.

✠ **A reading from the holy Gospel according to Mark**

All: **Glory to you, O Lord.**

Sell what you have, and follow me.

**[As Jesus was setting out on a journey, a man ran up,
knelt down before him, and asked him,
"Good teacher, what must I do to inherit eternal life?"
Jesus answered him, "Why do you call me good?
No one is good but God alone.
You know the commandments: *You shall not kill;
you shall not commit adultery;
you shall not steal;
you shall not bear false witness;
you shall not defraud;
honor your father and your mother.*"
He replied and said to him,
"Teacher, all of these I have observed from my youth."
Jesus, looking at him, loved him and said to him,
"You are lacking in one thing.
Go, sell what you have, and give to the poor
and you will have treasure in heaven; then come,
follow me."
At that statement his face fell,
and he went away sad, for he had many possessions.**

**Jesus looked around and said to his disciples,
"How hard it is for those who have wealth
to enter the kingdom of God!"
The disciples were amazed at his words.
So Jesus again said to them in reply,
"Children, how hard it is to enter the kingdom of God!
It is easier for a camel to pass through the eye of a needle
than for one who is rich to enter the kingdom of God."
They were exceedingly astonished and said among
themselves,
"Then who can be saved?"**

Jesus looked at them and said,
"For human beings it is impossible, but not for God.
All things are possible for God."]
Peter began to say to him,
"We have given up everything and followed you."
Jesus said, "Amen, I say to you,
there is no one who has given up house or brothers or sisters
or mother or father or children or lands
for my sake and for the sake of the gospel
who will not receive a hundred times more now in this present age:
houses and brothers and sisters
and mothers and children and lands,
with persecutions, and eternal life in the age to come."

The Gospel of the Lord. All: **Praise to you, Lord Jesus Christ.**

PRAYER OVER THE OFFERINGS

Accept, O Lord, the prayers of your faithful
with the sacrificial offerings,
that, through these acts of devotedness,
we may pass over to the glory of heaven.
Through Christ our Lord. All: **Amen.**

COMMUNION ANTIPHON (Cf. Psalm 34[33]:11)

The rich suffer want and go hungry,
but those who seek the Lord lack no blessing.

Or:

(1 John 3:2)

When the Lord appears, we shall be like him,
for we shall see him as he is.

PRAYER AFTER COMMUNION

We entreat your majesty most humbly, O Lord,
that, as you feed us with the nourishment
which comes from the most holy Body and Blood of your Son,
so you may make us sharers of his divine nature.
Who lives and reigns for ever and ever. All: **Amen.**

Twenty-Ninth Sunday in Ordinary Time

October 17, 2027

(World Mission Sunday)

Reflection on the Gospel

In today's gospel, James and John seek to sit on either side of Christ when he enters into glory. How can they be so unabashed about pursuing exactly the wrong thing? The Christian virtue of temperance can help. The Catechism of the Catholic Church *quotes St. Augustine: "To live well is nothing other than to love God with all one's heart, with all one's soul and with all one's efforts; from this it comes about that love is kept whole and uncorrupted (through temperance)" (CCC 1809).*

—Living Liturgy™, *Twenty-Ninth Sunday in Ordinary Time 2027*

Entrance Antiphon (Cf. Psalm 17[16]:6, 8)

To you I call; for you will surely heed me, O God;
turn your ear to me; hear my words.
Guard me as the apple of your eye;
in the shadow of your wings protect me.

Collect

Almighty ever-living God,
grant that we may always conform our will to yours
and serve your majesty in sincerity of heart.
Through our Lord Jesus Christ, your Son,
who lives and reigns with you in the unity of the Holy Spirit,
God, for ever and ever. All: **Amen.**

Reading I (L 146-B) (Isaiah 53:10-11)

A reading from the Book of the Prophet Isaiah

If he gives his life as an offering for sin, he shall see his descendants in a long life.

The LORD was pleased
to crush him in infirmity.

If he gives his life as an offering for sin,
he shall see his descendants in a long life,
and the will of the LORD shall be accomplished
through him.

Because of his affliction
he shall see the light in fullness of days;
through his suffering, my servant shall justify many,
and their guilt he shall bear.

The word of the Lord. All: **Thanks be to God.**

RESPONSORIAL PSALM 33

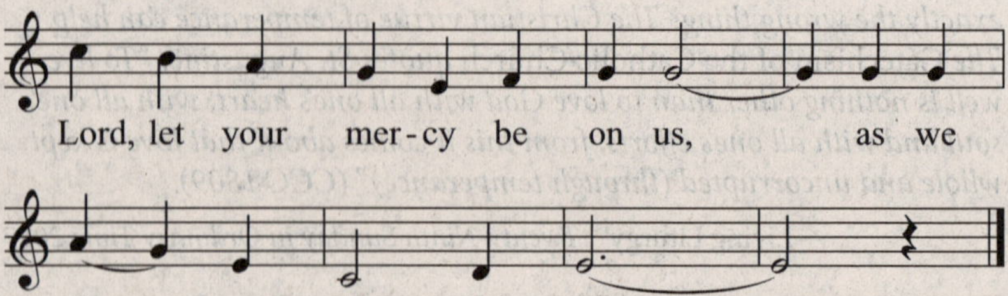

Psalm 33:4-5, 18-19, 20 and 22

℟. (22) **Lord, let your mercy be on us, as we place our trust in you.**

Upright is the word of the LORD,
and all his works are trustworthy.
He loves justice and right;
of the kindness of the LORD the earth is full. ℟.

See, the eyes of the LORD are upon those who fear him,
upon those who hope for his kindness,
to deliver them from death
and preserve them in spite of famine. ℟.

Our soul waits for the LORD,
who is our help and our shield.

May your kindness, O LORD, be upon us
who have put our hope in you. ℟.

READING II (Hebrews 4:14-16)

A reading from the Letter to the Hebrews

Let us confidently approach the throne of grace.

Brothers and sisters:
Since we have a great high priest who has passed through the heavens,
Jesus, the Son of God,
let us hold fast to our confession.
For we do not have a high priest
who is unable to sympathize with our weaknesses,
but one who has similarly been tested in every way,
yet without sin.
So let us confidently approach the throne of grace
to receive mercy and to find grace for timely help.

The word of the Lord. All: **Thanks be to God.**

GOSPEL

A Longer Form (Mark 10:35-45)

ALLELUIA (Mark 10:45)

℣. Alleluia, alleluia. ℟. **Alleluia, alleluia.**
℣. The Son of Man came to serve
and to give his life as a ransom for many. ℟.

✠ **A reading from the holy Gospel according to Mark**

All: **Glory to you, O Lord.**

The Son of Man came to give his life as a ransom for many.

James and John, the sons of Zebedee, came to Jesus and said to him,
"Teacher, we want you to do for us whatever we ask of you."
He replied, "What do you wish me to do for you?"
They answered him, "Grant that in your glory
we may sit one at your right and the other at your left."
Jesus said to them, "You do not know what you are asking.

Can you drink the cup that I drink
or be baptized with the baptism with which I am baptized?"
They said to him, "We can."
Jesus said to them, "The cup that I drink, you will drink,
and with the baptism with which I am baptized, you will be baptized;
but to sit at my right or at my left is not mine to give
but is for those for whom it has been prepared."
When the ten heard this, they became indignant at James and John.
Jesus summoned them and said to them,
"You know that those who are recognized as rulers over the Gentiles
lord it over them,
and their great ones make their authority over them felt.
But it shall not be so among you.
Rather, whoever wishes to be great among you will be your servant;
whoever wishes to be first among you will be the slave of all.
For the Son of Man did not come to be served
but to serve and to give his life as a ransom for many."

The Gospel of the Lord. All: **Praise to you, Lord Jesus Christ.**

Or:

B Shorter Form (Mark 10:42-45)

✠ **A reading from the holy Gospel according to Mark**

All: **Glory to you, O Lord.**

The Son of Man came to give his life as a ransom for many.

Jesus summoned the Twelve and said to them,
"You know that those who are recognized as rulers over the Gentiles
lord it over them,

and their great ones make their authority over them felt.
But it shall not be so among you.
Rather, whoever wishes to be great among you will be your servant;
whoever wishes to be first among you will be the slave of all.
For the Son of Man did not come to be served
but to serve and to give his life as a ransom for many."

The Gospel of the Lord. All: **Praise to you, Lord Jesus Christ.**

Prayer over the Offerings

Grant us, Lord, we pray,
a sincere respect for your gifts,
that, through the purifying action of your grace,
we may be cleansed by the very mysteries we serve.
Through Christ our Lord. All: **Amen.**

Communion Antiphon (Cf. Psalm 33[32]:18-19)

Behold, the eyes of the Lord
are on those who fear him,
who hope in his merciful love,
to rescue their souls from death,
to keep them alive in famine.

Or:

(Mark 10:45)
The Son of Man has come
to give his life as a ranson for many.

Prayer after Communion

Grant, O Lord, we pray,
that, benefiting from participation in heavenly things,
we may be helped by what you give in this present age
and prepared for the gifts that are eternal.
Through Christ our Lord. All: **Amen.**

Thirtieth Sunday in Ordinary Time

October 24, 2027

Reflection on the Gospel

"Master, I want to see." Often we struggle to see our faith community for who we actually are: the Body of Christ, the full and consciously engaged and active people of God. We can decide for ourselves, in any given context, what manner of speaking the truth might be best received, might best achieve a desired result. Those whose hearts and minds are most in need of change are often also the folks we think might need to be spoken to most forcefully. But remember: sometimes kinder voices are needed.

—Living Liturgy™, *Thirtieth Sunday in Ordinary Time 2027*

ENTRANCE ANTIPHON (Cf. Psalm 105[104]:3-4)

Let the hearts that seek the Lord rejoice;
turn to the Lord and his strength;
constantly seek his face.

COLLECT

Almighty ever-living God,
increase our faith, hope and charity,
and make us love what you command,
so that we may merit what you promise.
Through our Lord Jesus Christ, your Son,
who lives and reigns with you in the unity of the Holy Spirit,
God, for ever and ever. All: **Amen.**

READING I (L 149-B) (Jeremiah 31:7-9)

A reading from the Book of the Prophet Jeremiah

The blind and the lame I will bring back: I will console them.

Thus says the LORD:
Shout with joy for Jacob,
exult at the head of the nations;
proclaim your praise and say:
The LORD has delivered his people,
the remnant of Israel.

Behold, I will bring them back
from the land of the north;
I will gather them from the ends of the world,
with the blind and the lame in their midst,
the mothers and those with child;
they shall return as an immense throng.
They departed in tears,
but I will console them and guide them;
I will lead them to brooks of water,
on a level road, so that none shall stumble.
For I am a father to Israel,
Ephraim is my first-born.

The word of the Lord. All: **Thanks be to God.**

Responsorial Psalm 126

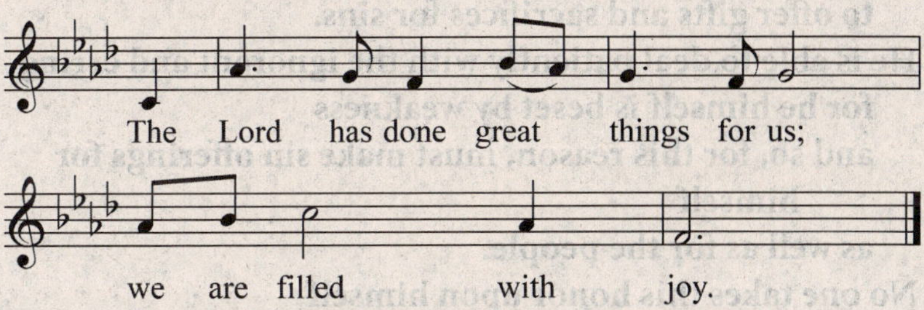

Psalm 126:1-2ab, 2cd-3, 4-5, 6

℟. (3) **The Lord has done great things for us; we are filled with joy.**

When the Lord brought back the captives of Zion,
we were like men dreaming.
Then our mouth was filled with laughter,
and our tongue with rejoicing. ℟.

Then they said among the nations,
"The Lord has done great things for them."
The Lord has done great things for us;
we are glad indeed. ℟.

(continued)

Restore our fortunes, O LORD,
like the torrents in the southern desert.
Those that sow in tears
shall reap rejoicing. ℟.

Although they go forth weeping,
carrying the seed to be sown,
they shall come back rejoicing,
carrying their sheaves. ℟.

READING II (Hebrews 5:1-6)

A reading from the Letter to the Hebrews

You are a priest forever according to the order of Melchizedek.

Brothers and sisters:
Every high priest is taken from among men
and made their representative before God,
to offer gifts and sacrifices for sins.
He is able to deal patiently with the ignorant and erring,
for he himself is beset by weakness
and so, for this reason, must make sin offerings for himself
as well as for the people.
No one takes this honor upon himself
but only when called by God,
just as Aaron was.
In the same way,
it was not Christ who glorified himself in becoming high priest,
but rather the one who said to him:
You are my son:
this day I have begotten you;
just as he says in another place:
You are a priest forever
according to the order of Melchizedek.
The word of the Lord. All: **Thanks be to God.**

GOSPEL (Mark 10:46-52)

ALLELUIA (*See* 2 Timothy 1:10)

℣. Alleluia, alleluia. ℟. **Alleluia, alleluia.**
℣. Our Savior Jesus Christ destroyed death
and brought life to light through the Gospel. ℟.

✠ **A reading from the holy Gospel according to Mark.**

All: **Glory to you, O Lord.**

Master, I want to see.

As Jesus was leaving Jericho with his disciples and a sizable crowd,
Bartimaeus, a blind man, the son of Timaeus,
sat by the roadside begging.
On hearing that it was Jesus of Nazareth,
he began to cry out and say,
"Jesus, son of David, have pity on me."
And many rebuked him, telling him to be silent.
But he kept calling out all the more,
"Son of David, have pity on me."
Jesus stopped and said, "Call him."
So they called the blind man, saying to him,
"Take courage; get up, Jesus is calling you."
He threw aside his cloak, sprang up,
and came to Jesus.
Jesus said to him in reply, "What do you want me to do for you?"
The blind man replied to him, "Master, I want to see."
Jesus told him, "Go your way; your faith has saved you."
Immediately he received his sight
and followed him on the way.

The Gospel of the Lord. All: **Praise to you, Lord Jesus Christ.**

PRAYER OVER THE OFFERINGS

Look, we pray, O Lord,
on the offerings we make to your majesty,
that whatever is done by us in your service
may be directed above all to your glory.
Through Christ our Lord. All: **Amen.**

Communion Antiphon (Cf. Psalm 20[19]:6)
We will ring out our joy at your saving help
and exult in the name of our God.

Or:

(Ephesians 5:2)
Christ loved us and gave himself up for us,
as a fragrant offering to God.

Prayer after Communion
May your Sacraments, O Lord, we pray,
perfect in us what lies within them,
that what we now celebrate in signs
we may one day possess in truth.
Through Christ our Lord. All: **Amen.**

Thirty-First Sunday in Ordinary Time

October 31, 2027

Reflection on the Gospel
Both we and our communities change over time—our needs, experiences, and perspectives shift. These changes should shape how we engage with Scripture and how we prepare for worship. One way to re-engage creatively and prayerfully is through lectio divina*—a tradition of reading Scripture not just for study but for transformation. This practice can be used by anyone looking to listen more deeply to God's word, alone or in a group, in one sitting or over several days.*

—Living Liturgy™, *Thirty-First Sunday in Ordinary Time 2027*

Entrance Antiphon (Cf. Psalm 38[37]:22-23)

Forsake me not, O Lord, my God;
be not far from me!
Make haste and come to my help,
O Lord, my strong salvation!

Collect

Almighty and merciful God,
by whose gift your faithful offer you
right and praiseworthy service,
grant, we pray,
that we may hasten without stumbling
to receive the things you have promised.
Through our Lord Jesus Christ, your Son,
who lives and reigns with you in the unity of the Holy Spirit,
God, for ever and ever. All: **Amen.**

Reading I (L 152) (Deuteronomy 6:2-6)

A reading from the Book of Deuteronomy

Hear, O Israel! You shall love the Lord your God with all your heart.

Moses spoke to the people, saying:
"Fear the Lord, your God,
and keep, throughout the days of your lives,
all his statutes and commandments which I enjoin on you,
and thus have long life.
Hear then, Israel, and be careful to observe them,
that you may grow and prosper the more,
in keeping with the promise of the Lord, the God of your fathers,
to give you a land flowing with milk and honey.

"Hear, O Israel! The Lord is our God, the Lord alone!
Therefore, you shall love the Lord, your God,
with all your heart,
and with all your soul,
and with all your strength.
Take to heart these words which I enjoin on you today."

The word of the Lord. All: **Thanks be to God.**

Responsorial Psalm 18

Psalm 18:2-3, 3-4, 47, 51

℟. (2) **I love you, Lord, my strength.**

I love you, O Lord, my strength,
O Lord, my rock, my fortress, my deliverer. ℟.

My God, my rock of refuge,
my shield, the horn of my salvation, my stronghold!
Praised be the Lord, I exclaim,
and I am safe from my enemies. ℟.

The Lord lives! And blessed be my rock!
Extolled be God my savior,
you who gave great victories to your king
and showed kindness to your anointed. ℟.

Reading II (Hebrews 7:23-28)

A reading from the Letter to the Hebrews

Because he remains forever, he has a priesthood that does not pass away.

Brothers and sisters:
The levitical priests were many
because they were prevented by death from remaining in office,
but Jesus, because he remains forever,
has a priesthood that does not pass away.
Therefore, he is always able to save those who approach God through him,
since he lives forever to make intercession for them.

It was fitting that we should have such a high priest:
holy, innocent, undefiled, separated from sinners,
higher than the heavens.

He has no need, as did the high priests,
to offer sacrifice day after day,
first for his own sins and then for those of the people;
he did that once for all when he offered himself.
For the law appoints men subject to weakness to be high priests,
but the word of the oath, which was taken after the law,
appoints a son,
who has been made perfect forever.

The word of the Lord. All: **Thanks be to God.**

GOSPEL (Mark 12:28b-34)

ALLELUIA (John 14:23)

℣. Alleluia, alleluia. ℟. **Alleluia, alleluia.**
℣. Whoever loves me will keep my word, says the Lord;
and my Father will love him and we will come to him. ℟.

✠ **A reading from the holy Gospel according to Mark**

All: **Glory to you, O Lord.**

Love the Lord your God. Love your neighbor.

One of the scribes came to Jesus and asked him,
"Which is the first of all the commandments?"
Jesus replied, "The first is this:
Hear, O Israel!
The Lord our God is Lord alone!
You shall love the Lord your God with all your heart,
with all your soul,
with all your mind,
and with all your strength.
The second is this:
You shall love your neighbor as yourself.
There is no other commandment greater than these."
The scribe said to him, "Well said, teacher.
You are right in saying,
'He is One and there is no other than he.'

And 'to love him with all your heart,
with all your understanding,
with all your strength,
and to love your neighbor as yourself'
is worth more than all burnt offerings and sacrifices."
And when Jesus saw that he answered with understanding,
he said to him,
"You are not far from the kingdom of God."
And no one dared to ask him any more questions.

The Gospel of the Lord. All: **Praise to you, Lord Jesus Christ.**

Prayer over the Offerings

May these sacrificial offerings, O Lord,
become for you a pure oblation,
and for us a holy outpouring of your mercy.
Through Christ our Lord. All: **Amen.**

Communion Antiphon (Cf. Psalm 16[15]:11)

You will show me the path of life,
the fullness of joy in your presence, O Lord.

Or:

(John 6:58)
Just as the living Father sent me
and I have life because of the Father,
so whoever feeds on me
shall have life because of me, says the Lord.

Prayer after Communion

May the working of your power, O Lord,
increase in us, we pray,
so that, renewed by these heavenly Sacraments,
we may be prepared by your gift
for receiving what they promise.
Through Christ our Lord. All: **Amen.**

All Saints

November 1, 2027

Reflection on the Gospel
Who is the holiest person you know? What is it about them that causes you to see holiness? Call to mind this person's face: their smile, their eyes, their hair . . . Yet if we want to see holiness, we must turn our gaze elsewhere. In the Sermon on the Mount, Jesus tells us to look to the poor in spirit, to the peacemakers, to those who hunger and thirst for righteousness. Seeing people in this way is the closest we will come to seeing the face of God.

—Living Liturgy™, *All Saints 2027*

Entrance Antiphon

Let us all rejoice in the Lord,
as we celebrate the feast day in honor of all the Saints,
at whose festival the Angels rejoice
and praise the Son of God.

Collect

Almighty ever-living God,
by whose gift we venerate in one celebration
the merits of all the Saints,
bestow on us, we pray,
through the prayers of so many intercessors,
an abundance of the reconciliation with you
for which we earnestly long.
Through our Lord Jesus Christ, your Son,
who lives and reigns with you in the unity of the Holy Spirit,
God, for ever and ever. All: **Amen.**

Reading I (L 667) (Revelation 7:2-4, 9-14)

A reading from the Book of Revelation

I had a vision of a great multitude, which no one could count, from every nation, race, people, and tongue.

I, John, saw another angel come up from the East,
holding the seal of the living God.
He cried out in a loud voice to the four angels
who were given power to damage the land and the sea,

"Do not damage the land or the sea or the trees
until we put the seal on the foreheads of the servants of our God."
I heard the number of those who had been marked with the seal,
one hundred and forty-four thousand marked
from every tribe of the children of Israel.

After this I had a vision of a great multitude,
which no one could count,
from every nation, race, people, and tongue.
They stood before the throne and before the Lamb,
wearing white robes and holding palm branches in their hands.
They cried out in a loud voice:

"Salvation comes from our God, who is seated on the throne,
and from the Lamb."

All the angels stood around the throne
and around the elders and the four living creatures.
They prostrated themselves before the throne,
worshiped God, and exclaimed:

"Amen. Blessing and glory, wisdom and thanksgiving,
honor, power, and might
be to our God forever and ever. Amen."

Then one of the elders spoke up and said to me,
"Who are these wearing white robes, and where did they come from?"
I said to him, "My lord, you are the one who knows."
He said to me,
"These are the ones who have survived the time of great distress;
they have washed their robes
and made them white in the Blood of the Lamb."

The word of the Lord. All: **Thanks be to God.**

Responsorial Psalm 24

Psalm 24:1bc-2, 3-4ab, 5-6

℟. (*See* 6) **Lord, this is the people that longs to see your face.**

The LORD's are the earth and its fullness;
the world and those who dwell in it.
For he founded it upon the seas
and established it upon the rivers. ℟.

Who can ascend the mountain of the LORD?
or who may stand in his holy place?
One whose hands are sinless, whose heart is clean,
who desires not what is vain. ℟.

He shall receive a blessing from the LORD,
a reward from God his savior.
Such is the race that seeks for him,
that seeks the face of the God of Jacob. ℟.

Reading II (1 John 3:1-3)

A reading from the first Letter of Saint John

We shall see God as he is.

Beloved:
See what love the Father has bestowed on us
that we may be called the children of God.
Yet so we are.
The reason the world does not know us
is that it did not know him.
Beloved, we are God's children now;
what we shall be has not yet been revealed.
We do know that when it is revealed we shall be like him,
for we shall see him as he is.

Everyone who has this hope based on him makes himself pure,
as he is pure.

The word of the Lord. All: **Thanks be to God.**

GOSPEL (Matthew 5:1-12a)
ALLELUIA (Matthew 11:28)

℣. Alleluia, alleluia. ℟. **Alleluia, alleluia.**
℣. Come to me, all you who labor and are burdened,
and I will give you rest, says the Lord. ℟.

✠ A reading from the holy Gospel according to Matthew

All: **Glory to you, O Lord.**

Rejoice and be glad, for your reward will be great in heaven.

When Jesus saw the crowds, he went up the mountain,
and after he had sat down, his disciples came to him.
He began to teach them, saying:

"Blessed are the poor in spirit,
for theirs is the Kingdom of heaven.
Blessed are they who mourn,
for they will be comforted.
Blessed are the meek,
for they will inherit the land.
Blessed are they who hunger and thirst for righteousness,
for they will be satisfied.
Blessed are the merciful,
for they will be shown mercy.
Blessed are the clean of heart,
for they will see God.
Blessed are the peacemakers,
for they will be called children of God.
Blessed are they who are persecuted for the sake of righteousness,
for theirs is the Kingdom of heaven.

Blessed are you when they insult you and persecute you
and utter every kind of evil against you falsely
because of me.
Rejoice and be glad,
for your reward will be great in heaven."

The Gospel of the Lord. All: **Praise to you, Lord Jesus Christ.**

Prayer over the Offerings

May these offerings we bring in honor of all the Saints
be pleasing to you, O Lord,
and grant that, just as we believe the Saints
to be already assured of immortality,
so we may experience their concern for our salvation.
Through Christ our Lord. All: **Amen.**

Communion Antiphon (Matthew 5:8-10)

Blessed are the clean of heart, for they shall see God.
Blessed are the peacemakers,
for they shall be called children of God.
Blessed are they who are persecuted for the sake of righteousness,
for theirs is the Kingdom of Heaven.

Prayer after Communion

As we adore you, O God, who alone are holy
and wonderful in all your Saints,
we implore your grace,
so that, coming to perfect holiness in the fullness of your love,
we may pass from this pilgrim table
to the banquet of our heavenly homeland.
Through Christ our Lord. All: **Amen.**

The Commemoration of All the Faithful Departed

ALL SOULS' DAY

November 2, 2027

Reflection on the Gospel

We are all familiar with the expression "true colors," when someone lets their "real selves" show through, revealing more of their heart and soul to the community. The liturgy itself has true colors too, which reveal something of the inner character of the celebration or season. For example, black is symbolic of death and mourning and may be used at funeral Masses or the feast of All Souls. Following Vatican II norms, however, white is the preferred color since it reminds us of the resurrection and our baptism.

—Living Liturgy™, *All Souls 2027*

Entrance Antiphon

(Cf. 1 Thessalonians 4:14; 1 Corinthians 15:22)

Just as Jesus died and has risen again,
so through Jesus God will bring with him
those who have fallen asleep;
and as in Adam all die,
so also in Christ will all be brought to life.

Collect

Listen kindly to our prayers, O Lord,
and, as our faith in your Son,
raised from the dead, is deepened,
so may our hope of resurrection for your departed servants
also find new strength.
Through our Lord Jesus Christ, your Son,
who lives and reigns with you in the unity of the Holy Spirit,
God, for ever and ever. All: **Amen.**

The following readings, other options for All Souls' Day *from the Lectionary (L 668), or those given in the Masses for the Dead (nos. 1011–1016), may be used.*

Reading I (L 668) (Wisdom 3:1-9)

A reading from the Book of Wisdom

As sacrificial offerings he took them to himself.

The souls of the just are in the hand of God,
and no torment shall touch them.
They seemed, in the view of the foolish, to be dead;
and their passing away was thought an affliction
and their going forth from us, utter destruction.
But they are in peace.
For if before men, indeed they be punished,
yet is their hope full of immortality;
chastised a little, they shall be greatly blessed,
because God tried them
and found them worthy of himself.
As gold in the furnace, he proved them,
and as sacrificial offerings he took them to himself.
In the time of their visitation they shall shine,
and shall dart about as sparks through stubble;
they shall judge nations and rule over peoples,
and the Lord shall be their King forever.
Those who trust in him shall understand truth,
and the faithful shall abide with him in love:
because grace and mercy are with his holy ones,
and his care is with his elect.

The word of the Lord. All: **Thanks be to God.**

Responsorial Psalm 23 (L 1013.1)

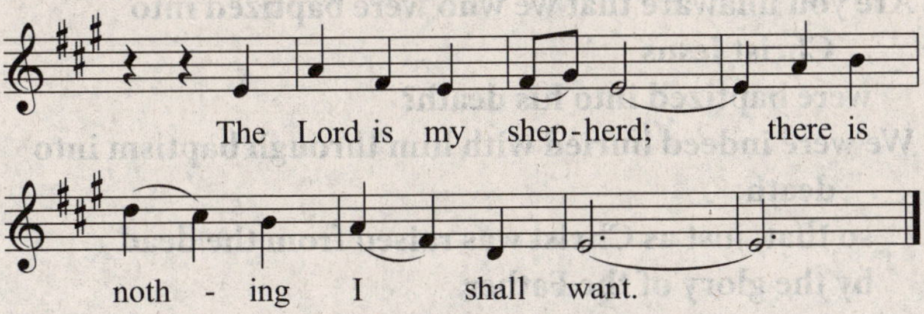

Psalm 23:1-3, 4, 5, 6

℟. (1) **The Lord is my shepherd; there is nothing I shall want.** *or:* ℟. (4ab) **Though I walk in the valley of darkness, I fear no evil, for you are with me.**

The LORD is my shepherd; I shall not want.
In verdant pastures he gives me repose;
beside restful waters he leads me;
he refreshes my soul. ℟.

He guides me in right paths
for his name's sake.
Even though I walk in the dark valley
I fear no evil; for you are at my side
with your rod and your staff
that give me courage. ℟.

You spread the table before me
in the sight of my foes;
You anoint my head with oil;
my cup overflows. ℟.

Only goodness and kindness follow me
all the days of my life;
and I shall dwell in the house of the LORD
for years to come. ℟.

READING II (L 1014.3) (Romans 6:3-9)

A reading from the Letter of Saint Paul to the Romans

Let us walk in newness of life.

Brothers and sisters:
Are you unaware that we who were baptized into Christ Jesus
were baptized into his death?
We were indeed buried with him through baptism into death,
so that, just as Christ was raised from the dead
by the glory of the Father,
we too might live in newness of life.

For if we have grown into union with him through a death like his,
we shall also be united with him in the resurrection.
We know that our old self was crucified with him,
so that our sinful body might be done away with,
that we might no longer be in slavery to sin.
For a dead person has been absolved from sin.
If, then, we have died with Christ,
we believe that we shall also live with him.
We know that Christ, raised from the dead, dies no more;
death no longer has power over him.

The word of the Lord. All: **Thanks be to God.**

GOSPEL (L 1016.12) (John 6:37-40)

ALLELUIA (L 1015.5) (John 6:40)

℣. Alleluia, alleluia. ℟. **Alleluia, alleluia.**
℣. This is the will of my Father, says the Lord,
that everyone who sees the Son and believes in him
may have eternal life. ℟.

✠ **A reading from the holy Gospel according to John**

All: **Glory to you, O Lord.**

Everyone who believes in the Son will have eternal life and I shall raise him up on the last day.

Jesus said to the crowds:
"Everything that the Father gives me will come to me,
and I will not reject anyone who comes to me,
because I came down from heaven not to do my own will
but the will of the one who sent me.
And this is the will of the one who sent me,
that I should not lose anything of what he gave me,
but that I should raise it on the last day.

For this is the will of my Father,
that everyone who sees the Son and believes in him
may have eternal life,
and I shall raise him on the last day."

The Gospel of the Lord. All: **Praise to you, Lord Jesus Christ.**

PRAYER OVER THE OFFERINGS

Look favorably on our offerings, O Lord,
so that your departed servants
may be taken up into glory with your Son,
in whose great mystery of love we are all united.
Who lives and reigns for ever and ever. All: **Amen.**

COMMUNION ANTIPHON (Cf. John 11:25-26)

I am the Resurrection and the Life, says the Lord.
Whoever believes in me, even though he dies, will live,
and everyone who lives and believes in me will not die for ever.

PRAYER AFTER COMMUNION

Grant we pray, O Lord, that your departed servants,
for whom we have celebrated this paschal Sacrament,
may pass over to a dwelling place of light and peace.
Through Christ our Lord. All: **Amen.**

Thirty-Second Sunday in Ordinary Time

November 7, 2027

Reflection on the Gospel

Jesus warns the crowds in today's gospel to beware of the scribes who "as a pretext, recite lengthy prayers." Some of us, especially in moments of improvised prayer, tend to ramble on and on because moments of prayer like these lack structure. Here is a pattern you can follow: Name God. Then name something that God has already done for you. Ask or petition God to do something for you. Close your prayer "through Jesus Christ," because he is our connection to God.

—Living Liturgy™, *Thirty-Second Sunday in Ordinary Time 2027*

ENTRANCE ANTIPHON (Cf. Psalm 88[87]:3)

Let my prayer come into your presence.
Incline your ear to my cry for help, O Lord.

COLLECT

Almighty and merciful God,
graciously keep from us all adversity,
so that, unhindered in mind and body alike,
we may pursue in freedom of heart
the things that are yours.
Through our Lord Jesus Christ, your Son,
who lives and reigns with you in the unity of the Holy Spirit,
God, for ever and ever. All: **Amen.**

READING I (L 155-B) (1 Kings 17:10-16)

A reading from the first Book of Kings

The widow made a little cake from her flour and gave it to Elijah.

In those days, Elijah the prophet went to Zarephath.
As he arrived at the entrance of the city,
a widow was gathering sticks there; he called out to her,

“Please bring me a small cupful of water to drink.”
She left to get it, and he called out after her,
“Please bring along a bit of bread.”
She answered, “As the LORD, your God, lives,
I have nothing baked; there is only a handful of flour in my jar
and a little oil in my jug.
Just now I was collecting a couple of sticks,
to go in and prepare something for myself and my son;
when we have eaten it, we shall die.”
Elijah said to her, “Do not be afraid.
Go and do as you propose.
But first make me a little cake and bring it to me.
Then you can prepare something for yourself and your son.
For the LORD, the God of Israel, says,
‘The jar of flour shall not go empty,
nor the jug of oil run dry,
until the day when the LORD sends rain upon the earth.’ ”
She left and did as Elijah had said.
She was able to eat for a year, and he and her son as well;
the jar of flour did not go empty,
nor the jug of oil run dry,
as the LORD had foretold through Elijah.

The word of the Lord. All: **Thanks be to God.**

RESPONSORIAL PSALM 146

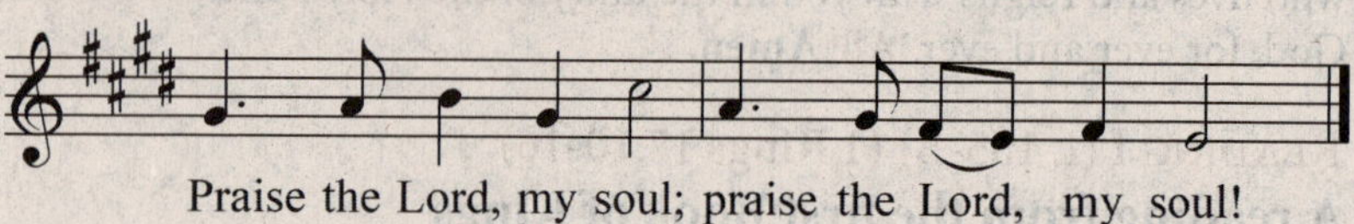

Psalm 146:7, 8-9, 9-10

℟. (1b) **Praise the Lord, my soul!** *or:* ℟. **Alleluia.**

The LORD keeps faith forever,
  secures justice for the oppressed,
  gives food to the hungry.
The LORD sets captives free. ℟.

The LORD gives sight to the blind;
  the LORD raises up those who were bowed down.
The LORD loves the just;
  the LORD protects strangers. ℟.

The fatherless and the widow he sustains,
  but the way of the wicked he thwarts.
The LORD shall reign forever;
  your God, O Zion, through all generations. Alleluia. ℟.

READING II (Hebrews 9:24-28)

A reading from the Letter to the Hebrews

Christ was offered once to take away the sins of many.

Christ did not enter into a sanctuary made by hands,
  a copy of the true one, but heaven itself,
  that he might now appear before God on our behalf.
Not that he might offer himself repeatedly,
  as the high priest enters each year into the sanctuary
  with blood that is not his own;
  if that were so, he would have had to suffer repeatedly
  from the foundation of the world.
But now once for all he has appeared at the end of the ages
  to take away sin by his sacrifice.
Just as it is appointed that human beings die once,
  and after this the judgment, so also Christ,
  offered once to take away the sins of many,
  will appear a second time, not to take away sin
  but to bring salvation to those who eagerly await him.

The word of the Lord. All: **Thanks be to God.**

Gospel

A Longer Form (Mark 12:38-44)

Alleluia (Matthew 5:3)

℣. Alleluia, alleluia. ℟. **Alleluia, alleluia.**
℣. Blessed are the poor in spirit,
for theirs is the kingdom of heaven. ℟.

✠ **A reading from the holy Gospel according to Mark**

All: **Glory to you, O Lord.**

This poor widow put in more than all the others.

In the course of his teaching Jesus said to the crowds,
"Beware of the scribes, who like to go around in long robes
and accept greetings in the marketplaces,
seats of honor in synagogues,
and places of honor at banquets.
They devour the houses of widows and, as a pretext recite lengthy prayers.
They will receive a very severe condemnation."
He sat down opposite the treasury
and observed how the crowd put money into the treasury.
Many rich people put in large sums.
A poor widow also came and put in two small coins worth a few cents.
Calling his disciples to himself, he said to them,
"Amen, I say to you, this poor widow put in more
than all the other contributors to the treasury.
For they have all contributed from their surplus wealth,
but she, from her poverty, has contributed all she had,
her whole livelihood."

The Gospel of the Lord. All: **Praise to you, Lord Jesus Christ.**

Or:

B Shorter Form (Mark 12:41-44)

✠ **A reading from the holy Gospel according to Mark**

All: **Glory to you, O Lord.**

This poor widow put in more than all the others.

Jesus sat down opposite the treasury
and observed how the crowd put money into the treasury.
Many rich people put in large sums.
A poor widow also came and put in two small coins worth a few cents.
Calling his disciples to himself, he said to them,
"Amen, I say to you, this poor widow put in more
than all the other contributors to the treasury.
For they have all contributed from their surplus wealth,
but she, from her poverty, has contributed all she had,
her whole livelihood."

The Gospel of the Lord. All: **Praise to you, Lord Jesus Christ.**

PRAYER OVER THE OFFERINGS

Look with favor, we pray, O Lord,
upon the sacrificial gifts offered here,
that, celebrating in mystery the Passion of your Son,
we may honor it with loving devotion.
Through Christ our Lord. All: **Amen.**

COMMUNION ANTIPHON (Cf. Psalm 23[22]:1-2)

The Lord is my shepherd; there is nothing I shall want.
Fresh and green are the pastures where he gives me repose,
near restful waters he leads me.

Or:

(Cf. Luke 24:35)

The disciples recognized the Lord Jesus in the breaking of bread.

PRAYER AFTER COMMUNION

Nourished by this sacred gift, O Lord,
we give you thanks and beseech your mercy,
that, by the pouring forth of your Spirit,

the grace of integrity may endure
in those your heavenly power has entered.
Through Christ our Lord. All: **Amen.**

Thirty-Third Sunday in Ordinary Time

November 14, 2027

Reflection on the Gospel

Speaking of the end times, as is typical for mid-November liturgies, Jesus points our attention to the budding fig tree. When its outward appearance changes and its tender branches sprout leaves, one knows what that signifies: summer is near. In the Rite of Baptism, those gathered hear the celebrant speak of the white garment. The dignity and purity the white garment represents is linked to a burning and zealous faith, the light of Christ for all to see. This is how our Scriptures this weekend call us to live.

—Living Liturgy™, *Thirty-Third Sunday in Ordinary Time 2027*

Entrance Antiphon (Jeremiah 29:11, 12, 14)

The Lord said: I think thoughts of peace and not of
affliction.
You will call upon me, and I will answer you,
and I will lead back your captives from every place.

Collect

Grant us, we pray, O Lord our God,
the constant gladness of being devoted to you,
for it is full and lasting happiness
to serve with constancy
the author of all that is good.
Through our Lord Jesus Christ, your Son,
who lives and reigns with you in the unity of the Holy Spirit,
God, for ever and ever. All: **Amen.**

Reading I (L 158-B) (Daniel 12:1-3)

A reading from the Book of the Prophet Daniel

At that time your people shall escape.

In those days, I, Daniel,
heard this word of the Lord:
"At that time there shall arise
Michael, the great prince,
guardian of your people;
it shall be a time unsurpassed in distress
since nations began until that time.
At that time your people shall escape,
everyone who is found written in the book.

"Many of those who sleep in the dust of the earth shall awake;
some shall live forever,
others shall be an everlasting horror and disgrace.

"But the wise shall shine brightly
like the splendor of the firmament,
and those who lead the many to justice
shall be like the stars forever."

The word of the Lord. All: **Thanks be to God.**

Responsorial Psalm 16

Psalm 16:5, 8, 9-10, 11

℟. (1) **You are my inheritance, O Lord!**

O Lord, my allotted portion and my cup,
you it is who hold fast my lot.
I set the Lord ever before me;
with him at my right hand I shall not be disturbed. ℟.

Therefore my heart is glad and my soul rejoices,
my body, too, abides in confidence;
because you will not abandon my soul to the netherworld,
nor will you suffer your faithful one to undergo corruption. ℟.

You will show me the path to life,
fullness of joys in your presence,
the delights at your right hand forever. ℟.

Reading II (Hebrews 10:11-14, 18)

A reading from the Letter to the Hebrews

By one offering he has made perfect forever those who are being consecrated.

Brothers and sisters:
Every priest stands daily at his ministry,
offering frequently those same sacrifices
that can never take away sins.
But this one offered one sacrifice for sins,
and took his seat forever at the right hand of God;
now he waits until his enemies are made his footstool.
For by one offering
he has made perfect forever those who are being consecrated.

Where there is forgiveness of these,
there is no longer offering for sin.

The word of the Lord. All: **Thanks be to God.**

GOSPEL (Mark 13:24-32)

ALLELUIA (Luke 21:36)

℣. Alleluia, alleluia. ℟. **Alleluia, alleluia.**

℣. Be vigilant at all times
and pray that you have the strength to stand before the Son of Man. ℟.

✠ A reading from the holy Gospel according to Mark

All: **Glory to you, O Lord.**

He will gather his elect from the four winds.

Jesus said to his disciples:
"In those days after that tribulation
the sun will be darkened,
and the moon will not give its light,
and the stars will be falling from the sky,
and the powers in the heavens will be shaken.

"And then they will see 'the Son of Man coming in the clouds'
with great power and glory,
and then he will send out the angels
and gather his elect from the four winds,
from the end of the earth to the end of the sky.

"Learn a lesson from the fig tree.
When its branch becomes tender and sprouts leaves,
you know that summer is near.
In the same way, when you see these things happening,
know that he is near, at the gates.
Amen, I say to you,
this generation will not pass away
until all these things have taken place.
Heaven and earth will pass away,
but my words will not pass away.

"But of that day or hour, no one knows,
neither the angels in heaven, nor the Son, but only the Father."

The Gospel of the Lord. All: **Praise to you, Lord Jesus Christ.**

Prayer over the Offerings

Grant, O Lord, we pray,
that what we offer in the sight of your majesty
may obtain for us the grace of being devoted to you
and gain us the prize of everlasting happiness.
Through Christ our Lord. All: **Amen.**

Communion Antiphon (Psalm 73[72]:28)

To be near God is my happiness,
to place my hope in God the Lord.

Or:

(Mark 11:23-24)

Amen, I say to you, whatever you ask in prayer,
believe that you will receive,
and it shall be given to you, says the Lord.

Prayer after Communion

We have partaken of the gifts of this sacred mystery,
humbly imploring, O Lord,
that what your Son commanded us to do
in memory of him
may bring us growth in charity.
Through Christ our Lord. All: **Amen.**

Our Lord Jesus Christ, King of the Universe

November 21, 2027

Reflection on the Gospel

We belong only to Christ, who is eternal. Our identity is far greater than any world leader can bestow, and our lives are owed to Christ alone. It is his kingdom we strive to build, his peace we work to bring. No matter who wins any election, we all have work to do. In our liturgies and in the world, we must strive—in the words attributed to a few different saints—to pray as if it all depends on God, and act as if it all depends on us.

—Living Liturgy™, *Our Lord Jesus Christ, King of the Universe 2027*

Entrance Antiphon (Revelation 5:12; 1:6)

How worthy is the Lamb who was slain,
to receive power and divinity,
and wisdom and strength and honor.
To him belong glory and power for ever and ever.

Collect

Almighty ever-living God,
whose will is to restore all things
in your beloved Son, the King of the universe,
grant, we pray,
that the whole creation, set free from slavery,
may render your majesty service
and ceaselessly proclaim your praise.
Through our Lord Jesus Christ, your Son,
who lives and reigns with you in the unity of the Holy Spirit,
God, for ever and ever. All: **Amen.**

Reading I (L 161-B) (Daniel 7:13-14)

A reading from the Book of the Prophet Daniel

His dominion is an everlasting dominion.

As the visions during the night continued, I saw
one like a Son of man coming,
on the clouds of heaven;
when he reached the Ancient One
and was presented before him,
the one like a Son of man received dominion, glory,
and kingship;
all peoples, nations, and languages serve him.
His dominion is an everlasting dominion
that shall not be taken away,
his kingship shall not be destroyed.

The word of the Lord. All: **Thanks be to God.**

Responsorial Psalm 93

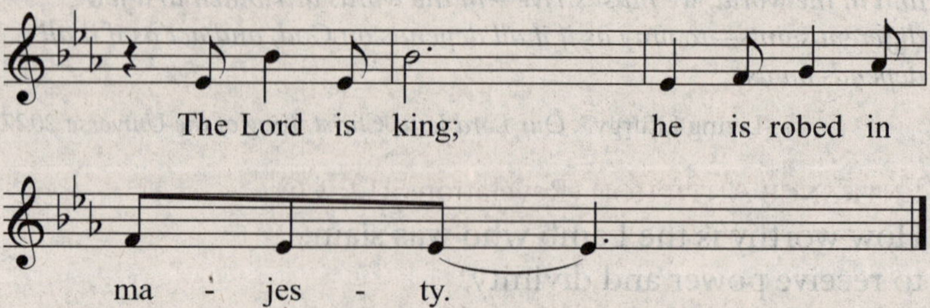

Psalm 93:1, 1-2, 5

℟. (1a) **The Lord is king; he is robed in majesty.**

The Lord is king, in splendor robed;
robed is the Lord and girt about with strength. ℟.

And he has made the world firm,
not to be moved.
Your throne stands firm from of old;
from everlasting you are, O Lord. ℟.

Your decrees are worthy of trust indeed;
holiness befits your house,
O LORD, for length of days. ℟.

READING II (Revelation 1:5-8)

A reading from the Book of Revelation

The ruler of the kings of the earth has made us into a kingdom, priests for his God and Father.

Jesus Christ is the faithful witness,
the firstborn of the dead and ruler of the kings of the earth.
To him who loves us and has freed us from our sins by his blood,
who has made us into a kingdom, priests for his God and Father,
to him be glory and power forever and ever. Amen.

Behold, he is coming amid the clouds,
and every eye will see him,
even those who pierced him.
All the peoples of the earth will lament him.
Yes. Amen.

"I am the Alpha and the Omega," says the Lord God,
"the one who is and who was and who is to come,
the almighty."

The word of the Lord. All: **Thanks be to God.**

GOSPEL (John 18:33b-37)

ALLELUIA (Mark 11:9, 10)

℣. Alleluia, alleluia. ℟. **Alleluia, alleluia.**

℣. Blessed is he who comes in the name of the Lord!
Blessed is the kingdom of our father David that is to come! ℟.

✠ **A reading from the holy Gospel according to John**

All: **Glory to you, O Lord.**

You say I am a king.

Pilate said to Jesus,
"Are you the King of the Jews?"
Jesus answered, "Do you say this on your own
or have others told you about me?"
Pilate answered, "I am not a Jew, am I?
Your own nation and the chief priests handed you over to me.
What have you done?"
Jesus answered, "My kingdom does not belong to this world.
If my kingdom did belong to this world,
my attendants would be fighting
to keep me from being handed over to the Jews.
But as it is, my kingdom is not here."
So Pilate said to him, "Then you are a king?"
Jesus answered, "You say I am a king.
For this I was born and for this I came into the world,
to testify to the truth.
Everyone who belongs to the truth listens to my voice."

The Gospel of the Lord. All: **Praise to you, Lord Jesus Christ.**

Prayer over the Offerings

As we offer you, O Lord, the sacrifice
by which the human race is reconciled to you,
we humbly pray,
that your Son himself may bestow on all nations
the gifts of unity and peace.
Through Christ our Lord. All: **Amen.**

Communion Antiphon (Psalm 29[28]:10-11)

The Lord sits as King for ever.
The Lord will bless his people with peace.

Prayer after Communion

Having received the food of immortality,
we ask, O Lord,
that, glorying in obedience
to the commands of Christ, the King of the universe,
we may live with him eternally in his heavenly Kingdom.
Who lives and reigns for ever and ever. All: **Amen.**

Eucharistic Prayer for Reconciliation I

Preface

It is truly right and just
that we should always give you thanks,
Lord, holy Father, almighty and eternal God.

For you do not cease to spur us on
to possess a more abundant life
and, being rich in mercy,
you constantly offer pardon
and call on sinners
to trust in your forgiveness alone.

Never did you turn away from us,
and, though time and again we have broken your covenant,
you have bound the human family to yourself
through Jesus your Son, our Redeemer,
with a new bond of love so tight
that it can never be undone.

Even now you set before your people
a time of grace and reconciliation,
and, as they turn back to you in spirit,
you grant them hope in Christ Jesus
and a desire to be of service to all,
while they entrust themselves
more fully to the Holy Spirit.

And so, filled with wonder,
we extol the power of your love,
and, proclaiming our joy
at the salvation that comes from you,
we join in the heavenly hymn of countless hosts,
as without end we acclaim:

Holy, Holy, Holy Lord God of hosts.
Heaven and earth are full of your glory.
Hosanna in the highest.
Blessed is he who comes in the name of the Lord.
Hosanna in the highest.

Priest:

You are indeed Holy, O Lord,
and from the world's beginning
are ceaselessly at work,
so that the human race may become holy,
just as you yourself are holy.
Look, we pray, upon your people's offerings
and pour out on them the power of your Spirit,

that they may become the Body and ✠ Blood
of your beloved Son, Jesus Christ,
in whom we, too, are your sons and daughters.

Indeed, though we once were lost
and could not approach you,
you loved us with the greatest love:
for your Son, who alone is just,
handed himself over to death,
and did not disdain to be nailed for our sake
to the wood of the Cross.

But before his arms were outstretched between heaven and earth,
to become the lasting sign of your covenant,
he desired to celebrate the Passover with his disciples.

As he ate with them,
he took bread
and, giving you thanks, he said the blessing,
broke the bread and gave it to them, saying:

TAKE THIS, ALL OF YOU, AND EAT OF IT,
FOR THIS IS MY BODY,
WHICH WILL BE GIVEN UP FOR YOU.

In a similar way, when supper was ended,
knowing that he was about to reconcile all things in himself
through his Blood to be shed on the Cross,
he took the chalice, filled with the fruit of the vine,
and once more giving you thanks,
handed the chalice to his disciples, saying:

TAKE THIS, ALL OF YOU, AND DRINK FROM IT,
FOR THIS IS THE CHALICE OF MY BLOOD,
THE BLOOD OF THE NEW AND ETERNAL COVENANT,
WHICH WILL BE POURED OUT FOR YOU AND FOR MANY
FOR THE FORGIVENESS OF SINS.

DO THIS IN MEMORY OF ME.

The mystery of faith.

People:

A **We proclaim your Death, O Lord,
and profess your Resurrection
until you come again.**

B **When we eat this Bread and drink this Cup,
we proclaim your Death, O Lord,
until you come again.**

C **Save us, Savior of the world,**
for by your Cross and Resurrection
you have set us free.

Priest:
Therefore, as we celebrate
the memorial of your Son Jesus Christ,
who is our Passover and our surest peace,
we celebrate his Death and Resurrection from the dead,
and looking forward to his blessed Coming,
we offer you, who are our faithful and merciful God,
this sacrificial Victim
who reconciles to you the human race.

Look kindly, most compassionate Father,
on those you unite to yourself
by the Sacrifice of your Son,
and grant that, by the power of the Holy Spirit,
as they partake of this one Bread and one Chalice,
they may be gathered into one Body in Christ,
who heals every division.

Be pleased to keep us always
in communion of mind and heart,
together with N. our Pope and N. our Bishop.*
Help us to work together
for the coming of your Kingdom,
until the hour when we stand before you,
Saints among the Saints in the halls of heaven,
with the Blessed Virgin Mary, Mother of God,
the blessed Apostles and all the Saints,
and with our deceased brothers and sisters,
whom we humbly commend to your mercy.

Then, freed at last from the wound of corruption
and made fully into a new creation,
we shall sing to you with gladness
the thanksgiving of Christ,
who lives for all eternity.

Through him, and with him, and in him,
O God, almighty Father,
in the unity of the Holy Spirit,
all glory and honor is yours,
for ever and ever.

* Mention may be made here of the Coadjutor Bishop, or Auxiliary Bishops, as noted in the *General Instruction of the Roman Missal*, no. 149.

People: **Amen.**

Then follows the Communion Rite, page 30.

Eucharistic Prayer for Reconciliation II

Preface

It is truly right and just
that we should give you thanks and praise,
O God, almighty Father,
for all you do in this world,
through our Lord Jesus Christ.

For though the human race
is divided by dissension and discord,
yet we know that by testing us
you change our hearts
to prepare them for reconciliation.

Even more, by your Spirit you move human hearts
that enemies may speak to each other again,
adversaries may join hands,
and peoples seek to meet together.

By the working of your power
it comes about, O Lord,
that hatred is overcome by love,
revenge gives way to forgiveness,
and discord is changed to mutual respect.

Therefore, as we give you ceaseless thanks
with the choirs of heaven,
we cry out to your majesty on earth,
and without end we acclaim:

Holy, Holy, Holy Lord God of hosts.
Heaven and earth are full of your glory.
Hosanna in the highest.
Blessed is he who comes in the name of the Lord.
Hosanna in the highest.

Priest:
You, therefore, almighty Father,
we bless through Jesus Christ your Son,
who comes in your name.
He himself is the Word that brings salvation,
the hand you extend to sinners,
the way by which your peace is offered to us.
When we ourselves had turned away from you
on account of our sins,

you brought us back to be reconciled, O Lord,
so that, converted at last to you,
we might love one another
through your Son,
whom for our sake you handed over to death.
And now, celebrating the reconciliation
Christ has brought us,
we entreat you:
sanctify these gifts by the outpouring of your Spirit,
that they may become the Body and ✠ Blood of your Son,
whose command we fulfill when we celebrate these mysteries.

For when about to give his life to set us free,
as he reclined at supper,
he himself took bread into his hands,
and, giving you thanks, he said the blessing,
broke the bread and gave it to his disciples, saying:

TAKE THIS, ALL OF YOU, AND EAT OF IT,
FOR THIS IS MY BODY,
WHICH WILL BE GIVEN UP FOR YOU.

In a similar way, on that same evening,
he took the chalice of blessing in his hands,
confessing your mercy,
and gave the chalice to his disciples, saying:

TAKE THIS, ALL OF YOU, AND DRINK FROM IT,
FOR THIS IS THE CHALICE OF MY BLOOD,
THE BLOOD OF THE NEW AND ETERNAL COVENANT,
WHICH WILL BE POURED OUT FOR YOU AND FOR MANY
FOR THE FORGIVENESS OF SINS.

DO THIS IN MEMORY OF ME.

The mystery of faith.

People:

A **We proclaim your Death, O Lord,**
and profess your Resurrection
until you come again.

B **When we eat this Bread and drink this Cup,**
we proclaim your Death, O Lord,
until you come again.

C **Save us, Savior of the world,**
for by your Cross and Resurrection
you have set us free.

Priest:
Celebrating, therefore, the memorial
of the Death and Resurrection of your Son,
who left us this pledge of his love,
we offer you what you have bestowed on us,
the Sacrifice of perfect reconciliation.

Holy Father, we humbly beseech you
to accept us also, together with your Son,
and in this saving banquet
graciously to endow us with his very Spirit,
who takes away everything
that estranges us from one another.

May he make your Church a sign of unity
and an instrument of your peace among all people
and may he keep us in communion
with N. our Pope and N. our Bishop*
and all the Bishops
and your entire people.

Just as you have gathered us now at the table of your Son,
so also bring us together,
with the glorious Virgin Mary, Mother of God,
with your blessed Apostles and all the Saints,
with our brothers and sisters
and those of every race and tongue
who have died in your friendship.
Bring us to share with them the unending banquet of unity
in a new heaven and a new earth,
where the fullness of your peace will shine forth
in Christ Jesus our Lord.

Through him, and with him, and in him,
O God, almighty Father,
in the unity of the Holy Spirit,
all glory and honor is yours,
for ever and ever.

People: **Amen.**

Then follows the Communion Rite, page 30.

* Mention may be made here of the Coadjutor Bishop, or Auxiliary Bishops, as noted in the *General Instruction of the Roman Missal*, no. 149.